RAMBLES ABOUT PORTSMOUTH.

SECOND SERIES.

SKETCHES

OF

PERSONS, LOCALITIES

AND

INCIDENTS OF TWO CENTURIES:

PRINCIPALLY FROM TRADITION AND UNPUBLISHED DOCUMENTS.

By Charles W. Brewster.

WITH A

BIOGRAPHICAL SKETCH OF THE AUTHOR,

BY WM. H. Y. HACKETT.

PORTSMOUTH, N. H.
PRINTED AND PUBLISHED BY LEWIS W. BREWSTER,
Portsmouth Journal Office.
1869.

PREFACE.

THE compilation of this Second Series of the RAMBLES ABOUT PORTSMOUTH was mostly the work of the author, as is stated in the biographical sketch by Hon. Wm. H. Y. Hackett, his life-long friend, that composes the first chapter. Slight changes in the text and arrangement were, however, left to the discretion of the editor, who has endeavored to adhere as closely as possible to the original details of the work, studying in all particulars to give them in accordance with the judgment and taste of the writer.

The plan of the Second Series is in all respects similar to that of the First. Gratified by its kind reception, the author continued his Rambles until the closing days of his life with little if any change in their character. In the Portsmouth Journal, his newspaper, in which they first appeared, apt writings of others were adopted as part of his series. In this book credit is due to Mr. John Henry Bowles, of Brooklyn, N. Y. (the Journal's correspondent "H∘∘∘∘,") in whole or in part for Rambles 85, 96, 113, 126, 131, 132, 140 and 141, Others of his interesting productions are omitted for want of room.

LEWIS W. BREWSTER.

PORTSMOUTH, N. H., Nov. 1, 1869.

CONTENTS.

RAMBLE. PAGE.

Biographical Sketch of the Author. 9

84. Site and Associations of the New City Rooms—Brick Market and Jefferson Hall. 23

85. Odiorne's Point—The First House and First Cemetery in New Hampshire........ 35

86. Marquis de Chastellux's Visit in 1782—French Fleet—Views of Portsmouth, &c.... 38

87. Sketch of Henry Sherburne and Descendants.................................... 44

88. Langdon and Sherburne Families.. 53

89. Lafayette Road—Langdon Farm—Family Monument—New Rank of American Nobility.. 58

90. Atkinson's Silver Waiter—The Record of Deaths in Portsmouth—Lady Wentworth's Picture, &c... 62

92. Theodore Atkinson's Estate—Will of Susanna, widow of George Atkinson.... ... 75

93. Peter Livius the Loyalist—Building of the North Bridge and Mill—Chief Justice of Quebec—His efforts to win Gen. Sullivan to the British Cause.............. 78

94. Legislation in Portsmouth in 1699—First Prison—Mark Noble.................... 83

95. The Old Stavers Hotel—The Party—The Daniel Street Apparition—The Dance—A Fragrant Interruption.............. 86

96. Sketches from an ancient copy of the N. H. Gazette............................ 90

97. Christian Shore—Freeman's Point—The Ham House—The Waterhouse Family.... 95

98. The Pickering Family.. 103

99. Pickering House in Vaughan Street—Edward Hart—Gen. Peabody's Perfidy—Capt. Cullam, &c.. 106

100. More of Pickering's History—Col. Atkinson—Woodbury Langdon—Revolutionary Incidents.. 111

101. Things of 1790 to 1800—Old School Gentlemen—Respect by Youth—Minor Offences—Prompt Punishment of Criminals—Justice Penhallow's Impartiality—First Pavement—Buck-Street Promenade—North and Southenders—Smoking not Allowed—Edward Hart elected Police Officer—His Success, and what produced it.. 117

102. The Hart Family—Quint and the Wolf.. 123

103. The Sheafe Family.. 126

104. James Sheafe—Jay's Treaty—The Effigies—The Riot—The Arrest—The Triumphal Procession, &c... 132

105. Insurrection in New Hampshire, 1786.. 138

106. The Cutts Family.. 142

107. Residence of Richard Cutts—Capt. Thomas Leigh's Sea Adventure—William Bennett, the Hostage—His Fate.. 147

108. The Cutts and Penhallow Cemetery on Green Street.......................... 151

109. The Residence of Dea. Samuel Penhallow.. 153

110. The Old Clock—The Four George Jaffreys—The Jaffrey House.................. 156

111. Rev. Samuel McClintock,.. 160

112. Sketch of Newcastle... 166

113. Newcastle Reminisences of Forty-Five Years Ago.............................. 174

114. The Court Martial at Fort Constitution in 1814—The Providential Witness....... 177

115. Fort Constitution—The Explosion in 1809....................................... 182

116. The Sparhawk Family... 185

117. Centennial Celebration, 1823—The Parchment Unrolled.......................... 188

118. The Yellow Fever of 1798... 193

119. Old Land Proprietors—The March Farm—The Family.............................. 196

120. Incendiary Sketches—Pilgrim Day—The Great Fire of 1813—The Incendiary.... 201

121. Central Portsmouth previous to the Great Fire—Portsmouth Pier—New-Hampshire Hotel—Jacob Sheafe's—Daniel Webster's—North side of Buck Street—The Haunted House.. 207

RAMBLE. PAGE.

122. Central Portsmouth before the Great Fire—Nicholas Rousselet—The Museum—Sailor Anecdote, &c. 214

123. Central Portsmouth before the Great Fire—Nicholas Rousselet's Courtship—The eccentric Josiah Shackford—His Unparallelled Feat of crossing the Atlantic alone—The Founder of Portsmouth, Ohio 218

124. Central Portsmouth before the Fire of 1813—North Side of Buck Street 223

125. Central Portsmouth before the Fire of 1813.—James Sheafe's Residence—Abraham Isaac, the Jew—Jonathan M. Sewell, the Poet 229

126. Central Portsmouth before the Fire of 1813.—Stories of Escapes, Rescues, &c. 233

127. State Street in 1793—Drown Family—Dr. Lyman Spalding—Capt. Peter Coues—Samuel E. Coues 239

128. Seizure of Arms and Powder at Fort William and Mary—The finale of Provincial Government in New Hampshire 248

129. The Navy Yard 254

130. Capt. Daniel Fernald—Residence—Ownership of the Navy Yard—War Adventures—Diddling the Spencer 74—Putting a British Frigate on the rocks 258

131. Shapley's Island—Small Pox Parties—Incidents and Pastimes 262

132. The Old Spring Market—The Neptune and River Nymphs of the Piscataqua 270

133. A step over the River—The Celebrities of Kittery in former days—The Spinney Family 282

134. Our Wharves—Privateering—The Portsmouth Record 285

135. Our Wharves—West-India Trade—Capt. Gilman—Admiral Nelson—Emperor of Russia. &c 290

136. The Old Welch House on Bridge Street—Johnny Cunningham 294

137. John Simes and his Descendants 296

138. Toppin Maxwell—"Commodore" Mifflin 298

139. My Brother Bob 307

140. The Brick School House in State-Street—Teachers, former and recent—School Dramatic Exhibitions—Struck by Lightning 316

141. School-House Hill—School Books—Amusements—Slides—Mrs. Maloon's Shop—The Catastrophe—Parson Walton's Meeting-House—Services—The Beloved Disciple 326

142. The Old South Church 332

143. The Old Bell Tavern 339

144. Witchcraft in Portsmouth and Newcastle—Death of Molly Bridget—Stone Throwing Devils of Newcastle 343

145. The Former Men of Portsmouth—Ancient Furniture 354

146. The Episcopal Church Yard 356

147. The Oldest House in our State 358

148. The Dead Elm on South Road 360

149. Fifty Years in a Printing Office—Our Own and the World's Progress 363

INDEX OF NAMES.

All the names used in the Rambles are intended to be printed in this index, except the following lists:

For those engaged in the Centennial Celebration, 1823, see pages 189 and 190.

For list of Master Taft's Scholars, see pages 319 and 320.

For list of "The former men of Portsmouth," see page 355.

Abbott, 71 240 329 366
Abercrombie, 124
Adams, 24 72 92 101 202 230 304 320 335 352 354 366 371 374
Akerman, 15 224 343 366
Albertz, 184
Alden, 174 351 354
Allen, 66 128 161
Amazeen, 347 352 353
Andrews, 227
Andross, 66
Anuable, 79
Appleton, 69 77 185 188
Arnold, 94
Arundel, 55
Atkinson, 49 50 62 77 112 185 191 219 253 357
Audubon, 10
Austin, 90
Ayers, 201
Badger, 113
Bailey, 178 to 182 367
Bainbridge, 328
Bampfylde, 56
Bancroft, 353
Banfield, 58 to 60
Barber, 353

Barefoot, 331 352
Barnes 366
Barnum, 94
Barrell, 49 57 60 263
Barry, 280
Barsantee, 280
Bass, 50 225
Bartlett, 11 12 16 31 182 186 366
Beck, 224
Belcher, 60 125 144 862
Belfour, 179
Belknap, 111
Bell, 171 223 336
Bellmont, 84
Bennett, 148 to 150
Berry, 196
Berthier, 92
Berthollet, 244
Bettenham, 226
Bigelow, 93
Billings, 27 367
Bire, 40 41
Bishop 366
Blaisdell, 77 240 270
Blay 362
Blunt, 110 242
Bold, 45
Bonaparte, 92 371
Borden, 351
Borland, 144
Borthwick 59
Bourne, 320
Bowles, 27 90 93 136 233 263 277 316 322 367
Boyd, 137 295
Brackett, 42 44 105 195 196
Bradley, 115
Bray 69 71 73
Brewster, 9 to 21 52 60 99 100 109 201 341 354 366
Briar, 146
Briard, 201
Bridget, 344
Brierly, 93
Brown, 49 159 260 286 287 335 341 358 367
Bruce, 230
Brummel, 266
Buchanan 371
Buckminister, 39 195 259 318 366
Burgoyne, 82 163
Burke, 114
Burnet 362
Burr, 161
Burroughs, 11 358 364
Butler, 45 143
Call, 153 294 366
Campbell, 324
Carr, 296
Carter, 32 271
Caswell, 339
Chadbourne 224
Chadwick, 341
Chamberlain, 105
Chambers, 65 73
Champernoone, 146
Chandler, 215 272
Charlton, 45
Chase, 146 201 202 209 31? 321
Chastellux, 38
Chauncey, 136
Cheever, 31
Cheney, 68
Chesley, 72
Childs, 11
Chipman, 188
Christie, 226 310
Cilley, 142
Claggett, 12
Clapham, 280
Clapp, 110
Clark, 10 52 224 343 351 352 366
Clay 374
Cleaves, 110
Clifton, 66
Clough 362
Cochran, 100 168 240 252 253 321
Coffin, 49 93 293
Coggeshall, 287
Coggswell, 75
Colbath, 206 207
Colby, 101
Coleman, 74 104
Coleridge, 277
Cook, 351
Cooper, 287
Cotton, 97 127
Coues, 240 to 247
Cowfield, 45
Craigie, 90
Cranfield, 157
Crawford, 144 374
Crockett, 1.2
Cromwell, 145
Crooker, 179 180
Cullam, 100 108 109
Cunnigham, 295
Currier, 12 108 224
Cushing, 75 228
Cushman, 12
Cutt, 48 49 69 70 97 142 to 153
Cutts, 12 31 117 142 to 149 192 195 248
Cutter, 12 31 77 107 108 183 194 195 200 268 317 363 366
Cutting 12
Daguerre 371
Dalby, 83
D' Allemagne, 92
Dame, 91 223 224
Daniel, 64 69 144
Darling, 164
Dartmouth, 251 253
Davenport, 182 228 229
Davidson, 184
Davis, 222
Day, 285
Dean 366
Dearborn, 11 28 366
Deering, 134 251
Delande, 212
DeMovan, 244
Dennett, 101 196 254 260
Dodge, 328
Doig, 91
Dow, 214 362
Downing, 64 65 67 71 74 106
Drake, 196 359
Drisco, 335
Drown, 15 31 114 132 133 136 180 182 224 240 to 244
Dudley, 57 128
Dummer, 144
Dushan, 44
Dwight, 231
Eastman, 15 310
Eaton, 74 127 223
Edwards, 203 225
Elliot, 69 144 146 246
Elwyn, 12 58
Emerson, 72 129 130 192 337
Emery, 335
Endicot, 53
Evans, 60

Fabyan, 104
Fairbanks, 93
Farmer, 111
Felt, 353
Fenton, 252
Fernald, 11 15 56 59 98 195 212 217 258 262 274 283 286 288 297 333 335 366
Fillmore 371
Fisher, 24 154 231
Fitch, 335
Fitzgerald, 16 366
Flagg, 100 193
Flanders, 271
Folsom, 195 250 366
Ford, 229
Foss, 99 to 101 109 340
Fourcroy, 244
Fowle, 90 91 95
Franklin, 327
Freeman, 12 62 191
Fremont, 374
French, 28
Frink, 297
Frost, 64 69 146 171 258
Frye, 343
Fulton, 371
Furber, 104
Furbish, 271
Furbisher 99
Furniss, 225
Fursell, 340
Gage, 250 252
Gains, 26 27 99 100 195 207 339 355 366 367
Gambling, 65 74 144 151 191
Gardner, 224 259 295 357
Geddis, 209
Gee, 111
Gerrish, 145 201 240 366
Gibbins, 45 51 to 53 111
Gibbons, 53 57 71
Gibson, 52
Gibbs, 127 to 129 365
Gillett, 279 280
Gilman, 12 49 65 73 93 141
Gilpin, 370 228 291 292 324 335 342
Goddard, 231 366
Goff, 124
Goldsmith, 176
Goldthwaite, 57 60
Goodrich, 126 158
Goodwin, 16
Gorges, 111
Gotham, 100
Gould, 272
Gove, 28 60
Grace, 232
Grafforth, 144 316
Grant 374
Graves, 144 250 253
Gray, 11 226 292
Green, 23 94
Greenleaf, 116 137 155 285 340
Gregory, 224
Griffes, 334
Griffin, 239
Gross, 144
Grouard, 25
Grow, 105

Hackett, 12 104 138 141 310 320
Haines, 196 359
Hale, 50 317 321
Hall, 57 59 60 66 109 184 199 200 209 357
Halliburton, 366
Ham, 9 96 98 101 156 202 224 306 329 366 367
Hammond, 145
Hancock, 27 302
Handy, 286
Hardy, 100
Harris, 195 211 293 320
Harrison, 371 374
Hart, 106 to 108 122 to 125 130 147 153 154 296 334 335
Harvey, 144 310
Hatch, 230
Hathaway, 320
Haven, 11 12 93 127 179 181 188 192 203 215 to 216 292 363 365 366
Hayes, 99 310
Henderson, 90 130 132 228
Hicks, 99
Higginson, 127
Hill, 18 57 60 110 296 365 366
Hilliard, 85
Hilton, 36 75
Hirst, 72
Hizeures, 41
Hobbs, 75
Hodges, 185
Hoes, 145
Holmes, 209
Holyoke, 188
Horny, 224 225
Hooton, 351
Howe, 115
Hoyt, 66 280
Hubbard, 56 59 68
Hughes, 291
Hull, 204 261 262 328
Humphreys, 76 77 203
Hunking, 73
Hunt, 223
Huntress, 209
Huske, 64 67
Hutchings, 113
Hutchings, 71
Hutchingson, 128
Huzzy 351
Irving, 251
Isaacs, 208 230
Jackson, 10 49 91 93 97 102 135 196 199 209 215 222 223 246 263 268 269 310 334 338 343 366 371 374
Jaffrey, 49 64 68 69 70 117 128 156 to 159 191 200 352 357
James, 272
Janvrin, 106 157 230
Jarvis, 186 187
Jay, 134 135 371
Jefferson, 29
Jeffries, 68 69 70 159
Jenness, 44 57 59 155 241
Jennings, 351
Johnson, 196 212 241 371
Jones, 75 77 109 226 230 297 325 326 340
Jose, 67
Keese, 67
Kelley, 111
Kennard, 16
Kenney, 67
Kettle, 241
Kimball, 320
King, 75 76 185 365
Kneill, 112
Knight, 46 52 72 74 97 144 151
Ladd, 145 188 230 247 318
Laighton, 56 59 246 297
Lake, 152
Lakeman, 10 209 366
Lanagan, 225
Lang, 93 334
Langdon, 41 42 46 to 60 73 116 125 134 149 196 241 334 335 338 366
Langford, 28
Larkin, 93
Lashley, 261
Lavoisier, 244
Lear, 46 52 53 56 59 68
Leach, 259
Leavitt, 291
Leigh, 93 148 149 150
Lewey, 279
Libbey, 239
Lincoln, 61 371
Little, 195
Livermore, 134 135 140 155 156 334 335
Livius, 78 to 83
Lloyd, 71
Locke, 343 353
Logging, 65
Long, 12 93 147 209 243
Lord, 24 114 231 340 366
Lovering, 178
Lowe, 153 209 211
Lowell, 146
Lowd, 343 367
Lunt, 297
Lyman, 148 182

MacCobb, 57 60
MacDonough, 251
Macklin, 339
Macpheadris, 65
Madison, 327 371
Manning, 136 137 155 209 339 357
March, 64 71 196 to 200 339 340 344
Mariner, 176 272 283
Marsh, 130 292 357
Marshall, 136 170 219 223

Marston, 154 310
Martin, 79 90 263
Martyn, 53 56
Mason, 12 31 53 78 111 154 155 158 159 168 199 260
Massena, 92
Massey, 297
Mather, 53 345 346
Matthew, 269
Maul, 351
Maxwell, 298 to 303 307
May, 83
Maynard, 227
McClintock, 160 to 165 199 209 296
McDaniels, 184
McIntosh, 366
McIntyre, 93
McNeil, 227
McPhededris, 69
Melcher, 91 227 366
Mendum, 11 71 219 296 297 363
Meserve, 65 72 79 124 226 239
Merlin, 367
Middleton, 45
Mifflin, 304 to 307
Miller, 11 12 298 363
Mills, 148 149
Mitchell, 77 184
Moffatt, 146 192 215 218
Montgomery, 162 164 192
Monroe, 371
Moody, 157 354
Moore, 64 70 91 111 144 146 196
Morrell, 56 59
Morrison, 296
Morse, 317 343
Mortegues, 41
Moses, 46 99 196 203 242 340
Moulton, 24
Mountford, 224
Mowatt, 187
Mudge, 286
Mussel, 168
Neil, 93, 226, 227 228
Nele, 51
Nelson, 99 291 292 325
Newmarch, 65 73 192 339
Nichols, 274 259
Noble, 85 93 186 194 297
Norris, 60
North, 90
Nutter, 201 212 227 297
Onell, 12
Odiorne, 35 36 37 49 64 65 63 69 73 146 196 216
Odlin, 64 68 73
Orcutt, 136
Orne, 185
Packer, 65 66 73 104 196
Parish, 320
Parker, 90 150 186 194 296 297
Parrott, 166
Parry, 93 209 226 297
Parsons, 72
Partington, 304 342
Payne, 194
Payson, 320
Peabody, 107 116 188 259 291
Pearse, 69
Pearson, 64 70
Peavy, 297
Peduzzi, 367
Peirce, 12 49 56 59 64 66 68 to 70 196 199 200 310 335 357 371
Pemberton, 144
Penhallow, 33 47 74 90 118 119 143 146 151 to 154 157 191
Perkins, 104 144
Perry, 328
Pepperell, 64 69 71 73 101 185 186 192
Pettigrew, 53
Philbrick, 59
Philpot, 328
Phips, 144
Pickering, 36 60 74 103 to 115 125 130 184 193 196 210 232 242 336 340 361
Pierrepoint, 230
Pike, 66 225
Pinkham, 115
Plaisted, 67 217
Plummer, 64 65 101 194 223 280
Polk, 371
Pomeroy, 93 227
Porter, 185 328
Potter, 117 209 320 343
Prescott, 188
Prince, 186
Pritchard, 343 367
Purcell, 49
Putnam, 178 188
Quincy, 67 145
Quint, 124 224
Rand, 170 196
Randolph, 352
Rea, 343 367
Redford, 66
Reding, 11 365
Reed 136 241
Reid, 287
Remick, 194 272
Revere, 92 248
Rice, 195 231 366
Ringe, 64 68 74 104 110 337
Rioms, 39 41
Robinson, 11 211 343 366
Rochambeau, 38
Rogers, 49 65 192 335 366
Rollins, 104 335
Ropes, 77 185
Rousselet, 215 to 218 223
Rowe, 343
Rowland, 140
Royall, 186
Ruck, 74
Rundlett, 93
Ruspert, 39 43
Russell, 145 194 235
Rust, 145
Rymes, 49 64 66 357
Salter, 334
Saltonstall, 145
Sandeman, 243
Sands, 57
Schaffer, 279
Schuyler, 80
Scott, 374
Scrivener, 146
Seavey, 59 60 105 129 130 196
Seaward, 97 212 225 239
Serat, 217
Sewell, 30 95 231 to 233
Shackford, 74 219 to 223 240
Shakespeare, 324
Shannon, 73
Shapley, 56 59 93 209 269
Shaw, 230 286 287 288
Sheafe, 36 67 90 93 105 106 126 to 136 193 194 204 210 226 228 to 230 292 293 357 358 366
Sheldon, 28
Shepherd, 28
Shepway, 143
Sherburne, 44 to 59 60 64 to 73 152 192 201 202 209 212 214 219 239 357
Sherive, 212
Sherman, 314
Shillaber, 304 307 to 315
Shores, 222 223 366
Shortridge, 43 44
Shurtleff, 333 335 336 338
Siber, 41
Sigourney, 165
Simes, 10 11 110 207 225 226 296 297 298
Simpson, 57 60 67
Sinclair, 286
Sise, 227
Slade, 64 67
Sloper, 46 51 52 56 144 151
Smart, 286
Smith, 11 12 65 66 72 13 139 202 204 211 244 320
Snell, 320
Solley, 64 63 69 70
Somerby, 367
Sowersby, 366
Spalding, 183 244 245 246
Sparhawk, 76 77 78 93 185 186 187 192
Spinney, 99 274 278 232 283 284
Spofford, 68
Stark, 113
Stavers, 85 135 226
Stevens, 214 320 323
Stewart, 202
Still, 229
Stone, 104 366
Stoodley, 75 212 366
Storer, 57 59 60 209 263 306
Story, 325 366
Stover 112
Stow, 332
Strong, 73 333 to 336
Sullivan, 50 57 60 79 81 140 141 155 156 169 249 250
Sumner, 92
Taft, 10 31 316 318 321
Tailor, 66
Tappan, 318 321
Tarlton, 227
Tash, 65 72
Tasker, 320
Taylor 49 371 374
Tetherly, 323
Thatcher, 127 128
Thomas, 92 242
Thompson, 12 42 166 193
Thornton, 113
Tilton, 341, 343
Tomson, 36
Toppan, 74 242
Townsend, 286
Treadwell, 69 90 242 366
Trecothie, 70
Tredick, 126 136 230
Trefethen, 136 170 184
Tripe, 223
Tripyear, 272
Trumbull, 162
Trundy, 211
Tuckerman, 98 367
Turell, 10 11 227 272 279 363
Turner, 186 317
Tyler, 188 371
Usher, 69
Van Buren, 371 374
Varney, 72
Varrell, 209 211 212
Vassell, 144
Vandreuil, 39 to 43
Vaughan, 64 69 71 144 to 147 150 152 153 191 195
Victor, 324
Yeaton, 136 203 223 239
Young, 100
Wadleigh, 363
Wainwright 200
Walbach, 276 179 to 284
Walden, 155
Waldron, 64 66 70 71 72 143 145 153 191 366
Walker, 12 64 68 128 256 209 337 338 342
Wallingford, 65 75
Walls, 143
Walton, 64 66 129 330 331 345 347 350 353 367
Wannerton, 111
Ward, 185
Warner, 46 65 117 122 235
Warren, 91 160
Washington, 50 92 114 133 163 169 232 361
Waterhouse, 98 to 102 117 284
Waters, 116
Watkins, 73
Watson, 286 289
Weare, 60 100
Webb, 127
Webster, 31 113 203 210 300 374
Weeks, 105 196 358 to 366
Welch, 228 294 295
Weld, 45 54
Wendell, 47
Wentworth, 30 41 42 44 46 49 50 54 60 62 to 69 71 to 75 90 93 112 116 119 129 131 154 155 190 191 199 203 219 243 248 251 253 263 316 357 362
Westbrook, 64 68 71
Wheeler, 227
Wherren, 272
Whidden, 59 60 153 196
Whipple, 41 93 112 113 146 192 210 230
White, 12 60 374
Whitefield, 127
Whtiham, 184
Whyddon, 56
Wibird, 64 66 191
Wildes, 366
Wiggin, 197 325
Willard, 131
Williams, 53
Willis, 112 114 115
Wilson, 64 70
Windmill, 156
Winkley, 59 74 99 144
Winn, 217 239
Winslow, 77 185
Winthrop, 53 55
Wise, 335
Woodbury, 12 31 57
Woodward, 203 207 239
Wyatt, 203 242 335

BIOGRAPHICAL SKETCH OF THE AUTHOR:

PREPARED AT THE REQUEST OF HIS FAMILY,

BY WILLIAM H. Y. HACKETT.

In offering to the public the second and concluding volume of the "Rambles about Portsmouth," it has been thought appropriate to accompany it with a sketch of the life and character of the Author. This idea was suggested by the circumstance that the finishing of this volume and the close of his life were contemporaneous. This volume not only comprises his last work; but his last days, so far as his failing strength would allow, were occupied and solaced by a careful revision and preparation of it for the press.

Charles Warren Brewster was born September 13, 1802, in Portsmouth, in the house on Islington Street, a few rods north of that in which he died. He was the son of Samuel and Mary (Ham) Brewster, and a descendant of Elder William Brewster, who came over in the Mayflower.

Few have exemplified better than Mr. Brewster, in life and conversation, the principles and character of his distinguished ancestor. Few have ever more fully embraced, and lived by, those precepts—religious and political—which made Elder Brewster and his associates exiles from home, and the founders of a great nation. Few have more firmly and successfully shaped for themselves a life and character independent of surrounding circumstances. So much did his life spring out of inward principles, that he was to some extent unmoved by the enterprises and fashions of the times in which he lived and labored. It was, perhaps, owing to this circumstance that his life was what is usually regarded as an uneventful one. Although it was one of ceaseless and systematic toil, it was wanting in that restless and expansive activity which have made or marred so many fortunes. He always had his home in one and the same spot,—rarely went abroad; and this turn of mind, in connection with the regularity required and formed by the publication of a weekly journal, centered and intensified his interest in his occupation, his home and town. It was because he did not roam abroad, that he rambled so perseveringly and so satisfactorily at home. It was because he lived so entirely by the inward light, that he avoided those foibles which checker, and those enterprises which modify, the lives of most men. It was because he delighted and to some extent lived in the past, that the public are favored with this and the preceding volume. It was because in his tastes and aspirations he was unlike most men, and sought a fact as resolutely as he would adhere to a principle; because he hesitated at no toil which would establish a date, or illustrate a character; because he would take as much pains to authenticate an anecdote as Audubon to find a new bird,—that we have an accurate and trustworthy account of the men and events of past times—a work which will inseparably connect the name of Charles W. Brewster with the history of Portsmouth and the State.

I applied to the schoolmates of Mr. Brewster for some account of his boyhood and youth. One of them replied, that it "was so even that there was nothing to relate, except that he was better and more sedate than the other boys." Another said: "His boyhood was as even and regular as his subsequent life." He first attended the school of "Aunt Betsey" Lakeman, a well known teacher of young children, sixty years ago. He then attended the North School, taught by Deacon Enoch M. Clark, and subsequently the school taught by Mr. Taft, in what was then called the Brick School-house, on State Street. The last school he attended was that of the late Henry Jackson, in 1817.

Having completed, under the tuition of Mr. Jackson, his school education, in his sixteenth year, on the 16th day of February, 1818, he began to learn the business of a printer in the office of the "Portsmouth Oracle," then published by Charles Turell, and his connection with that paper continued from that day until his death,—a period of more than half a century. At the end of that time Stephen H. Simes was the only person then remaining in business on Market Street, who was in business there in the early years of his apprenticeship on that street.

The first manuscript he put in type was an article written by the late Dr. Burroughs, who afterwards became a frequent and valued contributor to his paper.

Mr. Brewster was one of the earliest, as well as one of the most valued acquaintances that I made when I first came to Portsmouth in April, 1822. He was at that time foreman in the office of the Portsmouth Journal, then edited by Nath'l A. Haven, Jr., and published by the late Mr. Turell. About that time his intimate associates were Tobias H. Miller, who then kept a book-store on Congress Street ; Ammi R. H. Fernald, then a clerk in the store of Shadrach Robinson, Jr., on Bow Street ; George Dearborn, then a clerk in the book-store of Harrison Gray & Eben L. Childs, on Pleasant Street; Bray U. Simes, a clerk in the store of M. B. Trundy, on that part of Market Street then called Fore Street ; and the writer of this sketch. Two other gentlemen, who afterwards became distinguished members of Congress, about this time also were our acquaintances,—Francis O. J. Smith and John R. Reding, the latter of whom was for a short time in the office of the Portsmouth Journal, and the former then published a paper to which Mr. Brewster occasionally contributed.

The entrance to the office of the Portsmouth Journal was from what was then Lunt's Court, opening into Market Street, about where C. H. Mendum & Co.'s store now is. At this time it was the fashion for apprentices, as well as law-students, to work evenings. It was my practice, upon leaving Mr. Bartlett's office toward ten o'clock on Friday evenings, to go into the Journal office and make a friendly call upon Mr. Brewster ; see him "work off" (as he called it,) the inside of the Journal, and ascertain if any article which he or I had previously written had passed the editorial ordeal. He had schooled himself in writing for the press before he began to edit. He worked a hand press, which required two energetic pulls for each impression, and three or four hours of severe labor to print the whole inside of the paper. He usually worked, on Friday evening, till midnight, and the paper was distributed on Saturday morning. When making such calls, it often happened that one or more of the above-named friends were present, and one at least, at times, aided him in his work and was quite expert in inking the types. During his apprenticeship, and until he became proprietor of the Journal, in his walk from the office to his home, he passed by, or in sight of, every Law office in town. That of Jeremiah Mason was over the southern part of the First National Bank, with Geo. M. Mason, Lory Odell, John Elwyn, Charles W. Cutter, S. P. Long, Hampden Cutts, Thomas Currier, and Wm. A. Walker, as students at law; Levi Woodbury's, over the northern part of the same Bank, with Franklin Peirce, John Thompson and Jos. W. White as students; Ichabod Bartlett's, at the corner of Market and Bow streets, with Wm. H. Y. Hackett and Francis O. J. Smith as students; Nathaniel A. Haven, Jr.'s, at the corner of Market and Congress streets, with Alfred W. Haven as a student; Edward Cutts's, on the same corner, with J. Trask Woodbury as a student, and Wm. Claggett's, with Jonas Cutting as a student; Samuel Cushman's, where the Aqueduct Company's office now is, on Market Square; and James Smith's, in the Piscataqua House. Peyton R. Freeman's office was then a little north of the Journal office.

Several of these young gentlemen contributed to some one of the newspapers in town, and in this way became acquainted with Mr. Brewster. During his apprenticeship he wrote more frequently for other papers than for that with which he was connected. He took pains with his articles, regarding the exercise as a preparation for the position of an editor. He put most of Mr. Haven's editorial articles into type, and had an admiration for his style as a writer, and a veneration for his character as a man, traces of which were seen in his subsequent writings and life.

In July, 1825, Mr. Brewster and Tobias H. Miller assumed the joint proprietorship of the Journal. This connection was maintained for about ten years, when, in 1835, he became sole proprietor and editor. In 1853 he associated with him his son, Lewis W. Brewster, in these positions, who upon his father's death became sole proprietor.

Mr. Brewster married, May 13, 1828, Mary Gilman, daughter of Ward and Hannah Gilman. They had nine children. His wife and four of their children, Lewis W., Charles G., Mary G. and Helen A. G., survive him. At about the time of his marriage he became a member of the North (Congregational) Church, a position which he adorned through the remainder of his life.

To the Journal he gave his thoughts, his labors and his talents. The forty-three volumes of that paper, commencing in 1825 and ending in 1868, are at once the record of his industry, the illustration of his taste, the photograph of his character, his real biography. During the whole of that period he was the principal writer, and every volume, every number, shows his taste as a printer, his ability as a writer, and his discriminating judgment in making selections. It has been well remarked, that the success of an editor depends quite as much on what he keeps out of his columns, as on what he puts into them. It would be difficult to find a newspaper more free from every thing offensive to good taste. He aimed to make, and he did make, his Journal a good and valued family paper. Although it was always decided in its political principles, yet it supported them in a manner so free from bitterness, and was in other respects so judiciously managed, that it went into many families in which there was no sympathy with its politics.

Although his paper was the organ, in this part of the State, of the party to which he belonged, and although he gave to his party a firm and uniform support, yet he found more satisfaction in getting up the miscellaneous than the political part of his paper. I have called upon him more than once in the midst of an exciting political campaign, and found him absorbed in writing a " Ramble, " or delighted with an ancient manuscript, or some scrap of history or biography.

In the early part of his editorial experience, while the matter for his paper, during the week, was being put into type, he was arranging in his mind the location of it for the making up of his paper. Every article was thus assorted and located, by a rule as inflexible as that by which the naturalist classifies animals. And when on Friday he began to make up his paper, each article fell into its assigned place as regularly as the types of which it was composed fell, when distributed, into their proper boxes.

Mr. Brewster did not regard his paper only or chiefly as a means of making an income, but he viewed it as an instrument through which he was to perform important social duties. He felt as much responsible for the influence that his Journal exerted upon the community as for his personal example in his family or upon his employees. And he used every available means to make his influence felt for good. He thought not only the tone of his paper should be pure, but he believed that a correct style in arranging the matter, and beauty in the printing, aided in improving the taste and elevating the morals of his readers. He not only made the duties, toils and routine of life minister to the formation of his own high character, but he also made them the medium of a healthful and beneficent influence upon others.

The publication of a weekly newspaper for a half-century tends to form habits of regularity and routine. In him the tendency to regularity pre-existed; his occupation merely developed and established it. The idea that he could be away from his newspaper appeared not to have occurred to him. It would be safe to say that in forty-three years he was not absent from his office on Friday at the making up of his paper, more than a dozen times. He allowed himself no relaxation. He did not seem to desire any. He found his pleasure in his toil, his relaxation in his duty, and his happiness in his home. He did not carry the cares of business or the unfinished labors of the day to the fireside. Like most editors, he worked most easily and freely at his office-desk. His office was but a little more than two thousand feet from his house, and yet he walked more than the distance round the globe between those two localities. He was rarely seen in any street, except in that which led either to the church or to his office. He was as regular in attending church on Sunday, as he was in publishing his paper on Saturday. Although not averse to improvements, his tendency was to adhere to old habits, old principles, old friends, old books, and old ways of making money. For more than forty years he occupied the same office, and the same dwelling-house.

He recently said, in his "Fifty Years in a Printing Office," that one of the first paragraphs he ever put into type was,—"The follies of youth are drafts on old age, payable forty years after date, with interest." Few men so successfully escaped this kind of drafts. His youth was as free from foibles as his manhood from faults.

Through life he avoided every thing unbefitting a good man, as well from taste as from principle. He loved the beautiful in nature, art, and character. To him it was another name for purity. No one among us exerted a better, few a wider influence. It was not so much a demonstrative power, a sudden effort which invited public attention, as a quiet, persevering, effective influence, which gained and grew with advancing years—the blended influence of character and action, which benefitted the object more than it revealed the cause.

To the benevolent organizations he gave his sympathy and cordial and liberal co-operation. For more than half his life-time he was the Secretary of the Howard Benevolent Society, one of the best charitable organizations in the city, and for many years Treasurer of the Portsmouth Bible Society. He was for some time Superintendent of the Sunday School connected with the North Church.

The "Rambles about Portsmouth" were a labor of love, and, while indicating the direction of his reading, they afford a fair and favorable specimen of his style and taste. Plain Anglo-Saxon language flowed naturally from his pen. He commanded an easy and direct mode of expression, which formed an excellent narrative style. A pleasing story or a bit of romance always attracted him. He rescued it from the past, and lent it fresh charms by the simple, graceful mould in which he cast it. It is worthy of marked commendation, however, that he avoided the temptation of giving credence to pure fiction. Whatever was of doubtful origin never gained currency from him without being stamped as such. There was the quaint humor of the chronicler, the fidelity of the historian.

His labor in obtaining biographical facts, anecdotes and incidents, as materials for history, was such as no man would perform unless his heart were in his work. These articles were originally prepared for and published in his paper, and were compiled, through many years, from all accessible sources, manuscripts, letters, family records, city records, old newspapers, old deeds, wills, tombstones, and the recollections of aged people who have passed away. He was a long time in collecting the materials—some parts of a "Ramble" would be prepared years before a fact or incident necessary to complete it was obtained. He compared the statement of one aged person with that of another, and, when to be found, consulted contemporaneous accounts and incidents as well as collateral facts. Among others, he often conversed with, and obtained important facts from, the following named persons:

Capt. Daniel Fernald, born Nov. 19, 1767, died Mar. 7, 1866, age 99.
Renald Fernald, born Apr. 13, 1752, died Apr. 10, 1844, age 92.
Daniel P. Drown, born June, 1784, died Mar. 24, 1863, age 80.
Benjamin Akerman, born Feb. 3, 1776, died Feb. 20, 1867, age 91.
Mary Brewster, born Feb. 15, 1775, died May 2, 1866, age 91.

Richard Fitzgerald, born Sept. 14, 1771, died Nov. 24, 1858, age 87.

Oliver P. Kennard, now living.

George G. Brewster, now living.

From these and other sources he obtained merely the elements,—the data and crude material from which he worked. But as piled up on his desk, stowed away in drawers, or bound up for future use, they no more resembled a "Ramble," as the reader now sees it, than the paper-maker's uncleansed rags resembled the fair sheet upon which it is printed. Those unacquainted with like undertakings can form no adequate idea of the labor, patience and perseverance necessary to prosecute such a work,—of the interruptions and delays which attend it,—the research and discrimination requisite to discover and reproduce a trait of character, a telling anecdote or incident, or to confirm or confute a tradition. In all this the family and friends of Mr. Brewster saw him often employed for years. But much of the inward work, which was from time to time, amidst the cares and toils of life, moulding the matter thus elaborated into narratives so life-like, so attractive, so genial, as often to remind one of the writings of Washington Irving, gave no outward token of its process. The structure of these narratives, which is the blending of history, biography and romantic incidents, and constitutes the great merit and attractiveness of both volumes of the "Rambles," was in preparation while the writer appeared to others to be doing something else, or nothing,—walking the street, making up his paper, or sitting by the fireside.

Mr. Brewster was a man of marked ability, untiring industry, and high-toned character, but of diffident and retiring habits. He was called, literally called, to fill several positions of trust. At the time of his death he was one of the Trustees of the Portsmouth Savings Bank. He served for two years as President of the Mechanics and Manufacturers Association. He was for thirty-four years Secretary of the Howard Benevolent Society, was for several years in one or the other branch of the City Government, was Representative in the State Legislature in 1846-7, and in 1850, with Gov. Goodwin and Ichabod Bartlett, was a delegate from his ward to the Convention to amend the State Constitution. He declined being candidate for other positions, among them that of Mayor. In these and the other positions which he filled, he discharged his duties with diligence and ability, and to general acceptance. He occasionally delivered addresses before the Lyceum, the Association of which he was President, and other public bodies. These addresses were always heard with pleasure, and were marked by good taste and sound thought.

He was not only a good writer, as his forty-three volumes of the Portsmouth Journal and his two volumes of Rambles will abundantly show, but he was an historian, a lecturer, a biographer and a poet. His favorite reading was biography and poetry. He was very discriminating and just in his biographical sketches of prominent men and of his townsmen. He had considerable poetic ability which he exercised too rarely. He occupies a prominent position in the "Poets of Portsmouth," from which volume is selected, as here appropriate, the following Ramble in rhyme:

THE VANE OF THE NORTH CHURCH.

The vane of the North Church bore the date of 1732, when it was put up. It was not gilded until 1796. When destined to come down, in 1854, the vane is thus personified, to enable it to tell its story.

I can't come down—I can't come down!
Call loudly as you may!
A century and a third I 've stood;
Another I must stay.

Long have I watched the changing scene,
As every point I 've faced,
And witnessed generations rise,
Which others have displaced.

The points of steel which o'er me rise
Have branched since I perched here—
For Franklin then was but a boy,
Who gave the lightning gear.

The day when Cook exploring sailed,
I faced the eastern breeze;
Stationed at home, I turned my head
To the far western seas.

I 've stood while isles of savage men
Grow harmless as the dove;
And spears and battle axes turned
To purposes of love.

I looked on when those noble elms
Upon my east first sprung,
And heard, where now a factory stands,
The ship-yard's busy hum.

When tumult filled the anxious throng,
I found on every side
The constant breezes fanned a flame,
And freedom's fire supplied.

William and Mary's fort I 've oft
Through storms kept full in view—
Queen's Chapel in the snow squalls faced,
And west—looked *King street* through.

Fort Constitution now takes place
To meet my south-east glance;
The shrill north-easters from *St. John's*,
Up *Congress street* advance.

In peace I once felt truly vain—
For 'neath my shadow stood
The man whom all the people loved,
George Washington the good!

I 've seen—oh, may I ne'er again!
The flames thrice round me spread,
And hundreds of familiar homes
Turned to a light ash-bed!

But why recount the sights I 've seen?
You 'll say I 'm getting old—
I 'll quit my tale, long though it be,
And leave it half untold.

The fame of Rogers, Fitch and Stiles,
And Buckminster—all true;
And later men, whom all do know,
Come passing in review.

Their sainted souls, and hearers too—
Your fathers—where are they?
The temple of their love still stands—
It's mem'ries cheer your way.

Till that old oak, among whose boughs
The sun my first shade cast,
Lays low in dust his vig'rous form,
A respite I may ask.

This little boon I now must crave—
(Time's peltings I will scorn)—
Till coward-like I turn my head,
Let me still face the storm.

It was formerly the custom among the publishers of newspapers, to circulate, in or with the number of the paper issued on the first of January in each year, a poetical address to their patrons, called the Carrier's Address. Many years ago, and while the late Isaac Hill published the New Hampshire Patriot, he offered a set of Sir Walter Scott's Poetical Works for the best "Carrier's Address" for the then approaching first of January. Mr. Brewster with several others competed for this prize. Among the many Addresses offered was one to which Mr. Hill, himself a poet, gave the decided preference, and it was the same to which the Committee afterwards awarded the prize. Mr. Hill, supposing the successful Address to have been the production of a lady, remarked that this circumstance would somewhat moderate the disappointment of the unsuccessful competitors. When the award was made and the opening of the envelope revealed Mr. Brewster as the writer, Mr. Hill was quite as much disappointed as any of the authors of the "rejected addresses." He was not more surprised to find that the prize was not to be given to a lady than that it was to be given to an editor and a political opponent. The reader will see that he judged much better of the merits than of the source of the successful Address. The prize was duly forwarded, and is now a cherished treasure in the library of the family of Mr. Brewster.

This successful Address was the "History of News—Birth of the Press;" and it is presented here as being appropriate, alike from its origin and subject, to the profession of the writer, and as giving a fair specimen of his poetical writings.

HISTORY OF NEWS.—BIRTH OF THE PRESS.

Lo! when the Eternal planned his wise design,
Created earth, and, like his smile benign,
With splendor, beauty, mildness, decked the skies,—
Waked from eternal sleep, with wondering eyes
Man viewed the scene, and gave to News its rise.

New of himself, to Adam all was new,—
The concave canopy, the landscape's view;
The murmuring rivulet, and the zephyr's sound;
The songster's carol, and the deer's light bound;
The fruit luxuriant, where no brier sprung;
No weary toil, from morn to setting sun;
But every gale sweet odors wafted on,
His joys to freshen. Though he yet was lone,
This news was good indeed: such riches given,
Enough almost to make of earth a heaven.

But better news by far did Adam hear,
When woman's voice first hailed his raptured ear,—
News which, in later days, full well we know,
Lightens life's load of many a heavy woe.

But scarce our common parent rose from earth,
Inhaled the breath of life, and Eve had birth,
When twined the monster round the fatal tree,—
Dispelled their joy, content, and purity:
Then agonizing Nature brought to view
Ills which in Eden's bowers they never knew;
Then, at that hour accursed, that hour forlorn,
Bad News—the demon's first bequest—was born.
But, though ignobly born, to seek we 're prone
The bad as well as good, and make our own
The knowledge of the griefs and woes of all
On whom the withering frowns of Fortune fall.

Bad news abundant since has filled our world;
War's bloody garments oft have been unfurled,—
The kindly parent oft been called to yield
His earthly hope to dye the ensanguined field;
Disease oft torn our dearest hopes away,
Tyrannic princes borne despotic sway;
And every day the reckless bearer 's been
Of evil tidings to the sons of men.

But change this picture of a darkened hue;
Let scenes more bright now open to the view:
Though things may change with ever-varying flow,
They do not bring to all unmingled woe.
Do millions mourn a kingdom's fallen state?
A Cæsar hails the news with joy elate.
Does drought or frost destroy the planter's hope,
And climes more genial yield a fruitful crop?
Enhanced by contrast, these delight the more
In the good tidings of their bounteous store.
Does "the insatiate archer" claim a prize?
The weeping friend, the heir with tearless eyes,
Show joy is oft the associate of grief,
And pain to some, to others is relief.

Full many ages, centuries rolled along,
Ere news a record found, the press a tongue.
From sire to son, tradition's tale was told,
Or musty parchment spoke the days of old;
No minor incidents of passing time
Ere filled a page or occupied a rhyme;
No wars of politics on paper fought,
And few the favored ones by science taught.
Minerva saw the dreary waste below,
And urged the gods their bounties to bestow,
The mind of man to chaste refinement bring,
And ope to all the pure Pierian spring
The gods convened; but still Minerva frowned:
Not one of all their gifts her wishes crowned,

Till Vulcan thus,—and simple the address,—
"My richest gifts behold,—the TYPES and PRESS!"
The goddess smiled, and swiftly Mercury flies
To bear to earth the god's most favored prize.
Auspicious hour! hail, morn of brighter day!
Ages of darkness, close! to light give way!

The morn is past, the splendid sun is high!
The mist dispelled, and all beneath the sky
Feel its kind influence; and its cheering ray
Enlivens all, and shines in brilliant day.
The sacred writ, which once was scarcely known
To teachers, now (almost a dream!) is thrown
Into a book,—all, in one little hour,
Alike in king's and lowest menial's power;
And bounteous given—scarce is felt the task—
In every work which use or fancy ask.
Thousands of years a dreary night had been,
Ere Vulcan's art surpassed the tedious pen,—
Ere down from heaven this precious gift was brought
To lend the speed of lightning unto thought.

From necessity and practice Mr. Brewster early acquired the habit of writing rapidly. He also had the power of abstraction, and the current of his thoughts and the preparation of his editorial matter were not disturbed or impeded by the clatter of a printing office. He wrote, as he lived, from the light within. Sedate and retiring as he was, he had a fund of humor and wit which he sought rather to repress than exhibit, but which at times enlivened his friends and his paper.

His habits and tastes made him averse to newspaper controversy. What editor in the country, of his extended experience, has so generally avoided it? When forced into it, however, he was quick to "make the opposer beware" of whom he had attacked. His criticisms were pungent, his wit not seldom caustic. He undoubtedly possessed great powers of sarcasm. That they were used so sparingly, and never by way of display, but invariably in defence of what he was convinced was the right, or in exposing error and deceit, is characteristic of the man.

Mr. Brewster, like many of our prominent and able men, was educated in a printing office and at the editor's desk. There is something in the constant and powerful pressure upon an American editor—obliging him to record and comment upon the events as they occur, and to discuss those principles which are growing and ripening in the public mind and bringing him daily to a searching examination of the moral, social, economical and political problems which crowd and succeed each other with such rapid succession—that tends to quicken his powers and concentrate his energies; to give a decisive and practical cast to his character, and to force him into prominence and success.

This pressure developed Mr. Brewster. He was naturally retiring—unwilling to be before the public. His position compelled him to write; and he was found in this, as well as in all other positions in which he was placed, equal to the demands made upon him. This discipline made him a good and able writer and author and a successful business man, and gave him the tastes and habits of a scholar, a wide influence and a high position. The life of an editor makes some persons aggressive and irritable. But Mr. Brewster yielded to no such influence. He never alienated a friend or made an enemy. He early formed a plan of life, and faithfully acted upon it to the end. He was more anxious to be right than to be thought so; more intent upon doing his duty than in obtaining the reward for it; thought more of publishing a good than a profitable paper—more of being a useful than a prominent man. And at his death the universal feeling of respect for his memory, was his best eulogy.

But the great, rounded and ripened feature in Mr. Brewster's character, that which as years passed over him in his quiet walk of labor and usefulness, gained, deepened and fixed the public confidence and respect, was his integrity and purity. He was a remarkable man, not only for his industry and ability, his purity and success, but for his self-culture and wise self-control. His life was harmonious and symmetrical. His impulses were so under subjection that he appeared not so much to resist temptations as to avoid them. He was so diligent in the line of duty that he had as little opportunity as inclination to depart from it. Such a life, sweetening and cementing the domestic and social relations, was as full of happiness as of beauty. He died as calmly and serenely as he had lived, in the enjoyment of the affectionate respect of his townsmen and of the public.

To a neighbor, and life-long friend, who in taking leave of him a few evenings before his death referred to his approaching end, he said, "It matters not whether to-morrow finds me in this world or the next." A few hours before his death, as I approached his bed-side to take leave of him, he made me sit down, and then with labored breath reminded me of our life-long intimacy, and of the pleasure it had been to him. And as he calmly gave me his hand and said, "Good bye, I shall not be alive to-morrow," he was the only one unmoved in the room. His appearance indicated that the prayer of his youth, uttered in a poem from which the following is extracted, was fulfilled:

* * * * * *

" O how sweet, when the curtain of twilight 's o'erspreading,
And weary nature is sinking to rest,
O how sweet to recur, with conscience undreading,
To scenes where fond pleasure illumin'd the breast:

Those scenes where friendship waked anew,
Misconduct past forgiv'n—
Where hatred fled, like morning dew
By warming sun-beams driv'n.

O how sweet, when the last ray of twilight is gleaming,
And gath'ring shadows remind of the tomb,
O how sweet to behold *Luna* radiant beaming,
In majesty mild, dispersing the gloom.—

Thus when shades of death come o'er us,
And earthly joys are riven,
Star of Bethlehem, rise before us—
The wand'rer lead to Heaven."

Portsmouth Sketches.

RAMBLE LXXXIV.

Site and Associations of the New City Rooms—Brick Market and Jefferson Hall.

MR. MAYOR AND GENTLEMEN:

I am called upon to give a historical sketch of the site and associations of the New City Rooms, which have to-night,* for the first time, been thrown open for the use of the City Government. As we have passed from room to room it has been a matter of surprise to many of us that the old Jefferson Hall, spacious though it seemed, could have been transformed into so many capacious, well proportioned, cleanly and pleasant rooms—all just large enough for the purposes for which they are needed; and approached too by an easy flight of stairs, instead of winding up as heretofore around spiral columns. The whole internal arrangements are such as rest pleasantly upon the eye, and do credit to our city.

In the history of our ancient town, there is no period more marked by public enterprise than the five years at the close of the last century. In 1798, of the six hundred twenty-six dwelling houses in Portsmouth, there were only sixteen of three stories. In three years after, there were five of the latter class of houses added. In 1795 the

*NOTE.—This address was made at the request of the City Government of Portsmouth, by the Rambler, at the celebration of the opening of the new City Rooms, Thursday evening, Nov. 10, 1864.

Portsmouth Pier Company was incorporated. Their block of fourteen stores, three hundred twenty feet long and three stories high, was said to have no equal in New England. Seventeen vessels for foreign trade were built here in the year 1801. It was in 1799 that this spirit of enterprise brought the Aqueduct into Portsmouth; and our home enterprise was also the means of building Piscataqua Bridge about the same time. It was then, too, that the Salt works were constructed on our river.

It was in this age of enterprise, nearly seventy years ago, that our fathers came to the conclusion that a second public Market House was needed in a more central position; and in 1794 the town purchased of John Fisher, of London, for the sum of £450, the land on which the Brick Market House now stands. The condition of the sale was, that the land shall be "used and occupied for a public market place for the town of Portsmouth forever." Fisher purchased this lot with a house upon it, of Josiah Moulton, in 1744.

Previous to 1744, the whole of the land now occupied by the Exchange Buildings, and about 100 feet deep, was owned by Capt. Nathaniel Adams, the father of the late Nathaniel Adams, Annalist of Portsmouth. In 1744, John Fisher bought of the heirs of Adams about two-thirds of their land on the north side. Up to 1813, the Fisher mansion stood on the site of the Rockingham Bank; was a gambrel-roofed house very nearly resembling the residence of Samuel Lord on Middle street, and like that house its end was toward the street, within an open fence, and facing a garden on the south. There was then no house between Fisher's and Adams's. The latter was of two stories, on the corner of State-street; outside of the present corner, 19 feet on Pleasant, and 12 feet on State street. A row of large elms grew on the outside of the unpaved side-walk between the two houses. Under these trees was a place of much resort in the summer. Here the military companies found a place for drilling in the shade; and these military displays doubtless gave the name to the *Parade*, as Market Square was formerly called.

On the spot where the Market House now stands was an old two-story house occupied by James Grouard, who kept a hat store in front, and, in a one-story building adjoining on the north, manufactured his felts and cocked hats. This old house was furnished with a large chamber fronting on the Parade, which was rented for public uses. Here day-schools were kept, and here were held the evening singing schools some of our mothers and grandmothers delighted to attend. We know little of Mr. Grouard excepting that he was a matter-of-fact sort of man, fond of good living, and blessed with a good appetite—for to him, he said, a roast goose was a very awkward dish, being more than he could comfortably eat, but not enough to ask a friend to dine with him.

A few rods to the northwest of this house was the old State House, where the General and County Courts were held, and all public meetings for elections and other purposes were called. Here too, in the lower room, the independent military companies held their meetings,—while the Masons held convivial sessions in the East Chamber. The lower room of the old State House was also burdened by the hooks, ladders and other apparatus of the fire department.

Notwithstanding, the need of a public Hall as well as a Market House was so apparent, the committee appointed in 1799, to take into consideration the expediency of building a Market House, reported that it was expedient to erect a building for a Market, on the lot purchased. The building to be 80 feet long, 30 wide, and one-story high, with a roof supported by pillars, and projecting four feet on each side. The pillars to be of brick, and so

3

constructed that the building may be cool and airy in summer, and that the northerly side may be closed by doors against the storms in winter. The expense was estimated at one thousand dollars.

This report, it appears, did not meet the public approbation; so after further consideration, at a town meeting held on the 7th of April, 1800, it was decided to erect a Market House and Hall over it. The building to be 80 feet long and 35 feet wide. The lower story 12 feet high, and the upper 14—intended, as was said at the time, for "a commodious and elegant Town Hall." The town passed a vote that the Market roof be covered with tar and gravel to protect it from fire. As we find one hundred dollars were expended for shingles, it is probable that this vote was not regarded.

In four days after the vote to build was passed, the building committee, of which Col. Gains was chairman, advertised for bricks, lime, stone, &c. Soon the land was cleared, and the work commenced; and it is recorded as a remarkable fact for those times, that in 39 days, all the bricks, amounting to 145,000, were laid. We find that no less than eighty-nine persons were employed in constructing the building, of whom only two are now living. It is not probable that the work proceeded as noiselessly as that on Solomon's Temple, for we find among the bills one of $129, for a hogshead of rum, and also a bill of $70 for brads, lead and *rum*. This is some indication of the *spirit* of those times. The whole expense of the building, aside from the land, was $7,565.90.

The chairman of the building committee, who superintended the work, brought in no bill for his services, but left the matter with the town. The town readily voted to give Col. George Gains $150. He gave his receipt accordingly.

Here a word for that father of Portsmouth, who so long

retained his popularity with the people. Col. Gains was an honest, upright man, somewhat self-willed; but a high sense of justice was his predominant trait. With a single eye to the public good, he would readily take responsibilities which others would be slow to assume—doing himself the business which belonged properly to a whole board. He was in fact *the* Selectman.

As he never abused the confidence placed in him, to promote his own pecuniary interest, the public kept him continually in office. For thirty years he was regularly elected a Selectman, and as many years a Representative to the General Court. One of the keys to his popularity may be found in the above matter. Leaving the town to fix his compensation, instead of bringing in a bill—which if ever so small some might object to—shows that he knew how to promote his own interest as well as preserve the public favor.

In November, 1800, we find the Market is ready for occupancy, and Richard Billings (who had been a clerk to John Hancock) was appointed Clerk of the Market. He gives public notice that he will be happy to accommodate all his country friends with convenient stands in the new Brick Market, and insure them good prices and quick sales for their provisions. "This Market," he says, "has been built at great expense to shelter people from the weather. He is sorry to observe at this inclement season persons shivering in their open sleighs, when they could be more comfortable in the house—and he is sorry to observe gentlemen of the town hovering round the sleighs, when they ought to recommend the general use of the Market, and prevent forestalling."

Mr. Billings, a citizen of some distinction, was clerk but one year, when his place was filled by Deacon Samuel Bowles, who died in 1802.

Forestalling, to which Mr. Billings refers, was in those

days, as in previous years, regarded as a grievous offence. It was for a time finable for any storekeeper to offer meat to sell before three o'clock in the afternoon, thus reserving to those who brought in meat or poultry from the country for sale, the right of retailing until the dining hour had passed.

We find among the series of rules adopted for the government of the Market, that no meat of any kind should be carried into the west front arches of the Market; that no meat of any kind should be left in the Market over night, on penalty of forfeiture; that the market be closed at 4 P. M. except on Saturdays; and that the regular market days be Tuesday, Thursday, and Saturday. It would appear by this that at first the Market was opened only three days in the week.

There were six stalls for regular merchants, and four stalls at the east end for the use of the country traders. Among the first regular occupants were Anthony Langford, Joseph and Isaac Shepherd, Asa Dearborn, John French, Amos Sheldon, and Capt. Edward Gove.

The New Market House and Jefferson Hall, with their good finish, had hardly been soiled by use when, on the 26th of Dec. 1802, its internal work and roof were consumed in the first great conflagration in Portsmouth. For a time its standing walls and open arches on every side presented the appearance of some ancient ruin,—but such it was not long left to remain.

In 1804 it was rebuilt and in use again, with the same appearance as before the fire. The roof of the Hall, by a vote of the town, was better protected against fire, by being covered with tin. The roof at that time was quite flat, and hipped—the handsomely projecting eaves in the front and rear of the building being on a line with those on the sides. The roof of the Piscataqua Bank building was made in imitation of that of the Market. This good architectural symmetry was wholly destroyed when, about twenty years ago, the roof was raised and slated, and the eaves drawn in. Up to 1826, the arches of the Market, on the north and south sides, were filled with large loose doors without lights. In the coldest weather the doors were kept open through the day, and the hardy butchers kept their blood warm by stamping the feet and thrashing with the arms—for a stove in the Market had never been thought of. In 1826 the arches were contracted by brick work, and tight doors put in, with windows over each to admit the light. For a quarter of a century the only light to the Market when it was closed had been that from the semi-circular window over the front entrance, which is still retained there. This desire for light, as well as the arrangement made for warming the Market, were certainly evidences of progress.

Now we will leave the Market for the room over it, which, like many children, was several months old before it had a name. In Jan. 1801, we find it spoken of as "the Town Hall." At the annual town meeting held in the Court House March 25, 1801, it was voted, that the chamber of the Brick Market be hereafter called *Jefferson Hall.* Thus it appears that Jefferson Hall received its name just three weeks after Thomas Jefferson had taken his seat as President of the United States. The first public use of the Hall we can find was on the 24th of June, 1801, when the Grand Lodge of New Hampshire convened at Jefferson Hall on St. John's Day, and after proceeding to St. John's Church returned to Jefferson Hall, where an elegant repast was partaken.

On the 4th of July, 1801, a company dined in Jefferson Hall. We find no record of any other use of the first Jefferson Hall until the next 4th of July, in 1802. In that year there were celebrations by both political parties. The *Federalists* dined at Piscataqua Bridge, in *Washington*

Hall, and the *Republicans* took their dinner at *Jefferson Hall*. We have the original odes sung by both parties on that day. That sung at Jefferson Hall was by JOHN WENTWORTH. One verse will serve as a specimen:

That man so revered, so virtuous, so great,
Who saved a WHOLE PEOPLE, and then *saved a State*,
By wisdom and firmness,—'t is him we extol,
And ring JEFFERSON'S praises through JEFFERSON HALL.
Derry Down, etc.

The other ode, sung at Washington Hall, was from the pen of J. M. SEWELL. It shows a rather bitter party feeling in classing the room over the Market with the shambles below, and calling it Jefferson's *stall*. One verse will suffice:

But ah! what dire planet o'ershadows the day
On which Freedom's Sun lately beam'd forth benignant?
What comet portentous sheds death and dismay?
'T is *Jefferson's orb*, like the *dog star*, malignant.
But decreed is its doom!
The blest period will come
When the Day Star of Reason will scatter the gloom!
Away then to FREEDOM! leave JEFFERSON'S *stall!*
And court the bright goddess in WASHINGTON HALL!

It appears that the first Hall, through feelings of prejudice arising from the name, was used by one party only for meetings decidedly political. The Hall was kept very carefully as a public ornament, the Selectmen being unwilling to devote it to any common purposes. There was at first some difficulty experienced by the Artillery, Light Infantry, and Gilman Blues (the independent companies of that day,) in obtaining it for drill meetings. A town meeting was called on the subject, and they voted to give the companies the use of it. In August, 1802, we notice a meeting there of the Artillery Company—and this is the last meeting recorded in the first Jefferson Hall, before the fire not only cleared away all that was combustible, but also purified the partisan animosity which its name had so unwisely created. Nobody after the fire appears to have objected to the name of Jefferson Hall.

The entrance to Jefferson Hall was originally in the east end, by two easy flights of stairs, and through ante-rooms. It was for many years the place from which public processions were formed—the place for 4th of July and other public dinners, and for meetings of citizens on public occasions; but it was not until 1818 that it was used for town or state elections. Up to that year all meetings for election took place in the Old State House. In 1814, after the third great fire, the boys' high school, under Master Taft, was kept there for about a year. In 1819 it was for one season used as the great Sabbath School Room of Portsmouth, which the children of all parishes attended.

Of the scenes of the last forty years which Jefferson Hall has presented on town meeting days, many of you must have vivid recollections. The turmoil which arises where party spirit is inflamed by other spirits, (we speak of other days,) has often burst forth here like a volcano. For some men, who are sedate all the year, will somehow get excited on these occasions, where every man knows that his vote is of as much value as that of any one else. Jefferson Hall has been the forum where native eloquence has flourished. Here have been heard the voices of Webster, Mason, Woodbury, Cutts, Bartlett, Cutter, Cheever, Drown, and a host of those now living who were ready with the voice of wisdom to guide their fellow citizens—and there might be enumerated another class of orators, whose rough-hewn arguments never lacked fire and quaintness. The life of Jefferson Hall on election days was however almost extinguished by the adoption of the City Government in 1849. The North and the South wards withdrew the leading spirits, and since that time the Old Hall has seemed to say to the voters on election day, as they silently come and go, Where is the spirit of the former day? It seems to have expired with "that night" which followed March 13, 1849, when for only once in the history of Jefferson Hall, the morning sun rose with the Moderator of the former day yet in his chair.

But old Jefferson Hall has occasionally presented a better spectacle. Arrayed in the flags of various nations, with well covered and well attended tables, many a visitor has been made happy, according to the number of shillings he has bestowed for some object of benevolence. Here too has been the pleasant promenade, where the band and songsters have imparted life to the gathering.

Unlucky was the effort, three years since, of that well-meaning individual* who attempted in Jefferson Hall a State Mechanics Fair on his own responsibility. A temporary addition in the rear, nearly as capacious as the Hall, was erected. The expected articles for exhibition, however, did not appear. It was a sad failure; but the manager, too honest to wrong any one, at once enlisted in the army, and with his bounty money paid his debts. In a few months he rested with the honored dead.

Whether the spirit of this noble soldier still hovered around the scene which was the disturbing cause of his earthly comfort, we cannot say; but a military spirit was visible in Jefferson Hall soon after his death, when the Hall became a barrack for soldiers—and to this service of the country its last days were mainly devoted. In what more appropriate service could that Hall, which for sixty-three years has borne the name of JEFFERSON, be closed, now that it will bear that name no more forever!

In its place, what have we seen to-night? We have passed up an easy stairway and through a wide entry to a series of five capacious rooms, each independently warmed and lighted, and fitted for its particular purpose. As we pass under the City Safe, we cannot overlook it. We really have at last a *safe*. For more than 200 years the manuscript records and documents of great value have had less care taken of them than almost any merchant takes of his day-book. In the great fire of 1813, the town clerk's

* Henry M. Carter.

room, which was in the northeast corner of the Brick school-house on State street, was burnt. In this room, in a wooden chest, were the old and new records and papers of the town, which but for the thoughtfulness and efforts of an individual, Hon. Hunking Penhallow, would have been consumed. Had he not timely entered the room and secured the papers, we should now have been without any town record previous to that time. Yet even after this narrow escape, the town and city records have never, until now, been deposited a single day in a place secure against fire. The expenditure of $20,000 for a city hall, or any other public purpose, would have been a small item in comparison with the loss of the city papers, which are safe at last.

The door of the west room, in which the safe opens, is labelled "City Clerk." This important city official is always expected to be on hand, and so the most pleasant room is assigned him. At that table, filled with books and papers, the unwearied pilot of the City Government may in all future time be found, called often to the exercise of the grace of patience, which will fit him for enduring any of the varied evils of life.

In another room, with scarcely less of care, but cheered by the current of money which at particular seasons flows through that channel, may be found the Collector and Treasurer, sitting at his receipt of customs, seemingly as unconscious as the dentist extracting teeth, of the pain felt by those who pay over their hard-earned money for the support of the city. Only a small proportion of the visitors will leave this room richer pecuniarily than they entered, but every patriot will feel richer in the consciousness that his arm aids in keeping in motion the machinery which protects his property, his rights and his life, and keeps a good house always in reserve for him.

In another room, for a century to come, may be found the man whom the city delights to honor, filling the dignified position of the Mayor's chair. The room is well finished and furnished,—but his presiding seat in the adjoining room, and the tasteful chairs and desks of the Aldermen, with the whole finish and decorations, make it almost equal to an Italian Senate Chamber. Around the walls, instead of the works of the old masters, the portraits of the past Mayors are displayed, and vacancies are kept to be filled by the long train of honorables who are to succeed the present worthy incumbent. In the eight easy chairs and at that desk the consolidated wisdom of the City will be annually placed by the public voice; and to them will be committed the very hard task of pleasing everybody. If this is not done, faint will be the praises they may expect to receive from those whom they do not obey.

In that great room in the east, over the door of which the bust of the eloquent Webster is placed, will the people be represented by a Common Council, who will hold the purse strings and the check reins, and do all manner of wise things to regulate the machinery of the City Government. Here the germs of eloquence will be developed upon all sorts of appropriations; and scrutinizing committees will often think they discover measures introduced to promote some party purpose of their opponents. Here the practice of vigilance, in a right spirit, will ever promote the public good. Long may the interest of the people here be rightly represented!

We are now, Mayor and gentlemen, done with Jefferson Hall and its surroundings. May the future doings of the City Rooms of Portsmouth be marked with that wisdom and harmony of action which will give it a pleasant record in future history.

RAMBLE LXXXV.

Odiorne's Point --- The First House and First Cemetery in New Hampshire.

> " Here the dark forest's midnight shade began
> To own the power of cultivated man;
> Here is the shore, whose wide-extended breast
> First gave its borders for the wanderer's rest."

THE locality which should be the most venerated, not only by our own townsmen, but by every citizen of New Hampshire, is certainly where the first emigrants landed, and the spot on which was erected the first house in New Hampshire. How many associations cluster around this beginning of the history of our State. Less sacred they may be than those which surround the Plymouth Rock,—for the first settlers of New Hampshire came here to trade and fish, while the Pilgrims landed there for the enjoyment of religious freedom.

This place, of so much historic interest, is only about three miles from Market Square, and an hour's walk through interesting scenery will find you there. It may seem strange to residents elsewhere that any direction is needed from us to point out the spot to our home readers,—but when it is known that probably not fifty of our population of ten thousand ever visited the spot with any distinct knowledge of the several localities connected with our early history, that wonder will cease.

From the Sagamore House, on the south, is the road which leads to Odiorne's Point. On this road is but one house, which is a quarter of a mile distant. It is owned and occupied by Mr. Eben L. Odiorne, who inherits the farm which extends to the Point, where his ancestors resided for more than two centuries. We find the name of John Odiorne occupying this locality in 1660. Forty-three acres were then owned by him. He was a citizen of Portsmouth in 1657, and probably then resided there; but of this we are not certain. He gave name to the Point. Councillor Jotham Odiorne, who died in 1748, at the age of 73, was the son of John.

ODIORNE'S POINT should be respected as our Plymouth Rock. Here, in 1623, the little band landed, who were commissioned by the Laconia Company in England to found a plantation. In a ramble to the Point a week or two since, we found enough of tradition in the occupant, and visible remains left, to locate the spot where the first house, called Mason's Hall or the Manor House, was erected,—to designate also the locality of the first smith's shop. The well of the Manor House is yet to be seen in the field—and the cool, fresh water running from beneath the ledge on the shore, scarcely above the tide water, flows as freely now as when Tomson, the Hiltons and their companions quenched their thirst at it two hundred and forty-six years ago. Perhaps this inviting spring decided to them the site of their habitation.

The present proprietor of the ancient Manor does honor to his ancestors in presenting well cultivated land and a handsome farm residence. He seems however not much to pride himself upon his ancestry or the externals of his locality. So little of inquiry has been made of late years, that even the "garrison field" and "fish flake field" are spoken of as names that were formerly used.

Just before reaching the house, on the opposite side of the road, is a lane which leads nearly to the beach. The site of the old smith's shop was on the north side of this lane, on the highest point of land. Pieces of iron are now occasionally turned up in ploughing there. It is near the end of this lane on the beach that the spring flows. Here in former times, when the memory of the spot was more regarded, might be seen the Sheafes, the Pickerings and others, enjoying a social remembrance pic-nic and drawing their libations from the ancient fountain of the first residents.

But where was the site of Mason's Hall? Come this way, said Mr. Odiorne. And he led us through his spacious and shady farm yard, and down about twenty or thirty rods, in a southwest direction, from his house. Here, on a spot now covered with cabbage plants, tradition says the first house in New Hampshire was erected. Pieces of brick are yet turned up in ploughing, a small piece of ancient brown ware we picked up, and pieces of metal are here sometimes found. Although no monument designates the spot, yet here undoubtedly the Manor House stood. On the south of this site, a few rods distant, is the old well of the Manor; and eight or ten rods on the north is the resting place of those who first sank beneath the toils and privations incident to emigration to a new country.

This first cemetery of the white man in New Hampshire occupies a space of perhaps 100 feet by 60, and is well walled in. The western side is now used as a burial place for the family, but two-thirds of it is filled with perhaps forty graves, indicated by rough head and foot stones. Who there rests no one now living knows. But the same care is taken of their quiet beds as if they were of the proprietor's own family. Large trees have grown up there—one of them, an ancient walnut, springs from over one of the graves. In 1631 Mason sent over about eighty emigrants, many of whom died in a few years, and here they were probably buried. Here too doubtless rest the remains of several of those whose names stand conspicuous in our early State records.

"History numbers here
Some names and scenes to long remembrance dear,
And summer verdure clothes the lowly breast
Of the small hillock where our fathers rest.
Theirs was the dauntless heart, the hand, the voice,
That bade the desert blossom and rejoice;

Their restless toil subdued the savage earth,
And called a nation into glorious birth;
Their living floods with tides extending still,
Poured o'er the vales and climbed the highest hills;
And now the cottage that o'erlooks the scene
Of youthful revels on the village green;
The laughing fields where earliest verdure springs,
And Nature glories in the gifts she brings;
The flocks that gather in the peaceful shade,
Where once the deer in careless freedom played,
The spires that redden in the rising sun—
All these will tell you what their hands have done."

Were there a locality of similar historic interest north of the White Mountains, many an annual pilgrimage it would receive, its locality would be designated by some enduring monument, and a pebble from the first cemetery would be treasured as a mantel curiosity. But now, within a pleasant foot ramble, it is rarely visited, and seems to be almost unknown. When will some proper Monument be erected to identify the spot, and secure to posterity a locality which will with years increase in interest?

RAMBLE LXXXVI.

Marquis de Chastellux's Visit in 1782 — French Fleet — Views of Portsmouth, &c.

The year 1782 was noted locally as that in which the French fleet laid in our harbor. We have already in previous rambles given a record of some of the events which occurred, and now present a few more sketches, mainly gathered from the account the Marquis de Chastellux gave of his visit to Portsmouth while the fleet was lying in our harbor. The Marquis was a Major-General in the French army, serving under the Count de Rochambeau, with whom he came from France to this country in 1780. In 1782, in November, having some leisure, he left Hartford on a visit to Massachusetts and New Hampshire. His route brought him through Andover, Haverhill and Exeter. He speaks highly of the general appearance of the latter town, and goes on to say:—

"We stopped at a very handsome inn kept by Mr. Ruspert, which we quitted at half past two; and though we rode very fast, night was coming on when we reached Portsmouth. The road from Exeter is very hilly. We passed through Greenland, a very populous township, composed of well built houses. Cattle here are abundant, but not so handsome as in Connecticut, and the state of Massachusetts. They are dispersed over fine meadows, and it is a beautiful sight to see them collected near their hovels in the evening. This country presents, in every respect, the picture of abundance and of happiness. The road from Greenland to Portsmouth is wide and beautiful, interspersed with habitations, so that these two townships almost touch. I alighted at Mr. Brewster's, where I was well lodged; he seemed to me a respectable man, and much attached to his country.

"In the morning of the 10th of Nov. I went to pay a visit to Mr. Albert de Rioms, captain of the Pluto, who had a house on shore, where he resided for his health; he invited me to dinner, which he advised me to accept, as the Comte de Vaudreuil was in great confusion on board his ship, the mizzen-mast of which had been struck by lightning five days before, and which penetrated to his first battery; but he offered me his boat to carry me on board the Auguste. In returning for my cloak, I happened to pass by the meeting, precisely at the time of service, and had the curiosity to enter, where I remained above half an hour, that I might not interrupt the preacher, and to show my respect for the assembly; the audience were not numerous on account of the severe cold, but I saw some handsome women, elegantly dressed. Mr. Buckminister, a young minister, spoke with a great deal of grace, and reasonably enough for a preacher.

I could not help admiring the address with which he introduced politics into his sermon, by comparing the christians redeemed by the blood of Jesus Christ, but still compelled to fight against the flesh and sin, to the thirteen United States, who, notwithstanding they have acquired liberty, and independence, are under the necessity of employing all their force to combat a formidable power, and to preserve those invaluable treasures. It was near twelve when I embarked in Mr. Albert's boat, and saw on the left, near the little Island of Rising Castle, the America, (the ship given by Congress to the King of France,) which had been just launched, and appeared to me a fine ship. I left on the right the Isle of Washington, on which stands a fort of that name. It is built in the form of a star, the parapets of which are supported by stakes, and was not finished. Then leaving Newcastle on the right, and Kittery on the left, we arrived at the anchoring ground, within the first pass. I found Mr. Vaudreuil on board, who presented me to the officers of his ship, and afterwards to those of the detachment of the army, among whom were three officers of my former regiment of Guienne, at present called Viennois. He then took me to see the ravages made by the lightning, of which M. de Bire, who then commanded the ship, M. de Vaudreuil having slept on shore, gave me the following account: At half past two in the morning, in the midst of a very violent rain, a dreadful explosion was heard suddenly, and the sentinel, who was in the gallery, came in a panic into the council chamber, where he met with M. Bire, who had leaped to the foot of his bed, and they were both struck with a strong sulphureous smell. The bell was immediately rung, and the ship examined, when it was found that the mizzen-mast was cut short in two, four feet from the forecastle; that it had been lifted in the air, and fallen perpendicularly on the quarter-deck, through which it had penetrated, as well as the second battery. Two sailors were crushed by its fall, two others, who never could be found, had doubtless been thrown into the sea by the commotion, and several were wounded.

"At one o'clock we returned on shore to dine with M. Albert de Rioms, and our fellow guests were M. de Bire, who acted as flag captain, though but a lieutenant; M. de Mortegues, who formerly commanded the Magnifique (lost at the same period at Lovel's Island in Boston harbor) and was destined to the command of the America; M. de Siber, lieutenant *en pied* of the Pluto; M. d'Hizeures, captain of the regiment of the Viennois, &c. After dinner we went to drink tea with Mr. Langdon. He is a handsome man, and of noble carriage; he has been a member of Congress, and is now one of the first people of the country; his house is elegant and well furnished, and the apartments admirably well wainscotted: he has a good manuscript chart of the harbor of Portsmouth. Mrs. Langdon, his wife, is young, fair, and tolerably handsome, but I conversed less with her than with her husband, in whose favor I was prejudiced, from knowing that he had displayed great courage and patriotism at the time of Burgoyne's expedition.

" On leaving Mr. Langdon's, we went to pay a visit to Col. Wentworth, who is respected in this country, not only from his being of the same family with Lord Rockingham, but from his general acknowledged character for probity and talents. He conducted the naval department at Portsmouth, and our officers are never weary in his commendation. From Mr. Wentworth's, M. de Vaudreuil and M. de Rioms took me to Mrs. Whipple's, a widow lady, who is, I believe, sister-in-law to General Whipple; she is neither young nor handsome, but appeared to me to have a good understanding, and gaiety. She is educating one of her nieces, only fourteen years old, who is already charming. Mrs. Whipple's house, as well as that of Mr. Wentworth's, and all those I saw at Portsmouth, are very handsome and well furnished.

"I proposed, on the morning of the 11th, to make a tour among the islands in the harbor; but some snow having fallen, and the weather being by no means inviting, I contented myself with paying visits to some officers of the navy, and among others to the Count de Vaudreuil, who had slept on shore the preceding night; after which we again met at dinner at Mr. Albert's, a point of union which was always agreeable. After dinner, we again drank tea at Mr. Langdon's, and then paid a visit to Dr. Brackett, an esteemed physician of the country, and afterwards to Mr. Thompson. The latter was born in England; he is a good seaman, and an excellent ship-builder, and is besides a sensible man, greatly attached to his new country, which it is only fifteen years since he adopted. His wife is an American, and pleases by her countenance, but still more by her amiable and polite behavior. We finished the evening at Mr. Wentworth's, where the Count de Vaudreuil lodged; he gave us a very handsome supper, without ceremony, during which the conversation was gay and agreeable.

"The 12th I set out, after taking leave of M. de Vaudreuil, whom I met as he was coming to call on me, and it was certainly with the greatest sincerity that I testified to him my sense of the polite manner in which I had been received by him, and by the officers under his command.

"The following are the ideas which I had an opportunity of acquiring relative to the town of Portsmouth. It was in a pretty flourishing state before the war, and carried on the trade of ship-timber, and salt fish. It is easy to conceive that this commerce must have greatly suffered since the commencement of the troubles, but notwithstanding, Portsmouth is, perhaps, of all the American towns, that which will gain the most by the present war. There is every appearance of its becoming to *New*-England, what the other Portsmouth is to the *Old:* that is to say, that this place will be made choice of as the depot of the continental marine. The access to the harbor is easy, the road immense, and there are seven fathoms water as far up as two miles above the town; add to this, that notwithstanding its northern situation, the harbor of Portsmouth is never frozen, an advantage arising from the rapidity of the current.

"When I was at Portsmouth the necessaries of life were very dear, owing to the great drought of the preceding summer. Wheat cost two dollars a bushel, (of sixty pounds weight) oats almost as much, and Indian corn was extremely scarce. I shall hardly be believed when I say, that I paid eight livres ten sols (about seven shillings and threepence) a day for each horse. Butcher's meat only was cheap, selling at two-pence-halfpenny a pound. That part of New Hampshire bordering on the coast is not fertile; there are good lands at forty or fifty miles distance from the sea, but the expense of carriage greatly augments the price of articles, when sold in more inhabited parts. As for the value of landed property, it is dear enough for so new a country. Mr. Ruspert, my landlord at Exeter, paid seventy pounds currency per annum, (at eighteen livres or fifteen shillings the pound) for his inn. Lands sell at from ten to sixteen dollars an acre. The country produces little fruit, and the cider is indifferent.

"The road from Portsmouth to Newbury passes through a barren country. Hampton is the only township you meet with, and there are not such handsome houses there as at Greenland."

Col. Wm. Brewster at that time kept the Bell Tavern. Here the Marquis lodged. Mr. Albert's abode was probably at Mrs. Richard Shortridge's boarding-house, where some of the officers of the fleet, among them Vaudreuil, boarded. This boarding-house was in Deer street: the house, remodelled, was long the residence of the late Peter

Jenness and his family. Richard S. is the same individual who was impressed by arrangement of Gov. Benning Wentworth, with the hopes of obtaining his wife, as related in the 17th Ramble. Shortridge received a commission in the Revolutionary army, and died before the close of the war, somewhere in the vicinity of Lake Champlain, when returning from an expedition to Canada. He left three sons, Richard, Samuel and John. John H. Shortridge, who afterwards occupied the same house, was of another family.

It is said by those who have a knowledge of the fact, that the officers of high grade of the French fleet were industrious, and had their knitting-work ready to take in hand when in their boarding-houses. They knit silk gloves, which were bestowed as presents on the ladies.

In Ramble No. 50, an account was given of the murder of a Frenchman which gave name to "Frenchman's Lane." Since that was written we find a minute entered in a manuscript Register kept at the time by Dr. Brackett, (who is mentioned by the Marquis in the sketch given in this Ramble,) at the date of Oct. 23, 1778, as follows:

"John Dushan, a French-Man, was found murdered at the creek, hav'g his throat cutt, & robed, by night."

By this it appears that the murder of the Frenchman was four years previous to the visit of the French fleet—the recollection of the old gentleman who gave the account being thus much at fault.

RAMBLE LXXXVII.

Sketch of Henry Sherburne and Descendants.

Richard Sherburne, of Stoneyhurst, with others of the nobility and gentry, was called upon in the year 1543 to furnish his quota of men and arms against the Scotch, under the Duke of Somerset, and was knighted on 11th May, 1544, then 22 years old.

Sir Richard married Maud, the fifth child of Sir Richard Bold, Knight of Bold, in the time of Henry VIII., by his wife, Margaret, daughter of Sir Thomas Butler, Knight of Bewsey.

Sir Richard Sherburne, probably son of first Sir Richard, died in prison Aug. 6th, 1589, and was succeeded by his son Richard, who married Anne, daughter of John Cowfield, Esq.; and dying without issue, the princely mansion of Stoneyhurst and the many mansions and lordships appertaining to it, devolved on his brother, Sir Nicholas Sherburne, Bart., who married Catherine, daughter and co-heiress of Sir Edward Charlton, of Wesley Tidehaust, and had three children: *Catherine*, who died an infant; *Richard Francis*, born 1693 and died 1703; also *Mary Winnefrida Francisca*, who married Thomas, eighth Duke of Norfolk, and at his death married the Hon. Peregrine Middleton, but had no issue by either marriage. Sir Nicholas Sherburne died in 1718, bequeathing his large estates to his only surviving child, Mary, Duchess of Norfolk, who dying in 1754, all their estates were bequeathed *conditionally* (that no other heirs were living to claim the estates) to the issue of Elizabeth Weld, her aunt, sister of the deceased Baronet.

Such is the family in England from which it is said the Sherburnes in Portsmouth descended; but the connecting link for a generation we have not at hand. We find Henry Sherburne in the company which came to Portsmouth with the early settlers in 1631. He married Rebecca, the only daughter of Ambros Gibbins, who was of that company. Henry died in 1680. His wife died in 1667. The children of Henry Sherburne were *Samuel* and *Elizabeth*, twins, born 1638; *Mary*, in 1640; *Henry*, in 1642; *John*, in 1647; *Ambros*, in 1649; *Sarah*, in 1651; *Rebecca*, in 1654; *Rachel*, in 1656; *Martha*, in 1657; *Ruth*, born in 1660, and married Aaron Moses, 1677.

Elizabeth married Tobias Langdon in 1656; their son Honor (Onner) Langdon was born in 1664. Tobias L. died in 1664, and in 1667 his widow married Tobias Lear, and in 1669 their daughter Elizabeth Lear was born. She probably had other children by each marriage.

Mary married Richard Sloper. He died in 1716, aged 85; and she in 1718, aged 78. Their children were Bridget, born in 1659, (married John Knight); John, in 1661; Mary, in 1663; Sarah, in 1667; Susannah, in 1669; Elizabeth, in 1671; Rebecca, in 1673; Martha, in 1676, Tabitha, in 1679; Richard and Henry, twins, in 1682; Ambros, in 1684.

Henry Sherburne, grandson of the first Henry, but by which son we know not, was born in 1674, and was married to Dorothy Wentworth, born in 1680, sister of the first Gov. John. Henry Sherburne's house was at the head of the Pier, on the corner of State and Water streets, next the spot now occupied by the stone yard. It was of two stories and probably the first brick house built in Portsmouth. For many years previous to its destruction by fire in 1813, it was a public house, known as "the Portsmouth Hotel." He was a Provincial Councillor, and died in 1757, at the age of 83. His wife died in 1754, aged 74.

Henry Sherburne, son of the above, was born in 1709, and graduated at Harvard in 1728. In 1740 he married Sarah Warner, daughter of Daniel. He was for ten years after 1728 Clerk of the Court. He was a Selectman, Representative, and Provincial Councillor. He was also a member of the Colonial Congress held at Albany in 1754; and a Justice of the Court of Common Pleas in 1765. He occupied his father's mansion, and died there in 1767. He had eight sons and five daughters:—Henry, Daniel, Samuel, Nathaniel, Jonathan, Edward, Richard, Andrew, Sarah, (the ife of Woodbury Langdon), Hannah (the wife of Samuel 'enhallow), Dorothy (the wife of John Wendell), Mary nd Margaret.

Samuel Sherburne, whose will follows, (a brother of Ienry) died in 1765, unmarried. He was the owner of he estate in North Portsmouth where the Misses Sherburne the daughters of Col. Samuel) now live. That with other aluable property he gave to his nephew, who bore his name.

SAMUEL SHERBURNE S WILL.

In the name of God, Amen. — I, SAMUEL SHERBURNE, of 'ortsmouth, in the Province of New Hampshire in New England, Esquire, being affected with bodily pain and ndisposition, though at present of a perfect mind and nemory, blessed be God therefor, do ordain this as my ast Will and Testament, as follows: First, I give back my mmortal soul to the Almighty Giver thereof, hoping he will through the merits and mediation of Jesus Christ my Redeemer, be graciously pleased to accept it. My body I desire may be *entombed* near the south-easterly corner of the Queen's Chapel, in Portsmouth, in a decent, but not extravagant manner; which unnecessary expense I disapprove of. Then as touching the worldly estate which God in his providence has been pleased to bestow upon me, I hereby settle and dispose of as follows, viz:

Imprimis. — I direct that all my just debts and funeral charges be paid as soon as may be conveniently done by my Executors herein hereafter named in this my will.

Item. — I give and bequeath to the Church of England as by law established in the town of Portsmouth and province aforesaid, £2000 of the present value of old Tenor, so called, to be under the care and direction of the Vestry and Church Wardens of the Queen's Chapel in said town for the time being; and this I give for a perpetual fund for that end, and the interest and income of the same to be appropriated and expended if necessary, for the support of an organist in said Church or Parish, without any diminution of the principal sum.

Item. — I give and bequeath to the said Church or Chapel

my moiety or half part of a pasture or lot of Land and meadow, supposed in the whole twelve acres more or less, situated in Portsmouth aforesaid and lying on the southerly or south-easterly side of the highway leading from the Hay market to Wibird's Hill, so called, which said Tract was given me by my honored father in his last will and testament; and this bequest to be under the direction of the Church Wardens of said Parish for the time being and to remain a perpetual glebe to the said Church and Parish and their successors forever.

Item.—I give and bequeath to the said Church or Chapel my lot of land in Portsmouth which I bought of George Allmary, bounded and described as per his deed will appear, to be under the care and direction of the Church Wardens and Vestry as above mentioned; and this I intend as a place to build a school house upon, to have and to hold the same to the Church Wardens and Vestry for the time being forever.

Item.—I give and bequeath to my sister Ann Langdon during her natural life the interest or income of £2000 old tenor, to be paid to her annually by my Executors hereafter in this Will mentioned; and after her decease my Will is and I hereby give and bequeath the said principal sum of £2000 to the Church of England aforesaid, to be added to the two thousand pounds old tenor bequeathed to said parish in this my will above, and to be held and applied and improved and disposed of as in and by this my Will and Testament. The above legacy (to the Church) of two thousand pounds is mentioned to be applied and improved.

Item.—I give and bequeath to my said sister Ann Langdon, four pair linen sheets, also a pair of half pint silver cans, also one dozen China plates and three Dishes, all blue and white.

Item.—I give and bequeath to Mrs. Lydia Cutt during her natural life the Interest and income of fifteen hundred pounds old tenor, to be annually paid her by my Executors; and after her decease I give and bequeath the said principal sum of fifteen hundred pounds old tenor to the above mentioned Church of England in Portsmouth, to be held and improved as in and by this my Will, the money legacies to the said Church is directed and mentioned.

Item.—I give and bequeath to the said Lydia Cutt four pair linen and four pair cotton sheets, and one dozen China plates and three dishes, blue and white; I also give her one of my silver cans which holds about two-thirds of a pint.

Item.—I give to the children of my sister Dorothy Gilman deceased, and to be paid by my Executors, viz: to Christopher Rymes, Nathaniel Rogers and Dorothy Taylor, each two hundred pounds old tenor; I also give and bequeath to Nancy Barrel, grand child of my said sister, two hundred pounds old tenor—these legacies to be paid to the minors when they come of age.

Item.—I give and bequeath to Mrs. Hannah Atkinson, one pair of silver butter boats, so called.

Item.—I give and bequeath to Mrs. Sarah Jaffrey my silver tea kettle, lamp and stand.

Item.—I give and bequeath Gregory Purcel, Esq., and to his heirs and assigns forever, a tract of land of about one hundred acres, more or less, situated in Nottingham in this Province, near or adjacent to the estate of Joshua Peirce, Esq., deceased, and is that tract I bought of Mr. Coffin of Newbury.

Item.—I give and bequeath to Mrs. Rebecca Wentworth, daughter of John Wentworth of Portsmouth, one hundred pounds old tenor.

Item.—I give and bequeath to the Rev. Mr. Arthur Brown, two hundred pounds old tenor.

Item.—I give and bequeath to Miss Hannah Jackson, daughter of Elisha Jackson late of Portsmouth, deceased, one hundred pounds old tenor, and paid by my executors when she comes of age.

Item.—I give and bequeath to Mr. Thomas Odiorne of Exeter in this Province, merchant, three hundred pounds old tenor, to be paid him by my Executors hereafter mentioned.

Item.—I give and bequeath to Peter Gilman of Exeter, in this Province, Esquire, three hundred pounds old tenor, to be paid by my Executors hereafter mentioned.

Item.—I give and bequeath to my nephew Samuel Sherburne, Esq., all the residue of my Estate, both real and personal, of what kind or nature soever, to have and to hold to him the said Samuel and to his heirs and assigns forever.

Lastly. — I do hereby nominate, constitute and appoint Theodore Atkinson and Hunking Wentworth, both of Portsmouth in the Province of New Hampshire aforesaid, Esquires, to be the Executors of this my last will and testament, hereby impowering to see the same duly executed according to the intent and design thereof. In testimony whereof I have signed and sealed the same. Done at Portsmouth this fifth day of February, Anno Domini one thousand seven hundred and sixty-five, 1765.

SAMUEL SHERBURNE. [L.S.]

In presence of Theodore Atkinson, jr.
Samuel Hale, Joseph Bass.

This Will was proved 18th day of Feb. 1765.

Edward Sherburne, one of the sons of the Hon. Henry Sherburne, at the commencement of hostilities in the revolutionary war repaired to Cambridge and entered as a volunteer in the service of his country at his own expense. Soon after he became Aid to General Sullivan. At the evacuation of Boston, the army being ordered by General Washington to New York, he proceeded thither at his own expense, and was in all the battles in New Jersey. When the army evacuated New York in consequence of the enemy taking possession, the army was ordered to Philadelphia. At the battle of Germantown he was severely wounded. While carrying orders in front of both armies he received the wound of which he died. The General commended him much for his bravery, and said much to his family in praise of his general character. He spent most of his property in the service.

There are several other branches of the first Sherburne family of Portsmouth — from one of which Judge John S. Sherburne descended — from another the late Col. John N. Sherburne descended — and from another the late Joseph

Sherburne of the Plains descended. We have not the data to give a more connected genealogy of a family, which, if any of them come into the possession of the property in England awaiting an heir, will become the richest in New Hampshire.

We copy the following, verbatim, from a handsomely written old family record on parchment, by Mrs. Mary Sloper, who died one hundred and fifty-one years ago. The closing lines, recording her death, were added by another hand. The several families named were located between Sagamore Creek and the Plains. There are doubtless many families in Portsmouth which can be traced back to the early residents who are recorded below. In 1693, we see Lieut. Sloper and Capt. Nele were honored by having places assigned them in the second seats in front of the minister. Ambros Gibbins, it will be recollected, was the Assistant Governor in 1840.

An Acc't of the Birth, Marriage and Death of my Father and Mother, and other relatives; my husband's birth and mine, the year we was married, and the Births of our Children.

My Father Henry Sherborne and my mother Rebekah was married the 13th November, 1637. My father Henry Sherborne died about the year '80 or '83. His death we was not sensible of.

My brother John Sherborne was born the 3d of April 1647 and was Baptised at Newbury the 4th of October 1657. Sarah Sherborne was borne the 10th January 1651; and was Baptised at Hampton by Mr. Cotton. Rebekah Sherborne, 26th Aprill 1654, but was not Baptised. Rachel Sherborne was borne April the 4th, 1656, but not Baptised — dyed the 28th December, 1656.

My husband Richard Sloper, was borne November 1630. We was married the 21st October, 1658.

My mother Rebekah Sherborne, dyed the 3d June 1667 about noon, and was buried by four of her children. Tobias Langdon dyed the 27th July 1664, and was buried y his children. Martha Sherborne dyed the 11th November, 1658.

My grandmother Elizabeth Gibbins dyed the 14th May, 1655. My grandfather Ambros Gibbins, dyed the 1st July, 1656.

Elizabeth Sherborne was married to Tobias Langdon the 10th of June 1656. Onner Langdon was borne the 30th April 1664. Elizabeth Langdon was married unto Tobias Lear the 11th April 1667. Elizabeth Lear was born the 1st Feb. 1669.

Martha Sherborne was born the 4th December, 1657. Rebekah Sherborne dyed the 29th June 1696, aged 43 years. Ambros Sherborne was borne 3d August, 1649, and baptized at Newbury. Elizabeth Sherborne was borne 4th August 1638, baptised by Mr. Gibson. Mary Sherborne was borne the 20th November 1640, baptised by Mr. Gibson. Henry Sherborne was borne 21st January, 1642 — went to sea in '58 with Solomon Clark, and coming home the 10th July, 1659, dyed at Sea and was buried in the Sea. Ruth Sherborne was borne of Sunday 3d of June 1660. Samuel Sherborne was married to Love 15th December 1668.

Bridget Sloper was borne 30th August 1659. — John Sloper was borne 13th January 1661, being Sabbath day. Mary Sloper* was borne on Tuesday, the 11th Feb. 1663. Sarah Sloper was borne of Thursday the 26th July, 1667. Susanna Sloper was borne of Tuesday the 21st March, 1669. Elizabeth Sloper was borne the 26th June, 1671, being Friday. Rebeckah Sloper was borne Wednesday 23d October 1673. Martha Sloper was born of Monday the 26th December 1676. Tabitha Sloper was borne 17th December 1679. Richard and Henry Sloper was borne of Thursday 19th June 1682. Ambros Sloper was borne 20th January 1684.

Bridget Sloper was married unto John Knight 29th March 1684. Elizabeth Knight was borne of Saturday 8th July, 1687. John Knight was borne 29th January, 1684.

Richard Sloper deceased October 16, 1716.

Mary Sloper, [the writer of the above record,] wife of Richard Sloper, deceased Sept. 22, 1718.

* She married John Brewster, jr., and was scalped by the Indians at the Plains in 1696.

RAMBLE LXXXVIII.

Langdon and Sherburne Families.

At the request of the Rambler, the following family sketch has been prepared by one of the descendants of Gov. Langdon:

The earliest English settlers to which the Langdons of Witch Creek (or Sagamore Creek) go back, are Ambrose Gibbon and his wife: where in England lived Gibbon, Gibbons, Gibbens or Gibbins, for they spell his name any way, (who was the leading servant of Captain John Mason here after Mr. Francis Williams,) we cannot say: his name is in English books of heraldry spelled all four ways, also Gibbines and Gibbings, all with mostly the same arms: but we don't think our revered forefather knew much about his rightful armorial bearings. He was, it is like, the uncle or elder brother of Edward Gibbon of the Bay, a distinguished candlestick of the Bay puritans, but first was jailed by Endicot for the maypole business, with others from Gorges's country. This Edward is the hero of a long story of Winthrop and Mather's, by which we find that he had lived many years in Piscataway, and was a bosom friend, partner it is like, of a French protestant gulf cruiser of Santo Domingo and Piscataway, already on the seas, whose descendants are still, we think, amongst us, and write their names yet Petgru or Pettigrew. There was also a James Gibbins of Saco in Gorges's country; it is like, one of the same lot.

Ambrose's daughter, Rebecca Gibbon, married Henry Sherburne, one of his companions, and was the mother of Elizabeth Sherburne; afterwards Elizabeth Langdon, Elizabeth Lear and Elizabeth Martyn; for she had at least three husbands. But before saying more of her, we will speak of a Sherburne claim that is spoken of in the newspapers.

As we undertand it, it is to the estates in the counties of York and Lancaster, of the very ancient house of the Sherburnes of Stonihurst, always papists, and intermarried with leading papist families in England; the last baronet, Sir Nicholas Sherburne, dying in 1714: when they are understood to have gone to his only child, the Duchess of Norfolk, she and the duke papists, and at her death to the heirs of her father's sister, in 1754, she having no children to take them, which heirs are still the Welds of Lulworth Castle, county of Dorset, always papists, of which one was the late well known Cardinal Weld. These estates are to be claimed through Henry Sherburne of Piscataway, who must have been born not long after Queen Elizabeth died.

The then lord of Stonihurst was Richard Sherburne, who married into a noble family. Now we have first to show beyond all cavil in a court of law that Henry Sherburne of Piscataway was the heir of this Richard, or some still earlier Sherburnes, if he or they had no descendants of their own that could take; which would be hard, for Richard Sherburne died a good deal more than two hundred years ago: next also beyond all cavil in a court of law that they have not left a single descendant in all that long while, before we can look for the revered Henry to help us out. After all, then, we have to look up his male line, or else we can't get the Welds out to save our souls. His eldest son, Samuel, was killed by the Indians in Maine in 1691: then an old man. Henry, said to be the eldest son of Samuel, married Dorothy Wentworth, and had three sons, Henry, Sam'l, John, as we understand: Henry Sherburne, the last one, had a good many children, and we believe Colonel Samuel Sherburne of North Portsmouth, commonly called of Christian Shore, was his eldest son; he had a son Henry we think, who may have left another, which we do not know.

The whole estates can only go to one heir, if we can get the Welds and the jesuits out of Stonihurst: and though

Henry was so perseveringly their leading christian name here, it is only found once in a great many Sherburnes of Stonihurst. The estates went rightfully to the heirs of Maria Winifreda Francisca Sherburne, duchess of Norfolk, (here is a sounding name for the magazines,) and we can't drive them off.

There is a certain enticing plausibility to the business in the extreme possibility that Henry Sherburne of Piscataway may have been a papist: he was the church-warden of our church of England chapel, 1640, spoken of by Winthrop, broken up by the Bay puritans, the document about which is the only thing, if we remember rightly, left of our early town records, which were burnt by the Bay puritans in the civil wars, when they re-annexed Maine and New Hampshire to their empire: it would look as if he turned puritan though, in the civil wars, and went to meeting, and wouldn't again after the king was brought back. His son-in-law, Tobias Langdon, is said to be of the ancient house of the Langdons of Keverel in Cornwall, near Saint German's, which whether he was we cannot say, but his son didn't call either of his seven sons by the family name of Walter. The antiquity of those Langdons is indisputable, whose name at the conquest was the Cornish one of Lizard: for Carew of Anthony, the poet and scholar, speaks of them as his neighbors of ancient lineage, rather gone to decay in the days of Elizabeth. That they may have continued papists very late may be too, for a Walter Langdon of Keverel was fined on his estate during the rebellion, taken in arms for the king, when he and other gentlemen of the county held out with their wives and children in Pendenis Castle under an Arundel of Trerice, one of the heroic actions of the civil wars. This Cornish Arundel was not an open papist, but the other great Cornish Arundels of Lanhearne, as the lords Arundel of Wardour, are still, the lords Arundel of Trerice being gone. Arundel and Sherburne are both papist names, and the eldest of a Sir John Whyddon, also from the same corner of England, a justice in special favor with the bloody Mary, married the heiress of Langdon of Keverel. There was also a Langdon sent here, to New York we believe, by the papist James the second. And as the second Tobias Langdon got his commission of ensign from James, it may be, as he was very young, that it was that the name may not have escaped the loyal ears of Sir Edmund Andross, James's governor of New England. There is a possibility that Henry Sherburne of Piscataway may have been a papist, and a distant relation of the great papist Sherburnes of the North, but there isn't any, we think, that his male line in the States will ever get their estates.

One of Henry Sherburne's daughters married with a Sloper, a race gone from here in the male line, but their cellars and gravestones are left on Sloper's hill and Sloper's plain. Another, Elizabeth, married the young Mr. Tobias Langdon, who died early; next, Tobias Lear, the ancestor of General Washington's Tobias Lear—the Lears lived on the eastern side of the Langdons, and the Slopers on the west, all now in one farm—and next she married Mr. Richard Martyn.

By Tobias Langdon she had four children: Tobias, Elizabeth, who married with a Fernald, and Honour with a Laighton, both in Kittery, and Margaret with a Morrel.

Captain Tobias Langdon, her son, who is buried in his field, married Mary Hubbard of Salisbury in the Bay, and they had at least nine children; that is they had, if we remember, three sons-in-law, Bampfylde, Peirce and Shapleigh, all very ancient west country names; and they had seven sons: their eldest son Tobias, we do not know what became of him: Richard, their second, born 1694, lived and died at Newton on Long Island, and has descendants both in England and here, of very good standing in the world: some of them were royalists and went home, but Capt. Joshua Sands, once written Sandys, of the American navy, who knows all about them, is his great grandson. Joseph, their third son, lived near Witch Creek, and has two or three hundred descendants, though hardly any named Langdon, some of them at least the eleventh generation of English colonists at Witch Creek, counting Gibbon and his wife for the first: Mark, the fourth son, was a tanner at the south end: Samuel, their fifth son, married with a Jenness in the south part of Rye, where his gravestone is by the road, and died there young, of the locked jaw, a making shingles: William was a tanner at the north end, their sixth son; and his son William, also a tanner, many people remember, a very good looking, and a very worthy man. John, their seventh son, lived and died on the homestead. He married Mary Hall of Exeter, her mother a Woodbury of Beverly, her father the son of Kinsley Hall of Exeter and Elizabeth Dudley, the daughter of Samuel Dudley, who has numberless descendants in New Hampshire, who was the eldest son of the great puritan Thomas Dudley of the Bay.

John and Mary Langdon had six children, Mary Langdon, Woodbury Langdon, John Langdon, Elizabeth Langdon, Martha Langdon and Abigail Langdon. Mr. Woodbury Langdon and Mr. John Langdon were well known people. Mary married three husbands in Maine: Storer, Hill and MacCobb; Elizabeth a Barrel of Portsmouth, a royalist, Abigail a Goldthwait of Boston, also a royalist, Martha another Barrel, next a Simpson, and lastly Governor James Sullivan of Massachusetts Bay.

RAMBLE LXXXIX.

Lafayette Road—Langdon Farm—Family Monument—New Rank of American Nobility.

Before Lafayette road was laid out in 1825, the way to Newburyport as well as to Rye, was over Portsmouth Plains. The opening of Lafayette road brought the head of Sagamore Creek more directly in contact with the city, and within a pleasant walk of Market Square. The head of this Creek on the south side is noted as the locality where the Langdon family first settled, over two hundred years ago,—and from the family that farm has never been alienated. The seat of the first Tobias Langdon has descended to the sixth generation and is now owned by Hon. John Langdon Elwyn, grandson of late Gov. John Langdon who was there born.

On the north side of the same Creek, bounded on Lafayette road, is the farm of Samuel Langdon, Esq., a descendant of the first Tobias Langdon, also of the 6th generation, being the son of Maj. Samuel Langdon, who died in 1834 at the age of 81, as reported in the inscription below.

The farm of Samuel L. extends from the South road to the Creek, and contains about 150 acres. The house is of good size, and does not on the outside show marks of its age — but although in excellent preservation inside, in its heavy frame projecting into the rooms, it bears marks of having been built more than a century and a half. It was built by Capt. Samuel Banfield about the year 1700. In 1743 Banfield died, and the property came into Joseph Langdon's possession, and it has ever since remained in the family.

In the rear of the house towards the South road, is an enclosure for a family burial place, in which is visible to every passer-by an elevated monument of Italian marble, ected as a family memorial by the present owner of the :emises.

The plinth of the monument rests on a granite base. he die, which is surmounted by a frieze and cap, is a uare block of marble presenting four sides of about 21 ches in width by 42 in height. Two of the sides are ain; on the other two are the following inscriptions, which ve a very full genealogical history of the family. The onument is from Mr. Philbrick's establishment — the letring deep and clear, in Mr. Borthwick's best style.

I. Tobias Langdon, from England, died 1664; married 656 Elizabeth, daughter of Henry Sherburne, (she afterards m. Tobias Lear,) and had Tobias L., born 1660, died eb. 20, 1725; m. in 1686 Mary Hubbard. Elizabeth, m. Villiam Fernald. Oner, m. 1686 John Laighton. Mararet m. Nicholas Morrel.

II. Capt. Tobias and Mary Langdon had Mary, born Nov. 7, 1687, m. George Pierce. Tobias, born Oct. 11, 1689, . 1714 Sarah Winkley. Martha, b. Mch. 7, 1693, m. July , 1715, Nicholas Shapley. Richard, born Apr. 14, 1694, . Thankful ——, and died at Newton, Long Island. Joeph, born Feb. 28, 1696, died Aug. 10, 1767, m. Mary, aughter of Capt. Sam'l Banfield. She died Aug. 10, 1753, ged 49. Mark, born Sept. 15, 1698, died 1776; m. 1st Iehitable, who died Oct. 7, 1764, aged 63. Samuel, born ept. 6, 1700, died Dec. 2, 1725; m. Hannah Jenness. Villiam, born Oct. 30, 1702, died 1766. John, born May 8, 1707, died Feb. 27, 1780; m. Mary Hall, who died April 1, 1789, aged 72 yrs.

III. Capt. Joseph and Mary L. had Samuel, born 1721, died 779; m. Sept. 29, 1748, Hannah, daughter of John Storer, Esq. Wells, Me., who died Sept. 8, 1796, aged 73. Mary, orn 1725, died Feb. 23, 1807; m. Amos Seavey, who died Feb. 19, 1807, aged 89. Hannah, m. James Whidden. Elizabeth, died July 14, 1804; m. James Seavey.

III. Dea. Mark and Mehitabel Langdon had Joseph, born 1724, died Oct. 30, 1749.

III. Wm. and Sarah L. had William, born 1748, died Sept. 30, 1820; m. Mary Pickering, who died Feb. 8, 1802, aged 52. John, born 1748, died May 21, 1789; m. Mary Evans, died Mar. 10, 1825, aged 61. Mary m. Nicholas Pickering.

III. John Langdon married Mary Hall; had Mary, m. Storer, Hill and McCobb. Judge Woodbury Langdon, born 1738, died Jan. 13, 1805; m. Sarah Sherburne. Gov. John, born 1738, died Sept. 18, 1819; m. Elizabeth Sherburne. Elizabeth m. Barrel. Abigail m. Goldthwait. Martha, m. Barrel, Simpson and Gov. James Sullivan.

IV. Capt. Samuel and Hannah L. had Mary, born April 16, 1751, died 1836; m. Joseph White. Maj. Samuel, born June 9, 1753, died July 5, 1834; m. Lydia Brewster, daughter of Samuel Norris, died May 21, 1840, aged 62. Anna born Nov. 3, 1755, died May 24, 1690; m. James Whidden. Rev. Joseph L. born May 12, 1758, died July 27, 1824; m. Dec. 9, 1790, Patience Pickering, died April 8, 1846, aged 88. Elizabeth, born March 18, 1761, died 1831; m. Andrew Sherburne. Hannah, born June, 1766, died 1812; m. Edward Gove.

I. Capt. Samuel Banfield died 1743; m. Mary Seavey, who died 1753, and had Mary, who married Capt. Joseph Langdon.

The monument to Mr. Langdon's family ancestors is not confined to the burial enclosure. Around the sitting room of the mansion, displayed under glass in frames, are the military commissions of his fathers for four or five generations, signed by Gov. Belcher, Gov. Wentworth, President Weare and Gov. Langdon. It is a novel collection, exhibiting three various state seals, and showing too, that under the crown as well as in Revolutionary times, there never has been a lack of military spirit and patriotism at the head of Sagamore Creek.

It is probable that the royal ancestry of the family very nearly corresponds with that of one in the immediate neighborhood, which is illustrated by the following true story.

A descendant of one of the earlier families in Portsmouth which resided between Sagamore Creek and Great Swamp, was travelling in a stage coach with a stranger who found that they both bore the same family name. On inquiring for descent, the stranger, of somewhat high notions, said he was connected with the family of Sir David B., of Scotland. The native of Portsmouth, who thought his claims to aristocratic descent no less prominent, replied that he was descended from a family of Aldermen.

"*Family of Aldermen*," said the sprig of nobility, "why, you must be very ignorant to think that there is any such hereditary order—it is only a temporary city office, sir."

"You are mistaken," was the reply, "it is an order which ranks a little higher than knighthood. My forefathers for five generations bore the insignia of their high honors. They wore the Aldermen's aprons with as much honors and pride as any Knights Templar. Those aprons were no fragile silk or linen fabric—they were the pure hide, such as were used when the ark was constructed; and they date their nobility at as early a day. Perhaps you may yourself one day arrive at the honors, and then you will fully comprehend them. These aprons they wore six days in the week—and the ravages they made around Great Swamp and Sagamore Creek, are now manifest in the well cleared and productive farms of their descendants. Yes, sir, I am a regular descendant of the family of *Aldermen*, and shall never lose my aristocratic pride, but will endeavor to respect those who may be of lower rank."

To be descendants of the *Family of Aldermen* should be the pride of American nobility. Of such was President Lincoln.

RAMBLE XC.

Atkinson's Silver Waiter---The Record of Deaths in Portsmouth,---Lady Wentworth's Picture, &c.

In the 18th Ramble will be found a reference to the great amount of plate owned by Theodore Atkinson. Among the articles was a massive silver waiter, which for many years decorated his home on Court street, and must have been ever before him in his merry moments, as a *memento mori*. This waiter is now owned in the family of Hon. Asa Freeman of Dover, where are also the silver knives and forks, and other valuables, formerly in the Atkinson family, inherited by Mrs. F. from the estate of the last Theodore Atkinson, of this city, she being a daughter of the late Hon. William K. Atkinson, of Dover.

There are also portraits by Copley, of Hon. Theodore Atkinson and his lady, Hannah, the daughter of Lieut. Gov. John Wentworth. Not the least valuable in the collection (which we recently had the privilege of seeing) are the portraits of Theodore Atkinson, Jr. and of his wife, the beautiful Frances Deering Wentworth (who in ten days after her husband's death married Gov. John Wentworth.) They were painted in 1763, the year after their marriage. Her age was then about nineteen, and Atkinson's about twenty-seven. His countenance does not denote much force of character, but his russet dress and long embroidered vest are truly beautiful; and as a painting, it is a piece of superior workmanship. The portrait of his lady is by Copley, and is one of his best. Although it has been painted a hundred years, it now stands out in all the richness of its early days. There are some portions of it which have the appearance of small cracks in the paint, which a portrait painter a few years ago wished to daub over with his brush : but a close examination of the work shows that these marks were carefully made by the painter, and were necessary to bring out the display in the back-ground. The countenance is handsome, intellectual, full of life, and a little roguish. The painting as a work of art has been highly valued by connoisseurs, and five hundred dollars have been offered for it.

But the silver waiter is more particularly the subject of this Ramble. On this waiter are inscribed the names, ages and times of death of 48 individuals who were acquaintances of the elder Atkinson. Many of the deaths inscribed occurred before there was any newspaper in New Hampshire, and it is probable that Secretary Atkinson took this as the best means of preserving a record of his particular friends. The names upon the waiter were in two columns. One column was filled down, and the other was filled about half way down, there being room enough for twelve or fifteen names more. From the appearance of the engraving of the names, it is thought that the inscriptions were made at different times, as the persons happened to die.

The first date was about eight years after his marriage. His wife died 12th Dec. 1769. It will be seen that but two names were added after her death. He died 22nd Sept. 1779, and the dates stopped eight years previous to his death. Although the last column was not filled up, there were many distinguished persons who died within those eight years.

It will be seen that neither the death of his son nor of his wife is noticed. He alludes to the death of one of Gov. Benning Wentworth's sons, and omits those of the other two. He also omits the death of Gov. Benning's first wife. Those acquainted with the history of Portsmouth will notice that he omits husbands and notices wives, and *vice versa*. Indeed, the most interesting point in this matter is to get at the standard of qualification for record upon the waiter.

1. Benjamin Plummer, May 8, 1740 — 24 [age.]
2. John Rindge, Nov. 6, 1740—45.
3. Christopher Rymes, April 3d, 1741—41.
4. Shadrich Walton, Oct. 3d, 1741—83.
5. Joshua Pierce, Feb. 7th, 1742—72.
6. Elizabeth Wibird, Feb. 12th, 1742—73.
7. John Downing, Sept, 16th, 1744—85.
8. Joseph Sherburne, Dec. 3, 1744—64.
9. Mary Sherburne, March 6th, 1745-6—61.
10. Mary Huske, March 8th, 1745-6—43.
11. Arthur Slade, Jan. 12th, 1746—64.
12. Dudley Odlin, Feb. 13th, 1747-8—37.
13. Jotham Odiorne, Aug, 16th, 1748—73.
14. Ann Pierce, Oct. 19th, 1748—25.
15. Mary Westbrook, Oct. 23, 1748—75.
16. George Walker, Dec. 7th, 1748—86.
17. George Jaffrey, May 8th, 1749—66.
18. Jane Frost, May 22, 1749—64.
19. Mary Sherburne, Nov. 27th, 1750—28.
20. Elizabeth Vaughan, Dec. 7th, 1750—68.
21. Jotham Odiorne, May 19th, 1751—48.
22. Nicholas Daniel, June 24th, 1751—31.
23. Sarah Odiorne, June 23, 1752—76.
24. Capt. William Pearson, Dec. 2nd, 1752—55.
25. Mary Moore, March 12th, 1753—45.
26. Elizabeth Solley, March 12th, 1753—34.
27. Mary Wilson, April 15th, 1753—71.
28. Richard Waldron, Aug. 23d, 1753—60.
29. Dorothy Sherburne, Jan. 3d, 1754—74.
30. Sarah Downing, Jan. 11th, 1754—70.
31. Mary Wentworth, June 13th, 1755—32.
32. Henry Sherburne, Dec. 29th, 1757—83.
33. Eliza Waldron, Oct. 16th, 1758—57.
34. Mary March, March 22d, 1759—80.

Sir William Pepperell, Bart., July 6th, 1759—63.

36. Mary Meserve, Aug. 8th, 1759 — 47.
37. Ann Tash, Aug. 25th, 1759 — 68.
38. John Wentworth, Nov. 8th, 1759 — 39.
39. Samuel Smith, May 2d, 1760 — 74.
40. Dorothy Gilman, Jan. 25th, 1761 — 49.
41. Ann Packer, Jan. 12th, 1762 — 61.
42. Hannah Sherburne, Feb. 10th, 1762 — 57.
43. Margaret Chambers, Aug. 6th, 1762 — 82.
44. Madame D. Newmarch, Jan. 8th, 1763 — 63.
45. M. Gambling, Aug. 29th, 1764 — 75.
46. John Downing, Feb. 14th, 1766 — 82.
47. His Ex. Benning Wentworth, Oct. 14th, 1770 — 75.
48. T. Wallingford, Aug. 4th, 1771 — 75.

1. Benjamin Plummer, died 1740, aged 24. He made his will 7th May, 1740, the day before he died. He calls himself of Portsmouth. His orders were that his wearing apparel be taken to Boston and there be sold for the most it would bring. He speaks of no relative in this country, but wills the most of the property to his mother and brothers in London. He makes Thomas Plummer, of London, merchant, and Theodore Atkinson, of Portsmouth, N. H., executors. He made presents to Theodore Atkinson, John Loggin, and to "my much esteemed friend" Mary Macpheadris. The presents to Miss Macpheadris were so numerous and valuable as to indicate intentions of marriage. The portrait of Miss Macpheadris can be seen in the house of the late Col. John N. Sherburne. She was the granddaughter of Lt. Gov. John Wentworth and wife of Hon. Jonathan Warner. Her family is more particularly described in Ramble 25.

2. John Rindge came to Portsmouth early in 1700, from Ipswich, Mass., when a minor. He married Ann, daughter of Jotham Ordiorne, Sr. He was made Counsellor the year he died. His children were as follows: Elizabeth *m* Mark Hunking Wentworth; Mehitable *m* Daniel Rogers;

John; Jotham, married Sarah ———. The widow of John Rindge probably was Anne, the last wife of Sheriff Packer.

3. Christopher Rymes was son of Samuel Rymes, who was married sometime previous to December, 1691, to Mary, sister of Lt. Gov. John Wentworth. She was afterwards the wife of Dr. John Clifton. Samuel was "Mariner," and was dead as early as 1712.

Their son Christopher had a wife, Dorothy, who as early as 1748 had married John Tailor of Milton, Mass. Christopher left property to his son Christopher Jr., daughter Ann, mother Mary Clifton, wife's brother Richard, brother Samuel, brother Samuel's son Christopher and brother Samuel's daughter Dorothy.

4. Shadrich Walton may have been son of —— Walton, who married Fanny, daughter of Gov. Samuel Allen. They had George, *Shadrich*, Samuel and Fanny, who married William Hoyt.

5. Joshua Pierce. He was the first of the Pierce family who arrived at Portsmouth (see Ramble 30, page 356.) Mr. Joshua Pierce of Newbury, Mass., married Dorothy, daughter of Major Pike, of Salisbury, Mass., and had a son Hon. Joshua Pierce who married Elizabeth, daughter of Joseph Hall of Piscataqua, N. H., who married Elizabeth Smith, who came here from England upon the desire of her uncle, the original Major Richard Waldron of Dover. This Elizabeth, widow of Joseph Hall, who died Dec. 19th, 1685, married 7th of August, 1687, Col. Thomas Packer, supposed to be the father of old Sheriff Packer. She died at Greenland, N. H., Aug. 14th, 1717, aged 62 years.

6. Elizabeth Wibird was the widow Elizabeth Redford when married to Richard Wibird, Sr., July 10th, 1701. She was the mother of Hon. Richard Wibird, Jr., who was born July 7th, 1702. Was her first husband William Redford, who was Register of Deeds at Portsmouth 1693 to 1697? Richard, Sr. was one of the King's Councillors from

1716 to his death in 1732. He is said to have erected the first brick house in Portsmouth, and was a very wealthy man.

7. John Downing, died 1744, aged 25.

He was one of the Provincial Counsellors from 1740 to his death. Letters of Administration were granted to his wife, Patience Downing. He was of Newington. He owned four houses in Portsmouth in 1727.

8. Joseph Sherburne, died 1744, aged 64.

He was one of the Provincial Councillors from 1733 to the day of his death. His wife was Mary, and he lived at Portsmouth. His son Joseph of Boston was his administrator.

9. Mary Sherburne, died 1745, aged 61.

In her will she gives property to grandson Nathaniel, who was son of her son John, deceased; also to sons Joseph and Nathaniel and daughter Mary. He was one of the justices that tried Sarah Simpson and Penelope Kenny in 1739, who were executed for murder.

10. Mary Huske was daughter of Ichabod and Mary (Jose) Plaisted. She was born Oct. 6th, 1702, and was sister to Samuel Plaisted, who married Lt. Gov. John Wentworth's daughter Hannah, afterwards Mrs. Theodore Atkinson.

Salem, Mass., records give the following:—"Capt. Ellis Huske married 25th Oct., 1720, Mary Plaisted." The will of Ellis Huske was proved April 30th, 1751; and from it we get his children as follows: John, Olive married Daniel Rindge, who died childless; Ann married Edmund Quincy, Jr., whose daughter Mary married Jacob Sheafe, Jr., of Portsmouth; Mary married John Sherburne, and died childless before her father.

11. Arthur Slade, died 1746, aged 64.

He was from New Market. Letters of administration were granted to Henry Keese and his wife Elizabeth. This Mrs. Elizabeth Keese may have been his daughter, but nothing is shown by the Exeter records of his having a wife or descendants.

12. Dudley Odlin, died 1748, aged 37.

His will indicates that he was a physician. He was of Exeter. He willed property to nephew John, son of his brother Elisha, on condition that he study medicine; to his father; to brothers John, Elisha and Woodbridge; to cousins Winthrop and William.

13. Jotham Odiorne, Sr., lived at New Castle. Was Counsellor 1724, and Judge from 1742 to 1747. He had son Hon. Jotham, Jr., and Ann, who married John Rindge and was mother of Mrs. Mark Hunking Wentworth.

14. This Ann Pierce has been claimed to be the Ann Pierce born Oct. 26th, 1723, and who was sister of Elizabeth who married Samuel Solley, and daughter of George Jaffrey, who married Sarah Jeffries of Boston, Jan. 10th, 1710. She married Dec. 20th, 1744, Nathaniel Pierce, and had two sons and a daughter Sarah, who married Col. Joshua Wentworth. Mr. Pierce died Aug. 27th, 1762, aged 50 years. On the 6th of Dec., 1769, she married Leveret Hubbard and died Dec. 1790, aged 67. So the above must refer to some other Ann Pierce. It is probable that she was the daughter of the first Joshua Pierce who came to Portsmouth in 1700.

15. Mary Westbrook, died 1743, aged 75.

Was she not the wife of Hon. Thomas Westbrook mentioned in Ramble 30 as one of the thirteen men who paid the highest taxes in Portsmouth in 1727?

16. George Walker, died 1749, aged 86.

He was of Portsmouth and left property to wife Abigail and to Walker Lear, son of his sister Elizabeth Lear. Also to cousins Ichabod Cheney and Hannah Spofford. There was a Capt. Walker in 1727 in Portsmouth who had four slaves.

17. George Jaffrey was born at Great Island (New Cas-

tle,) Nov. 22, 1682, graduated at Harvard College 1702, was Counsellor in 1716. He married Jan. 10th, 1710 Sarah, daughter of David and Elizabeth (Usher) Jeffries of Boston, who was born May 4th, 1695. She died Jan. 12, 1734, and was the mother of George, Jr. Elizabeth married Samuel Solley, Sarah married David Jeffries, and Ann married Nathaniel Pierce.

George Jaffrey married for a second wife, March 9, 1738, the widow of Hon. Archibald McPhederis, who was Sarah, daughter of Lt. Gov. John Wentworth, who survived him. He was only son and child of George and Anne Jaffrey of Great Island, who was Counsellor, Speaker, &c., and died at Col. Appleton's in Ipswich, Mass., aged 69, May 8, 1749.

18. Jane Frost was originally the wife of Andrew, son of Col. William and Margarey (Bray) Pepperell. He was the oldest child and was brother of Sir William. She had one daughter Margarey, who was the first wife of Capt. William, son of Lt. Gov. John Wentworth. She had another daughter Sarah, who married Charles Frost, Jr.; and she married his father Charles Frost, Sr., for her second husband. She had by him Elliot Frost, born June 29, 1718. Her father was Robert Elliot of New Castle, who was made Counsellor in 1683.

19. Mary Sherburne, died 1750, aged 28.

20. Elizabeth Vaughan, died 1750, aged 68.

21. Jotham Odiorne, Jr., married Mehitable, daughter of Robert Cutt of Kittery, Dec. 29th, 1725. Among his children were Sarah, married (1st) Henry Appleton (2d) William Appleton; Mary married Peter Pearse; Mehitable married William E. Treadwell.

22. Nicholas Daniel, died 1751, aged 31.

There is nothing at the Probate office at Exeter to indicate who either of these individuals were.

23. Sarah Odiorne is supposed to be wife of Jotham, Sr., and mother of Jotham, Jr.

24. Capt. William Pearson, died 1752, aged 55.

He made will at Portsmouth 18th Nov. 1748, and states that he was born 30th January, 1697 in ——, County of York, England. He appoints his wife executor and gives her his property. In case of his absence and his wife should die before him, he appoints Theodore Atkinson of Portsmouth, N. H., and Barlow Trecothie of Boston, Mass., his Attornies.

25. Mary Moore, died 1753, aged 45.

The Probate records at Exeter indicate nothing save that there was a Samuel Moore of Portsmouth, N. H., who made his will in 1744 and died 1749. He made his wife Mary sole executor. She died without a will and Joshua Peirce was made her administrator. She must have been the Mary Moore alluded to in Ramble 80, as daughter of Joshua Peirce, Sr., who died in 1763, and sister to Joshua Peirce, Jr., who was her administrator.

26. Elizabeth Solley, born July 20th, 1719, was daughter of George Jaffrey, who married Sarah Jeffries of Boston, Jan. 10th, 1710. She married Oct. 20th, 1741, Hon. Samuel Solley, who was made Councillor in 1740. Solley went to England in 1758, where his second wife Lucy ——, died 1761. He died in London June, 1785. There was in Portsmouth in 1702 Nathaniel Solley, who called himself "formerly of London." Probably father of Samuel. The above Elizabeth Solley was sister to Ann Jaffrey, who married Nathaniel Pierce. She died childless.

27. Mary Wilson, died 1753, aged 71.

Probate records show nothing in this case.

28. Richard Waldron was born at Dover, N. H., Feb. 21st, 1693, and graduated at Harvard College 1712. He was grandson of old Major Waldron, who was massacred at Dover, June 28th, 1689, by the Indians. He was son of Richard Waldron who married (1st) Hannah, daughter of President Cutt, who died Feb. 14th, 1692, and (2nd) Feb.

6th, 1692-3 Eleanor, daughter of Major William Vaughan. His father died Nov. 3d, 1730. He first lived at Dover, but early removed to Portsmouth, where he became Judge, Councillor, and Secretary of the Province. His wife was Elizabeth, daughter of Hon. Thomas Westbrook.

29. Dorothy Sherburne was daughter of Samuel and Mary (Benning) Wentworth, and was born June 27th, 1680. She was sister of Lt. Gov. John Wentworth. She married Henry Sherburne, described in another place.

30. Sarah Downing, died 1754, aged 70.

She was probably the wife of John Downing in Ramble 46, as he mentions no wife in his will.

31. Mary Wentworth was daughter of Nathaniel and Mary (Lloyd) Mendum, and wife of Ebenezer Wentworth, one of the sons of Lt. Gov. John. This Ebenezer had but one child, Rebecca, (who married her cousin George Wentworth, father of Ebenezer, late of this city.) He married Dec. 4th, 1746, and died Feb. 3d, 1757. He was born Aug. 1714, and she June 18th, 1723.

32. Henry Sherburne married Dorothy, sister of Lt. Gov. John Wentworth. He was son of Samuel Sherburne, who married Love Hutchins of Haverhill, Dec. 15th, 1668, and was killed at Casco Bay Aug. 4th, 1691. This Samuel was son of Henry Sherburne, who married (1st) Rebecca, daughter of Ambros Gibbons, and (2d) Sarah, widow of Walter Abbot. The Henry first alluded to was appointed Councillor in 1728, and was also Chief Justice.

33. Elizabeth Waldron was only child of Col. Thomas Westbrook. She was born Nov. 26th, 1701, and married, Dec. 31st, 1718, the above mentioned Secretary Richard Waldron.

34. Mary March, died 1759, aged 80.

Probate records show nothing in this case.

35. Sir William Pepperell, son of Col. William and Margarey (Bray) Pepperell, was born June 27th, 1696. He

married Mary, daughter of Grove Hirst, Esq., a merchant of Boston. He was knighted for his services, and his biography has been written by a descendant of his father, Dr. Parsons.

36. Mary Meserve, died 1759, aged 47.

Nathaniel Meserve of Portsmouth willed property to his wife Mary and died in 1758. Mary was to bring up the children under age. He had sons Nathaniel, John, George and Hanson; and daughters Annah Wills, Sarah Odiorne, Mary Batson, Esther, Jane, Elizabeth and Ann. See Ramble 35. He died at Louisburg of small pox in 1758. It is said that his last words to his wife on leaving were—"Don't break my will." She did break it, however, and the story is that his apparition harshly upbraided her in the entry of her place of residence, (the Boyd house by the mill.) It appears that she died the next year.

37. Ann Tash, died 1759, aged 63.

Exeter Probate records give nothing about Tash until 1811, when John Tash of New Market died at an advanced age.

38. John Wentworth was son of Gov. Benning, and was born Jan. 1720. He was never married. Adams alludes to his death in his Annals. He was christened at Boston, Jan. 29th, 1720, as his mother, the first wife of Gov. Benning, Abigail Ruck, was a member of the South Church there. His portrait is now at the house of the late Ebenezer in this city.

39. Samuel Smith, died 1760, aged 74.

He was a Provincial Counsellor from 1740 to the day of his death. He willed property to Mary, widow of Timothy Emerson; Elizabeth wife of Solomon Emerson; Hannah, wife of Richard Waldron; Temperance, wife of Joseph Varney; Sarah, wife of Lemuel Chesley; Joseph Knight, husband of deceased daughter Patience Knight; to his son Joseph Smith.

40. Dorothy Gilman was daughter of Henry and Dorothy (Wentworth) Sherburne, and sister to the fathers of Woodbury and John Langdon's wives. She married Hon. Peter Gilman of Exeter, who was Councillor from 1772, and Speaker for several years under the colonial government. He died Dec. 1st, 1788, aged 84 years. Their daughter Abigail married (1st) Dec. 6th, 1750, Rev. John Strong of Portsmouth, N. H., and (2nd) Oct. 23d, 1755, Rev. Woodbridge Odlin of Exeter, who died March 10th, 1776.

41. Ann Packer must have been a second wife of Hon. Thomas Packer, who was Sheriff from 1741 to the day of his death, June 22d, 1771. She was sister of Hon. Jotham Odiorne, Jr. The first wife of Sheriff Packer was Rebecca, daughter of Lt. Gov. John Wentworth, who died in 1768. She was, probably, the widow of John Rindge.

42. Hannah Sherburne, died 1762, aged 57.

She was of New Castle. She had grandson Thomas Odiorne of Greenland; son Noah, and daughter Catherine Odiorne of Portsmouth.

43. Margaret Chambers, died 1762, aged 82.

She died a widow, of Portsmouth. No will. Cutts Shannon was appointed Administrator. She had 70 acres of land at Gravelly Ridge; 57½ acres in upper and 2 in lower marsh, and half an acre of Gore, so called. Her estate was appraised £10,972.

44. Madame D. Newmarch was wife of Hon. Joseph Newmarch. He was born Oct. 29th, 1707, and was son of Rev. John Newmarch, who married Mary, widow of Mark Hunking, who was the father of the wife of Lt. Gov. John Wentworth.

Dorothy was born July 23d, 1698, and was daughter of Col. William and Margarey (Bray) Pepperell, and sister to Sir William. She married John Watkins March 26th, 1719, and had children by him. She subsequently married Mr. Newmarch, who was one of the Councillors in 1754.

45. Exeter Probate records show that there was a Benjamin Gambling of Portsmouth, who made his will in 1744, and left all his property to his mother Mary Gambling.

There is on file a will made April 2nd, 1764, from Mary Gambling, which was proved Sept. 26th, 1764, which proves her to have been the M. Gambling referred to on the waiter. She wills property to sister Elizabeth Toppan and her son; sisters Deborah Knight and Susanna Winkley; cousins Samuel Penhallow, John Penhallow, William Knight, Temple Knight, Mary Knight; children of cousin Henry Coleman, children of brother Samuel, deceased; to Benjamin Gambling, Carter land in Leicester, Mass.; to Mr. Eaton, present minister of Leicester, Mass., land in Leicester. Her estate was very large, and the Exeter records show nothing of her husband. She probably once lived in Leicester, Mass.

In 1738, John Rindge was appointed Councillor in place of Benjamin Gambling deceased. There was a Benjamin Gambling who was Register of the Council in 1681.

46. John Downing, died 1766, aged 82.

He was supposed to be son of John Downing, No. 7. He was of Newington and wills to grandsons John, Samuel and Jonathan, who were sons of his son John deceased; to grandsons Samuel and Josiah Shackford who were sons of his daughter Susannah S. deceased; to grandsons Nicholas, John and James who were sons of his daughter Mary Pickering, deceased; to his sons Richard and Harrison Downing.

47. His Excellency Benning Wentworth was son of Lt. Gov. John, who was son of Samuel, whose grave stone is still legible at the Point of Graves; and the fourth in descent from Elder William Wentworth of Dover, N. H. He was born July 24th, 1696. He married (1st) Dec. 31st, 1719, Abigail, daughter of John Ruck of Boston. He had had three sons, John, Benning and Foster, who died single

and before him. He married (2nd) Martha Hilton, and left her a childless widow. She subsequently married Col. Michael Wentworth of England, and had by him Martha Wentworth, who married John, son of Thomas and grandson of Mark Hunking Wentworth.

48. T. Wallingford refers to Col. Thomas Wallingford of Somersworth, one of the wealthiest men in New Hampshire. He lived near Salmon Falls, between that place and the old Somersworth meeting-house on the road to Dover, N. H. His tombstone is still readable in the old cemetery near were the old Somersworth meeting-house stood. His splendid mansion still exists to do honor to his memory. He was a Representative from Dover (Somersworth not then being a separate town) as early as 1739, and a great many years thereafter. He was one of the Judges of the Superior Court from 1748 to the day of his death, which took place at Mr. Stoodley's in Portsmouth. About 1855, his youngest child, the widow of Charles Cushing of South Berwick, Me., died, aged nearly a hundred years. Hon. H. H. Hobbs, of South Berwick, married her daughter. Col. Wallingford was father of Lt. Samuel Wallingford, who was killed on board the ship Ranger in her engagement, under John Paul Jones, with the Drake, leaving a widow who married Col. Amos Coggswell of Dover, and one child, late George W. Wallingford, whose family still lives at Kennebunk, Maine. Col. Wallingford had three wives, and at least thirteen children.

RAMBLE XCII.

Theodore Atkinson's Estate--Will of Susanna, widow of George Atkinson.

In a former Ramble (No. 18, page 106) it was stated that at the time of Theodore Atkinson's death in 1779, his property by bequest come into possession of William King, of Dover, who added Atkinson to his name. This we since find is not strictly correct. The property was conveyed to George King, a relative of Atkinson, who changed his name to George Atkinson. The entailed estate afterwards became the property of William K. Atkinson of Dover, a nephew of George.

Hon. George Atkinson, who was a man of some distinction, occupied the mansion house of Hon. Theodore Atkinson, on Court street. He was twice, we think, candidate for Governor of New Hampshire, and received nearly votes enough to elect him. The date of his death we cannot find, but it occurred not far from 1790. He married Susanna, the second daughter of Rev. John Sparhawk of Salem. She died in 1796, without issue. We find in her will the following bequests, showing somewhat of her style of living:

I give, and bequeath to my nephews, Wm. K. Atkinson, John Sparhawk and Thomas Sparhawk, all my public securities, monies in the funds, notes of hand, bonds, debts of every kind due to me; judgments, executions and mortgages, to be equally divided between them my said nephews in equal thirds, share and share alike.

To Daniel Humphreys, Esq., my brother-in-law, one hundred pounds, and my house and land, shop, wharf, &c., at Puddle Dock in Portsmouth.

To my beloved brother Samuel Sparhawk, £40 *per annum during his life.* To his son Samuel Sparhawk, jr., £50, to be paid in six months after my decease. To his daughter Eliza Sparhawk, £50, to be paid in six months after my decease.

To the relict of my dear departed brother John Sparhawk, £30 per annum during life.

To my nephew John Sparhawk, my dwelling house, garden and all my household furniture and plate, (except what is hereinafter bequeathed,) my book case, books, my horses and my carriages.

To my nephew Geo. King Sparhawk, my plain silver oval waiter, my largest silver teapot and teaspoons with the "King" crest.

To my nephew Thomas Sparhawk, the land fronting my dwelling house, and also my mowing field at the creek; also I give him £100.

To my nephew Samuel Sparhawk, my pasture land at the creek.

To my niece Susannah Sparhawk, £40 sterling.

To my nephew Daniel Humphreys, jr., the field this side the creek, with the barn on it, and £30 and 2 small silver salvers.

To my nephew George Humphreys, the lot near my coach house, which is now hired of me by Abner Blaisdell.

It is my will that my protege Eliza Winslow, be suitably provided with apparel, schooling, and all other conveniences, until she attains the age of eighteen; and at 20, or sooner if married, the sum of £60 sterling.

To my sister Priscilla, (widow of Judge Ropes,) my suit of black satin and my black laced shade.

To my niece Peggy Appleton, daughter of my sister Jane, my suit of Brussels and my leather wrought fan.

To my nephew, *Wm. K. Atkinson*, the *family pictures*, my silver wrought bread basket, my largest silver tankard, my new silver plated tea urn. 1 case silver handled knives and forks, my largest Wilton carpet, also sundry books.

Then all the jewels, watches, &c., are bequeathed to sundry persons.

To niece Katy, my white satin cloak trimmed with ermine.

Sister-in-law Abigail aforesaid, my black satin cloak trimmed with broad lace.

To Deborah, wife of Nath'l Sparhawk, my suit of dove colored satin.

The rest of her apparel to her nieces.

All the residue and remainder of my estate to my nephew aforesaid, John Sparhawk, and his heirs forever.

Nephews John Sparhawk and Thomas Sparhawk to be joint executors of the will.

Signed in presence of

A. R. CUTTER,
WM. CUTTER,
ABIGAIL MITCHELL.

The farm now owned by Hon. Frank Jones in North Portsmouth was the property of George Atkinson, and thither their coach might frequently be seen going in the summer season. It afterwards became the property of her nephew Col. George K. Sparhawk — although by the will it appears to have been given to his brother John Sparhawk.

RAMBLE XCIII.

Peter Livius the Loyalist — Building of the North Bridge and Mill — Chief Justice of Quebec — His efforts to win Gen. Sullivan to the British Cause.

OUR old town was noted in the Revolution as a place of Loyalists, or Tories as they were called, as well as for her Revolutionary Patriots. At the close of the Revolution, Portsmouth came in for its share of proscribed individuals, who had left the country to avoid any participation in the Revolution. They were forbidden to return without the assent of the representatives of the country. Among these individuals was Peter Livius, the subject of our present Ramble.

PETER LIVIUS was born in Bedford, England, in 1727. He was the second son of Peter Lewis Livius, of a Saxon family of distinction, envoy to the Court of Lisbon. Peter Livius was married in England to Anna Elizabeth, second daughter of John Tufton Mason, Esq., a cousin of the Earl of Thanet. Miss Mason was of Portsmouth, a resident at the Mason House, now on Vaughan street, and had gone to England to complete her education. Mr. Livius possessed a handsome fortune, and when he came to this town, about the year 1762, he not only brought his coach, but also a double set of wheels — supposing that the new world had not art enough to make a set when the first gave out. He first occupied the house next to the North Mill which the

Meserve family had vacated; and after a few years removed into the house No. 35 Deer street, afterwards Thomas Martin's, and now owned and occupied by George Annable. In 1764, he made proposals to the town to build a bridge over the mouth of Islington Creek, twenty feet wide, part thereof to consist of a lifting bridge thirty feet long, with flood-gates of the same length, upon condition that the town would allow him to dam the water course in the Creek, for the purpose of erecting mills. This was granted, and was the first laying of the North Mill bridge, which was a private enterprise of Mr. Livius. He was educated abroad, but received an honorary degree from Harvard University in 1767.

Of the members of the Council of New Hampshire, in 1772, seven were relatives of the Governor. Having been left out of commission as a Justice of the Common Pleas, on the division of the province into Counties, when new appointments were made, and dissenting from the views of the Council as to the disposition of reserved lands in grants made by a former governor, Livius went to England, and exhibited to the lords of trade several and serious charges against the administration of which he was a member. These charges were rigidly investigated, but were finally dismissed. Livius appears, however, to have gained much popularity among those in New Hampshire who were opposed to the Governor, and who desired his removal; and was appointed, by their influence, Chief Justice of the Province. But as it was thought that the appointment, under the circumstances, was likely to produce discord, he was transferred to the more lucrative office of Chief Justice of Quebec. Livius was of foreign extraction, and, as would seem, a gentleman of strong feelings. He wrote to General John Sullivan from Canada, to induce him to abandon the Whig cause.

This letter presents in a clear manner the arguments used

by those who opposed the Revolution, and is written with such openness that Livius seemed confident that his man was secure. The letter was sealed up in a canteen with a false bottom, and was taken out by Gen. Schuyler at Fort Edward, June 16th, 1777. There is an endorsement on the back of the manuscript in Gen. Sullivan's writing.

"FROM MR. LIVIUS TO GEN. SULLIVAN."

SIR:—I have long desired to write my mind to you, on a matter of the greatest importance to you; but the unhappy situation of things has rendered all intercourse very difficult, and has prevented me. I now find a man is to be sent for a very different purpose to you. By him I shall contrive to get this letter to you, a person having undertaken to put it in the place of that which was designed to be carried to you. You know me very well, and are acquainted with many circumstances of my life, and have seen me in very trying situations, that might perhaps have been some excuse, yet I am sure you never knew me guilty of an ungentlemanly action. I remind you of this, that you may safely trust what I say to you, as coming from a person who has never trifled with any man. You know better than I do the situation of your Congress, and the confusion there is among you, and the ruin that impends: you have felt how unequal the forces of your own people are to withstand the power of Great Britain; and foreign assistance, I need not tell you how precarious and deceitful it must be. France and Spain know they cannot embark in your quarrel without the greatest danger of Great Britain turning suddenly against and taking possession of their colonies, with so great a force collected and in America; besides their fears of raising views of independence in their own colonies, to which they are much disposed. But why should I enlarge on this subject? I am sure you know the futility of all hopes of effectual foreign assistance, and that these hopes have been thrown out to keep up the spirits of the deluded common people. You therefore will not suffer yourself to be deluded by them. The most you can expect from foreigners is, that they will help, at the expense of your countrymen's blood and happiness, to keep up a dispute that will ruin you and distress Great Britain. It is not the interest of France and Spain that America should be independent; but if it were possible you could entertain any thoughts that the hopes of effectual foreign assistance were well grounded, you cannot but know that such assistance must now arrive too late; the last campaign was almost consumed before the English army could get collected and in a position to act in America; but now the campaign is just opening, the whole army in the greatest health and spirits, plentifully provided with everything, most earnest in the cause, I do assure you, well acquainted with the country, and placed so as to act briskly with the greatest efficacy. A few months will therefore probably decide the contest; you must either fight or fly; and in either case ruin seems inevitable. *You were the first man in active rebellion,* and drew with you the province you live in. What hope, what expectation can you have? You will be one of the first sacrifices to the resentment and justice of government, your family will be ruined, and you must die with ignominy; or if you should be so happy as to escape, you will drag along a tedious life of poverty, misery and continual apprehension in a foreign land. Now, Sullivan, I have a method to propose to you, if you have resolution and courage, that will save you and your family and estate from this imminent destruction; it is in plain English to tread back the steps you have already taken and to do some real essential service to your king and country, in assisting to re-establish public tranquility and lawful government. You know I will not deceive you. Every one who will exert himself for government will be rewarded, and I do assure you firmly upon my honor that I am empowered to engage particularly with you, that it shall be the case with you, if you will sincerely endeavor to deserve your pardon. It is not desired of you to declare yourself immediately, nor indeed to declare yourself at all, until you can dispose matters so as to bring the province with you; in order to which you should as much as possible, under different pretences, contrive to send every man out of the province from whom you apprehend difficulty, and to keep at home all those friendly to government or desirous of peace. In the meanwhile endeavor to give me all the material intelligence you can collect (and you can get the best;) or if you find it more convenient, you can convey it to General Burgoyne, and by using my name he will know whom it comes from without your mentioning your own name; and as soon as you can do it with efficacy and success, declare yourself, and you will find assistance you very very little expect in restoring the province to lawful government. If you do not choose to undertake this, another will, and if you continue obstinate on the ground you are now on, you may depend upon it, you will find it suddenly fail, and burst under you like the springing of a mine. What I recommend to you is not only prudent, safe, and necessary; it is right, it is honorable. That you embarked in the cause of rebellion is true; perhaps you mistook the popular delusion for the cause of your country, (as many others did who have returned to their duty,) and you engaged in it warmly: but when you found your error, you earnestly returned, you saved the province you had engaged for from devastation and ruin, and you rendered most essential services to your king and country; for which I engage my word to you, you will receive pardon, you will secure your estate, and you will be further amply rewarded. Your past conduct has been unworthy; your return will be praiseworthy. What is all this expense of human life for? these deluges of human blood? Very probably only to set afloat some lawless despotic tyrant in the room of your lawful king. I conceive you must be surrounded with embarrassments; you may perhaps find difficulty in getting a letter to me. Possibly the fellow who carries this to you may be trusted; he thinks indeed he carries to you a very different letter from this, and I suppose will be frightened a good deal when he finds the change that has been put upon him, and that I am in possession of the letter he was intended to carry—yet I have understood that he has a family here, and will I suppose wish to return, and knows well enough it is in my power to procure him pardon and reward; and I imagine he thinks (as I trust most people do) that I am never forgetful of a man who does anything to oblige me. You will consider how far you may trust him, how far it is prudent to do it, and you can sound him, and see whether he wishes to return, and whether he is likely to answer the purpose; and if you think proper you may engage to him that I will protect him, and reward him if he brings me safely a letter from you. I could say a great deal more on this subject, but I must close my letter lest it should be too late. Be sincere and steady, and give me occasion to show myself

Your sincere friend,

MONTREAL, 2nd June, 1777. ***** ******

Livius had three slaves at his house, when he lived in Deer street. A man and a wife might have been seen one day driven from the house to a vessel at the wharf, to be sent to the West Indies to be sold, crying aloud for their child which they were not allowed to take with them. And on another day, a stout slave was sent on board another vessel on an errand, when he was seized and put in confinement by the request of his mistress, and sent also for sale in the West Indies. Mr. Livius went to Canada before his family, and his wife paid off some debts here with her household furniture. The large family bible with the family coat of arms, was given to a next door neighbor, and is still retained there in nearly as good condition as it was when received ninety-three years ago.

Peter Livius died in England in 1795, at the age of 68 years. He had three daughters—one of them died unmarried—the second married Mr. May of Blackheath; the third, Capt. Dalby.

RAMBLE XCIV.

Legislation in Portsmouth in 1699—First Prison—Mark Noble.

PORTSMOUTH was the seat of Government of New Hampshire at the time when the following proceedings took place.

Ancient documents in the office of the Secretary of

State contain the records of the formation at Portsmouth of Bellmont's government, and minutes of the proceedings of the first Legislative Assembly under him in the fall of 1699. Under the act passed at this session, the Courts of Justice were originated, and continued to operate under the organization for seventy-two years. The act is copied at length in the ancient records, being the most ancient Legislative document in the possession of the State. The Assembly consisted of fifteen members, three from each of the five towns—Portsmouth, Hampton, Dover, Exeter and New Castle. The "Lord's Speech" at the opening of the Assembly commences thus:

"Gentlemen—I have called you together at this time to give you an opportunity of serving the common interest of your country by Redressing the Greaveances this province lyes under."

Among "the articles to be observed for regulating the House" is one "Imposing a threepence fine for absence at calling over;" and another, "that none smoke tobacco in the House after calling over, on penalty of threepence for Cleark." Under date of Sept. 15, 1699, is the following record:

"Complaint being made to the Assembly by the sheriff that the prison is not sufficient, *Voted*—That a strong logg house be built in the Province for a prison of thirty foot long, fourteen wide, one story of seven foot high, two brick chimneys in the midst five foot each, to be done forthwith, strong and substantial, the Treasurer and overseer to be paid out of the next Province Assessment, to be sett in Portsmouth in or near the Great Fort."

[This first prison was built near Market Square. Church Hill was called the Fort.]

In July 1700, it was voted "that Clerk of the Assembly receive 18 pence per day to be paid out of publicque Treasury for writing for the Assembly, finding paper and registering its minutes in this book."

Under date 17 July 1701 is the following: "The Publicque affairs of the House being much obstructed by persons sitting and leying on the bed—Voted that whosoever henceforward either sett or lye down shall forfeit three pence to the House for a fine for every such Default after the House is called over." On the next day, July 18, 1701, is the following record: "Whereas the publicque affairs of this House is much obstructed by reason of several members thereof soe often withdrawing themselves into the chimney to take tobacco and sitt talking and not attend the affairs of the House, Voted, That whosoever shall soe doe for the future shall pay a threepence fine for every such offence except leave be given."

At the same session is the following minute:—"Mr. Timothy Hilliard dismissed, voted a person not fit to be a member hereof. Request sent to Upper House that notice be given to town to fill vacancy."

In the State records we also find the following letter from Mark Noble, asking for the discharge of John Stavers, after the famous riot of the Earl-of-Halifax Hotel. Noble was an insane man for forty years afterwards.

PORTSMOUTH, February 3, 1777.

To the Committee of Safety the Town of Exeter:

Gentlemen:—As I am informed that Mr. Stivers is in confinement in goal upon my account contrary to my desire, for when I was at Mr. Stivers a fast day I had no ill nor ment none against the Gentleman but by bad luck or misfortune I have received a bad blow but it is so well that I hope to go out in a day or two. So by this gentlemen of the Committee I hope you will release the gentleman upon my account. I am yours to serve.

MARK NOBLE,
A friend to my country.

RAMBLE XCV.

The Old Stavers Hotel – The Party – The Daniel Street Apparition—The Dance—A Fragrant Interruption.

THE following reminiscences of the old Pitt Tavern, in Pitt (now Court) street, presenting, as they do, a pleasant picture of social life in the olden time, are perhaps worth preserving from oblivion; not the less so from the fact that the ancient hostelry still survives, in a vigorous old age, the merry party, which on the occasion referred to, were assembled within its walls.

On a winter evening, in the latter portion of the last century, a party of half a dozen of the young men of Portsmouth met at the dwelling of one of their number to take part in a dramatic representation he had designed for the amusement of himself and of his friends; but in consequence of the illness of a member of the family, it was postponed until another evening. Feeling in a somewhat festive mood, it was proposed, by way of mitigating their disappointment, to adjourn to Stavers' Hotel, and there enjoy a quiet supper. On proceeding thither, the landlord informed them that in preparing for an expected sleighing party from out of town his larder was nearly exhausted, but he would do the best he was able for them. As they sat around the shining brass fender in the room assigned to them, enjoying the genial warmth of a blazing wood fire, it was suggested that while waiting for the preparation of their meal, each one in turn should sing a song or tell a story. A majority, being good singers, were thus enabled to fulfil their share of the agreement, and a young sailor, who had just returned from a voyage to London, gave them a description of some of the wonders of that famous city. When the last was called upon to contribute his share to the general fund of amusement, he informed them that he was neither gifted as a musician or as an *improvisatore*, but he would tell them what might pass for a ghost story, recently related to him by a female relative. On a summer night some thirty years before, a young friend, (who afterwards became her husband,) had been visiting her at her father's house, and on his way home, while passing through Ark (now Penhallow) street, was startled by a low whistle, and looking back to learn its source, he saw the figure of a man far above the ordinary stature, in a huntsman's dress, followed by a troop of twenty to thirty dogs. Astonishment at so strange a spectacle nearly rivetted him to the spot; and his wonder was still farther excited on observing that he could hear no sound of footsteps, nor was the dust in the least disturbed, although it was like ashes in its lightness, and two to three inches deep. Recovering somewhat from his surprise, he addressed the individual, who made no reply, and proceeding onwards, passed down Buck (now State) street, where the young man lost sight of him in the distance. On reaching home, instead of retiring at once to rest, he seated himself in a chair by the side of his bed, and fell into a profound fit of meditation at what he had witnessed, from which he was aroused half an hour afterwards by the entrance of his room mate, who, in a jocular tone, inquired if "Molly had given him the mitten?" On learning the cause of his abstraction, he replied, "Why, I saw them myself, just as the clock struck ten, while stopping a moment under Wentworth's elms. They passed me, and I watched them until they turned into Ark street." Determined, if possible, to learn if so unusual a visitor, with so large a troop of canine companions, was really in town, they arose at an early hour, and made inquiries at the various places where travellers were entertained in those days, but could gather nothing then, or at any time afterwards, that would enable them to elucidate the mystery. She further stated that the moonlight on that evening was of such remarkable brilliancy that she had tried the experiment of reading, by its aid, the fine print of a pocket Bible.

While commenting upon this curious story, supper was announced as in readiness, and proving excellent in quality as it was abundant in quantity, was fully enjoyed. A song or two succeeded, mingled with expressions of gratification at the pleasant evening they had passed, when the company prepared to depart for their homes; but encountering in the passage a portion of the party from out of town, and recognizing a couple of their school-boy friends of a few years previous, they accepted an invitation to remain and participate in the dance about to commence above-stairs, for which a colored professor of the violin had been included among the arrangements of the landlord. A further addition was made to their number in the person of a young gentleman, who came to the hotel to return a conveyance procured there for an excursion to Boston.

The ceremony of introduction being over, the dancing commenced with great spirit; the unexpected accession of so many young gentlemen, in providing them with partners, proving highly acceptable to the young ladies, who had previously been in a decided majority. They had not long enjoyed their exciting amusement, when an odor of onions became perceptible in the room, and imagining that it proceeded from the culinary regions below stairs, the doors leading into the entry were closed. Instead of diminishing the perfume, however, it rather increased, until it became quite overpowering. The person who seemed the most annoyed by it was the young gentleman from Boston, and while he was endeavoring to ascertain its cause, a sudden light broke upon him which caused his exit, for a season, from the room.

His excursion to Boston had been a combination of business and pleasure, and among many commissions he had been called upon to execute for others, was the purchase of a pound of that fragrant drug known as asafœtida, for an old lady of his acquaintance, a sort of Lady Bountiful, who went about among the sick and the needy, administering to their various wants, spiritual, temporal, and medicinal. Receiving it from the druggist in half-pound packages, it had been laying in the sleigh-box during his homeward journey, from whence it had been transported to the pockets of his coat, where it was totally forgotten until it made him aware of its presence, in the heat of the room and the excitement of the dance. It was soon restored to its original place of deposit, and the explanation given on his return as the cause of his sudden disappearance, afforded the company no little merriment. The dancing, interspersed with singing, was continued with unabated spirit until the small hours of the morning, when the out-of-town party took their departure, and the Portsmouth delegation sought their various homes. It was to the latter one of those unanticipated seasons of enjoyment that leave behind so pleasant an impression; and was not forgotten as such by one of them, at least, when nearly fifty years had passed away.

The writer of this heard the "ghost story" from its original relator when she had reached the age of more than four score years, and saw the fine-print Bible from which she read in that brilliant moonlight. She said that her husband and his friend often alluded to the incident in their maturer years, and in such a way, added to the fact that they were truthful men, as to convince her of their entire sincerity. Modern science would probably set it down as a case of optical illusion, which may be a correct solution of the mystery; one cannot but be puzzled a little, however, by the fact, that it occurred to two individuals at a distance from each other.

RAMBLE XCVI.

LYING before us* among the ancient newspapers of Portsmouth, is the "*New Hampshire Gazette*" from the 17th of January to the 14th of April, 1775, published by its original proprietor, Daniel Fowle, and bearing at its head the British coat of arms. The reading matter consists chiefly of the doings of the Continental Congress, and items of English and domestic news, relating to the one all-absorbing topic—the difficulties between King George and his American subjects. The number of April 7th contains the well-known eloquent and prophetic speech of the Lord Mayor of London "on the motion of Lord North for an address to His Majesty against the Americans." The following synopsis of the advertisements will show who were among the leading business men of Portsmouth the year previous to the breaking out of the Revolution:

Jacob Sheafe, Jr.—Malaga wine, feathers, choice lime and pitch.

Hugh Henderson, at his shop "opposite the Printing Office"—English and India goods.

Thomas Martin—English goods, hardware, groceries, china and earthern ware.

Benjamin Austin, at his shop on Spring Hill—Hardware and groceries, with "a genteel assortment of silver-plated shoe-buckles, of the newest fashion."

Richard Wibird Penhallow, Long Wharf—Russia duck, hardware, steel, cordage, &c.

Joshua Wentworth—Refined bar iron, anchors, &c.

Noah Parker—New ship bread, New York crackers and batter bread.

George Craigie—English goods, including dry goods and hardware.

Jacob Treadwell, offers for sale an assortment of prime moose hides.

* For this and a number of sketches used as Rambles, we are indebted to the pen of Mr. John H Bowles, now residing in Brooklyn, L. I.

John Moore—Day and night school at his residence near the Long Wharf. Also has for sale paper hangings, carpeting, Holland tiles* for chimneys, Jacob's Law Dictionary, onions, &c. [Rather a miscellaneous business.]

George Doig, painter, from London, executes coats of arms the neatest of any in the Province of New Hampshire. Shop in King street.

Thomas Warren, painter, from Boston, paints coats of arms.

NOTICE.—The person who took a gun out of *Dr. Hall Jackson's*† entry is requested to return the same to *George Dame*, or he will be prosecuted as a thief. [This sharp device for frightening a rogue into making restitution, resorted to sometimes in our own day, does not appear to have been very successful, as the notice is continued several weeks in succession.]

After a lapse of twenty years, during which the battles of the Revolution and of the Constitution had been fought and won, the Gazette seems to awake, like Rip Van Winkle from his long slumber, and finds itself reclining most lovingly in the arms of its ancient political opponent, the "*Oracle* of the *Day*." Its dimensions are considerably enlarged, and the name of Daniel Fowle has given place in the imprint to that of his apprentice, John Melcher. The lion and the unicorn have disappeared also, to continue their fight for the crown in some more congenial sphere. As these ancient contestants, the Gazette and Oracle, who threw so many paper bomb-shells into each other's camps in the olden time, lie so quietly together before me, they seem like a pair of venerable gentlemen, who forgetting the asperities of their earlier life, smoke the pipe of peace together in their declining years. May they both live—the Gazette under its time-honored title, and the Oracle under that of the "JOURNAL" which it has held for forty-seven years—for many generations yet to come.

* *Query.*—Were not these "tiles" the same article still to be seen in the Warner mansion, and others of the ancient dwellings of Portsmouth?

† Dr. Hall Jackson's residence, in its present modernized form, is still in existence at the northeast corner of Court and Washington streets.

There are some fifty or sixty copies of the "Gazette" and "Oracle," of various dates in the years 1796, '7 and '8, containing a large amount of interesting matter, much of which has passed into history, and much more equally worthy of being placed on permanent record, that, but for its preservation through some such method as this, would have been consigned to oblivion. Among the state papers are the annual and other messages of Presidents Washington and Adams, and the messages and proclamations of John Taylor Gilman, Governor of New Hampshire, and Increase Sumner, Governor of Massachusetts. There is also a letter of the Grand Lodge of Massachusetts to General Washington, signed by the familiar names of Paul Revere, Grand Master, and Isaiah Thomas, Senior Grand Master, with General Washington's reply—the original of which is at this day one of their most valued relics.

Much prominence is given to the interesting events then transpiring in Europe. France was in a transition state, between the period known as the Reign of Terror, and that when Napoleon assumed the reins of government and obliterated the last vestiges of what had been little else than an empty name—the French Republic. "Citizen Bonaparte, General-in-Chief of the Army of Italy," was winning for himself a name that will exist through all time. Many of his official letters to the Executive Directory, the then existing government of France, are published in full; among others, that relating to the battle of Lodi, in which while giving due credit to Berthier, Massena, D'Allemagne, and others of his generals for their heroic daring in the passage of the bridge across the Adda, modestly omits even the slightest allusion to his own participation in that world-renowned event. I find in these papers many proofs of the corrections of history in relation to the Little Corporal. Here is a confirmation of the truth of one of the many anecdotes respecting him, related by himself in one of his despatches to the Directory. "The day previous to our affair at Lodi, while seeing a brigade file off, a light-infantry man approached me and said, 'General, we must do so and so.' 'Sir,' said I, 'will you be silent?' when he immediately disappeared. I have since endeavored to find him—for what he hinted was exactly what I had secretly ordered—but much to my regret I sought for him in vain." The following incident of Napoleon's earlier life as a soldier, I have never met with before, and if not new to others, is worth repeating. On rejoining his regiment at Auxonne, in 1789, after a term of absence, he took with him a younger brother of but the age of twelve years. On being asked by one of his companions why he had brought with him a youth of so tender an age, he replied, "I wish him to enjoy a great spectacle—that of a nation which will speedily be either regenerated or destroyed." He little fancied, probably, at that period, in the subordinate capacity of lieutenant of artillery, how vast an influence he was destined to wield in the future destinies of France.

It is very evident, from the tone of these journals, that the American press were accustomed to regard Napoleon at this period through the medium of his own personal merits, rather than the blurred vision of British spectacles, as many were inclined to do in later years when the star of his fortunes was waning, or when his position as arbiter of the destines of Europe, was changed to that of a powerless exile upon the rock of St. Helena.

The following are a few of the names that appear in the advertisements of 1798: J. Whipple, Collector of Customs; Martin Parry, Samuel Larkin, James Rundlett, George Long, Clement Jackson, John Shapley, Edward Parry, Lang, Brierly & Co., Benj. Bigelow, Jr., Nathaniel A. Haven, Fairbanks & Sparhawk, George Wentworth, Leigh & Bowles, James Sheafe, Peter Coffin, Joseph Green, Neil McIntyre, John Noble & Co., Wm. Neil, John Pomeroy, (in Buck street, near the sign of "Noah's Ark.")

There was no lack of amusement, it would seem, at Portsmouth, in the latter portion of the last century, of which that venerable temple of Melpomene and Terpsichore, the old Assembly House, was the arena. At one time the advertisements announce the Boston company as performing tragedy and comedy; and at another, Mrs. and Miss Arnold, and Miss Green, of the dramatic profession, are aided by Portsmouth amateurs, in the production of light comedy and farce, with an occasional attempt at tragedy. Young Norval, in the tragedy of Douglas, "by a young gentleman of Portsmouth." Old Pickle, in the farce of the Spoiled Child, "by a gentleman of Portsmouth," etc. Here is a portion of the entertainment for March 21st, 1788, that from its exceeding novelty is worth bringing to light. It is well for Barnum that he did not flourish in those days; the Fejee Mermaid or Woolly Horse would hardly have saved him from being shorn of his laurels. "A favorite tragic piece called '*The Babes in the Woods*,' wherein will be displayed the father and mother lying on their beds, giving charge of their children to their brother, who promises to take care of them. After the death of the parents, which takes place before the audience, the uncle hires two ruffians to kill them; they fight, and one of them is killed; also the Death of the Babes; a Robin will descend and cover them with leaves; being one of the greatest curiosities ever exhibited. Likewise an Angel will descend, uncover the bodies, and fly away with them! To conclude with the fatal end of the cruel uncle, who is *carried off by a large Serpent!!*" The working up of the final catastrophe, the retribution that overtook the "cruel uncle" through the agency of that "large Serpent," was a stroke of genius, never excelled in the modern school of sensation dramas.

The most youthful and the last of these relics of ancient journalism, is "*The Literary Mirror*," of various dates in

1808, "published by Stephen Sewell, in Court street, opposite the Brick Market,"—neat and tasteful in its typographical execution, and containing a judicious variety of original and selected matter. It was published, I think, but a single year, though deserving a longer lease of life.

As I look upon these ancient sheets, especially those of ante-revolutionary date that have so long survived the generation who were their first readers, the thought occurs to me that among the many and great improvements time has made since they first issued from the press, there is none greater than that in newspaper-printing itself. Fancy presents to my view Mr. Daniel Fowle standing by the side of the quaint-looking structure, but little superior in its mechanism to an old-fashioned cider mill, on which these antique copies of the *Gazette*, at the rate of fifty to an hundred per hour, received their impression; while that eccentric specimen of colored humanity, *Prime*, his serving man, inks the types with a pair of sheepskin balls, black and glistening as his own face. Equally incredulous would have been both Prime and his master, to learn, that in the not far distant future a piece of mechanism would be produced, wondrous alike for grace, beauty and celerity, from whence twenty-five thousand sheets, printed, folded and counted, could be thrown in a single hour, nor less so that *steam* would be the power by which this marvellous machine could be set in motion.

RAMBLE XCVII.

Christian Shore—Freeman's Point—The Ham House—The Waterhouse Family.

In a former Ramble we said we were unable to state the origin of the name *Christian Shore*, given to the north part of our city. We since learn that a century ago, when there were but few families beyond where the North mill bridge now is, there were several who were strict adherents to puritan principles, while others were more loose in their habits, and might be found sometimes late at night at Foss's Tavern, enjoying their flip, and cracking their jokes. When the hour for parting arrived, "Well, we must leave for *Christian Shore*," was frequently the jocose remark; and from it that part of Portsmouth took its name. In the town books, that part of the town, two hundred years ago, was designated as "the land on the other side of Strawberry Bank Creek."

One of the most beautiful locations in Portsmouth for river proximity, extensive prospect and varied landscape, is that above Portsmouth Bridge, known of late years as Freeman's Point, but for nearly two centuries previously as Ham's Point. It is approached by Cutts's lane, and a ride of a third of a mile from North road brings you to the spot where the old deserted mansion house of William Ham, with the marks of where the corn-house and barn once stood, remained until it was taken down in 1868 or '69; and the enclosed square in its rear contains the graves of five or six generations. Rough stones mark the head and foot of each mound, but they tell not a name or date of those of olden time who sleep there.

It is said that three brothers of the Ham family came to this country previous to 1646: we have, however, the name of William only, who in 1652 had a grant of fifty acres of land at what is now called Freeman's Point, where he erected a dwelling, which is probably the building now standing there. In 1654, Matthew Ham was granted by the town "a lot of land next to his father's new dwelling house." In 1660, Matthew Ham was granted twenty five acres—which appears to have been between the Point farm and the present main road. In 1668, there was a John Ham in Dover, who might have been another son of William.

In 1664, it appears by the town book that "Wm. Ham, widow Ham, and the rest who live on the other side of Strawberry Bank Creek" made complaint that William Cotton was interfering with their rights by claiming his division of the public land on that shore, whereupon the selectmen decreed that William Ham should have sixty-six acres, joining on the north side Richard and John Cutt's two hundred acre farm.* That Matthew Ham should have twenty-five acres, on the west of William's, also bounded on the north-west by the Cutt farm. Roger Knight had thirteen acres, assigned between Matthew Ham's and Richard Jackson's. Richard Seaward had thirteen acres, east of Knight's; and Richard Jackson was decreed twenty-six acres.

On the latter grant the old Jackson house of two stories now stands, which was probably built as early as 1664, and is now more than two centuries old; probably the most ancient house in the city. It is a rare specimen of the architecture of the early times. The roof on the north side extends to the ground, covering a wood-house in connection with the dwelling. The frame is of oak, and the timber which forms the sills projects into the lower rooms, affording around them a continuous and stationary seat for the children of six generations. It is now owned by Mr. Nathaniel Jackson, a regular descendant of the original proprietor.

The farm of the first William Ham came down by entailment to the oldest sons through four or five generations. We have no early family genealogy, but as the name of *William Ham* is continued regularly in the tax lists for many years, there is little doubt that the eldest sons for

* This Cutt's farm was that which Madam Ursula occupied thirty years after, when she was killed by the Indians, and is now the beautiful country seat of Mark H. Wentworth, Esq.

several generations bore that name and in succession inherited the house and possessed the farm.

The owner in the year 1700 was Samuel Ham. His oldest son, William, who was born there about 1712, married Elizabeth Waterhouse and had seven sons—Samuel, who inherited the homestead) Timothy,† George, William, Ephraim, Nathaniel, and Benjamin,—and one daughter, who married Capt. John Tuckerman. The farm came by right of primogeniture into possession of Samuel, who broke the entailment, and more than forty or fifty years since the farm passed out of the family.

It was at a time when the hostile Indians were prowling in this neighborhood, just after Madam Ursula Cutt had been murdered on the adjoining farm, that the Ham boys were left at home one Sunday while the family boat had borne a load to the old mill-dam meeting. In the midst of the services, a powder explosion was heard. The meeting was closed instantly, and the worshippers, putting themselves in position to meet the Indians, proceeded to the Point. They were agreeably disappointed to find that the boys had affrighted themselves as well as the whole village, by the explosion of the great powder-horn.

About a third of a mile north of the old Ham mansion-house on the Point, between the great elm and the shore, in a grove, is the cellar of the house of Timothy Waterhouse. He was the third son of Richard Waterhouse, the tanner, who married Sarah, the daughter of Dr. Renald Fernald, and owned and occupied Peirce's Island, in 1688. The other sons of Richard W. were Richard, born in 1674, and Samuel, born in 1676.

Timothy Waterhouse located himself on this cove above Freeman's Point probably soon after the year 1700. He

---

† The children of Timothy Ham were Timothy. William, Supply, Henry, Elizabeth, Sarah (married Samuel Akerman,) Mary (married Samuel Brewster), Phebe (married Charles Reding), Ann and Jane.

was also a tanner and shoemaker. Here were his tan-pits, and his cultivated acres. His connection with the town was by the river. His wife was Miss Moses. Their children were three sons—John, Joseph and Timothy; and six daughters,—Margaret, Mary, Ruth, Sarah, Elizabeth and Lydia. The parents had the ability to instruct their children, and they gave them a better education at home than girls generally received in that day. *John* settled in Barrington. *Joseph* settled in some town in Maine, and *Timothy* removed to Rhode Island, where he became one of the Royal Council. Timothy had eleven sons; among them was the celebrated Dr. Benjamin Waterhouse, a Professor at Cambridge, and the father of vaccination in this country. [His own son in the year 1800 was successfully vaccinated for the kine pox by him,—the first experiment made in this country.]

Margaret became the wife of Samuel Brewster at the Plains, and was the mother of eight sons and five daughters. Their first daughter *Margaret* married Mr. Furbisher of Boston. *Samuel* removed to Barrington. *Moses* inherited the Plains house. *Timothy* died at 21. *John* went to sea and never returned. *Abigail* married Leader Nelson. *Mary* married Samuel Winkley of Barrington, and was the mother of Winkley the Shaker elder. *Daniel* occupied the house next east of the Steam Factory previous to the Revolution—in 1775 removed to Rochester, and in 1795 located in Wolfeborough. *David* married Mary Gains, daughter of John, and built the house in Deer street in 1766. *William* (Colonel) married Ruth Foss, daughter of Zachariah. *Paul* removed to Barrington. *Margaret* 2d (born after the death of the 1st) married Joseph Hayes of Barrington. *Lydia* married Joseph Hicks of Madbury, the owner of "Hicks' Hill."

Mary married Mr. Spinney, a ship-carpenter. She had one daughter and three sons, all of whom died nearly at the same time. Her desire that her children might be restored was answered—having again in due time three sons and a daughter.

Ruth married John Gains, the father of Col. George Gains of the Revolution, and of Mary the wife of David Brewster. From the latter descended Samuel, Mary and John G. Brewster.

Sarah was one day visiting her sister Ruth after marriage, when Capt. Zachariah Foss in passing saw her. He spoke to his associate on the beauty of Mrs. Gains, when he was informed that he mistook the person. "If that is not Gains's wife she is mine," was the reply. His suit was successful. On the total loss of his property in a few years his wife disposed of about ten dollars' worth of fine linen and obtained the means for opening a place of refreshment on a small scale. As their means increased, in after years they built a large stage and tavern house on the spot on Fleet street now occupied by the brick stable of the Franklin House. The house afterwards came into possession of John Weare, the father of Mrs. Mary A. Gotham.

The children of Zachariah and Sarah Foss were eight daughters. *Sally*, the wife of Capt. Cochran who had command of Fort William and Mary when captured by the Patriots in 1774. [Mrs. Charles Hardy was the youngest daughter of Capt. Cochran.] *Mary*, the wife of Joseph Young of Newmarket. *Elizabeth* married Thomas Flagg of Chester. [After living together three or four years her husband was detected coining money, and eloped with his own aunt to Virginia. He took his two young children, and the mother never saw her two sons again until they were married men.] *Ruth* married Col. William Brewster. *Margaret* married Capt. Cullom. There were also *Joanna*, *Olive* and *Abigail.*

Once in her husband's absence at sea, Mrs. Foss sold a rich brocade silk dress pattern and purchased the frame of a house with the proceeds. The house is now standing in Washington street, the Low house. What Foss acquired by the industry and frugality of his first wife, he lost by the extravagance of a second, who was a widow of Adams of Boston. Among her bills contracted before the marriage was one of several hundred pounds for sperm candles. It took nearly all his estate to pay her old debts.

Elizabeth married William Ham, above referred to, and lived on the farm at Freeman's Point. They had seven sons and a daughter, whose names are given elsewhere.

Lydia married Capt. Colby, who sailed in the employ of Sir William Pepperell. After Colby's death, Capt. Ephraim Dennett of Christian Shore took a liking to her, and to save the trouble of frequently visiting Kittery in the winter, paid her board at a relative's on Christian Shore by furnishing the family with their wood for the winter. In the spring they were ready to be married, and took up their residence in the prominent Dennett house, now better known as the "Bee Hive." After a few years she became a widow, and her reputation as belonging to a family of smart girls brought her to the notice of John Plummer of Rochester. For an account of his romantic interview when she was dressed in her leather apron, the reader is referred to the 75th Ramble, 345th page. Lydia had but one son, *Jeremiah Dennett.* [His children were George, Ephraim, John Plummer, Mark, Jeremiah, William, Lydia, Susannah, Ann and Catherine.

Thus have we almost unwittingly, while standing over the old Waterhouse cellar, conjured up an army of which the germs here first had existence. We can point also to some remains of the old house which was removed from the cellar about 92 years ago. It may be found in the ancient mansion house of the late Timothy Ham senior, at the corner of North and Dearborn streets. But those who gave life to the house a century and a third ago, are subjects of more interest.

There was no little life in that old house—which had under its roof six merry girls and three roguish boys and a slave—and sometimes the staid old folks would tell them that they almost raised the evil one. One winter evening, somewhere about 1725 the parents were absent for the night, the snow was fast falling, and the boys and girls resolved to have a good time. So the fire was enlivened with fresh wood, and the dance began. The slave had a good voice, and as he capered round in a "country dance" merrily sang—

"Don't you see how my head does wag—
Don't you see how my shoulders lag—
Don't you see how my hips do shake—
Don't you see what pains I take,
In dancing of my quivering shake!"

In the height of their hilarity, which would hardly have been enjoyed in the old folks' presence, there was a violent thumping at the door. In that stormy night, far away from any neighbors, and from any road, there was something frightful in that token. The singing was hushed, and that parental admonition to beware of "raising the evil one," seemed to flash suddenly over their superstitious minds. Margaret, the oldest and bravest, led the way to the door, but no sooner had she opened it than she saw what she thought Satan himself. The figure was white, with a horrible black face deep in a white lopped hat, which was hanging down over each shoulder! That the Old Scratch had now come they all believed, Margaret fainted, and it was sometime before the ugly looking but faithful slave of Nathaniel Jackson was recognized beneath his snow covering,—who had "come to get Massa's shoes."

Could those nine children now be recalled on this spot, the fright of that night would doubtless be one of the first events they would bring to remembrance.

The Rambler feels some personal interest in that family, for three of those sisters, Margaret, Ruth and Elizabeth Waterhouse, all hold to him in different lines the relation of great-grandmothers.

RAMBLE XCVIII.

The Pickering Family.

JAMES COLEMAN PICKERING died at Newington March 30, 1862, aged 90 years 6 months. He was in his manners, character and appearance a gentleman of the old school. He was tall, erect, of large frame, and comely in figure and feature. He owned and cultivated the ancient Pickering homestead; was the oldest person in town, and enjoyed through his long pilgrimage the confidence and respect of the community. He was a descendant, in the sixth generation, from Hon. John Pickering, Speaker of the Colonial Assembly and King's Attorney General of the Province of New Hampshire.* He lived and died where he was born, in the old Pickering mansion, and where were born his grandfather Joshua Pickering (father of late Ephraim Pickering) and his uncle, the late Hon. John Pickering, Chief Justice of the State.

By his death his beautiful homestead farm, which has been in this family from the first settlement of New Hampshire, and descended from father to son for nearly two hundred years without a deed in all that time, will pass into the possession of another generation. Incidents of this kind serve occasionally as landmarks to indicate how fast and far the present generation are drifting from the English habits which for many generations characterized the people of this section of the State.

He was the last of a family of twelve children, all of whom were alive at the death of their father, more than

* The wives of the late Dr. Nathan Parker, Isaac Lyman, Wm. K. Atkinson, and Charles Walker, who were sisters, and the late William Pickering, State Treasurer, were descendants of the same John Pickering, as are Thomas B Aldrich of Boston, James F. Joy of Detroit, Wm. P. Haines of Biddeford, Wm. P. Weeks of Canaan, Albert R. Hatch and John S. H. Frink of Portsmouth, the wife of Josiah Minot of Concord, and the wife of Wm. H. Y. Hackett of Portsmouth.

half a century ago, and followed him from the same house to the grave. They were—

Anna, the wife of Samuel Fabyan of Newington—born Feb. 28, 1758; died Dec. 26th, 1833, aged 75.

Sarah T., wife of Valentine Pickering—born April 11, 1760; died Jan. 1, 1823, aged 62.

Deborah Rollins, wife of Paul Rollins of Newington—born Jan. 15, 1762; died March 22d, 1846, aged 83.

Lydia, the wife of Theodore Furber of Portsmouth—born March 1, 1764; died Jan. 3, 1842, aged 78.

Olive Rindge—born March 22, 1765; died Sept. 16, 1840, unmarried, aged 75.

Joshua Pickering, of North Hampton—born March 8, 1768; died Jan. 25, 1852, aged 84.

Joseph W. Pickering, of Portsmouth—born March 15, 1770; died May 19, 1850, aged 80.

James C. Pickering—born Sept. 30, 1771; died March 30, 1862, aged 90½.

Mary, wife of Joseph Perkins of Kennebunkport—born Nov. 8, 1773; died Aug. 1, 1849, aged 76.

Elizabeth, wife of Jonathan Stone of Kennebunkport—born Oct. 23, 1775; died July 3, 1834, aged 59.

Abigail, wife of Matthew B. Packer of Greenland; born Oct. 4, 1777; died Sept. 3, 1857, aged 80.

Ephraim Pickering, of Newington—born Sept. 28, 1779; and killed by an explosion of a magazine at Fort Constitution, July 4, 1809; and died in the house now occupied by Mr. Hackett, 69 Congress street, aged 30.

The average age of the twelve children was 73; a case of family longevity rarely found. Their added ages, with that of their parents, was over a thousand years. Of the eleven married, all except Ephraim outlived their respective wives and husbands, by many years.

Lydia (Coleman) Pickering, the widow of the late Col. Ephraim P. whose twelve children are above named, died in the same house, February 16, 1832, aged 94. She was the mother of twelve children, ten of whom were alive at her death; 60 grandchildren, 43 of whom were then living; 93 great-grand children, 81 of whom were then living; and five of the fifth generation:—170 descendants, 139 of whom were living at her death.

Mr. James C. Pickering and two of his brothers, Joseph W. and Joshua, if we mistake not, were subscribers to the Portsmouth *Oracle* when it commenced in 1793, and continued to take it when the name of the paper was changed to the *Portsmouth Journal,* and as long as they lived. Whether that good state of mind which results from a consciousness of dealing justly with others tends to long life, is a problem in philosophy we will not attempt now to discuss,—but the fact that they all three paid promptly their annual subscriptions our books give evidence.

The first John Pickering, of whom an account is given in Ramble VII. had two sons; John, born in 1640, who inherited Pickering's Neck, and Thomas, who had his farm in what is now Newington. Thomas's first son James, born about 1680, was the first male Pickering born in Newingson. He was a lieutenant in the French war; was married in 1717. He had three brothers and eight sisters. One of his sisters married a Brackett, from whom descended the Brackett family now living in Greenland, one married a Seavey, of Rye, who was an ancestor of the Sheafe family—the mother of the wife of the first Jacob Sheafe;* another married a Weeks, of Greenland; one a Grow; one a Chamberlain. From the old Lieut. sprang all the Pickerings of Newmarket (some of whom have emigrated to the South),

* We will in this connection correct a mistake made in a former Ramble, respecting the locality of the mansion house, in which Hannah Seavey, the wife of the first Jacob Sheafe, was born. The house was on the beautiful spot where the new house of Mr. Eben L. Seavey now stands, at the head of Seavey's Creek, on the road leading from Sagamore Creek to Wallis's Sands. The old house was taken down but a few years since. His grandfather, Wm. Seavey, a brother of Hannah, inherited it from his father. Connected with the house is an excellent bathing house on the Creek, and the beauty and convenience of the locality attracts many boarders from abroad in the summer months.

all those in Rochester and Barnstead, besides what remain in Newington. The great-grandfather of Charles W. Pickering, of the U. S. Navy, was a son of Lt. James. Joshua, a brother of Lieut. James, married a Smithson, from Portsmouth. He had six sons. One of them, Judge Pickering, father of the late Jacob S. Pickering, married his second-cousin; a sister of Col. James Sheafe. His second brother, Thomas, married Col. Downing's daughter for his first wife; a Miss Janvrin of Portsmouth for his second. From him descended all the Pickerings now living in Greenland, and three or four families now living in Newington. The late Richard Pickering was his son. His grandson, Col. Thomas Pickering, commanded a regiment stationed on Peirce's Island during the last war with England; so it seems up to that time the old military spirit had not subsided.

RAMBLE XCIX.

Pickering House in Vaughan Street—Edward Hart—Gen. Peabody's Perfidy—Capt. Cullam, &c.

THE Pickering mansion, in Vaughan street, was built not far from the year 1780, by Mr. Edward Hart, a baker, the son of Col. John Hart, who in an excursion to Louisburg in 1758 died there of the small pox. Col. Hart left eleven sons by three wives: Thomas a mariner died in Europe, William a mathematician, George a blacksmith (father of the late George Hart of Deer street,) John a ropemaker, Benjamin (the father of the late venerable Hanson M. Hart,) Edward a baker, Richard who settled on a farm at Newington, Joseph, Henry and Nathaniel, blacksmiths, and Oliver a house carpenter. (Messrs. Richard Hart of Russell street and Daniel Hart were their cousins.)

Edward Hart, as above stated, built this house, and was at the time the baker of Portsmouth. The building on the north of the house, now a livery stable, was built for his store and bake-house. Between the dwelling-house and the bake-house was a shop for selling bread. At that day wheeled vehicles were scarce, and the hot bread was put in two large pannier baskets, and placed on the horse's back, behind the carrier. The customers had to be on the look-out, as there was no dismounting. In rainy weather and in hot sunshine, a wide-spread umbrella was raised, and the steam rising from the baskets and the horse's heated sides, gave some premonitions of the steam travel of later days. It was found, however, that horses could stand this business but a short time—the hot bread continually applied to their backs, was soon fatal. Bread carts were afterwards brought into use.

In a few years after Mr. Hart built this house, the Universalist Society purchased the lot in the rear and erected the meeting-house. Mr. H. was not pleased with its proximity to his premises, and remarked to its projector—"It is no matter, I shall have it for a stable one of these days." The reply was, "Well it may be so—for our Lord and Master was born in a stable." The house was used for public worship by different societies during the life of Mr. Hart—although there have been times since when it has sunk beneath the dignified name of a stable.

As Deputy Sheriff, Mr. Hart's bondsmen were Judge John Pickering and Dr. William Cutter. Imprisonment for debt was the law and custom of those times—and among the men who would not pay their debts was Gen. Nathaniel Peabody of Exeter. When on a visit to Portsmouth, a writ was put into Mr. Hart's hands, and he served it upon him taking him as a prisoner. "Money, bail, or jail," was the word. Money he could not command—bail he could not give—and so jail was the only horn of the dilemma left. Gen. P. said he preferred imprisonment in Exeter jail, and so the accommodating Sheriff, in respect for the high military position of his charge, started with him for Exeter. At Portsmouth Plains, the General told him he did not like to have the show of so long a ride in the custody of a sheriff, and if he would allow him to proceed alone, he would deliver himself to Hart the next day at Exeter. Hart took his personal promise. Gen. P. went home alone, and the next day the Sheriff was promptly on the ground. Gen. P. however on arriving home, made his house his castle, and kept out of sight. This made the Sheriff responsible for a large debt, and was his ruin.

The bondsmen paid the debt, and Judge Pickering took the house and building in Vaughan street, to which he removed when his residence in Market street was burned by the fire of 1802. Dr. William Cutter took a parcel of land on the west and north sides of the North burying ground, in consideration of what he had to pay as bondsman. This land was afterwards purchased of Dr. Cutter by the town, and added to the original acre which Mr. Hart's father had originally granted to the town for a burying ground.

This misplaced confidence of Mr. Hart was felt by him and his family through life, which closed some fifty years since.

We will not resuscitate the remains of one who at an earlier day was an occupant of the next house north.

When David Cullam came to Portsmouth, we do not know. As early as 1773 he was married to a Miss Currier. She had the reputation of being an excellent woman, and he an affectionate and kind husband. Their offspring were one son, who bore his father's name, and died in early life unmarried; and one daughter, Amy. She was born about the year 1774. Her mother died when Amy was not more than three years old. In 1776 Capt. Cullam was without much property, ranking with the lowest in tax assessment. In 1777 his taxes had increased about four fold, and in 1779 he was one of the rich men of Portsmouth, being one of the twenty highest tax payers. He was a lieutenant with Elijah Hall, under John Paul Jones, either in the Reliance, or the Ranger, or Bonne Homme Richard. There is a naval anecdote of Capt. Cullam which one of our old citizens, now dead, used to relate, as told him by Capt. Cullam. When sailing with Jones, they had on board a large number of green hands. One day a number of vessels hove in sight. The number was rather terrifying to the crew. Have we got to fight them? What are they?—were the general inquiries. "They are all seventy-fours," said Capt. Cullam, "we shall have to fight them, and they will kill you all—so prepare for the worst!" They did fight and take them—valuable merchantmen, and the five shares owned by Capt. C. as Lieut. was a fortune to him. Capt. C. had not been much in the habit of attending church. One Sunday, after he became rich, he was seen in his pew in the North Church, and the old gentleman to whom we just now referred, when they next met, referred to the rare occurrence. "O," said he, "they sent me the devil of a tax bill for my pew, and I mean to get my money's worth." (There was a property assessment on pews.)

After the death of his first wife, Capt. Cullam broke up house-keeping and boarded at a hotel, kept by Zachariah Foss, on the spot in Fleet street where the stable of the Franklin House now stands. Foss had three daughters. One of them married Col. Wm. Brewster, and another married Capt. Cochrane who had the command of Fort William and Mary, at Newcastle, when it was captured by the citizens in 1775; and the other daughter, Margaret, Capt. Cullam took as his second wife. She was handsome and neat in her personal appearance, but in disposition very passionate. They first went to housekeeping in the mansion on the corner of Hanover and Vaughan streets, afterwards occupied by Col. Supply Clapp, and now by the heirs of John Hill. Capt. C. removed into a house on the opposite side of the street, afterwards owned by Capt. George F. Blunt, on the spot where Samuel Cleaves' house now stands. In 1780 he lived in a house on Deer street, near where the Concord Depot now is. He still followed the sea,—but his prize money, like that of many others, went as easily as it came, and in 1784 he was again reduced to comparative poverty—paying only a poll tax. He died in some foreign port about the year 1785. By his second wife he had several children, all of whom died in childhood.

Amy, the daughter of the first wife, received from her stepmother rather cruel treatment. So apparent was it, that the friends of the child interposed in her behalf, and she was placed in the family of Mr. Daniel Rindge, who occupied a house on the corner of Market and Daniel streets. She became the companion and assistant of Mrs. R. and received the education of a daughter. It was here that the estimable merchant whose shop was in close proximity to the house on the north, first became acquainted with her—and no less fascinating were her attractions by seeing her, like Rebecca, bringing water from that well, which is now on the premises of S. H. Simes & Co. It was a remark one of our reverend doctors of divinity used to make, that while he had highly estimable daughters in his son's wives—there was none he loved better than Amy.

RAMBLE C.

More of Pickering's History—Col. Atkinson—Woodbury Langdon—Revolutionary Incidents.

SOON after the issue of the First Series of the RAMBLES, the following communication to the Rambler was received from one of the historians of New Hampshire, giving some incidents in the local history of Portsmouth, that have not before been recorded in this publication.

CONCORD, Feb. 13, 1860.

MY DEAR SIR:—Your "RAMBLES" have extended to this place,—for which receive my thanks, as I have been very much interested in them.

I have made some notes and corrections in my copy,—which as they refer to other authors, as well as to the "Rambles," I subjoin for your perusal.

On page 18th occurs the name *Warnerton.* This name is thus given by Belknap, Farmer and others, but it is Wannerton, as I have the *proof* in the *original* letters of Mason, Gorges and Gibbens, now before me. On same page is *Goe*. This word stumbled Belknap, Farmer, Moore, Kelley and others,—but should not stumble *you* or *me*, as *we* know the name still is *extant* in Newington and Greenland. It is Gee, as it occurs in—John *Gee* Pickering. *Gee* was a family connection of the Pickering's. It was right in the Appendix of Belknap, but Dr. Farmer altered it in a foot note to *Goe.* I have the *original* letter of Ambrose Gibbens, of 1633, given in Belknap's Appendix, in which the name is *unmistakably Gee.* This settles the question.

On page 47, you say, "as early as 1636 John Pickering," &c. John Pickering was here as early as 1633, as I have a bill of his now before me, the caption or heading of which reads thus:—

"John Pickering Creditor unto Mr. Ambrose Gibbens in the yeares 1633 and 1634 as foll."—

Then follows the labor of Thomas Crockett and the altering of frame and chimney of a certain house—furnishing boards, nails—and *plastering* a chimney,—all amounting to $21 —— —— showing that Pickering was a carpenter. This work was done at Newichewannock, and the bill is receipted thus:

His
John I Pickering.
Test, Charles Kneill. *signe.*

Page 49.—Capt. Thomas Pickering was killed at Annapolis, Nova Scotia. So says a petition from Mrs. Pickering.* He married Dorothy *Stover* of Cape Neddock.

Page 53.—Capt. John Pickering was also member of the Assembly in 1685 and speaker of the same—as I have a Bill passed by the House of that date and signed John Pickerin, Speaker. It was *non concurred* in by the Council.

Page 104.—Col. Atkinson also had the command of *the* Regiment in the "Canada Expedition," so called, of 1746. A thousand men were voted by June, and by the first of July 800 men were raised or enlisted, and Col. Atkinson, was ordered by Gov. Wentworth to occupy and repair Fort William and Mary, with his Regiment. He did as ordered, and added many guns to the batteries there and at "Jerry's Point." The first of November, the Regiment went into "Winter Quarters" at Sanbornton near "Union Bridge" where they built a Fort—which I have called "Fort Atkinson." The regiment remained there till the fall of 1747, when the Expedition to Canada and the Regiment was abandoned.

Page 113.—Gov. Wentworth was Knighted for his services—was he not?

Page 152.—Are you not mistaken as to Gen. Whipple's being appointed General by the Council—or being ordered

* We are happy to have this fact attested so well. It is said in the N. H. Historical Collections that Pickering was killed by the Indians at *Casco*. Mr. Willis, the historian of Portland, says that no such incident occurred at that time at that place. There is now no doubt that it occurred at *Annapolis*.

with one-fourth of his command to the North Western Frontier with Gen. Stark? I have thought such was the fact—but it was not so.

The General Court at a session of three days, commencing July 17, 1777, divided the militia of the State into two Brigades, and appointed Gen. Whipple to the command of the *first*, and Gen. Stark to the command of the *second*. The same day one *quarter* of Gen. Stark's Brigade and one *quarter* of Colonels Thornton's, Webster's and Badger's Regiment in Gen. Whipple's Brigade, were ordered to be drafted and sent to meet the enemy on the North Western Frontier. Gen. Stark was put in command of these forces. On the 19th they adjourned. There was none of Whipple's Brigade ordered out except the quarter of the three Regiments under Thornton, Webster and Badger. These troops gained (with the assistance of others from Massachusetts and Vermont joined) the battle of Bennington. Now I presume that *Whipple and his troops were ordered out by the* "Committee of Safety" in the *recess* of the Legislature and before its adjourned meeting on the 17th of September—at which time they resolved not to send any *General Officer* with their troops for the defence of the "North Western Frontier." This of course deprived Gen. Whipple of *any command* there—whether sent by the "Committee of Safety," or a volunteer.

The reason of this vote was, that Congress had taken umbrage at their sending Stark with an *independent* command, and had lectured New Hampshire by a sharp Resolution,—and after a committee had been appointed to address Congress upon the subject, this Resolution—of not sending any "General Officers with these troops"—was adopted.

Page 222.—Capt. Thomas Pickering fell in an engagement with a British "East Indiaman" of 32 guns,—24 nines and 8 fours.

Pickering and Hutchings stood on Union Wharf—that

formerly belonged to Sampson B. Lord, Esq.—w hen they fired upon the Scarborough's barge. The bullet-hole in the east end of the warehouse used to be pointed out.

Pickering finally took that barge and *impounded* it. The crew, for fear of being fired upon landed the Barge in the slip below Pickering's mill. "Tom" found it, and hitching four horses to it hauled it through the various streets, he standing in the Barge and assuming the command. After they had worn her bottom entirely off, they hauled her to the pound and locked her up. Deacon Drown's wife (his sister) stood in the door, and as "Tom" rode past in the Barge, cried out, "Tom, you'll be hanged, for you're rebelling against your King and Country." I will add two other *affairs* of some importance in which Capt Pickering was the principal actor.

Sometime in the night of October 1, 1775, the British ship "Prince George" came into the "Lower Harbor" at Portsmouth, in a storm. On the next day, Oct. 2, Pickering, with a picked crew in a boat—boarded and took the ship, and brought her up to town. This prize was very opportune—as the town of Portsmouth and Washington's army at Cambridge were *out of flour*, and the Prince George had on board 1894 barrels of that necessary article. She was bound from Bristol to Boston. About 50 barrels were kept in Portsmouth, and the rest was sent to the army at Cambridge, by Washington's request. His letter and that of the "Committee of Safety," are on file in the State Secretary's office—from which I gather the main facts.

Another. There was a Privateer called the Warren and commanded by Capt. Burke. This was taken by the British Frigate Milford and turned into a *tender* for that Frigate. This tender of about 80 tons, commanded by Capt. Willis, and with a crew of 50 men all told, besides the Captain, was a source of great annoyance along our coast, from 'Quoddy to Cape Cod—and in November and December of

1777 took eight prizes. On Friday, Dec. 20, of that year, she took a wood Sloop commanded by Richard Pinkham. Saturday, December 21, the valuables were taken from the sloop and the vessel set on fire. The 25th, there came up a storm when near York Ledges, and Capt. Willis being drunk, the under officers and crew gave the command of the schooner to Pinkham—and he *pretending* that he was going into Boston Harbor, put her into "Little Harbor" at Portsmouth and ran her ashore. The next day "Tom Pickering" boarded her with a picked crew and took vessel, officers, men and provision up to town. She had the Milford stores on board and was a valuable prize. Capt. Willis and the officers of the George were billetted on Jonathan Eastman and Philbrick Bradley, Esqs. in Concord. Their prisoners were exchanged and the names of the prisoners and their rank are upon the Cartel receipt now on file in the Secretary's office. Capt. Willis in his receipt *modestly* speaks of his vessel as being *wrecked* near Portsmouth. This was *permitted* to save him a lady love, as he was engaged to a daughter of Admiral Howe. Willis however concluded that this fiction would not keep his conduct a secret, and committed suicide by jumping overboard in Long Island Sound, rather than meet his Admiral and intended father-in-law!

Page 243.—You quote from N. H. Gazette of Nov. 18. Either you or I have copied erroneously. My extract is noted thus, "Under date of Aug. 1782, the N. H. Gazette has the following item of news. 'Thursday last *arrived* in this port an 80 and two 74 gun ships, with a frigate of 32 guns, being part of a fleet of our *magnanimous Allies*, the French, lately arrived on this coast from the West Indies.'" The ship struck with lightning Nov. 5, 1782, was the 80 gun ship 'L Auguste.

Page 244.—It may have been soldiers who *rolled* themselves in the chest, for I find from an old advertisement noted in my note-book, signed by Joshua Wentworth, of date Sept. 2, 1782, in which deserters are mentioned from the French Fleet, that "five soldiers of the regiment of Venois, their clothing *white* cuffed with blue" are particularized.

Page 359.—The house moved by me was not a *dwelling* house—it was a *pleasure* house. It had a Dining Hall below, and a Dining Hall above, with a Drawing Room to each, and attached to the old house by a narrow covered walk.

Page 390.—Woodbury Langdon was *taken prisoner* by the British and was liberated by exchange. When Judge, it seems he did'nt *always appear* to hold courts. Complaint was made and the House of Representatives voted and attempted to impeach him. The Senate met on a day appointed, but Langdon paid no more attention to the order of the Senate, than to the Statute appointing the time of holding the courts. The Senate adjourned to the following June, voting an order for Langdon to appear, but he paid no attention to them, and when the Senate met, he did not appear! Still the Senate took no further notice of the matter, and the House dropped the charges. It is probable that the Lobby or "Third House" saved him harmless.

I have thus suggested some corrections and a few *additions* to your "Rambles." I need not add that I have read it through with the greatest pleasure, and I hope for my pleasure and that of the public, as well as for the advantage of our local and general history, you will continue your Rambles and give us another volume.

By the way, Dr. Peabody, upon the authority of Mr. Greenleaf, has Charles Watrous* (I *think*,—I have not a

*The name of the individual was Charles Waters. He was a foreigner, an ingenious black and white smith. Many anecdotes are told of him—we have room but for one. A smith was needed on board of a public vessel, and several appeared at the place appointed for examination. After two or three had been interrogated, who professed to be perfect in their art, the turn of Waters arrived. "Well, sir," said the captain, "what can you do?" "I don't know any thing," was Waters reply. "How so?" "Why, those men know every thing in the world, and there is nothing left for me—but just take us to the forge." With the display of skill far above the rest, he at once secured the position.

copy at hand)—should it not be Waterhouse? I think so, and I have always heard the old people speak of 'Charley Water'ouse's coppers,'—the word was clipped "*a la cockney*" to Water'ous. Portsmouth people, as well as their forefathers, having a great dislike to the letter *h.* "Down in the *w'ite 'ouse* near the *w'arf*" was a direction I once heard a Portsmouth lady give a servant, and I give it in illustration of the above.

Yours respectfully, C. E. POTTER.

RAMBLE CI.

Things of 1790 to 1800 – Old School Gentlemen – Respect by Youth – Minor Offences – Prompt Punishment of Criminals – Justice Penhallow's Impartiality – First Pavement – Buck Street Promenade – North and Southenders – Smoking not Allowed – Edward Hart elected Police Officer – His Success, and what produced it.

IN the last ten years of the last century, the inhabitants of the quiet, good old town of "Portsmouth upon the Piscataqua" had not entirely outlived the salutary influence of the aristocracy of the colonists of earlier times, when scarlet colored broadcloth cloaks, worn by our *Warners Jaffreys*, *Cutts*, and *other gentlemen* of the *old school* of politeness, good order and decorum, warned the boys of the *severe reprehension*, if not of *rods*, which awaited them for any neglect of respectful recognition of the approach and presence of those august personages, by the *low bow*, or *doffed hat*, or by both, especially on Sabbath days, when *tithingmen* took due care that none were seen loitering about the streets while the bells were tolling the good people to meeting.

Nevertheless, it came to pass, in the course of time,

through the remissness of the *tithingmen* and other *conservatives* of *religion* and *morals,* that the good order of the town had so greatly deteriorated as to alarm the order-loving portion of its inhabitants, lest a worst condition of morals should ensue. Though the evils of which they complained were not in amount, a *tithe* of the abuses for which the good citizens of Portsmouth now have just cause of complaint, they required the most efficient and prompt measures to abate.

Then, *crimes* such as are now characterized as *rowdyism,* were unknown by the inhabitants of Portsmouth. If minor offences against personal rights were committed, which did not, in the estimation of a discerning public, require legal measures to be resorted to, either to punish the offenders or to serve as preventives of a repetition of them, the disapprobation of the good people of the town was a sufficient rebuke and corrective. In thos e days the offenders had *no apologists.*

Offences of graver consequence to the public, which were within the final jurisdiction of justices of the peace, and which subjected the offenders to corporeal punishment, were sure to meet with prompt attention by our vigilant officers of the law. Instance the case of a hostler employed in one of the stage stables, who in the night next preceding his detection, stole a water bucket full of West India rum from the cellar of his employer. He was arrested the next morning, upon a warrant issued by Justice Penhallow—arraigned—tried—found guilty, and sentenced by him, to suffer the infliction of *ten lashes upon his bare back,* which in about thirty minutes thereafter were faithfully applied at the town pump, in the presence of many witnesses; and before the town clock struck the hour of eleven, the convict was again at work in the stable of his employer! Such was then the majesty of the law, and the promptness of its execution.

Justice Penhallow was a *"strict constructionist,"* and fully agreed with Chief Justice JAY of the Supreme Court of the United States, that in conformity with the provisions of the Constitution, *justice* should be administered *"faithfully, impartially* and *without delay."*

As an instance of his impartiality in the administration of justice, we notice a case brought before him, of a complaint for assault and battery. The complainant, who was a kinsman of Governor John Wentworth, set forth in his complaint, that he, "being in the peace of God and the State," and quietly passing up Pleasant street, was then and there assaulted, beaten, bruised and wounded by two persons. [The names of the parties we will not mention. One of them was a tall limb of the law who had gained some celebrity professionally in our courts of justice, and subsequently attained a high distinction as an eminent jurist and counsellor-at-law in a neighboring State; the other was a person nearly related to one of our most opulent merchants, and afterwards succeeded to an honorable and lucrative office in Great Britain under the crown.] Upon complaint being made, Justice Penhallow issued his warrant for their arrest and arraignment before him, to answer to said complaint, and they soon after being brought before him, he found both of them guilty, and sentenced each of them to pay a fine for the use of the County of Rockingham, and to stand committed, (that is, to be locked up in jail,) until said sentence should be performed. The fines were paid, forthwith.

"Thus jails, those iron agents of the law,
Keep many a graceless wretch in awe."

Our venerable Justice recognized only two distinctions of character, of those living under and entitled to the protection of the laws of the State; namely, obedience to, and disobedience of those laws. Neither the possession of wealth, or any adventitious condition of life of the accused, ever influenced "the old Deacon," (for he was one of the deacons of the North Church) so as to allow the respondents to escape the penalty of the law, if upon a fair and impartial trial before him, he found them guilty.

In those days of which we write, the subject of laying side pavements began to be agitated; for until then, there were none in town except very narrow ones in *Paved street*, so called, now Market street, which at that period was only about one half of its present width. Said side pavement being a mere apology for the absence of more commodious accommodations for the ladies who resorted to the "Piece Good Stores" there located. And although the necessity of these were admitted by all our good ancestors, they *could not* or *would not* agree upon a location for the commencement of them.

The belligerent boys also had something to do about this matter. Strong prejudices were there operating between the "Southenders" and "Northenders," and the belligerents had made *Buck street*, now called State street, the line of demarkation between the respective parties. They had also made Buck street, by common consent, *neutral ground*, upon which declaration of war was made and parleys held.

Had not this practice and ill-feeling of the boys against each other been the result of the influences originating in *older heads*, if not in implacable hearts, the interests of the public would have been better promoted. But the antipathies engendered by the revolution between the *Whigs* and *Tories* not having fully subsided, operated injuriously in town affairs, and had prevented many improvements which otherwise the inhabitants would have enjoyed. So it was in respect to the laying of sidewalks. They could not agree upon the location of the commencement of them.

At length, however, at an annual town meeting, one of our wise, far-seeing and worthy townsmen, seizing upon the *neutral ground* influence which the boys had created, without their fathers discovering the use he was about to make of it, moved, "that the Northwest side of Buck street be paved with Durham flat stones for a side walk." The motion prevailed, and this event constitutes the epoch of the commencement of side-pavements in Portsmouth, and the memory of the "*old Tory*" is now blessed. Such was the effect of prejudice, and the result of wisdom and fore-sight.

As soon as this convenient promenade of Buck street was completed, those of our fair inhabitants whose domestic relation confined them much of the time to their homes, when the weather was suitable for the purpose, were seen promenading this flat stone side pavement, enjoying the pure, invigorating, health promoting and life prolonging atmosphere. It was indeed a luxury, as well to those enjoying good health, as to the feeble and the convalescent.

At that period of our history the smoking of tobacco, either in pipes or in the form of cigars, in the streets, was deemed a *nuisance* and made by law a penal offence. Ladies could then enjoy the rich blessing of the invigorating, uncontaminated atmosphere without being obliged, as now, at almost every step to encounter and even to contend with the *odious, filthy, sickening* fumes of *tobacco pipes* and *cigars*, and the contaminating odors of breath issuing from the reservoirs of lungs made still worse by poisoned alcoholic liquors imbibed by the smokers.

But we return to our subject of reform, which our good fathers had determined to effect. It had become a matter of universal observation and discussion, in the streets, in our work-shops, in our parlors, in our kitchens, in some of our public assemblages; and when the inhabitants assembled in town meeting to decide upon the adoption or rejection of by-laws which had been made to meet the emergency of the times, the question was proposed by the

Moderator, (the Hon. Jonathan Warner,) upon the acceptance and adoption of them, "Who shall execute these laws?" When profound silence had for sometime pervaded the meeting, the Moderator spoke again, and said, "Who will you trust with this important business? Who will faithfully carry your object into effect?" Silence again for a short time prevailed, when it was broken by a simultaneous announcement from different parts of the meeting, of the name of *Edward Hart! Edward Hart!!* and thus nominated he was thereupon unanimously elected *Police Officer* for the then current year. Some sketches are given of him in Ramble 99.

The power which that officer then possessed was similar to those with which our City Marshal is now clothed, and his duties were analogous. A call was then made for Mr. Hart, but he was not present. A constable was sent to announce to him his election, and to request his attendance. In a few minutes he presented himself, and addressing the Moderator said, "Mr. Moderator: I have been informed by your messenger, that the town has unanimously elected me Police Officer for the current year. The duties of the office are of the highest importance and responsibility, and it will require much labor and persevering effort to perform its duties to your satisfaction. No *one*, *ten* or *twenty* men can succeed acceptably, if at all, without the cordial co-operation of his good feeling townsmen: but with such aid, much may be effected even by one man. I will accept the office to which the town has elected me, and perform its duties according to the best of my abilities, upon *one condition.* That condition is, that in discharging my duties all my good fellow townsmen will LIFT THE HELPING HAND!" And rising on "*tip-toe*," suiting the action to the word, extended his right hand as high as he could reach. In an instant, as if by the power of *magic*, all hands present were *up-lifted*; which being observed by him as he took a cursory glance around the room to see what was passing, he turned to the moderator and thus addressed him: "Mr. Moderator, with this assurance of the co-operation of my fellow-townsmen so unanimously expressed, I accept of the office, and am ready to be qualified." Which being done, he left the meeting amid the approving cheers of all present, and immediately commenced active duties, in the performance of which he made himself *powerfully* effective, and ere twenty-four hours had elapsed, every school-boy in town; as also every offender against good order, was fully apprised of the appointment of the energetic officer with whom they had to deal. Public confidence in the ability and faithfulness of their Police Officer was every where apparent; a generous and ready aid always offered him when needed. Most of the evils which had been so obnoxious to the people of the town were soon abated, and Mr. Hart was very highly respected and regarded as one "sent for the punishment of evil doers and for the praise of them that do well."

The relater of this sketch was present at the election of Mr. Hart, and details as far as his memory enables him, his remarks upon his acceptance of the office in nearly the same words used by him on that occasion.

RAMBLE CII.

The Hart Family—Quint and the Wolf.

In Ramble 99 we say that Col. John Hart, the father of Edward, died at Louisburg of small pox in 1758. So we were informed, and stated in Ramble 79, but we have now conclusive evidence that the fact is otherwise. Col. Meserve, a neighbor of Hart, died at Louisburg that year, and the names were probably thus confounded.

In 1758, Col. John Hart took command of a New Hampshire regiment of several hundred men, and marched with them to Lake George to join Gen. Abercrombie. His forces were joined by those of Col. Goff; and under command of the latter they were ordered down the shores of Lake Champlain to cut off a body of French and Indians, who had been in what is now the State of New York, and had done some mischief there. But Col. Goff, regarding discretion the better part of valor, thought best to keep clear of bullets, and so landed on an island in Lake Champlain, drew his men up in a hollow square, went to prayer, and prayed that there might be *a long and moderate war and no bloodshed.* The religious services were extended to so great a length that the enemy had time to and did pass by,—so his prayer was answered in part, as there was no bloodshed. Although we have no knowledge that this fact has ever before appeared in print, yet "a long and moderate war and no bloodshed" was a by-word brought home by the New Hampshire militia men of the French war, which was in common use here during the Revolution, and is yet familiar in the ears of our old men.

Among the soldiers in this expedition was Joseph Quint, who afterwards, we think, lived in Newington. He was sent out on a skirmish in the neighborhood of Fort William Henry, and night coming on he found himself alone in the woods, without sufficient light to find his way out. He gathered a quantity of leaves for his bed, and laying himself down was soon asleep. Awaking in the night, he saw but a very few yards from him a large wolf, with glaring eyes directed towards him! He had his gun by his side, and while thinking what to do, he saw, or imagined he saw, hundreds of wolves' eyes glaring upon him in every direction! To discharge his gun would be regarded as a signal of alarm to the fort—so rising slowly, he took off his hat, brandished it round and then threw it at the wolf! This frightened him off—and the moon being now up, he was able to trace his way back to the fort, which was done without delay, and the adventure made a family story.

Col. John Hart's son Henry (not Richard, as we stated) settled in Newington, on the farm now belonging to Richard Pickering, Esq. He had a blacksmith's shop standing between the house and the road. He had a high reputation as a horse-shoer, and many sent their horses from Portsmouth to him to be shod. He had a son, Richard D. Hart. After he had passed middle-life, Henry removed to Wells and there died.

When Edward Hart built the Pickering house in Vaughan street, about eighty years ago, the thatch where the house stands was as high as a man's head. One of our old citizens tells us that he has seen the tide from the North mill-pond flowing near the spot where the house stands.

We will close this Ramble by a court scene in Portsmouth ninety-eight years ago, which contrasts with the republican simplicity of the present day.

In 1771 the province of New Hampshire was divided into counties, and on the 3d of March in the next year the first sitting of Superior Court in Rockingham county was held in Portsmouth. On that occasion, when the court bell rang, a procession moved in royal dignity to the Court House on Market Square, in which the honorable Judges might be seen in their full bottomed wigs and official robes, and all the members of the bar following in order with their white bands hanging conspicuously beneath their chins. Whether the Rev. Dr. Langdon, who was the chaplain for the occasion, led or followed in the procession, the record does not show.

RAMBLE CIII.

The Sheafe Family.

THE late James Sheafe resided on State street, where is now the house of J. M. Tredick, Esq., and his ownership extended over the entire square south of the City building. The premises are not yet alienated from the family. Here too was the residence of his father, Jacob Sheafe, who was born at Newcastle. As this family held a prominent place in Portsmouth for a century and a half, we think our readers will feel some interest in a sketch of its history.

Samuel Sheafe was of Cranebrook, England, as appears on the records of the Herald Office, London. On an ancient monument within the diocese of Norwich, Norfolk, England, is given the following inscription:

Here are buryed under this ston
Thomas Sheff and his wyff Marion;
Sometym we warr, as ye now be,
And as we arr, so be schall yee;
Wherefore of your charitie,
Pray for us to the Trinitie.
" " Obiit (Marion) MCCC lxxxxiii.

At this time, 1393, Richard 2d was King of England. Thomas Sheff as he was to be prayed for after his death, must have been of the Roman Catholic religion, as all English people were at that time. Afterwards, in the reign probably of Queen Mary, from some ancient records is extracted the following:

"Out of this town and places adjoining, good people in neighborhood met on week day, to pray melancholy providence to be sanctified to them; prosecuted by a neighboring Justice, and by him are fined, and for non-payment sent to Maidstone Jail for three months. Among the rest was one Harmon Sheaf, a man very kind to his parish minister, and who usually attended upon public worship in the way of the Church of England. He was imprisoned for nonconformity."—[Cranebrook, Wm. Goodrich's *Notes*, 1, 10.]

Edmund Sheafe was born in 1605, and was married to Elizabeth Cotton, daughter of Sampson Cotton of London. His children were, Rebecca, Elizabeth and Sampson Sheafe. Sampson was born in 1650, soon after his father's decease.

Jacob Sheafe was also from Cranebrook, born in 1616, and married to Margaret Webb, born 1625, died 1693, aged 68. She was the only daughter of Henry Webb of London, who came over to this country with his father, of Salisbury, England.

Two of the children perished in their house near the Court House in Boston, which was burnt in 1655. It is believed that Jacob Sheafe came over with Rev. Henry Whitefield, and in 1643 was one of the seven pillars in the Church of Guilford, Connecticut, so denominated or styled, to which was gathered the body of the Church. Whitefield was a member of the Church of England, but afterwards a conformist to the manner of worship of the church in New England. He left Guilford with Mr. Higginson, who came to Salem, and in 1650 returned to England. Mr. Eaton, one of the pillars, remained in Guilford, or New Haven; and prior to 1647, Jacob Sheafe came to Boston and there died in 1658, aged 42, and was buried in a tomb in the King's Chapel burying ground. This was the first tomb made there. He owned considerable landed estate, and 361 ounces of plate. Some of the plate was a few years since in the family of Mr. Henry Haven, a descendant of Jacob Sheafe. The widow of Jacob Sheafe married Rev. Mr. Thacher, and died 1693, aged 65. She was buried in the same tomb. Robert Gibbs, her son-in-law, was also buried there.

In the first church, Boston, Margaret wife of Jacob Sheafe, merchant, was admitted a member 15th of the third month, 1647. Jacob Sheafe was also admitted 4th of 2d month, 1658.

Inscription on the stone over the family tomb in the burial ground, King's Chapel:

"Here lyeth inter'd the Body of Jacob Sheafe of Boston, and for some time lived at Cranebrook, in Kent, Ould England. He deceased 22d March, 1658, aged 42 years.
Robert Gibbs."

"Here lyeth inter'd the body of Mrs. Margaret Thacher formerly wife of Jacob Sheafe and late wife of the Rev. Thomas Thacher, ætates 68. Obiit 29, Feb. 1693"

"Here lies inter'd the Body of Jacob Sheafe, who departed this life 26 of Dec, 1760, aged 79 years."

Mehitable Sheafe's grave stone, near the tomb is now destroyed.

Jacob Sheafe left two children; Elizabeth, born 1644, married Robert Gibbs, the father of Henry Gibbs of Watertown. Mehitable, born 1656, married Sampson Sheafe, the son of Edmund Sheafe, in year 1679.

Sampson Sheafe resided in Boston, and was a respectable merchant. In 1675, he came to Newcastle, N. H., and did business there in the mercantile line, and was at the same time Collector of the Customs. In 1677, he (then living in Boston) contracted with George Jaffrey to proceed to Great Island and take charge solely of his goods, housing, wharves and land and to do no other business, in consideration of 40 pounds lawful money of New England, for two years; and to be found and allowed good and sufficient meat and drink, washing and lodging.

In 1698, Sampson Sheafe probably returned to New Hampshire, being at that time appointed, under Gov. Allen, one of His Majesty's Council and Secretary of the Province. In 1711, he was appointed, by Gov. Dudley of Massachusetts Bay, Commissary of the New England forces on an expedition against Quebec, which failed, owing principally to the disaster of the fleet under Admiral Walker. The first intelligence of this, says Hutchinson (in his history of Massachusetts,) was by a letter of the 11th of Oct. received from the Commissary, Sampson Sheafe. He was at one time Collector of the Port of Piscataqua, where he made several seizures of vessels, as appeared by Superior Court records. He remained in New Hampshire several years, winding up his mercantile concerns, and then returned to Boston, where he died, aged 76. He had two children only, Jacob, born 1677, and Sampson 1681.

While a resident in Boston, Jacob Sheafe lived or had property in Salem street, then called Sheafe street, where he owned two parcels of pasture land which he sold to his brother-in-law, Robert Gibbs. His heirs owned land near the ferry. His property in Newcastle he gave to his son Sampson Sheafe. Jacob Sheafe the eldest son of Sampson, born in Boston where he always lived, was married to Mary. He had four children, Abigail, Mary, Elizabeth and Margaret. Mary born 1718, was married to Sampson Sheafe at Boston. The residence of Jacob Sheafe was near Frog street, now Tremont street.

Sampson Sheafe of Newcastle, second son of Sampson of Boston, was born 1681, educated at Harvard College where he graduated 1702. His business was in the mer, cantile line, in the fishery and West India trade. November 27th, 1711, he was married by the Rev. Mr. Emerson to Sarah Walton, the daughter of Col. Theodore Walton of Newcastle.

In 1740 he was appointed one of the King's Council, Belcher being at that time Governor, and continued a mandamus councillor as they were then styled, during the administration of Gov. Benning Wentworth, to the year 1761, when he resigned his seat at the board at the age of 80. He died 1772, aged 91, leaving 8 children,—Sampson, born 1712; Jacob, 1715; Henry, Matthew, Samuel, Sarah, Mehitable and Elizabeth.

Jacob Sheafe was born at Newcastle, Oct. 21, 1715, where he resided for 27 years. In 1740 he married Hannah Seavey, whose home was on the beautiful spot where the house of Mr. Eben L. Seavey now stands, at the head of Seavey's Creek, on the road leading from Sagamore

Creek to Wallis's Sands.* She was here born May 4, 1719. The name of Hannah's father we do not know—she had a brother Paul, the father of late Major Mark Seavey, who lived for many years at 65 Congress street. "Sampson's Point," at Little Harbor, was but a short distance from Newcastle, and Mr. Sheafe sometimes came to Portsmouth that way. On one occasion in a shower he took refuge in the farm house of Mr. Seavey, where for the first time he saw Hannah. He liked Hannah so well that he felt inclined to visit there in pleasant weather also, and finally she became Mrs. Sheafe.

In 1742 he purchased the house and lot of land next west of the brick school house in State street, on which Mr. George M. Marsh's house and the Episcopal chapel now stand. It had probably been the residence of Rev. John Emerson, who died in 1732, as Mr. Sheafe purchased it of his widow, for £550. How many years he resided here we have no record, but probably his house on the opposite side of the street was not built until twenty or thirty years after. He died in 1791, at the age of 76. His wife died in 1773, at the age of 54. Their children were—

Matthew, born Aug. 13, 1741, a shipmaster, was lost at sea.

Abigail, born April 26, 1744, m. Judge John Pickering. She died Dec. 10, 1805, aged 62.

Jacob, born Sept. 6, 1745, merchant. Died Jan. 25, 1829, aged 84.

Sarah, born Aug. 1, 1748, died June 8, 1839, a. 91. She married John Marsh, who died in 1777. She was the mother of Matthew S. Marsh, and g. m. of George M. Marsh.

Hannah, born April 26, 1750, m. Hugh Henderson; afterwards Mr. Hart. Died Sept. 1, 1845, a. 95.

Thomas, born April 16, 1752, merchant. He died Sept. 4, 1831, aged 80.

---

* The note at the foot of page 105 has reference to this paragraph; which is here corrected accordingly, the Ramble referred to not having been discovered by the compiler until the note had passed through the press.

Mary, born Nov. 22, 1753, m. Pres. Joseph Willard, Har. College, Cambridge. Died March 6, 1826, aged 72.

James, born Nov. 16, 1755, merchant. Died Dec. 5, 1829, aged 74.

William, born Sept. 11, 1758, merchant. Died March, 1839, aged 81.

Mehitable, born April 12, 1760, m. Eben. Smith, Durham. Died Sept. 4, 1843, aged 83.

John, born July 13, 1762, and died Jan. 24, 1812, aged 50.

The average age of nine of the eleven children was over 81 years. A truly remarkable case.

Mr. Sheafe was appointed by Gov. B. Wentworth Commissary to the N. H. forces at Louisburg, in 1745, soon after his removal from Newcastle to Portsmouth. Being bred a merchant, he pursued the mercantile business extensively, with shrewdness, reputation and success, until his death. His principal place of businnss was at the warehouses on Point of Graves, which of later years have, with the wharves around, sunk into decay. He was elected a Representative of the town for 1767 to 1774, when the provincial government expired.

He was quick in discernment, and shrewd in the management of his business. Many illustrative anecdotes are given of him. One day, after selling a customer a few pounds of wool and putting it into the bag, he went into his counting room, and looking into a glass which reflected the counter, he saw the man slip in a small skim cheese. Mr. S. on returning said, he thought he had by mistake put in more wool than was ordered, and would just place the bag in the scale again. The man objected, as he said the weight was all right—but Mr. S. threw it in, and finding it some eight pounds heavier, offered to take back a part of the contents. The customer however concluded that he would take the whole, and so to save exposure paid between two and three dollars for a cheese which might have been bought for twenty-five cents.

On another occasion, after missing a barrel of pork some months, a man said to him one day, Mr. Sheafe, did you ever find out who stole that pork? O yes, said Mr. S. Indeed, who was it? Nobody but you and I ever knew it was stolen: so pay for it at once, if you wish nobody else to know about it. The man paid for the pork.

It is a singular fact, that of the large number of the Sheafe family who resided in Portsmouth a few years since, there is not now one descendant here that bears the name.

RAMBLE CIV.

James Sheafe — Jay's Treaty — The Effigies — The Riot — The Arrest — The Triumphal Procession, &c.

THERE are many reminiscences in the history of Hon. James Sheafe which have a local relation, and while standing before his premises we will bring up one or two of them. He was a loyalist during the Revolution,—but did not, like many others, leave his home. With his brother-in-law, Hugh Henderson, he was summoned before the Committee of Safety at Exeter, and Mr. Samuel Drown had them under charge. While Mr. Sheafe rode his horse unmolested, the excited populace followed Mr. Henderson on foot, and compelled him to walk as far as Greenland Parade, pelting him with stones whenever he attempted to mount. They gave their bonds to the Committee that they would do nothing to impede the progress of the Revolution, and were dismissed.

After the Revolution, although Mr. Sheafe was a very popular man with his friends, and was captain of a company of cavalry, yet occasionally he was subject to rough abuse from political opponents. One of the strongest demonstrations of this sort was made by a mob attack upon his house in 1795, which, curious as it might be, resulted in summoning the same Mr. Drown to Exeter, although innocent of the offence charged.

It was in July, 1795, that the memorable "Jay's Treaty" was promulgated before final action was taken upon it by the Senate. Its appearance created great excitement throughout the country. The article which forbade the trading of American vessels of over 70 tons with any of the British colonial ports or islands, was far from being acceptable; and it was said that while the treaty conferred many important privileges on Great Britain, it secured no advantages but what might be claimed under the existing treaty of 1783. A public meeting was called by posters at the corners. To show the deep feeling we give the handbill.

"THE CRISIS!—*To the citizens of Portsmouth.*

This (citizens of every description) is the crisis of your fate. To-morrow you are warned to assemble at the State House, on the most momentous occasion of your lives. Your all is at stake. The Senate have bargained away your blood-bought privileges, for less than a mess of pottage. That perfidious, corrupting and corrupted nation whom you, vanquished with your sword, are now endeavoring to vanquish you, with their usual, but alas, too successful weapon, British gold! Your only remaining hope is in the President! Assemble then to a man! Shut up your shops and warehouses, let all business cease: Repair to the State House, remonstrate with coolness, but spirit, against his signing a treaty, which will be the death warrant of your trade, and entail beggary on us, and our posterity forever. If you regard yourselves, your children, and above all the honor of your country, assemble at the sound of the bells. Portsmouth, July 15, 1795."

This meeting, after voting that it was inconsistent with the interest and honor of the United States to adopt the treaty, agreed to an extended address to President Washington on the subject. They voted thanks to Senator

Langdon and his nine associates for the opposition they made to the ratification of the treaty, and without any opposition being shown, adjourned.

Nearly two months after, a counter address to the President was drawn up, approving of the treaty, and complimentary to Senator Livermore and Mr. Jay. It was presented by Mr. Jacob Sheafe for signatures. As soon as this proceeding was publicly known, the town generally, and south-end in particular, was in commotion. On the morning of the 10th of September, 1795, bills were posted at the corners, stating that the signers of the second address to the President, and the gentleman who had circulated it, had highly displeased the people, as the avowed design was to render the proceedings of the late town meeting contemptible. As Mr. S. (who was called by his opponents "Cunning Jacob") received some personal abuse in the forenoon of that day, disagreeable consequences were apprehended from the excited state of the public mind.

The opponents of the treaty, who had just taken the name of Republicans, held a meeting in the vicinity of Liberty Bridge in Water street, and a committee was sent to Mr. Sheafe, notifying him immediately to deliver the paper containing the address and signatures, or abide the consequences. This demand Mr. S. peremptorily refused to comply with: but to convince them that those who were advocating the measures of government were not acting in a clandestine manner, he offered them a copy of the address with every name thereto subscribed. This was received, but was by no means satisfactory.

Now the blood begins to boil, and the tug of war commences. In the shop of William Deering the carver, on Water street, were reposing two profile effigies, cut from boards, which had been made in July, when the treaty first arrived. These were brought out and nailed one on each side of a cart,—and a public crier, with bell in hand, was sent through the town, inviting the inhabitants to attend the execution of those two "bribed traitors," Jay and Livermore, who were to be hung and burnt in the evening on Warner's wharf. [Now Railway wharf.]

The cart was rigged, but without a driver, when London, a black of William Stavers, coming by, was placed in the cart and compelled to act as driver. A drum and fife soon gave the signal for forming, and the procession proceeded to the South Bridge, up Pleasant street, gathering in numbers until, three hundred strong, it passed over Market Square and down Daniel street, to Warner's wharf—the scene of the execution.

The effigies are erected on a pole, and being too high for the torch, a boy is held up to apply the flame. It was twilight when this mark of contempt was completed. As the evening came on, the procession followed the drum and fife to various parts of the town, paying particular attention to the residences of the thirty-nine individuals who signed the second address. Groans and denunciations were poured out in profusion. The residence of Jacob Sheafe received marked attention. That of his brother, James Sheafe, was assailed, the windows broken in by missels, and Mr. S. compelled to secrete himself from their fury. The residence of Dr. Hall Jackson was also assailed, and the large stones thrown into the chamber windows greatly endangered the lives of the family. Whether this assault was made by men of Portsmouth or of Rye, we do not know; but it is probable that the Doctor was not in very good repute with the inhabitants of the latter town at the time, as a story we have heard will explain.

When the news of the treaty arrived, information went to Rye that the country was sold; that Jay had sold Rye with it, and British gold would be the cause of its ruin. Dr. Hall Jackson was on a visit in Rye at the time, and was well convinced that a poorer town could not then be found in the county—as utterly different in wealth and prosperity from what it is now as black is from white. The Doctor listened to the story of being sold, and answered as follows:

"If Rye to Great Britain was really sold,
As we by some great men are seriously told,
Great Britain, not Rye, was ill-treated:
For if in fulfilling the known maxim of trade,
Any gold for such a poor purchase was paid,
Great Britain was confoundedly cheated."

This exercise of his ready wit perhaps cost him a few panes of glass on this occasion.

There might have been seen on the Parade on that day, sitting in his chaise, a lawyer of our town, taking down the names of those who were in the current of the procession. And a day or two after Gen. George Reed of Londonderry, the High Sheriff, attending the Court then in session at Exeter, visits Portsmouth officially, and summons some ten or twelve of the leading men of Portsmouth to appear before the Court, on a charge of being engaged in a riot and unlawful assemblage, and injuring the property of James Sheafe, &c. The names of all these individuals we have not been able to obtain, as the Court records do not present them; but among them were the names of Deacon Samuel Bowles and Samuel Drown (who passed the Parade at the time, but were not connected with the mob,) Capt. Thomas Manning, Nathaniel Marshall, Thales G. Yeaton, Wm. Trefethen, Wm. Tredick, Charles Chauncey. Some of them joined in the afternoon procession, but none of them were connected with the evening mob.

When the Sheriff saw who the men generally were, he took their word for their appearance at Exeter on the morning of the next day. So, before daylight, they were all on the way, and ere the Court opened in the morning, the culprits presented themselves at the Court House. Judge Orcutt was on the bench. Their case was stated by Mr. Drown, and readily understood by the Court, who suggested that a *nol pros.* should be entered, and they were discharged.

Their prosecution and summons to Exeter for trial made no little excitement, and the news of the speedy discharge no little joy. The matter was well known in the neighboring towns also, and every vehicle and horse were in requisition to go out and escort them home. William Boyd, no less enthusiastic, requested Mr. Greenleaf, the keeper of the Bell Tavern, to have refreshments in every room in his house. Just at sunset the carriages made their appearance in town. In the first was Thomas Manning, who on this occasion was first called Commodore, a title which he never after lost among his friends.

By a concerted arrangement, as soon as the first carriage arrived in sight of the Bell Tavern, three cheers went down the whole line of the procession. When the first coach passing down State street reached Market Square, the Commodore put his hat out of the window and gave the signal; another stationed where the new Post Office now is, repeated it, and on it went up State street to Middle street, and up Middle street to beyond Wibird's Hill—the whole cavalcade and procession giving such long three cheers as has scarcely been heard in our city since.

Of the high go at the Bell Tavern that night, it is only necessary to say that it was in full accordance with the "*Spirit*" *of the times*—"West-India."

The remembrance of that occasion is still held among our old inhabitants—but the full record has never before been made.

RAMBLE CV.

Insurrection in New Hampshire, 1786.

THIS incident in our State history, although its actual locality was a few miles from Portsmouth, yet from the deep interest it excited here at the time, and the terror of the mob at the bare idea that "Hackett's Artillery" from Portsmouth was marching upon them, is entitled to a place among the Rambles.

In the beginning of the year 1785, the complaints of the unhappy people, who had contracted debts during the time of the too great plenty of money, induced the Legislature to pass an act, making every species of property a tender at an appraised value. It was soon however found from experience, that this answered no other purpose but to prevent a demand on the part of the creditors and a neglect on the part of the debtors, to discharge their just debts. The scarcity of money still remained a complaint; for so far as goods and real property were substituted as a medium in commerce, so far specie, of course, ceased to circulate; and credit being thus injured, the money holders turned their keys on that cash which might otherwise have been loaned to the needy.

In August a convention of committees from about thirty towns assembled, and agreed upon and preferred to the General Court a long petition, setting forth their grievances on account of the scarcity of money, and praying for an emission of paper bills of credit, in which there is no single trace of an idea of redemption, or any one attempt to give the currency a foundation; but the whole seems predicated on a supposition that the General Court by a mere act of legislation by *words* and *signs* could *impress an intrinsic value on paper;* which is as fully absurd as it would be to suppose that the Legislature had the power of Midas, and could, from a single touch, turn stones and sticks into gold. Their great object was, however, to have this paper a tender for all debts and taxes, and no plan is hinted by which the people are to get this money out of the treasury; but it rather seems that they expected the General Court to apportion it among the people at large.

The Legislature formed a plan for the emission of fifty thousand pounds, to be let out at four per cent. and land security redeemable at a future period, carrying interest at four per cent., and to be a tender in taxes for the internal support of the State, and for fees and salaries of the officers of the government. This plan was sent as early as the fourteenth of September, 1786, to the several towns, to collect their minds upon the subject.

The following interesting account of the matter was drawn up by Judge Smith of Exeter not long before his death.

"It was at this period that the clamor for paper currency began. Many indulged the hope that a liberal emission of bills of credit, and a mere order on the part of Government that they should be received in all cases as equal in value to specie, would operate as an immediate and effectual remedy for all their grievances.

"On the morning of 20th September, we were informed that a large body of insurgents were on their march to Exeter, where the Legislature was then in session; and at three in the afternoon they made their appearance. I saw them as they passed down the street by the Academy. More than a hundred were tolerably well armed; but the rest (for they were upwards of two hundred in number) were mounted, and their arms consisted only of whips, cudgels, and such weapons as tradition has assigned to the Georgia militia. They pursued their march over the bridge, overturning or thrusting aside all who ventured within their reach. In a short time they returned, and invested the court house. Judge Livermore, who was then upon the bench, and the severity of whose countenance was not diminished at sight of the array, would not permit the business of the court to be interrupted, or allow any one to inspect the besiegers from the windows. In a short time, however, finding their mistake, and probably supposing it rather a hopeless business to ask redress of grievances from a court of law, they marched to the meeting house, where both houses of Assembly were met in conference. The meeting house, at that time, stood where Rev. Mr. Rowland's was afterwards erected, and the court house was just opposite. They here began to load all the muskets which had not previously been prepared, and to point them at the house. After spending some time in this parade, they sent in a deputation, to demand that the Legislature should allow an immediate issue of paper, which should be made a tender in all cases for debts and taxes; and laid close siege to all the avenues of the house, intending to detain the members until they should see fit to grant their request. Some who endeavored to make their escape were driven back with insult. It had been publicly known some hours before, that the insurgents were on their march, and a large concourse was assembled to watch their motions. Some gentlemen attempted to reason with them on the folly of their conduct, but without effect. President Sullivan soon came to the door. He addressed them with perfect coolness; expostulated with them for some time; assured them that their reasonable demands should not be neglected; but that they might at once abandon the idea of forcing the government into submission: that their array was not so formidable as to terrify an old soldier. It was now evening, and they still adhered resolutely to their post.

" President Sullivan, as I said before, addressed the insurgents without effect, and there seemed no mode remaining of liberating the Legislature from their imprisonment but a resort to force, until a plan was resorted to with good success. It was now twilight. The meeting house was surrounded by a high fence, which intercepted the view on all sides. A drummer was summoned, who stood at a little distance, and beat his drum with as much vigor and effect as if a regular army were advancing to the rescue, and a band, rendered most formidable in appearance by the indistinctness of evening, marched toward the rebel forces. The surrounding crowd at the same time shouted for Government, and loudly expressed their apprehensions that the enemy would be annihilated by the vengeance of Hackett's Artillery. The insurgents, unable to measure the extent of their danger, needed no second invitation to decamp. Their whole array was dissolved in a moment. They scampered through lanes, streets and fields, and clambered over walls and fences with a rapidity which nothing but fear could give them, and did not stop until they reached a place at the distance of a mile, where they considered themselves safe for the moment from the terrific host, whose sudden appearance had caused their flight. Here they endeavored to rally their broken ranks, and encamped for the night; while the Legislature immediately declared them in a state of rebellion, and authorized the President to issue his orders for calling in the militia of the neighboring towns.

" A company of volunteers was immediately enrolled under the command of Hon. Nicholas Gilman, afterwards a Senator in Congress from this State. They were ordered to meet at the President's quarters early the next morning. I went to the place appointed before daybreak; and the first person I met in the streets was President Sullivan, mounted, and in full uniform. He told me that he was about reconnoitering the enemy, and immediately rode away. In a short time the militia began to pour in, and by the hour of nine, a large body was assembled. Among their officers was Gen. Cilley, whose bravery and conduct in the revolutionary war is so well remembered. Many distinguished citizens also arrived, and attached themselves to the company of volunteers I have just mentioned.

"Before ten, the line was formed, and the troops commenced their march, commanded by the President in person. The enemy's line was formed on an eminence near the western bank of the river that crosses the Kingston ground. When the militia had advanced to a spot near the river, Gen. Cilley, at the head of a troop of horse, dashed into the enemy's ranks, which were instantly broken and put to flight, without firing a single gun. Many of their officers were taken prisoners upon the spot; and the same night, a small detachment seized several of the ringleaders, and committed them to goal in Exeter, whence they were shortly after discharged by the Court, after a proper submission. The vigorous measures of Government, and the fear which they had inspired, rendered it unnecessary, as well as impolitic, to resort to severer punishments."

RAMBLE CVI.

The Cutts Family.

PROMINENT among the early settlers of New Hampshire was the family bearing the name of Cutt, which in 1730 added an *s*, making the name *Cutts*. We have already (in Ramble 5th) given an account of the emigration from Wales of the three brothers, John, Robert, and Richard Cutt, previous to 1646. John was the first President of New Hampshire. His residence was not far from the corner of Market and Russell streets, about where the stone store now stands,—the grave yard on Green street, in which he was buried, being in his orchard near his house. There the grave stones of his family are still to be seen. We have procured a copy of the inscriptions on all these stones, and give them in Ramble 108.

Richard Cutt and John were owners of at least one half of what is now the compact part of Portsmouth. In 1660 the first fort on the present site of Fort Constitution, Newcastle, was erected, and Richard Cutt was the first in command.

Robert Cutt carried on ship building at Kittery.

Among the papers of the late Edward Cutts, Esq., was recently found an old manuscript, probably written about seventy-nine years ago, giving the Cutts family genealogy. We give it as a matter of record, in which many families are interested, adding a few explanatory words in brackets.

CUTTS GENEALOGY.

John Cutts, the eldest, afterwards President.

Richard, the next.

Robert, the third son.

A sister, whose husband's name was Shepway.

President Cutts had two wives. It is uncertain whether the first came with him; she left four children, viz:

Hannah, Mary, John and Samuel.

Hannah married Col. Rich'd Waldron, (son to Maj. Waldron who was murdered by Indians,) about 1681 or 1682, and died at the birth of her 1st child, whose name was Samuel, who lived 11 months only.

Mary married Sam. Penhallow, Esq., (the celebrated Justice,) and had 13 children—5 sons and 8 daughters. Sons were Samuel, John, Joshua, Joseph, Benjamin.

Sam. married in London, and left children there.

John married the widow Walls (maiden name Butler,) had 2 sons and 1 daughter. These sons are Sam'l and John, now living.

Mary died single, at about 20 years old.

Joshua [Penhallow] died single; Joseph married and

settled in London; Benj. died young. Of the 8 daughters, Hannah married Benj. Pemberton, Esq., Boston; Mary married Benj. Gambling, Esq., Portsmo.; Elizabeth, —— Dummer, Esq., Newbury.

Phebe had 4 husbands, viz: a Mr. Gross, of Boston; Mr. Vassell, the father of the present Mrs. Knight; Dr. Gràves, of Charlestown; and Francis Borland, a wealthy merch't of Boston. She had only one child, viz: Mrs. Knight.

Deborah married Mr. Knight, of Portsmo., merchant, and left 2 sons (Wm. and Temple) and one daughter (Deb'h Carter.)

Olympia died single, at 18 years of age.

Lydia married Henry Slooper, compelled by her father. She left one son, who died at sea.

Susannah married Wm. Winkley.

John Cutts [grandson] married a sister of Col. Moore. There was one son.

Samuel Cutts, the youngest, married Harvey [Hannah Perkins.] Had several children, who settled in Boston. His widow afterwards married Phips.

The above are descended from President John Cutts.

Richard Cutts, the second brother, married the daughter of an English officer, who left England on account of the public commotions there. Had 2 daughters, Margaret and Bridget.

Bridget had 2 husbands, viz: Daniel and Crawford, and died without children.

[Bridget Cutts wrote the name of her second husband *Graffort.* This is probably another mode of spelling and pronouncing Crawford, though it is possible that Graffort and Crawford are distinct names.]

Margaret married Maj. Wm. Vaughan. Had 2 sons and 6 daughters.

Cutts Vaughan died at Barbadoes, unmarried.

Geo. Vaughan, afterwards Lieut. Gov. of New Hampshire, married Mary sister to Gov. Belcher, who died with her first child 1699. He afterwards married to Elizabeth Elliot, of Newcastle, and had 11 children.

Wm. Vaughan, the first son, was the first projector of the Louisburg expedition in 1744 to 1746. He died unmarried, in London, in 1746.

Elliot Vaughan married Anna Gerrish, and left 5 children, William, George, etc., now living.

Elinor Vaughan, the eldest daughter, was the second wife to Col. Rich'd Waldron (aforementioned). Had 2 sons and 4 daughters. Rich'd Waldron, Esq., of Portsmo. was the eldest. He was Secretary of New Hampshire, and sustained many other offices.

The second son was a minister at Boston, whose only daughter married Col. Josiah Quincy, of Braintree.

Margaret Waldron, the eldest daughter, married Eleazer Russell, Esq., of Portsmouth, father of the present Eleazer Russell, Esq.

Anna married Henry Rust, minister of Stratham.

Abigail married Col. Saltonstall, of Haverhill.

Elinor died unmarried, at 19.

Robert Cutts.

He went from England to the West Indies, (Barbadoes or St. Kitt's,) where he married a wealthy widow, who died soon after, when he married a second wife, Mary Hoel, (who went from England to Ireland at 12 years of age, from whence she went to the West Indies,) who he brought to America. He first lived in Portsmouth, in the Great House, so called, at the bottom of Pitt street. He afterwards removed to Kittery, set up a carpenter's yard, and built a great number of vessels. He had 2 sons and 4 daughters.

Richard Cutts, the eldest son, married to ——, and had — children.

[Richard had four if not more sons. Samuel, of Portsmouth; Richard, of Cutts' Island; Col. Thomas, of Saco; and Judge Edward Cutts, of Kittery. From the latter the late Edward Cutts, counsellor at law, of Portsmouth, descended. Samuel Cutts, a merchant (whose residence was on Market street, next south of the residence of the late Alexander Ladd,) was the father of Edward Cutts, the merchant, and Charles Cutts.]

Robert Cutts, 2d son, married to Dorcas Hammond, daughter to Major Joseph Hammond (whose father left England on the death of Cromwell, whose side he had taken in the contest with King Charles, and here married to a daughter of —— Frost, who had left England before, being an adherent of Charles the 1st.) They had four daughters.

Mary, the eldest, married to William Whipple. She had three sons and two daughters, and died in 1783, aged 85.

Katharine married John Moffatt, and left one son and two daughters; and several children died before her.

Mehitable married Jotham Odiorne. Had a number of children, some of whom died young. She died in 1789, aged 86. She left three daughters and one son.

Elizabeth married Rev. Joseph Whipple, and lived at Hampton. Afterwards married the Rev. John Lowell, and lived at Newbury, whom she also survived.

The four daughters [of the first Robert Cutts] were

1st, ——, married to —— Briar.
2d, ——, married to —— Scrivener.
3d, ——, married to —— Moore.
4th, Elizabeth, married to —— Elliot.

Robert Cutts' widow married an English gentleman, named —— Champernoone, of a respectable family. He visited England afterwards, and carried his wife's daughter Elizabeth with him; which daughter afterwards married to a Capt. Elliot, with whom she went a voyage by stealth.

Champernoone died. His widow went to South Carolina with two or three of her daughters, who removed thither.

There are no descendants of President John Cutts bearing the family name.

Hunking, Benjamin, and John Penhallow, were the sons of John P., the grandson of President John Cutts.

The old house at the corner of Market and Deer streets, used for boarding by Mrs. Chase in late years, which was taken down about eight years since, was the residence of Lieut. Gov. George Vaughan, the grandson of Richard Cutt. From the Lieut. Gov. Vaughan all the family bearing the name in this vicinity descended. It was in this branch only that Richard Cutt had any descendants. That old house was a distinguished seat in its early days. To it came the sister of the Governor of Massachusetts as a bride,—and from it, in a year, the imposing ceremonies of her funeral were displayed. From 1715 to 1717 this house was the residence of the Governor of the State. Here, in 1703, was born William Vaughan, the projector of the Louisburg expedition, which shed a lustre upon American history. That old house should have been daguerreotyped before it passed away.

RAMBLE CVII.

Residence of Richard Cutts — Capt. Thomas Leigh's Sea Adventure — William Bennett, the Hostage — His fate.

In our last, reference was made to the old house recently taken down at the corner of Market and Deer streets, the former residence of Lieut. Gov. George Vaughan. A building on the north, bounded on Market street, was an old bake house; and a brewery, as early as 1790, was south-west of the house, on the opposite side of the street. The house where the late George Long for many years resided, was built by Samuel Hart, (father of the late Richard,) more than a century ago, on what was then called the "Malt House Lot." The localities are so nearly like those referred to in the Will of the first Richard Cutt [Ramble 5th,] that there seems a probability that the old house, demolished about eight years since, was his residence in 1675, when he made his Will,—and that George Vaughan, his grandson, inherited it from him. If so, President John and his brother Richard lived in the immediate neighborhood of each other.

Elizabeth, a daughter of Gov. George Vaughan, married

George Bennett. She was said to be a lady of excellent education, and highly accomplished for her times. She died nearly eighty years since, at the age of 93 years. William Bennett, referred to in the following narrative, was their son.

The residence of Mr. George Bennett was on the spot where John P. Lyman's iron store now stands, opposite and a little south of the house of Capt. Samuel Cutts. We may imagine, a few years before the Revolution, a ship of perhaps 250 tons—a large vessel for those times—fitted out by Capt. Cutts at a wharf near by, with a freight for the West Indies, to proceed thence to Spain or the Mediterranean for a return cargo. She is under command of a well-informed master, Capt. Thomas Leigh. Young William Bennett, who had been brought up under the eye of the owner, ambitious to be himself a master, performs the duties of the first officer with a diligent and scrupulous attention. We may see the opulent owner on the wharf as the vessel departs, wishing them a prosperous voyage. On and on they sail, day by day. After touching at various ports, at length, in a Spanish port, the vigilant officer of customs discovers an infringement of their revenue laws, and the vessel is seized and condemned as a forfeit to Government. [Another tradition says that the vessel was captured by the Algerines; we cannot decide which is correct.] In this emergency the clemency of the captors was extended in the offer to Capt. Leigh to release the vessel on the payment of several thousand dollars, considerably less than the real value of the vessel. But how could the money be paid? There was no way of sending for it direct, and to keep the vessel on expense for months was not the policy of calculating men. Leave two of your men as hostages, and depart, was the offer. "Leave me," said Bennett; and his friend Mills was also left, as his companion. The stipulation was that they should be boarded until a specified time, ample for a return,—after that time they should be put in close confinement, and after another stipulated time, if no return, they should be left without food, to die of starvation. For some time the two friends, confident in the good faith of the master, passed their time in as pleasant a manner as the circumstances would permit. At length an opportunity offered for them to escape. Mills availed himself of it; but no persuasion would lead Bennett, who had faith in the vessel's return, to join him. Bennett was at once imprisoned, when it was found that his partner was gone. Here we will leave him to follow the vessel home.

As dear as his own life was Bennett to Capt. Leigh; and the security of the lives of the hostages of far more value in his estimation than a dozen ships. They arrived safe in the Piscataqua, and the Captain, instead of keeping this vessel (which then belonged to a foreign power) below, until the terms of the ransom were complied with, brought her up to the wharf and delivered her to Capt. Cutts, having acquainted him with the condition on which she had been purchased, and receiving the promise that the conditions should be faithfully complied with. The lives of two valuable men depending on the fulfilment of the contract.

The vessel is unloaded, and the cargo disposed of — but Captain Leigh sees no movement towards paying the ransom. The anxious parents of Bennett entreated, and it was said that the ransom money had been forwarded. There is less anxiety for a time, but after the elapse of the earliest hour in which a return is expected, the anxiety increases. Sabbath after Sabbath now the notes of the distressed parents can be heard from the pulpit of Rev. Dr. Langdon, asking prayers for a son in bondage in a foreign land. And the blood of Capt. Leigh boils to his veins as he contemplates the dreadful result which the failure of the receipt of the ransom money must produce. He measures the time, he knows the day when his friends are to enter their prison house—he marks with feverish excitement that dreadful day when the pangs of starvation are to commence. Accounts received gave evidence that poor Bennett suffered the extent of the penalty imposed. This was too much for humanity to bear. Leigh's mind feels the shock—but it did not at once cut him off from his regular business. At length, however, he becomes insane, and the name of Bennett is one the most frequent on his lips in his ravings. In the last century there were no asylums for those bereft of their reason, and the quarters of the almshouse were the best abodes to be found for those who could not safely be kept at home. Sixty years ago, when William Vaughan took the superintendence of our almshouse, among the unfortunate persons under his charge was Capt. Thomas Leigh, who had been a boarder in the institution for more than twenty years. His son, a distinguished merchant of South Berwick, who bore his father's name, did every thing for his comfort a son could do, but there was no return of that reason which the dreadful end of William Bennett tended to overthrow; the remembrance of which was manifest in his violent ravings to the close of life.

The sister of William Bennett was the grandmother of William Bennett Parker, Esq., of this city.

Joseph Leigh, who was the only brother of Thomas, was a Commissary in the Revolution, and afterwards a shipmaster. He was truly patriotic in his feelings, and prided himself in being a citizen of the Republic,—the title so pleased him, that he was better known as "Citizen Lee" than by any other name. He died about fifty-eight years ago.

RAMBLE CVIII.

The Cutts and Penhallow Cemetery on Green Street.

THOUSANDS of the people of Portsmouth have never noticed the fifty feet lot on the north side of Green street, enclosed by a wall of "lime and stone," as directed by President John Cutt in his will made in 1680. It appears that his first wife Hannah died six years previous to that time, that several of his children had died and been buried in "the orchard," a few rods west of the President's house which was near the shore, where the stone store now stands.

After spending, recently, an hour or two in the enclosure rubbing off the moss from the old grave stones to decipher the inscriptions, a friend put into our hand the result of a similar visit some years ago, so that by comparing notes we are enabled to give the ancient inscriptions :

"Here lyes buried the body of Mrs. Hannah Cutt, late wife of Mr. John Cutt, aged 42 years, who departed this life on the —— day of November, 1674."

"Here lies interred ye body of Mrs. Mary Penhallow, late wife to Samuel Penhallow of Portsmouth, in ye Province of New-Hampshire in New England, Esq. She was born Nov. 17th, 1669, and died Feb'y the 8th, 1713."

"Here lies buried ye body of the Honorable Samuel Penhallow, Esq.—first of His Majesty's Council of ye Province of New Hampshire,—born at St Mabon, in ye County of Cornwall in Great Britain, July 2d, 1665—Dyed Dec'r 2d, 1726—aged 61 years and 5 months."

"Here lyes interred the body of the Hon Benjamin Gambling, Esq. a Member of his Majesty's Council in the Province of New-Hampshire, and Judge of the Probate of Wills—who departed this life the first of September, 1757—aged 56 yrs."

"Here lyes buried the body of Mr. Benjamin Gambling, who departed June 2d, 1744, in the 30th year of his age."

"Here lies buried the body of Mr William Knight, Merchant in Portsmouth—Deceased November 16th, 1730, in the 37th year of his age."

"Here lyes buried the body of Mrs Lydia Sloper, late wife to Capt. Henry Sloper—who departed this life August 17th, 1718—aged 16 years and 11 months."

"Here lyes interred the body of John Penhallow, Esq. who departed this life July 28th, Anno Domini 1735, aged 42 years."

"Here lyes buried the body of Mrs. Elizabeth Penhallow, the wife of John Penhallow, Esq. aged 47 years—who departed this life Feb. 25, 1736."

"Olympia Penhallow, 1693."

These were all, with the exception of those on one or two grave stones of modern date.

It is a little remarkable that the name of President Cutt

was not placed upon the monument of his wife Hannah, for which a blank was evidently left. Nor do we here find a stone for Ursula, the widow of President Cutt, who was killed by the Indians, although here she doubtless was buried.

The inscription on the monument of Hon. Samuel Penhallow shows him to be the first of the family that came to this country. The term "first of his Majesty's Council," means that he was President of that body. We have seen an extended sketch of his life and services, written by the author of the Annals of Portsmouth, but not inserted in that work. He built a brick house which stood at the head of the Pier, where he lived in a style of much grandeur for that day. This spacious house, which afterwards passed into the hands of the Sherburne family, and eventually became the *New Hampshire Hotel*, was situated on the south east corner of State and Water streets, and was consumed in the fire of 1813.

His son, Samuel Penhallow, the grandfather of Hunking, Benjamin and John, married the sister of Sir Ribye Lake. The letter-book of Samuel, which is still in the family, contains one letter in which he writes to Sir Ribye, and among other things for which he makes himself indebted, is a scarlet cloak trimmed with gold lace, that he desires him to purchase for his sister Elizabeth, (Mrs. Elizabeth Penhallow.) This was after he grew rich, for he had many troubles and much suffering in the early times of the country—but his enterprise, perseverance and upright course were crowned with success.

The following extract from a deed given by Gov. George Vaughan in 1702, who then lived in the house at the northwest corner of Market and Deer streets, will serve to show the localities of some of the houses at that time.

I, George Vaughan of Portsmouth, Gentleman, for £61

of and from Michael Whidden of the same town, have sold unto said Michael a certain piece of land containing one house lot whereon stands a dwelling house which formerly was made use of as a bake house by Mr. Richard Cutt, deceased, laying near said Vaughan's mansion house on Strawberry Bank, said lot being 40 feet fronting on that highway which runs from Maj. Vaughan's to Mr. Waldron's house, carrying the same breadth back and is 100 feet back from said street, is bounded with a street known by the name of *Dear* street, which runs between the said Vaughan's mansion house and that said lot.

I say bounded with this street of 46 feet wide on the south side, with Samuel Hart's land on the north-west, and with John Low's land on the south-west, together with the liberty of landing any goods, lumber, wood, &c. on a certain landing place, being given by the said Vaughan for the use of any such as may or have purchased land abutting on the aforementioned street known by the name of *Dear* street, which is 46 feet as aforesaid—together with all the privileges and advantages to the same appertaining or in any wise belonging: to have and to hold, &c.

RAMBLE CIX.

The Residence of Dea. Samuel Penhallow.

ANOTHER old landmark was removed in 1862 to give place to the more modern and sightly mansion built by Mr. Thomas E. Call. The old Penhallow house, which for more than a century formed the south-east corner of Court and Pleasant streets, is now among the departed. The exact date of its erection we cannot ascertain. It was here that the good Deacon Samuel Penhallow, and his prim lady lived and died. The little shop on the corner afforded to the public the needles, pins, thread, tape, snuff, and other useful and fancy articles—while in the adjoining room on Pleasant street, the penalties of violated law were decreed with all the rigor which a sense of the majesty of the law required. This little room of justice was only large enough to admit the magistrate, the culprit, two attornies, and four witnesses—if more appeared they could only look in at the door. The smallness of the room seemed to make the law operations work with more celerity. In this room was the trial of poor Cæsar Marston the slave, who stole the bucket of rum and received summary punishment therefor, as recorded on page 118.

We will give here a more detailed account of the incident recorded on page 119.

Jeremiah Mason came to Portsmouth in 1797. Not long after that time an article appeared in one of the papers by inuendo charging the administrator of the estate of Hunking Wentworth with unfair dealing. The article was so personal and so unjust, that the writer was sought out, and John Wentworth, the lawyer resident at Little Harbor, was found to be the man. Mr. Mason and his friend Mr. Fisher, determined to chastise him for the insult; and procuring cowhides they took a walk down Pleasant street at the time he usually came into town. They met Wentworth near the elm at the corner of Gates street, and after the application of the hide for a few times, he escaped by running down Gates street.

South-end was then easily excited; the sympathy of Water street was raised in favor of their Republican friend Wentworth, and their wrath boiled over against the Federalists who had assaulted him. It became at once a party matter. Mr. Wentworth entered his complaint, and Sheriff Edward Hart arrested Mason and Fisher. They promised to appear the next morning, agreeably to the summons, before Justice Penhallow, and so were released on their own recognizances. The next morning might be seen entering that little room the great gun of the law, with his friend, while around the door the sympathizers of Wentworth might be seen in hundreds, awaiting the result of the trial. After the warrant was read, Mr. Mason told the magistrate they should not contend, and asked for their fine. The Deacon made it some six or eight dollars—it was paid, and they were discharged. This was not satisfactory to the Republicans, who wished to have them bound over to the County Court, and some strong demonstration was attempted to be made. Mr. Mason, it will be recollected, was a man nearly six feet and a half in height. At that time he was much more slim than in after years, and his figure did not excel in gracefulness as it did in length. Capt. Thomas Manning saw that there was danger of his receiving rough treatment, and having a controlling influence over the party, he sat in the door of the shop, resting on his cane, when Mr. Mason passed out. "Hiss the Flamingo—hiss the Flamingo," said he, (knowing that something must be allowed,) "but don't lay a finger on him." There was a general hissing—and as Rome was once saved by a similar sound, so by it, Mr. Mason, somewhat affrighted, was protected. But it was hard work for him to press through the crowd. At this moment, Mr. Jacob Walden, a gentleman who had the general respect of the citizens, pressed forward and offered his arm to Mr. Mason, which was thankfully accepted, and they were able to reach the high steps of the Greenleaf house, then on the spot where Hon. Richard Jenness now resides, and going up the steps backward to keep an eye upon the hissing crowd, Mr. Mason retired. The excitement was soon over, and Mr. M. as he became more generally known as an able and distinguished lawyer, was subjected to no further molestation—nor did he ever give a like exciting cause for it.

It was in this little room, that in about the year 1760, John Sullivan, afterwards General, and President of New Hampshire, when a student with Matthew Livermore, successfully plead his first case—while Livermore, unknown to Sullivan, stood in the shop listening to the ingenuity of his student's argument.

Could all the incidents of the old house be gathered, they would form a Ramble too extensive for one week. It is a matter of regret that these old landmarks should be torn down and be forever forgotten.

RAMBLE CX.

The Old Clock—The Four George Jaffreys—The Jaffrey House.

At the residence of the late Mr. Supply Ham, one of the ancient and honorable clock and watch makers of Portsmouth, stands a monument of time, seven feet in hight, which notes the passing hours with the same regularity that the earth rolls upon its axis. It is an excellent piece of workmanship, showing no marks of wear in its machinery, although that bright pendulum for more than five thousand millions of times, has swayed "here"—"there"—as in obedience to the command of the "tick" above it. The case is of the English oak, handsomely veneered—the key to wind it up is of fanciful workmanship, and appears to be an imitation of that of the holy house of Loretto.—The clock, which was made by "J. Windmill, London," bears this inscription of its owners:

"1677—George Jaffrey. 1802—Timothy Ham.
1720—George Jaffrey, Jr. 1856—Supply Ham.
1749—George Jaffrey, 3d. 1862—Francis W. Ham"

The first George Jaffrey, who appears to have been the owner, was born in 1637 at Newbury, where he lived sometime. There he married Elizabeth Walker in 1665. About that time he removed to Newcastle, and was Speaker of the New Hampshire Assembly which convened sometimes at that place.

But, as in these days, the people of old made haste to be rich more rapidly than through the channels of regular trade. Mr. Jaffrey was a man of good repute, and a member of the Rev. Mr. Moody's church. But in 1684, for some attempt to import without paying regular duties, his vessel was seized and put under government charge. In the night the vessel mysteriously disappeared. Mr. Jaffrey took oath that he had no knowledge of the affair.

Although there was no doubt in the public mind in this respect, Gov. Cranfield was compounded with, and all legal proceedings against Jaffrey were stopped. But the conscientious Mr. Moody was not so easily satisfied. He preached a sermon on false swearing, and had an ecclesiastical trial of Jaffrey. He acknowledged his crime, made a public confession, and we know not that he afterwards went astray. This proceeding was an occasion of great offence to Cranfield, and led to the imprisonment of Moody. The Annals of Portsmouth, p. 72, endeavors to veil the matter by using the name " George *Janvrin,* "—the church records however give the trial as that of George Jaffrey. This old clock doubtless witnessed a sorry and anxious countenance frequently cast upon it in those days—when it occupied a place in the old Jaffrey house at Newcastle. That house still stands in the vicinity of Jerry's Point—originally, doubtless, Jaffrey's Point.

His son George Jaffrey, Jr., (whose name appears as an owner of the old clock,) was born at Newcastle in 1683, graduated at Harvard College in 1702, was a mandamus counsellor in 1716, and after the death of Samuel Penhallow in 1726, was Treasurer of the Province. He was also Chief Justice of the Superior Court to the time of his death in 1749.

He took up his residence in Portsmouth previous to 1719—as we find him holding various town offices from and after that year—and built, probably as early as 1730, that unique structure on Daniel street, occupied by the heirs of the late Col. John Goodrich, which still retains the name of the *Jaffrey House.* In the recollection of many, the fine front yard and elevated position of the mansion gave it a very inviting appearance from Daniel street. This yard and the extensive garden plot in the rear are now covered by many houses, but the old mansion stands yet conspicuous among them all.

George Jaffrey 3d, son of the above, was born in 1716, graduated at Harvard in 1736, and in 1746 was one of the purchasers of Mason's patent, and then became an extensive landed proprietor. He occupied this house to the day of his death in 1802. If he was ever married, the fact never reached us. This old clock was his companion his whole life of 86 years. He was a man of about five feet seven or eight inches in height, portly, and being one of his Majesty's Council was very dignified in his appearance. His red cloak, small clothes, silk stockings and heavy gold shoe buckles, are well remembered by our older citizens. He was appointed Clerk of the Supreme Court in 1744, which office he retained until he was admitted as one of his Majesty's Council in 1766. He was also Treasurer of the Province until the Revolution. He was strongly opposed to the change in the government.

One day, while mending his buckle, a goldsmith remarked, "I suppose you prize this highly not only for its intrinsic value, but also for its Tower mark and Crown stamp." "Yes," said he bringing down his cane with violence, "yes—we never ought to have come off."

The Jaffrey mansion was kept in the most perfect order, not only externally, but also internally. On one occasion no small offence was given to a neighbor, who was applied to for some of their cobwebs to put on a cut finger, as none could be found in the premises.

He was opposed to oral prayer, deeming those who thus pray hypocrites. But in church on one Sunday his voice was heard in response above all others. He had been much annoyed by encroachments on the boundaries of some of his extensive estates in the interior, and went to church with a vexed mind from that cause. In the course of the service, when "Cursed be he who removeth his neighbor's landmark" was read—"Amen!" said Jaffrey with a loud voice and hearty good will. At one time, the Rev. Dr. Brown chanced to come abruptly upon him when he was uttering a volley of oaths. "I am surprised, sir," said he, "that you should so soon, after denouncing praying men as hypocrites, be found offering to God a petition."

His will was drawn up by the Hon. Jeremiah Mason, whose kind efforts to alter some of its controlling features were ineffectual. That will bequeathed all the real and and personal estate of Mr. Jaffrey to his grand nephew and namesake, George Jaffrey Jeffries, then only thirteen years of age. The inheritance was on these conditions; that he should drop the name of Jeffries; become a permanent resident in this city; and never follow any profession except that of being a *gentleman.* As an heir to an estate supposed to be immense, and destined to a profession not specifically acknowledged among us, Mr. Jaffrey was of course to be furnished with the best possible education.

Mr. George Jaffrey (the fourth) accepted the name, and occupied the mansion here for several years,—led the life of a gentleman, and in 1856 died at the age of 66 years. As he left no son nor estate to continue the name, the line of George Jaffreys closed with him.

The old clock with other old furniture was sold in 1802, and it became the property of the grandfather of the present owner. It still goes on undisturbed by the succession of six generations, and its swaying pendulum is likely to say "pass on, pass on," to many generations to come.

RAMBLE CXI.

Rev. Samuel McClintock.

IN the picture of the battle of Bunker Hill, representing the fall of Gen. Warren, may be seen in the group a clergyman arrayed in his bands, who appears to be deeply interested in the battle. That man was the Rev. SAMUEL McCLINTOCK, D. D. of Greenland, N. H., the father of the venerable John McClintock, who died in Portsmouth a few years since at the age of 94, retaining his mental and physical faculties to the last.

We have recently been applied to for a history of Rev. Dr. McClintock, and have been enabled to collect the following from an authentic source, embracing some interesting facts which have never before appeared in print.

William McClintock, (the father of Dr. Samuel McClintock, the subject of this article,) was a respectable farmer, born in Scotland. From thence he early removed to Londonderry in Ireland, probably in the latter part of James the Second's reign. When his intrigues, in order to reinstate Catholicism, were creating great uneasiness among his people, James endeavored by taking sides with the Kirk to overthrow the Episcopacy, for by thus pitching one party against another and holding the balance of power, he hoped in the end to turn the scale and restore Catholicism. But the Presbyterians were too cunning for him: strong as was their hatred of Episcopacy, their dislike for Catholicism was greater, and uniting with their Episcopal brethren, they showed themselves ready to receive his favors but unwilling to enter into any of his plans. The civil wars of Charles the first were not however forgotten, and many were fearing new changes, and emigrated from all parts of the kingdom. Among these was Mr. McClintock. He went where he found friends; for the eastern coast of

Ireland and the west of Scotland have in all ages been inhabited by men of the same stock. But the war was transferred to Ireland, and James sat down before Londonderry, determined to press it by a slow siege. This was one of the most important and most obstinately contested sieges during the whole war. It continued from the month of December, 1688, until August, 1689. The garrison suffered all the miseries attendant on a protracted siege, which they bore with unflinching fortitude.

King William at length relieved the place. Mr. McClintock with some others emigrated to America when the war was over. Their fortunes had probably been dissipated, and they hoped to find that religious peace and those worldly comforts which they sought for in vain in their own country across the ocean.

Mr. McClintock settled on Mystic river, but his companions travelled on to Londonderry in this State, which they named after their parent town. Mr. McClintock continued quietly to till his farm without entering into any of the politics of the day, busy with Scotch thrift in increasing his property, and died at the advanced age of ninety. He was married four times, had nineteen children,—and left by his last wife one daughter and two sons.

Dr. Samuel McClintock was born in 1732. He was educated at Princeton College, under the care of President Burr, the father of the distinguished Aaron Burr.

We may suppose that he finished his course with honor, for his sermons bear the marks of great mental discipline, and we have been told that throughout his life he was distinguished as one of the finest Latin scholars in New England.

After having finished his studies, stopping on a journey to Portsmouth, he was invited to preach before the Congregational Society of Greenland, who were in want of an assistant for their pastor, Mr. Allen, then very infirm with age; and so favorable was the impression he made, that he was immediately invited to share his labors. He soon after accepted and entered upon his duties. It is reported that the charms of a certain Mary Montgomery, of Scotch extraction, and who resided in Portsmouth, had a great influence in inducing Mr. McClintock to accept a charge which offered so little in a worldly point of view. This lady Dr. McClintock married, and if she induced him to accept the offer of the Greenland Society he never repented it. His salary was but $300 a year, with the parsonage, a small and not over fertile farm. This seems little enough, when we recollect that the Dr. had fifteen children to support, and the tax upon his hospitality was somewhat heavy, as there were no hotels in those days, and the pastor was expected to entertain all the travelling clergymen of his own denomination, and other men of any note.

His children have amusingly related that whether the cow gave more milk or less, the quantity was always the same,—it was, to be sure, a trifle bluer. Dr. McClintock had many calls to richer churches, but he preferred his own people, to whom he was endeared by a long ministry of forty-eight years of uninterrupted usefulness. During the revolution he strongly espoused the side of the people, as his temper was ardent, and he very easily broke the bond of allegiance to a government to which his religious principles were opposed, and from which his ancestors had suffered so much.

His character gave weight to his opinions, and we must give him credit for courage, since he was so ready to stand forth boldly in a doubtful cause, when in case of defeat his ruin was certain. He was Chaplain at the battle of Bunker Hill, and is represented in Trumbull's picture of that battle; and he has left a sermon on the adoption of the constitution, exhibiting the enlarged views of a patriot and the temper of a Christian.

But Dr. McClintock suffered severely in the cause which he espoused with such boldness. Three of his sons perished in the war. One of them, Nathaniel, received a collegiate education at Harvard, but the war breaking out he joined General Washington, and was raised to the rank of Major of Brigade. He was in the New Hampshire line at the battles before the capture of Burgoyne on the 19th of September and the 7th of October. After the capture, his regiment was ordered South, and he was with Washington at the memorable capture of the Hessians at Trenton. He was then (although he had not reached 21 years of age,) raised to the rank of Major of the line, over all the older Captains. And as he was therefore regarded with jealousy by those lower than himself in rank, he resigned his commission and returned home. He was induced to take the command of a company of marines which went out in a ship-of-war, the Raleigh, and soon after perished in an engagement. Another son of Dr. McClintock was an officer at the battle of Trenton and there slain; and a third was lost at sea, serving as a midshipman, and afterwards as lieutenant in a ship-of-war. Doctor McClintock bore all these trials with christian fortitude.

He was loved and esteemed by his parish, and in the latter part of his life received the Diploma of Doctor of Divinity from Princeton College where he was educated.

He enjoyed uninterrupted good health, and was only ill a few days before his death, which took place at the age of 72. In his writing desk were found the following instructions to his son John:

I feel myself sinking in the vale of years, near the house appointed, and have had for some time a premonition that the time of my departure is near. It may be imagined. However, considering that I have exceeded the stated period of human life, it must be expected that I am drawing near the great period. My only hope of being happy beyond the grave is founded on the mercy of God and the merits of a Divine Redeemer. May you, long after I shall be here no more, enjoy happiness in the endearments of an agreeable companion and pleasant children. You know that I have appointed you executor of my will, and that therein I have expressed my desire that the solemnity of my funeral should be conducted in the manner that is customary at the funerals of my parishioners, without any parade or sermon which has commonly been the custom at the funerals of those who have sustained any public character in life. If you should think it proper, about which I am perfectly indifferent, to erect a head-stone at my grave, which in that case I wish may be quite a plain one, I would have you inscribe in it the following epitaph, without an addition or alteration, except filling up the blanks for the months and years of my decease and standing in the ministry.

To the memory of SAMUEL McCLINTOCK, D. D. who died —— in the — year of his age, and — of his ministry.

His body rests here in the certain hope of a resurrection to life and immortality, when Christ shall appear the second time to destroy the last enemy, Death, and to consummate the great design of his mediatorial kingdom.

The annual fast, which was the 19th of April, 1804, was the last of his preaching; and what was remarkable, on his return to his family he observed that he *had done his preaching*. He continued until the morning of the 27th of April, when he exchanged this world for another, and is, we trust, reaping the reward of a faithful servant in the kingdom of God.

His grave-stone, inscribed as above with the blanks filled, (died 27th April, 1804, aged 72—48th of his ministry,) may be seen in the Greenland Cemetery.

Dr. McClintock had two wives, his first wife, Mary Montgomery, died Aug. 4, 1785, aged 48. For his last wife he was married to a widow Mrs. Darling. The match was not very congenial. She was not so strictly the darling of his heart as his first love. She survived him.

Dr. McClintock's religious views were strictly calvinistical in the early part of his ministry. Some regarded them harsh and untempered by the law of love. This is not surprising when we consider the troubled times in which those men were educated in violent struggle for civil and religious liberty, when even their prejudices seemed sanctified by their blood. Men who had so long followed the pillar of fire might easily forget that there were souls who needed the refreshing shadow of the cloud. The opinions of Dr. McClintock were however much milder in the later portion of his life, but he was always strenuous in his appeals, with something of the enthusiasm and the better part of the perseverance of his Scotch ancestors. Full of simplicity and honesty, it is not too great praise to say that if his head sometimes erred his heart was nearly always right.

History informs us that during the battle of Bunker Hill this venerable clergyman knelt on the field, with hands upraised, and grey head uncovered; and, while the bullets whistled around him, prayed for the success of the compatriots, and the deliverance of his country. This rare incident prompted the following beautiful ode from the pen of Mrs. Lydia H. Sigourney.

THE PRAYER ON BUNKER HILL.

"It was an hour of fear and dread—
High rose the battle-cry,
And round, in heavy volumes, spread
The war-cloud to the sky.
'Twas not, as when in rival strength
Contending nations meet,
Or love of conquest madly hurls
A monarch from his seat:

"Yet one was there, unused to tread
The path of mortal strife,
Who but the Saviour's flock had fed
Beside the fount of life.
He knelt him where the black smoke wreathed—
His head was bowed and bare,—
While, for an infant land he breathed
The agony of prayer.

"The column, red with early morn,
May tower o'er Bunker's height,
And proudly tell a race unborn

Their patriot fathers' might;—
But thou, O patriarch, old and grey,
Thou prophet of the free,
Who knelt among the dead that day,
What fame shall rise to thee?

"It is not meet that brass or stone
Which feel the touch of time,
Should keep the record of a faith
That woke thy deed sublime:
We trace it to the tablet fair,
Which glows when stars wax pale,
A promise that the good man's prayer
Shall with his God prevail."

RAMBLE CXII.

Sketch of Newcastle.

THE history of Newcastle is of some interest, as the first settlement in New Hampshire was made in 1623, upon its borders, by a Scotchman named David Thompson. He was selected by the Company of Laconia, in England, to establish a permanent settlement in this province. Shortly after his arrival he built the first house on Odiorne's Point, a few rods distant from what resembles the remains of an ancient fort. It was afterwards called Mason Hall, in honor of a prominent member of the company under whose auspices the settlement was begun. The house remained standing for many years.

The original designation was *Great Island*, but in 1693, it was separated from Portsmouth, and incorporated under its present name. At the time of its incorporation a large portion of land on the west was included within its limits, but in consequence of the incorporation of Rye in 1719, its area was reduced to 458 acres. The soil, though thickly interspersed with rocks, has ever been made to produce abundantly; and owing to the plentiful supply of seaweed, the farmers need never fail for want of the proper means of enriching their lands.

The original copy of the ancient charter, written throughout in Old English or Black Letter, can now be seen in the office of the Selectmen, though the seal has been cut off by some individual ignorant of its real importance. It is a very interesting document, written upon parchment, and and is one of the many relics of antiquity to be found in Newcastle.

Formerly a bridge was built on the south-west side of the town, forming a means of connection between Rye and Newcastle; and, previous to the building of the new bridges in 1821, all travellers for Portsmouth went by way of the "Old Bridge." Owing to carelessness and neglect, nearly all signs of the "Old Bridge" have now vanished.

It it well known that the annual meeting in Newcastle for the choice of town officers takes place one week before the usual State election, yet but few seem to know when this custom originated. By referring to the charter, it is found that requisition was then made for this matter, concerning which we make the following extract:

"AND for the better order, rule and government of the said Towne, wee doe by these presents Grant for us and our Successors unto the men and Inhabitants of the said Towne, That yearly and every year upon the first Tuesday of March, forever, they, the said men and Inhabitants of our said Towne, shall elect and choose by the major part of them, two sufficient and able men, householders in the said Towne, to be Constables for the year ensuing, which said men so chosen and elected, shall be presented by the then next preceding Constables to the next Quarter sessions of the peace to be held for the said province, there to take the accustomed oaths appointed by Law for the execution of their offices under such penalties as the law of our said province shall appoint and direct upon refusall or neglect therein. AND we doe by these presents Grant for us, our Heirs, and Successors, unto the men and Inhabitants of the said Towne, That yearly and every year upon the said first Tuesday of March, forever, they, the said men and inhabitants of our said Towne, or the major part of them, shall elect and choose three men, Inhabitants and householders of our said Towne, to be overseers of the poor and highways, or selectmen for our said Towne for the year ensuing with such powers, privileges and authorities as any overseers or selectmen within our said province have and enjoy."

For the privileges enjoyed as an incorporated town, it is further stated that there shall be paid "the annual quitt rent or acknowledgment of onne Pepercorn in the said Towne on the five twentieth day of October yearly forever."

Soon after the settlement of Great Island, a fort was built upon Frost Point, to serve as a protection to the harbor. It was an earthwork "made with certain great gunns to it," and in the year 1660 was mentioned in the documents of that day as the means of distinguishing Great Island from other islands in the vicinity. It was several times remodeled, and for many years prior to the war of the Revolution, was called Fort William and Mary, named in honor of the King and Queen of England. In the eleventh year of the reign of Charles the first, of England, the Island together with the Fort came into possession of Mistress Anne Mason, widow of John Mason, of London, who, at the time of his death, was engaged in mercantile pursuits. Portions of the island were afterwards deeded to Robert Mussel and other individuals, by her agent, Joseph Mason of "Strawberry Bank" on the river of the "Pascattaquack."

At the time of the passage of an act in 1774, by George III. forbidding the exportation of gunpowder to America, the Fort was garrisoned by Captain Cochran and five men, and the ships-of-war Scarborough and Canseau were daily expected to arrive with several companies of British soldiers to re-inforce the garrison. On receipt of the news a company of citizens from Portsmouth determined upon seizing the arms and ammunition at the earliest period. They procured a gondola at midnight, and anchoring a short distance from the fort, waded ashore and scaled the walls. Shortly after their arrival they encountered the Captain, who delivered to them his sword. It was, however, immediately returned, for which favor he tendered his thanks. Having taken one hundred barrels of powder, they started on their return, and on leaving the Fort were rewarded for the favor before shown to the commanding officer, by his giving them a lunge with his sword. They tarried not at the insult, but hastened on board the gondola and rowed up the Piscataqua to Durham. On their arrival, the ammunition was taken to the cellar of the Congregational Church, where it remained for some time ; thence it was taken to Bunker Hill, where on the 17th June it was used to the disadvantage of the British. On the following day the Fort was again entered, and "fifteen of the lighter cannon and all the small arms taken away." The Scarborough and Canseau soon after arrived.

In the autumn of 1775, fearing an attack upon Portsmouth, General Sullivan, at that time a resident of Durham, N. H., was appointed by General Washington to take command of the militia of this State and to defend this harbor. Several fortifications had been thrown up, which he strengthened, and placed in them several companies of militia. In Fort William and Mary a company of artillery were placed who "were allowed the same pay as soldiers of the Continental Army."

In 1808 the Fort was again rebuilt under the name of Fort Constitution, and remained until a new structure was commenced in 1863, upon the same spot.

The Fort on Jaffrey's Point at the entrance of Little Harbor, was once thought to be a very important post. It was garrisoned in the war of 1812 by citizens of this and other towns, under command of Capt. William Marshall, who remained stationed at that post for several years. Nine guns, 6 and 9 pounders, were placed in position, and on several occasions full one hundred and twenty men were stationed there.

A short distance from this Fort may be seen another Fort, situated upon rising ground near the bridge leading from Newcastle to Portsmouth. This post was not considered of much importance, yet several cannon were held in readiness to be placed upon it at short notice.

During the visits of the English ships to this harbor in 1775–6, a spirit of hatred seemed to prevail against the British seamen, but by the major part of the citizens they were respectfully treated. The sailors would often conduct badly, and if reprimanded would threaten to fire upon the town. Oftentimes the lives of the inhabitants were endangered, and on some occasion, a committee of citizens waited upon the commander of the Scarborough, offering an apology for some fancied insult to his men, to prevent him from permitting the threats of the sailors to be carried into execution. Owing to the state of public excitement at that early period of the Revolution, many citizens left the town and many more were prepared to leave at a moment's warning.

In the rear of the Congregational Church is a well in which some of the citizens once placed their silver ware for safe keeping: and near the fish yard of Veranus C. Rand may be noticed a depression of the ground, showing the site of an old revolutionary house, which was then occupied by a Mrs. Trefethren, who was noted for refusing water to the British sailors on account of her hatred to them. It is stated that notwithstanding her positive refusal to permit the sailors of the Scarborough to get water there, they once succeeded in filling their casks; and leaving them near the well, visited the central part of the town. No sooner were they out of sight than she emptied the casks. Upon their return they demanded of her why she had turned away their water. She promptly replied that she did not turn away *their* water; the water was *her own.* On returning to the ship they rewarded her by firing a ball through the room in which her family were sitting.*

Portsmouth, in its proximity to the ocean, and the many convenient landing places between the city and the islands outside of the light-house, has peculiar advantages for the water excursions that have ever been so popular with its inhabitants. Newcastle, previous to the construction of the bridges that connect it with the city, was a favorite resort, where they were wont to cook their fish and partake of their refreshments, generally at some favorable spot on the rocky shore, or obtain permission to occupy apartments for the purpose at one of the dwellings at the water-side. A public house, kept a Mr. Bell, also received a share of of patronage on some of these occasions. On the premises was an out-door bowling-alley, or, in ancient phrase, "a bowling-green," of which one of the memories that survive is the dilapidated condition of the pins from long and hard usage, and the reply of a visitor to the landlord who complimented him on his skill at the game. "Oh," said he, "it does not require much skill to *knock down* the pins, but if it were as hard to *upset* them as it is to *set them up*, I should never have got that tenstrike." The following, copied from the graceful chirography of a former much esteemed citizen of Portsmouth, is a record of a winter excursion, under unusual circumstances, to Newcastle :

"Feb. 17th, 1817.—In consequence of the severe weather of last week, I was enabled to-day in company with my brother-in-law, D**** M*****, to walk to Newcastle on a substantial bridge of ice. We stopped at George Bell's,

*The foregoing portion of this Ramble was prepared by Mr. Thomas B. Frost of Newcastle.

who furnished us with a dinner of fine fresh cod, taken at the edge of the ice, 172 yards from the end of his wharf. We measured the ice on our return, and found it 18 inches in thickness, over which sleighing parties were merrily gliding on their way to the Island. T. G. M."

There are few, if any, of the natives of our city, who have not remembrances, at some period of their lives, of pleasant hours passed upon the water. In my childhood, writes one whose early life was passed on the shores of the Piscataqua, there were five brothers in one family circle, of whose aquatic adventures, in their youth at the close of the last century, I never wearied, as they were recalled when they met at each other's dwellings. One fine summer night, when the moon was shining brightly, they went to one of the small islands outside of the light-house—Wood Island I think—in pursuit of lobsters. After setting their nets they landed and built a fire among the bushes a short distance back from the beach, and making a kettle of chocolate, enjoyed a hearty meal from the stock of refreshments always taken into consideration among the requisite accompaniments of such expeditions. This pleasant performance over, they went to look for their boat, but great was their consternation, instead of finding it, as they anticipated, high and dry upon the sand, to discover that it had got loose from its moorings, and was fast travelling, with the tide, in the direction of the Shoals. The misfortune was increased by the fact that it was a new one, the property of a relative, who had given them many injunctions as to its good usage. Like the man in the play, they were in a peculiarly perplexing 'predicament,' but trusting as a last extremity, to their usual good luck, in the product of their nets, which were within reach by swimming, for something to eat, and in the hope that some passing boat would take them off in the morning, they took the most philosophic view of the matter possible, and wrapping themselves in the rough overcoats always taken in their nocturnal voyages, they retired again to the shelter of the bushes, and ere long were fast asleep. They awoke just as the first rays of the sun appeared above the horizon, and looking seaward, to their great satisfaction discovered a fishing-boat in the distance, with another boat in tow, which they had no doubt was their lost craft, as it eventually proved when within hailing distance. An abundant supply of lobsters was found in their nets, which were shared with the men who had restored their boat, and they reached home in season to relate their adventures around the family breakfast table. On their return from another trip by moonlight to the dominions of Neptune, they brought with them a supply of eels, of an unusually large size, which, to facilitate the process of preparing for the frying-pan, were deposited in the ashes of the kitchen fire-place. At an early hour of the morning, before daylight had fully appeared, the family "help," an eccentric and rather superstitious specimen of feminine humanity, descended to the apartment, and, on opening the door, obtained a glimpse of a dozen or more strange looking animals, of serpentine form and of a dusky hue, disporting themselves among the sand upon the floor. A moment later the mistress of the mansion was awakened from her slumbers by a knock on her door, and a familiar voice exclaiming, "Oh, Miss ——, I believe *the old serpent and his whole family* are in the kitchen and I am afraid to go down there." A few words of explanation settled the matter, and in a brief space of time the eels were retreating before energetic thrusts from a birch broom, that received from its holder an additional impetus for the fright she had received. Two of the brothers were shipmasters in after years, and spent the largest portion of their lives upon the ocean. They have *all* sailed upon their last voyage, but the legends of their youth will long survive them.

RAMBLE CXIII.

Newcastle Reminisences of Forty-Five Years Ago.

Anterior to the erection of the bridges that now connect it with Portsmouth, many of the least cultivated among the older inhabitants of Newcastle, isolated as they were from the outer world, especially during the inclement seasons of the year, were about as primitive in their ideas as the dwellers at the Shoals, and scarcely less peculiar in their dialect. Separated by some three miles of water communication from Portsmouth, it was no uncommon occurrence to hear quiet, stay-at-home bodies among the old ladies acknowledge that they "had not been to town" in ten to a dozen years, and inquiries would be made as to individuals they had once known, as if the place were a thousand miles away.

A more antique locality, previous to the consummation of that achievement in the march of improvement, the construction of the bridges, could not have been found in all New England. While many of the dwellings were spacious and comfortable, there were very few of modern construction; by far the larger proportion gave evidence of having been erected in the early part of the last century; many were so dilapidated by age as to be almost untenantable, and others had reached that point in their history, and were undergoing the process of being converted into firewood.

One of the most antique of these moss-covered structures of the olden time, was the ancient church that occupied the site of the modern edifice, of which the Rev. Mr. Alden is pastor. Though sadly fallen to decay, traces existed to show that taste had not been omitted in its construction. Erected originally for the service of the English Church, the chancel remained in good preservation, and relics survived of ornamental devices that had once surmounted the creed and decalogue. The sills had gone to decay, and the floor had consequently sunk some inches below its original position, but the building served for summer use, and the people loving the old place of worship where their ancestors had been wont to gather, continued to to occupy it every season until the cold winds of autumn drove them to the shelter of the less spacious but more comfortable structure, where on week-days,

"The village master taught his little school."

Among the many improvements upon the island none are more conspicuous than those visible in the vicinity of the spot occupied at a former day by the ancient sanctuary. The tasteful and well-kept flower garden, with its gravelled walks, wrought out of the once rough, uncultivated ground, attached to the modern church, has in its season of bloom a most bright and cheerful appearance, highly complimentary to him to whose good taste citizens and strangers are annually indebted for so pleasant a feature; and the neat enclosure around the little cemetery, with the order in which it is kept, are a great improvement upon our earlier remembrances of the place, when a rough board fence or dilapidated stone wall, *which* the writer has forgotten, alone protected it from the incursions of stray animals in search of pasture.

At the time of which we write, there was much of social and neighborly intercourse among the people of the island, as they met and discussed the news brought by some one who had returned from a trip to town, an event oftentimes not of daily occurrence in unpropitious weather, especially during a sharp, cold spell of mid-winter. The receipt of the Journal and Gazette were semi-weekly events of rare interest, and their contents from the title to the last line of the advertisements on the fourth page, were duly digested. A Boston paper was about as much of a novelty to the inhabitants as is now one from Canton or Honolulu.

The writer has some especially pleasant recollections of the friendly intercourse referred to, that seemed in a measure a realization of the scenes in rural life so delightfully pictured forth by Goldsmith in the Deserted Village, and in the London story-books that then formed so prominent a feature in juvenile literature. One place of sojourn was at the residence of the village teacher, still in existence at the summit of a high bluff on the seashore. Opposite the house was a large and thriving garden, and higher up, on an elevation too rocky for culture, was a delightful spot, embracing a view of Portsmouth, and the ocean far out to sea, where the youth of both sexes used to gather at the close of day, and on moonlight evenings, and participate in the ever-popular sports of childhood.

One of the incidents of life to the people of Newcastle was the frequent appearance, during the summer season, of a fleet from Kittery and Eliot upon their shores, for the purpose of bartering vegetables and fruit for dried codfish and halibut, and other products of the brisk fishing trade then carried on from the island. As a general thing the values of articles on both sides were so well understood as to render the business a very simple one, but an amusing scene occasionally occurred between a pair of sharp bargainers, each affecting to depreciate the other's goods, that would have done honor to the parties in a horse-trade. Such a scene between an attache of Hannah Mariner's squadron, with a stock of green corn and whortleberries, and an old lady of the island with dried halibut to dispose of, each boasting, when the trade had been concluded, of having outwitted the other, left, in its oddity, an ineffacable impression upon our memory.

Fort Constitution imparted much animation to the island, and not a little to Portsmouth, being still under command of Col. Walbach, and with a larger force stationed there than at any other period within our memory. The band numbered every instrument then known in martial music, and with such an attraction, the morning and evening parades were well worth attending. Musicians were not then very plenty in our good city, none making it a profession, and it was a well appreciated luxury when the old hero; while in the service of his native Prussia, of twenty-six pitched battles against Bony, occasionally came to town with his command, and the fine band stirred up the people with such airs as "Wreaths for the Chieftain," "Washington'sMarch," "Paddy Carey," etc.

RAMBLE CXIV.

The Court Martial at Fort Constitution in 1814 – The Providential Witness.

ALTHOUGH now beyond our present city line, Newcastle was once a part of Portsmouth; and the fortification on that island being for the defence of Portsmouth harbor, still attaches it to us. Several references have been made to the fortification in previous Rambles—showing that at the old Fort William and Mary, since called Constitution, was the first scene of seizure of British property by the patriots at the commencement of the Revolution,—a circumstance which should give it a place in history scarcely less prominent than Lexington or Bunker Hill.

Our present object is to record an event which took place in the Fort nearly half a century ago, which did not appear in the papers of the day, nor has it since until now been published.

In the spring of 1814, when our country was at war with England, the 40th regiment of U. S. Infantry was designated as rendezvoused at Boston, but its companies were rarely if ever collected there together, being raised principally for the defence of the eastern seaboard. Col. Joseph Lovering, jr. of Boston, had command of it, and Perley Putnam, of Salem, was Major. In this regiment, one company of a hundred men from Newport, R. I., commanded by Capt. Bailey of Mass., of which a son of Capt. Bailey was Ensign, was detached and ordered to garrison a fort at Wiscasset. Their most direct course from Boston was through Portsmouth. Soldiers then had none of the present advantages of railroad conveyance, and the marching of a company then meant that they went on foot. The marching through country roads was done "at ease," but the soldiers were held in such positions that when they approached any town or village, they could readily be brought into regular sections at a tap of the drum or word of command. It was in this way that Capt. Bailey's company was marching when it approached Greenland parade. Soon after the word was given to form rank and shoulder arms, Ensign Bailey touched with his sword the gun of a soldier to remind him that he should change its position to shoulder arms, at the same time giving the order. Capt. Bailey, hearing the order, stepped to the flank to ascertain whether there was any trouble, when instantly a bullet from a gun just grazed his side. It appears that the soldier, instead of shouldering his gun, had dropped it into a horizontal position on his left arm, and pulled the trigger. It was supposed the shot was intended for the Ensign, but the lives of the Captain and many others were equally endangered. The soldier was immediately arrested, put under guard, and brought with the company to Portsmouth. Fort Constitution being the nearest garrison, he was sent there to await the charges to be made out against him. Capt. Bailey and his company passed over Portsmouth ferry and proceeded into Maine. In a few days the specifications were made, containing the names of the four witnesses to the act. There was, however, too much of other service required for officers to admit of a court martial being held for several months, and the prisoner in the mean time was kept securely at the fort.

It was on a pleasant day in that summer that Col. Walbach, who, it will be recollected, for a long time had command of the garrison, was walking with a gentleman around the fort, that they came to a room in the arsenal in which a squad of soldiers were busily engaged in making musket cartridges, in great demand at that time. As they passed along, Col. W., in a private way, directed his guest's attention to one of the workmen, who seemed to be very active and deeply interested in his work. After they had passed out of the arsenal and were proceeding outside the fort, said Col. W., "did you notice that man who was making cartridges twice as fast as any other? O, I pity him, for that man, well as he appears, *is soon to be shot!* Nothing can save him, poor fellow! He it was who a few months since came near shooting two officers in the Newport company. I cannot think that he intended murder or mutiny with which he stands charged,—but if such doings are overlooked, what officer is safe? It is a pity, but poor Haven's fate is sealed.

In the fall of 1814, a general court martial was held at Fort Constitution for the trial of several cases which had accumulated within course of the season. Major Crooker, of the 9th regiment, was President, and Lieut. Belfour, of the Artillery, was Judge Advocate. Capt. Bailey had been notified of the time of the trial, and was directed to send the four witnesses mentioned in the specifications accompanying his charge against the soldier.

When the witnesses arrived, it was noticed that there were five soldiers instead of four—but when the witnesses were summoned before the court only the four appeared. *They testified* all alike, that they were near Haven and saw him discharge his gun when it was laying on his arm. The prisoner was allowed to interrogate the witnesses: his only question, which was asked to each of them in turn, was, "Did you see Ensign Bailey strike me before I fired?" They all replied, No.

Just in this stage of the proceedings the clock struck three. In those days, and we know not but at the present time, no proceedings in a court martial can be held after that hour, and so the court adjourned without coming to the fatal verdict which, had half an hour's more time been allowed, would doubtless have been arrived at.

On this court martial was the late Hon. Daniel P. Drown, of this city, then a Lieutenant in the army. When the court came together the next morning, the case of Haven came up as it was left, with every prospect that the fate anticipated by Col. Walbach would rest upon him. At this stage, Lieut. Drown stated that it appeared that five soldiers had been sent here from Wiscasset, instead of the four detailed as witnesses. He made inquiry of the President why the fifth man had been sent. Maj. Crooker could see no reason for making an inquiry on this subject, as the specifications, which were their only guide, made no mention of any one beyond the four witnesses. At length, however, it was decided that the fifth soldier should be brought before the court.

After the preliminary questions as to what regiment and company he belonged to, when he enlisted into Capt. Bailey's company, &c., had been satisfactorily answered, he was asked—Were you in the company when this act of mutiny on the part of Haven took place? I was. Was you near him when he fired? I was. Your name is not on the detail of witnesses, how came you to be sent here on this trial? I don't know. All I know of the matter is, that when the corporal who had charge of the witnesses had just left the fort at Wiscasset, he was ordered to halt, and I was sent for by Capt. Bailey to come into his quarters. He asked me if I knew Haven. I told him I did—had worked with him at the shoe business at Dartmouth, Mass. Capt. Bailey said no more, but ordered me to be supplied with rations, and march with the squad to Fort Constitution. Did you expect that you were coming here as a witness? I had no instructions, and do not know for what purpose I was ordered here.

It now appearing to the court that this man might have been sent to give what information he might possess of the prisoner, he was at once sworn. The witness was then directed to state what he knew of the prisoner.

He had worked a year or so with Haven. Had found him a man singular in his habits,—sometimes a very talkative, and then a very silent man. He was an excellent workman, and careful in fulfilling his obligations; was a kind-hearted man, and beloved by all his fellow workmen. The shoe-shop in which they worked was on the side of the road opposite a stone wall. At one time, when in a desponding state of mind, he suddenly laid down his work on his seat, ran across the road with great rapidity, and dropping his head as he approached the wall, he ran against it with his full force. It was thought he had killed himself. He scarred his head very badly. The court on examination of the prisoner's head found the deep scars.

After answering a few more questions, the witness was dismissed, and the examination closed.

It should be here stated that the prisoner had said to the court that he had no hostile feelings against Lieut. Bailey. He had no doubt of the truth of the statement of the witnesses that he discharged the gun, although of the act he had no recollection.

The Judge-Advocate summed up the evidence which went to sustain the charge of mutiny. The question was put by the President to each member of the court, Is the prisoner guilty of the crime with which he is charged? Lieut. Drown, being the youngest in commission, was first called upon. He replied, No. The other eleven replied, No. And the President was well satisfied that the verdict was just.

It was found that, suffering as he was under partial insanity, he was not a safe man for the army, and the court recommended that he be honorably discharged from the public service.

No one rejoiced more than Capt. Bailey, at the happy result of sending a witness not in the specification. And frequently our venerable friend Drown (who was the summer guest of Col. Walbach above referred to) congratulated himself with the thought, that if while in the army he never killed a man, he was by his position instrumental in saving one innocent man from being shot.

RAMBLE CXV.

Fort Constitution—The Explosion in 1809.

In our last Ramble some reference was made to incidents occurring at this point of our harbor defence. We take this occasion to give a sketch of a disaster which took place at this fort in 1809, when the garrison was under command of Col. Walbach. The circumstances will be new to many of the present generation.

On the 4th day of July, 1809, there were two public political celebrations in Portsmouth. The Federalists marched to the Old South Church to listen to an oration from Isaac Lyman, Esq., and partook of a dinner at the old Assembly House. The Democrats marched to the North Church, were addressed by Joseph Bartlett, Esq., and dined at Davenport's.

There were a few, however, who accepted an invitation of Col. Walbach to dine with him at the Fort,—among them Dr. L. Spalding, Capt. Jacob Cutter, the officers of the Fort, and a few others. The company were enjoying the hospitalities of the Colonel in his quarters, and the outside visitors were just collecting on the platform on the northwest corner of the Fort, where a fiddler just arrived had invited them to form a contra-dance. On the northeast point of the Fort, two of the 24-pounders had been removed to make way for a brass 6-pounder from which it was intended to fire salutes after dinner. Two ammunition chests, containing about 350 pounds of powder, and one containing balls, were placed on the side of the platform near the house where the company were at dinner, and on the platform were also seventeen cartridges of two pounds each, for the salute. The company had been at the table about three-quarters of an hour, when a tremendous explosion took place—the sides and ceiling of the room were driven in, the tables upset, and everything on them shivered to atoms! The company were prostrated, and the lady of Col. W. came running into the room, bloody from slight injuries. None of the company were, however, materially injured. They ran out to witness the distressing scene of men dead and alive, their clothes burning, and the ground covered with fragments of timber and boards, scattered balls and pieces of iron on every side. The sides and wainscot of the house were beaten in; balls were sent through the windows, and five 24-pound balls were carried beyond the house. One poor fellow was carried over the roof of the house, and the upper half of his body lodged on the opposite side near the window of the dining room; the limb of another was driven through a thick door over the dining room, leaving a hole in the door the shape of the foot; parts of the other bodies were carried nearly a hundred yards from the fatal spot. Of the killed were three soldiers, one citizen and three boys. Six soldiers and several citizens were wounded. The scene was heart-rending. Col. Walbach exclaimed, "I have faced death in its most dreadful form—I have witnessed the desolations of war, and have mingled in all the hazards and havoc of battles, but never before did I feel a pang so terrible and intolerable as this."

The persons killed were Ephraim Pickering, Esq., of Newington, (a brother of the late Joseph W. P. of this city,) James Trefethen and Joseph Mitchell, lads of Newcastle; another lad named Paul, belonging to Kittery; Sergeant Joseph Albertz; privates Peletiah McDaniels and Theodore Whitham.

It appeared that the seventeen small cartridges, which were to have been placed in the ammunition chest on the rampart, the sergeant thought best to leave for a short time in the sun, as he fancied they felt damp. A spark from one of the lighted linstocks was probably driven by the wind to the exposed cartridges, and was the occasion of the explosion.

We have before us a short record of the event, made in the Fort morning report of the 5th. It appears that there were stationed at the Fort at that time, a captain, two 2d lieutenants, one surgeon's mate, three sergeants, four corporals, four musicians, six artificers, and fifty-three privates—in all seventy-four.

The body of McDaniel was found near the light-house below low water mark. The remains of the three soldiers were buried with the honors of war in the same grave on the 8th of July. The countersign given out on the 4th was "Dreadful."

Capt. Davidson, now at the Fort, is the connecting link between the days when Col. Walbach was stationed here and the present time. Through his gentlemanly attentions we are enabled to give such of the above facts as appear on the records of the Fort.

RAMBLE CXVI.

The Sparhawk Family.

In Ramble 92 we gave the Will of the widow of George Atkinson, in which most of the bequests were made to members of the Sparhawk family. This leads to an investigation of the family pedigree, and gives an opportunity for a few historical sketches.

In a bundle of manuscripts of Sir William Pepperell in our possession, we find some incidents relating to Nathaniel Sparhawk, who married the only daughter of Sir William, and settled at Kittery Point, in the vicinity of the old Meeting House.

It appears that the Rev. John Sparhawk, a minister of Bristol, in Mass., who died in 1718 at the age of 45, had two sons. One of them was the Rev. John Sparhawk of Salem, who married Jane Porter, and died in 1755 at the age of 43. The other son was Hon. Nathaniel Sparhawk of Kittery, who married Elizabeth, the only daughter of Sir William Pepperell.

The children of Rev. John S. of Salem were:

1. Priscilla, who married Judge Ropes of Salem, and died in 1798, [leaving three sons, John, Nathaniel and Samuel; and three daughters—Jane, who married S. C. Ward; Priscilla, who married Jonathan Hodges; and Abigail, who married William Orne.]

2. Susannah, who married George Atkinson of Portsmouth, and died in 1796. [Her Will is given in Ramble 92.]

3. Jane, who married John Appleton.

4. Margaret, who married Isaac Winslow of Boston.

5. Katy, who married her cousin, Nathaniel Sparhawk, Jr., of Kittery.

6. John, who married Miss King. [Their children were

Thomas, Samuel, John, and George King Sparhawk. The latter spent most of his days in Portsmouth, and died at Conway. He was the father of Col. George S. who died at Kittery Point in 1857.]

The children of Nathaniel Sparhawk of Kittery were:

1. Nathaniel, whose first wife was his cousin Katy Sparhawk, his second Miss Bartlett, and his third Miss Parker.

2. Mary, who married Dr. Charles Jarvis of Boston.

3. Sir William Pepperell, Bt., who married Miss Royall of Medford, and died in 1816, aged 60.

4. Samuel Hirst, who married in England. His daughter, Harriet Sparhawk, is now living in this city, his only descendant.

5. Andrew Pepperrell, who married Miss Turner, and died in 1783, aged 30.

Nathaniel Sparhawk was married to Elizabeth Pepperrell, June 10th, 1742. Her father sent to England for her wedding dress, as follows:—

PASCATAQUA IN NEW ENGLAND,
October 14th, 1741.

Francis Wilks, Esq.: SIR—Your favors of ye 16th May and 24th June last, I received by Capt. Prince, for which am much obliged to you. Inclosed you have a receipt for 46 ps. of gold, weighing twenty ozs., which will be delivered you, I hope, by Capt. Robert Noble, of ye ship America, which please to receive and cr. to my account with; and send me by ye first opportunity, for this place or Boston, *Silk* to make a woman a full suit of clothes, the ground to be white paduroy and flowered with all sorts of coulers suitable for a young woman—another of white watered *Taby*, and *Gold Lace* for trimming of it; twelve yards of *Green Paduroy;* thirteen yards of Lace, for a woman's head dress, 2 inches wide, as can be bought for 13s. per yard; a handsome Fan, with a leather mounting, as good as can be bought for about 20 shillings; 2 pair silk shoes, and cloggs a size bigger than ye shoe.

Your servant to command.

WILLIAM PEPPERRELL.

If the tale of tradition is true, to the beauty of Mary Sparhawk, who became the wife of Dr Jarvis, Portsmouth is more indebted for its protection in 1775, than to its forts. The story goes, that Capt. Mowatt, of the Canceaux, a British ship of 16 guns, connected with a large armed ship, a schooner and a sloop, were off our harbor in the month of October, 1775. Capt. Mowatt went privately on shore at Kittery Point, and was received at the loyal house of Nathaniel Sparhawk. Here he became so much fascinated with Mary that the intent of his voyage to destroy Portsmouth, was, by her influence, changed, and he made sail for Falmouth (now Portland) and burned more than 400 of the best houses and stores—leaving only about 100 of the poorest houses, and they much damaged. How much our city is indebted to the influence of the beauty of Mary we can now hardly estimate.

After the death of her husband, (Dr. Jarvis of Boston,) Mary returned to Kittery Point, where she died in 1815. The old mansion of Col. Sparhawk, east of the village church, is preserved in all its primitive beauty. The long avenue of noble trees through which it was formerly approached have disappeared—but the mansion is yet one of the attractive features of the ancient town.

The following is from the memorandum book of Rev. John Sparhawk of Salem, relating to his settlement:

"Feb. 29th, 1735-6, I preached the first time at Salem, by the desire of Committee of the Confederate Society of Salem, having been a preacher about the space of one year, and by desire of the same committee, engaged for a term and continued preaching to my call."

"Aug. 5th, 1736, I was chosen minister of ye Confederate Society by a great majority in the Society. Voted 220 oz. of Silver for my salary, and afterwards, upon my desire in ye answer I gave them, they added 100 £ Bills of the Province for help."

"Dec. 8th, 1736. On this day was the ordination. Mr.

Chipman began with prayers. Mr. Appleton preached, Prov. 11: 30. Mr. Holyoke gave the charge, and Mr. Prescott ye Right hand of Fellowship. The whole service was performed with the greatest order and decency."

RAMBLE CXVII.

Centennial Celebration, 1823—The Parchment Unrolled.

THE two-hundreth anniversary of the first settlement of New Hampshire, at Portsmouth, was celebrated here on the 21st day of May, 1823. It was a matter of State interest, and called together the leading men from many distant as well as adjoining towns. The Collections of the N. H. Historical Society, vol. 6, contains a very full account of the whole proceedings, embodying many historical facts, collected by our late townsman, Alexander Ladd. N. A. Haven, Jr., Esq., was the orator of the day, O. W. B. Peabody of Exeter delivered the poem, and Rev. Bennet Tyler of Hanover, and Rev. I. W. Putnam performed the religious services at the old North Church.

In the evening a splendid ball was given at Franklin Hall, at which nearly four hundred were present. Grandsires and grandmothers danced in the same sets with their children and grandchildren—and in the numerous ancient portraits, by the best masters which covered the walls on every side, the representatives of the past centuries seemed to be mingling with their descendants on the joyous occasion.

Most of those present, as well as those who had taken an active part in the services of the day, inscribed their names and ages on a parchment roll, which was deposited in the Portsmouth Atheneum at the time and has there remained undisturbed for nearly half a century. As bad ink was used for some of the signatures, which already begin to grow obscure, we herewith present a copy for preservation. It will be read with some interest by those now alive who participated in the scenes and festivities of that day, and is a matter of history worthy of preservation on other accounts.

Elijah Hall, 80 years
Bennet Tyler
Timo. Upham
Charles B Haddock
Nathan Parker
Israel W Putnam, 36
Frederick Clark, 26
J Mason
Dan'l Webster
Jacob Sheafe, 78
Clement Storer, 62
Edw'd Cutts 59
N A Haven. Jr, 33
Jacob Cutter, 51
Charles W Cutter, 23
Benjamin Penhallow, 55
John Haven, 57
Joseph Story
Samuel Hartt, 37
W Jones, Jr. 38
John F Parrott, 56
E G Parrott 43
William Gardner
George Blake
Joshua W Peirce, 32
Jacob Wendell, 34
J F Shores 31
Samuel Larkin, 50
Isaac Waldron, 49
Nathan Hale
Alex'r Ladd
Eben Wentworth, 43
Nath'l B March, 41
Ichabod Rollins, 33
Benjamin Brierly, 48
Thos. T Brierly, 23
John Ball, 30
James Rundlet, 50
Samuel Larkin, Jr.
Hampden Cutts, 20
Alfred Mason
Joshua W Larkin
John G Palfrey
Hunking Penhallow, 57
T W Penhallow, 39
Oliver W Penhallow, 26
Henry Haven, 55
William Haven, 53
Peter Pearse, 56
Charles Turell, 36
Robert Rice, 42
William Claggett, 33
Langley Boardman, 48
Nich's Gilman, 23
Isaac D Parsons, 24
Cyrus P Smith, 22
Eben Smith, Jr. 36

Wm Berry, U S N, 26
John Sullivan 22
Jonathan Brown, 27
Oliver Sheafe, 23
Harrison Gray, 28
Theodore Sheafe, 27
Samuel E Coues, 25
Nath'l A Haven, 60
Wm P Adams, 38
Charles Cushing, 46
Joshua H Hall, 29
Samuel T Gilman, 22
John H Sise, 27
Jno S Place, 40
Charles Hardy, 43
Chas. Cushing, 36
Charles A Cheever, 29
Eben L Childs, 24
William Smith, 23
John A Haven 31
John M Whidden, 21
John H Sheafe, 27
Robert Cross, 22
John Rice, 35
William Clark, 28
Jno. W Foster, 34
Rich'd Russell Waldron, 20
Henry P Salter, 21
Edw'd F Sise, 23
Charles Seaver, 26
M W Peirce, 50
William Rundlet, 23
J M Tredick, 20
Herman B Harris, 23
Aug. Lord, 25
Sam'l P Long, 24
J Woodward Haven
Alfred W Haven
Washington Haven, 24
William Hill
J G Joy, 36
Daniel Taylor, 25
Hermon Orne, 20
Geo. Melcher, Jr. 25
Wm. L. Pickering, 19
George Sparhawk, 23
Jeffrey Richardson, 33
George Briard, U S N, 20
Daniel Sparhawk, 20
Thomas Curtis, 23
Jacob Sheafe, Jr. 59
Geo. Humphreys, 39
L G S Boyd
Wm. Haven, Jr.
J B Ball, 28
Jos. Margaund, Mass.
Wm. Stone, "

G Horney, 29
Thos. B Coolidge, 21
Edmund Roberts, 39
Robert M Mason
Samuel Cushman, 40
James Ladd, 41
Wm H Y Hackett, 23
H Bufford, 43
N. Sheafe Waldron
Wm F Carter
Chas C Adams
Charles W Chauncy
Wm Salter, 18
Edward Rundlet, 17
Thomas Sheafe, 71
Sam'l Sheafe, 35
Enoch Mudge, 47
Joseph Haven, 65
Ichabod Bartlett, 35
Levi Bartlett, 30
James Bartlett, 20
Mary Mason
Grace Webster
Mary Sheafe
Dorothy Storer
Mary H Cutts
Eliza W Haven
Miriam Cutter
Frances Cutter
Susan Penhallow
Ann Haven
Sarah Waldo Story
Mary T Hartt
Ann P Jones
Martha B Parrott
Sarah P Parrott
Sarah Gardner
Sarah Olcott Blake
Emily S Peirce
Mehitable R Wendell
Elizabeth Oliver Shores
Ann J Larkin
Mary C Waldron
Sarah P Hale
Maria T Ladd
Catharine H Wentworth
Sarah H March
Mary Ann Rollins
Susan Brierly
Ann B Brierly
Jane S Ball
Frances Rundlet
Sarah P Larkin,
Mary Cutts
Mary E Mason
Anne C Larkin
Mary Ann Palfrey

Harriet Penhallow
Margarett E Scott
Lucy E Penhallow
Sarah Sheafe
Eliza Langdon Elwyn
Ann H Cushing
Dorothea Gilman
M Jane Haven,
Eliza C Porter
Mary H Sheafe,
Ann Mary Haven,
Adaline Haven
Charlotte Ann Haven
Margaret F Lamb
Sarah P E Rice
Sarah Simes
Eliza Delia Tudor Toscan
Caroline Haven
Elvira Haven
Augusta Haven
Eleanor J Williams
Ruth W Cushing
Louisa Sheafe
Elizabeth P Abbott
Charlotte Sheafe
F M M'Clintock
C G Stevens
Sarah P Hardy
Lydia Fernald
Eliza C Melcher
Georgianna Toscan
Sarah B Brierley
Elizabeth Cushing
Elizabeth March
Mary C Shapleigh
Emily S Langdon Elwyn
Caroline Jones
Jane M Andrews
Mary Jane Durell
Mary L Storer
Lydia Foster
Catharine M'Clintock
Lydia R Hale
Susan W Haven
A T Cross
E W Shapleigh
E W Hill
Olivia Ann Prescott
M E Long
M Cutter
Eliza Jane Larkin
Arianna Smith
Geo. Douglas Ramsay, U S A
Augusta Willard
Eliza B Rice
Lucinda Willard
Elizabeth Glover
Sarah J Wentworth
Mary B Appleton
Mary Sherburne Simes
Sarah Ann Salter
Sarah S Langdon Haven
Susan Sheafe
Ann E Salter
Sarah E Appleton
Elizabeth S Durell
Rebecca J Wentworth
L Hodges
Caroline Cross
Emily S Pearse
Clara L Haven
Mary Hardy
Mary P Hodges
Frances L Brierley
Ann M Simes
Anna H Cutts
Margaret Sparhawk
Susan Sparhawk
Mary Oliver Larkin
Mary Appleton
Margaret Foster
Lucy Clapham
Harriet Morris
Susan Purcell

The ages of many of the ladies are given on the parchment,—but as a matter of courtesy to those living we have thought best to omit them. One thing however is pretty certain, that most of them are now full *forty-six* years of age.

The following interesting account of the distinguished persons whose portraits were exhibited at this Centennial Celebration, taken from the Historical Collections, shows how rich Portsmouth and its neighboring towns are in portraits of our distinguished ancestors :

John Wentworth, son of Samuel Wentworth, and grandson of Elder William Wentworth. He was a native of Portsmouth, and was born January 16, 1671. He was a counsellor from 1712 to 1717, and lieutenant governor from 1717 to his death, December 12, 1730. Of his sixteen children, fourteen survived him.

Benning Wentworth, son of the preceding, graduated at Harvard College in 1715, and afterwards went to England and Spain, where he remained several years. He was appointed counsellor in 1734, and was governor from 1741 to 1767, when he was superseded by his nephew, John Wentworth. He died Oct. 14, 1770, in his 75th year.

John Wentworth, son of Governor Wentworth.

Lady Frances Wentworth, wife of governor John Wentworth. Now owned by the family of Asa Freeman of Dover.

Theodore Atkinson, son of Hon. Theodore Atkinson of New Castle, where he was born Dec. 20, 1697. He graduated at Harvard College in 1718; was a counsellor in 1734; subsequently a judge of the superior court and secretary of the province. He died Sept. 22, 1779, aged 82. He is painted with a roll in his hand, with the inscription, "Expenses of Government."

Theodore Atkinson, jr. son of the preceding, graduated at Harvard College in 1734; was a counsellor and secretary; died in 1769. Now owned by the family of Asa Freeman of Dover.

Richard Waldron, son of Capt. Richard Waldron, and grandson of Major Richard Waldron, who was killed by the Indians at Dover in 1689. His mother was Eleanor Vaughan, daughter of Maj. William Vaughan. He was born Feb. 21, 1694. He was a counsellor, and secretary of the province to about the time of his death, in 1753.

Thomas Westbrooke Waldron, son of the preceding, was a captain in the expedition against Louisburg—and died in 1785.

George Jaffrey, counsellor from 1702, to his death in 1706.

George Jaffrey, son of the preceding; appointed a counsellor in 1716. He was also treasurer of the province; died in 1749.

George Jaffrey, was counsellor in 1766; was also treasurer. He died in December 1802, aged 86.

Benjamin Gambling, judge of probate and counsellor from 1734. He was born in 1681; married a daughter of Samuel Penhallow; died 1737.

Richard Wibird, son of Richard Wibird, of Portsmouth, was born July 7, 1702. He was appointed collector of customs for the port of Portsmouth in 1730, and counsellor in 1739. He died 1765, aged 63.

Thomas Wibird, brother of the preceding, was born at Portsmouth, Oct. 1, 1707. The father of these brothers was counsellor from 1716, and died in 1732.

Col. William Pepperrell, who came from England during the reign of William and Mary. He lived many years at the Isles of Shoals; afterwards removed to Kittery Point, where he became an eminent merchant. He died Feb. 15, 1734.

Sir William Pepperrell, Bart. son of the preceding, was born at the Isles of Shoals. He died at Kittery, July 6, 1759, aged 63.

There were also portraits of the mother of Sir William and two sisters, one of whom was Mrs. Newmarch, wife of the Hon. John Newmarch.

Hon. Henry Sherburne, a counsellor, and chief justice of the province from 1735 to 1744.

Nathaniel Sparhawk, a counsellor of Massachusetts, a colonel of the militia, and an eminent merchant. Col. Sparhawk married the only daughter of Sir William Pepperrell, and died at Kittery in 1776.

John Moffatt, a merchant of Portsmouth. Born in England in 1692. Died in 1786, aged 94.

Catharine Cutt Moffatt, wife of John, grand-daughter of President John Cutt.

Catharine Moffatt, their daughter, married Wm. Whipple, a signer of the Declaration of Independence. Mrs. W. was living in 1823.

Rev. John Emerson, minister of New Castle, 1703; of Portsmouth, 1715; died June 21, 1732.

Madam Emerson, wife of the preceding.

Rev. Nathaniel Rogers, (painted 1623,) son of Rev. John Rogers, of Dedham, in England, who died Oct. 18, 1639, aged 67. The latter was a grandson of Rev. John Rogers, prebendary of St. Paul's, who was burnt at Smithfield, 1555. Mr. Rogers came to New England in Nov. 1636; settled in Ipswich, Mass. 1639; died July 2, 1655, aged 57.

Rev. Samuel Haven, D. D., ordained minister of the 2d Church in Portsmouth, May 6, 1752; died March 3, 1806, aged 79.

Madam Montgomery, (painted in Scotland in 1555.) One of her descendants came to New England and settled in Portsmouth in 1720.

RAMBLE CXVIII.

The Yellow Fever of 1798.

AMONG the dividing points of the eras in Portsmouth history, is "the year of the yellow fever," 1798. We rarely pass among the old houses at the north end of Market street, without being reminded (not unfrequently by the noxious air of the present day,) of the scenes which there transpired about seventy years ago, when the "Yellow Malignant Fever" prevailed, finding victims almost every day for eight weeks.

At that time Thomas Sheafe, one of the most respectable merchants of the day, father of the late Samuel Sheafe, and occupant of the house on the corner of Market and Deer streets, was largely engaged in commerce. On the 22d of July, 1798, the ship Mentor, belonging to him, of which John Flagg was master, arrived in a short passage from Martinique, where the yellow fever had prevailed to a great extent. At that time but little regard was paid to such quarantine laws as stood on the statute book, and the Mentor came up immediately to the wharf. One or two of the crew had been sick on the passage, but having recovered, no precautions were taken, as in later days, by cleansing the ship. The Mentor was fully laden with sugar, molasses and coffee, and discharged at Sheafe's wharf in the rear of the store now occupied by Pickering & Tompson. A laborer assisting in discharging, was the first victim of that fever,—and then another who had worked on board was taken down with the like symptoms. The owner of the ship was still unwilling to believe that any malignant fever was brought by the vessel: but soon the melancholy fact was brought directly home to him by the death of two promising sons—Thomas at the age of 14, and Horatio at the age of 6, and an only daughter Sally at the age 17 years. The existence of the malady now became too manifest. The selectmen sent the ship off and had her properly cleansed,—but it was too late to stop the pestilence which now began to spread with fearful rapidity in the neighborhood. The north part of the town was soon depopulated. Every family that could conveniently remove left for other places, and people from the country abstained from visiting the town. A strict guard was kept to prevent intercourse below the infected district and other parts of the town. The fever raged principally in Green, Russell and the east end of Deer streets, and from Rindge's wharf down Market street to the house next south of late Thomas Sheafe's mansion, now occupied by Albert A. Payne. At that time the widow of Noah Parker kept a boarding house there. The victims in this house were her daughter Zerviah, her neice Rebecca Noble, and William Plummer, a merchant. In the house in Russell street, now occupied by Joseph Remick, Mrs. Hannah Noble and two daughters, Eliza and Mary, died—none could be found to bury them, and the brothers of the girls were compelled to bear their sisters and mother to their grave. There were some cases elsewhere. Dr. William Cutter was dangerously sick with the fever, on Congress street. In two months ending on the 5th of October, when the frost terminated the course of the fever, there were 96 cases, of which 55 proved fatal. In the same time there were 52 deaths from dysentery and other diseases, making over a hundred deaths in two months, and that too at a time when our population was only about 6000, and a large number of inhabitants had fled to other towns.

Eleazer Russell, mentioned in the 47th Ramble, died at the time of this fever but not of it. He was said to be so much in fear of the fever of which his sister died, that he refused to have any one come to his assistance, and died alone.

The sickness was not confined to those who remained in

Portsmouth. Moses Little, Esq. who had just married the widow of Humphrey Fernald of this town, to escape the danger, with his wife and her only son, John Fernald, aged 20, went to Dover. Mr. L. and son were soon attacked at the same time and died at Dover.

Among those who were dangerously attacked but recovered were Robert Rice, Abel Harris, Nathaniel Folsom, Thomas Cutts, and many others with whose names our readers are not familiar.

There fell in that season many who sacrificed their lives in devotion to the sick—whose good deeds yet rest in the remembrance of our older citizens.

None or few were seen in the street where the fever raged. Nothing was heard there but the groans of the sick and the awful shrieks of the dying. If persons were met, they would have handkerchiefs to their faces wet with vinegar or camphor, and passing with hasty steps. There were however some noble hearted men and women, who, fearless of consequences, stood by the bedsides of the sick and dying, to wet their parched lips; and when the spirit was about quitting, some were there to smooth the passage through the dark valley. The Rev. Dr. Buckminister, Col. George Gains who at that time was selectman, Mr. Vaughan the sexton, were among those who were ever faithful in their duties. Also Dr. A. R. Cutter, and Dr. Bracket, senior. These men stood firm through the whole and never took any fever. In consideration of the devoted service of Col. Gains, the town made him a present of $100.

As at the time of the plague in London, no bells were heard at funerals; and when the fever abated, the tolling bell was hailed as a signal of returning health. People were hurried to their graves hastily. No procession attended. Soon as the breath left the body, and perhaps sometimes before, it was immediately put in a tarred sheet and rough box, slid from a chamber window to a cart or dray, conveyed to the north cemetery and deposited in one common grave or trench. The grave of no friend was afterwards found. Like the burial of Sir John Moore, they were hurried off "at dead of night, by the lantern dimly burning."

Such a pestilence had never before, nor has since visited our town, which ranks among the healthiest in the Union.

RAMBLE CXIX.

Old Land Proprietors—The March Farm-The Family.

THE possessions of ancestors seem to be made more sacred by the length of time they have been held in a family. The path which a parentage of three or four generations has passed over, becomes endeared by the associations which are spread along it. This feeling has kept no small amount of landed estate around Portsmouth in the same families which took the original grants at the first settlement, more than two centuries ago, or soon after purchased the land. Among those families which have kept their first localities, are the Odiorne, Pickering, Seavey, March, Peirce, Moses, Whidden, Langdon, Dennett, Jackson, Drake, Johnson, Berry, Weeks, Haines, Packer, Brackett, Rand, and other families which do not occur to us now, whose ancestors of the same name, where there has been a line of male descendants, located themselves two centuries ago on the spot, or in the immediate vicinity of where their descendants now reside. Some who had located in Portsmouth then, by a change of town lines have had their farms transferred to the neighboring towns.

If it is pleasant to those who thus show their veneration

for their ancestors, it is scarcely less so to those who in passing along can point to the localities where the labors of five or six successive generations have been turning the wild forest into a fertile garden, and the original log cabin into a palace. There are various localities to which this remark might apply, but we shall in this Ramble speak more particularly of one, which is prominent in the eye of every traveller who passes beyond the western bounds of Portsmouth.

The farm now owned by J. Bartlett Wiggin, Esq., on the Winicott road in Stratham has never been out of his own direct family since it was first granted by the crown. No deed has ever been made or given of said farm, but it has descended from father to son, by will, to its present owner, and he will pass it down, for he has sons; and "that farm is not for sale," if for no other reason, because the owner does not wish, nor has he a heart or occasion, to dispose of it out of the family.

On the south side of the road in Greenland, near the Portsmouth line, begins the farm of the March family, of two hundred seventy-five acres, now owned by the Hon. Clement March, which has been in the family seven generations. Its extent on the road is readily defined by the handsomest stone wall to be found in New Hampshire. It is built of clouded granite, from a quarry in Raymond belonging to Mr. March, the foundation sunk eighteen inches below the surface. In front of the house for several hundred feet, the wall is made of dimension stone, every block beaded. On this wall, and even with the ground in front of the house, is an open iron fence. The house of Dr. Clement March was burnt on this spot in 1812. Its place was soon supplied by a large house of three stories, which was consumed by fire in 1826. The present house was soon after erected on the spot. Large additions have been made the present season, under the direction of a distinguished Newburyport architect, rendering the mansion, in the extent of its accommodations, its spaciousness, its elegant furnishing, its rich ornaments, a residence of which any baron might be proud. The improvements, however, do not here terminate. In the several fires, the large old barn on the east of the house escaped conflagration. It was built full a century ago, as its oak posts testify. Its place has recently been supplied by another of far greater extent, and finished in the best style. It is several rods south of the mansion. Another group of buildings is also rising up several rods west of the barn—in one, stalls with iron hay racks for a dozen horses may be seen—another is the carriage house—and the third, resembling the first story of an octagon pagoda, is a well ventilated corn house. The air circulates through a half inch opening under every clapboard, which is not apparent without examination. The grapery is near the house. For the use of the mansion and the out buildings, water is being brought from a pond nearly half a mile distant, and, by the aid of hydraulic rams raised to the upper story of the buildings. It is a matter of doubt whether the beauty of the scenery from the house, or the richness of the treat to those who travel by, is most gratifying.

Passing through the curved avenue from the door to the iron gate on the west, and crossing the road, we come to another iron gate which opens to a wide tesselated path, made of the largest sea beach stones, of variegated colors, making a good mosaic. The path winds up a slight eminence, where on the declivity beyond is the family tomb, "Erected by Clement March in 1759, and repaired by Charles and Clement March in 1859." In it rest the remains of the family for a century. The care which is taken of these homes of the departed is another link in the chain which holds the affection to the names of our ancestors.

And here we will take occasion to trace the family so long located on this farm.

This farm was first owned and occupied by John Hall. The date of his grant we cannot find, but as the road through Great Swamp was opened in 1663, it is probable he occupied it about that time. By his will, dated in 1677, in the reign of his "most excellent Majesty Charles of that name the Second, by the Grace of God, of France, Great Britain and Ireland King, Defender of the Faith, &c., we learn that Greenland was regarded as a "Township of Dover."

His son Joseph Hall, succeeded him as proprietor. He had three daughters. One of them became the wife of Dr. Clement Jackson, and the mother of the celebrated Dr. Hall Jackson; another married Joshua Peirce, and was the grandmother of the late distinguished John Peirce of Portsmouth; and another was married to Israel March, who came from Massachusetts somewhere between 1690 and 1700, and by the will of his father-in-law he came into possession of the farm, which for 160 years has now been in the same family name.

Clement, the son of Israel March, born in 1707, added largely to his patrimonial estate, and by purchase from one of the original assignees of Mason's Patent became one of the largest landed proprietors in the county or State. He commanded the Horse Guards under Gov. Benning Wentworth; by whom he was appointed Aid, and also Judge of the Court. He possessed great influence in his vicinity, and represented the town of Greenland in our General Court for twenty years or more. We recollect of hearing the late Capt. McClintock speak of being present when Col. March, in brief and emphatic phrase, laid down his functions as Representative: "Fellow citizens," said he, "I have served you to the best of my ability for many years; I purpose to do so no longer; you will now bring in your votes for my son-in-law, the Major." The Major was accordingly elected.

His son Clement succeeded to the estate in Greenland. He graduated at Harvard University, and studied medicine with Dr. A. R. Cutter, of Portsmouth. He married Miss Lucy Dudley Wainwright, a ward of the Hon. George Jaffrey, and niece of his wife—by whom he had six sons:

Thomas, who died in Brooklyn in 1850, aged 71. Charles, who died in New York in 1855, aged 74. Clement, who died in St. Louis in 1830, aged 47. Joseph Wainwright, who died in Greenland in 1843, aged 58. Francis, who died in New York in 1858, aged 71. John Howard, who died in Paris in 1863, aged 72.

Dr. March gave his children a good education. All the above brothers were merchants. Joseph W. (the father of the present owner) although doing business for some years in Portsmouth, remained as the occupant of the homestead, while his brothers went abroad in the world, acquired a high standing as merchants, and accumulated much wealth. The youngest, John Howard, was for over forty years the American Consul at Maderia. He was the last deposited in the family tomb.

The extensive, and highly cultivated farm of Col. Joshua W. Peirce, adjoining the March farm and extending to Great Bay, is made up in part of the paternal property descended from his ancestor Hall. The original Hall house was on the premises of Col. Peirce, near the spot where the sharp roofed cottage now stands.

RAMBLE CXX.

Incendiary Sketches—Pilgrim Day—The Great Fire of 1813—The Incendiary.

AMONG the most fearful pests of society, the most reckless of desperadoes—the most fiendish in human form—may be classed the incendiary. While there is a certainty of his presence shining out from conflagrations here and there, the whole community are in disquietude, each fearing that his own neighborhood will be the next visited.

There is a monomania pervading the incendiary, which shuts out all ideas of the rights and safety of others. The burning building and the excitements of a fire seem the subject of the highest gratification. There are others who are guilty of incendiarism from motives of malice.

In December, 1804, the incendiary torch was applied to several buildings in Portsmouth. On the 8th, to a large barn belonging to Moses Brewster, at the Plains, consuming fifteen head of cattle and seventeen tons of hay. On the 10th, a barn of Samuel Sherburne at the Plains with valuable contents was consumed. Eight days after, another of Mr. Sherburne's barns, with fifteen head of cattle, thirty tons of hay, etc., were burned. Efforts also were made to set fire to a building near Joseph Chase's, between Pitt and Buck streets.

Large rewards were offered, but no disclosure was made. Sometime after, an attempt was made to fire the barn of Mr. Perkins Ayers, who occupied the house now of A. D. Gerrish in School street, opposite the School House. The incendiary left a tin pot in the barn, which was exhibited to the public to find an owner. It was recognized by Mr. Oliver Briard, who occupied the house No. 26 Hanover street, near the barn. Suspicion rested upon the girl living there, named Sukey Nutter. She had lived with Capt.

Joseph Chase, on Pitt street; and while attending Elder Elias Smith's meetings, in which she exhibited a wonderful gift in prayer and exhortation, was guilty of bad conduct out of meeting, which Capt. Chase told her he would expose to the brethren. "If you do, I'll burn you up," served to keep the Captain quiet, but did not keep her long on his premises. It was also found that she lived at Mr. Sherburne's, at the Plains, when the barns were burnt.

Such strong circumstances led to her arrest; but Sukey being a girl of great beauty, her facinating appearance saved her from the stern clutches of the law. Although one of the investigating committee declared that he would never agree to a verdict of acquittal, he gave way on condition that she should leave Portsmouth never to return. Sukey went at once to a town in the upper part of Strafford County, found a husband in one Charles Stewart, (by some called Ham,) who had been arrested for firing a barn of Nathaniel Adams in 1805. Of their after life we know nothing, but probably they became better persons than hanging would have made them. Whether the political party bearing the name of "*Barnburners*," descended from them, history does not say.

The 22d of December is the anniversary of an event of much national importance, and is also the anniversary of a local calamity of a deeply appalling character.

This day, in 1620, our Pilgrim fathers landed at Plymouth, and laid the basis of those institutions which have made New England what she now is—the abode of freedom,—freedom of conscience,—freedom from political tyranny,—and freedom from hereditary titles and power. On the rich blessings we enjoy from the stern devotion of our honored ancestors, we will leave the reader to meditate, for this is not our present purpose.

On the 22d December, 1813, Portsmouth suffered a calamity the effects of which it took many years to hide from sight. With the "panoramic view of the burning of Moscow," most of our readers are familiar. The commencement of the fire in that panorama, and its gradual extension until one half the horizon presented one continuous flame, gives an idea of a Portsmouth night scene in 1813.

About half past seven, on that evening, flames were seen bursting forth from the barn of Mrs. Woodward, on the corner of Church and Court streets, where the Stone Church now stands. By the brightness of the light the citizens were soon collected, but all their exertions were ineffectual to subdue the fire, which before eight o'clock, had so spread over every part of the house of Hon. Daniel Webster and Thomas Haven in Pleasant street, between Court street and State street, and to the house of Mrs. Woodward, at the corner of State street and Church street, that it was with difficulty any part of the property was preserved. From the violence of the wind and flames, immense flakes were driven through the air to a great distance, and fell in showers upon the roofs in the direction of the wind. The next building that took fire was Mr. Yeaton's barn at the corner of Chapel street and State street, which was distant from Mrs. Woodward's barn fifty-six rods, about one-sixth of a mile. The fire soon spread from Yeaton's barn, passing over thirteen rods and caught the house occupied by D. Humphreys, at the corner of Mulberry and Daniel streets. This happened about half past eight. The flames then took the shop of Miss Wentworth, the Union Bank and the store at the corner of State and Pleasant streets. These were scarcely on fire at half past nine o'clock, when the shop of Mr. Moses the tailor, at the corner of Penhallow and State streets, the house occupied by Mr. Wyatt in State street opposite Mr. Moses the tailor, the house of the widow Edwards in State street near the corner of Chapel street, and several houses on the opposite side of it, and the house, at the corner of Daniel and Chapel streets, were all blazing upon the roofs. By eleven o'clock almost every house in State street and on the south side of Daniel street was in flames. The house of Jacob Sheafe, Esq., in State near Penhallow street, was now the only building in State street, east of where the fire commenced, for the whole extent of a quarter of a mile, that was not burning. This however was wrapped by a tempest of fire from the surrounding houses, but was defended to the last extremity by the persevering energy of some generous souls—among them Commodore Hull and Captain Smith of the Frigate Congress, and other officers from the Navy Yard, who were enjoying that evening the hospitality of the Navy Agent, and on the top of the house they fought the fire as though it were the declared enemy of their country. But the fire insidiously entered some inner apartment and this building shared in the fate of its neighbors. The destruction of the whole town nowseemed inevitable. Despair was upon every face, and each individual seemed to feel grateful for his personal safety. A few persons entertained some faint hopes that the fire-proof stores in Water street, between State and Court streets would have been safe themselves, and would have served as a barrier against the fire. But the heat was so intense that it burnt through the walls, and the composition roofs of tar and gravel melted like ice before the fury of the burning flakes.

The fire acknowledged no other barrier than the shores of the Piscataqua. It was not until five o'clock of the morning of the 23d that it ceased its ravages. That morning presented in the midst of our city fifteen acres of ruins, studded over by hundreds of chimneys, tottering walls and charred stumps of fruit and ornamental trees. There had disappeared in one short night 108 dwelling houses (occupied by 130 families,) 64 stores and shops, and 100 barns, &c., making in the whole 272 buildings. From west to east the fire extended one third of a mile, and from north to south, the width of the ruins in the widest part was an eighth of a mile.

So rapid was the progress of the fire, that nothing was saved from cellars. Few people had time to go into their upper chambers, and a vast amount of property which had been removed from houses to what were regarded places of safety, was overtaken by the flame and consumed.

On the dreadful night of the fire numerous and painful were the sensations experienced. Many were apprehending the entire loss of their property, impoverishment of their friends, the blasting of their fairest hopes, the destruction of some valuable acquaintance and the ruin of the town. They saw the widow, deprived of her house and everything it contained, wringing her hands in agony,—they saw the "aged man and bowed down" supporting himself on his staff and crawling to some place of safety,—they saw the aged and diseased mother borne in a chair by the arms of an affectionate son,—they saw the child emaciated by a lingering disorder, snatched from the couch of maternal tenderness to encounter the piercing wind of night; and the victim of distraction borne from confinement to find a refuge from death. The mighty roaring of the wind and flames, the awful crash of the buildings, and the shrieks of distress, almost drove some to distraction.

None however could fail to be struck with the sublimity of the prospect as viewed from the tops of the buildings. The fire seemed a torrent of desolation rushing through the midst of the town, and with humility they saw its destructive energies mocking the impotence of man. Not only this place, but the whole adjacent country was illuminated with a crimson splendor. The deep and majestic river, awfully reflected the blazing deluge of ruin, and contributed greatly to heighten the grandeur of the scene.

The atmosphere was remarkably clear on the night of

the fire, which could consequently be seen at an immense distance. It was seen at Boston and was supposed to be in Charlestown. In Ipswich and Gloucester, thirty-five miles distant, books could be read in the streets. It was seen at Providence, about one hundred miles from us in a southwesterly direction. It was seen in a town ten miles beyond Windsor in Vermont, about one hundred miles from us in a northwesterly direction, and was supposed to be in Windsor. The persons who saw it mounted their horses and went to Windsor expecting to be of use to people suffering there from fire. It was so light in Berwick, fifteen miles from us, they could discern a pin in the streets; and in Dover, ten miles from us, it was so light they could read.

A large number of persons arrived from Newburyport in season to be useful at the fire, and at three o'clock in the morning forty men arrived from Salem, having come forty-three miles in six hours, and were in season to afford efficient aid. Eighty men from Newburyport remained over the second night, to complete their work of philanthrophy in watching the ruins.

In those days but few persons had insurance upon property, so that the loss of nearly $300,000 was severely felt by our citizens. To a call by the Selectmen for donations, there was a noble response, not only from neighboring towns, but also from some as distant as the city of brotherly love. Philadelphia sent a donation of $13,291, New York $4,055, Boston over $20,000, Portland $1,421, Providence $2,750, Newburyport $1,858; and from a hundred other towns, in the aggregate making up $77,273, or about 25 per cent. of the whole loss. This sum was as equally divided as the circumstances would permit.

For more than forty years the public were left without a kowledge of the cause of that desolating fire. It now appears that a girl who bore the name of Colbath had been a domestic at the house of Mrs. Woodward, and had taken offence because Mrs. W. had taken from her some bottles of wine which a gentleman boarder at the house had given her. She left the house and procured a place in the kitchen of Mr. John Gains, then occupying the house where Mayor Simes now resides. She there told her story, and made an avowal of revenge—"I'll burn her out." She was remonstrated with in vain. With a threat of vengeance upon her lips she left Mr. G.'s house early in the evening of the 22d of December, and in the course of an hour there was an alarm—"Woodward's barn is on fire!" She never again returned to Mr. G.'s but sent a messenger for her clothes the next day. The fear of experiencing a like revengeful, fiendish act, led the family to keep the matter to themselves,—and it was not until her death, many years after, that the facts were made known. This Colbath led a dissolute life, and become an inmate of our almshouse.

It is our intent in a number of Rambles, to reconstruct, as well as the materials will permit, that portion of Portsmouth as it was before that fire, and introduce to the stage of life some of the men who might have been seen in that part of our city half a century ago.

RAMBLE CXXI.

Central Portsmouth previous to the Great Fire—Portsmouth Pier—New-Hampshire Hotel—Jacob Sheafe's—Daniel Webster's—North side of Buck St.—The Haunted House.

Before the conflagration of 1813, the principal business mart of Portsmouth was State (then Buck) street. At its eastern termination was the Portsmouth Pier; near it was the New Hampshire Hotel; in this street the Post Office was located for many years, and also the Custom House. Here too was *the* public grammar school of the town. The street was very narrow and irregular, not averaging much more than half its present width of sixty feet. Between Washington and Atkinson streets it was only about twenty five feet wide—comparing well with Hunking street of the present day. On the north side of the street, outside of the side-walk, in front of the Episcopal chapel, can now be seen the stone covering of a well. This well was in the front yard of Abraham Isaac's house before the fire. Measuring the same distance from the opposite side of the street so as to reduce the width just one-half, will give an idea of State street before the fire.

This street was the first to be furnished with paved side-walks, and here was the place of promenade of the *elite* of the town. There were continual arrivals at the Pier, of ships, brigs and schooners; and through this street there were more goods transported than through any other in Portsmouth. Then the commerce of our merchants was extended to Europe, South America and the East and West Indies. We find that in 1800, no less than twenty-eight ships, forty-seven brigs, ten schooners and one bark were employed on foreign voyages, belonging to Portsmouth. Seventeen of these vessels were built here in the year 1800. Twenty coasting vessels were also employed.

The *Portsmouth Pier* in those days was a corporation of some magnitude. The company was chartered in 1795. They constructed the Pier or wharf which still bears the name, 340 feet in length and averaging sixty feet in breadth. On the south side of it they built an edifice which was not at that day equalled by anything in New England, not excepting the warehouses of Boston of that day. It was three hundred and twenty feet in length and thirty feet in breadth—three stories high. It was divided into fourteen stores. On the north side of the Pier was another building of the same height, divided into two stores. The site of the latter is now occupied by Mr. Hall Varrell's coopery.

The occupants of the large Pier building were, first on the east end, Thomas Manning, then Daniel Huntress, Aaron Lakeman, John McClintock, Elisha Lowe, James Shapley, Theodore Chase, Clement Storer, Clement Jackson, Martin Parry, Elijah Hall, George Long and William and Joseph Chase. In the third story was Joseph Walker's sail loft. Benjamin Holmes and others occupied the other Pier building for counting rooms and storage.

These stores at the time of the fire were full of merchandise—such as liquors, molasses, sugar, salt, coffee, and one store was filled with yellow ochre, much used for painting in those days.

On the west of the Pier edifice and nearly adjoining it, on the north corner of Water street, was the *New Hampshire Hotel*, a large brick building, where ship masters, mates and the public generally, found accommodations. In this hotel the celebrated ventriloquist Potter, whose fame was world-wide in his day, was in his early life a servant. This hotel as well as the site of the Pier wharf, was formerly the property of the Sherburne family—Capt. Benjamin Sherburne occupied the hotel about seventy years ago, and it was disposed of by him to the Pier Company. The last landlord of the hotel was Mr. Geddis.

Water street before the fire varied in width from twenty-two to thirty feet. Daniel street, from Penhallow street east, was about thirty-five feet wide. There was a front yard to the mansion of Elijah Hall—and the building opposite set out five feet into the present street line.

State street being so narrow, and very compactly filled with wooden buildings, the fire extended through it with irresistible fury. The flames from both sides of the street uniting in a grand but terrific arch over the centre. How powerless then was the feeble force of the only three small engines owned by the town; and how hard to collect a company at any point, when almost every one thought his own premises in danger. On, on it swept, and its voracious appetite not only took in all of the edifices that were combustible, but much of smaller matters that had been treasured up as invaluable. Prized heirlooms were burned to ashes; valued paintings gave their oil and coloring to feed the flames; treasured manuscripts, souvenirs, books, jewels, all disappeared; and those carefully hidden bank notes, or coins, laid up in some hidden crevice for a rainy day, it is vain to seek for among the ruins.

The Hon. Daniel Webster lived in a house on the corner of Court and Pleasant streets. It was built by Oliver Whipple, about the time and in the same style of the house of the late John K. Pickering. Mr. Webster was enjoying the festivities of an entertainment at Jacob Sheafe's, whose house was on State street, near the east corner of Penhallow street. The house was large, of two stories, with gambrel roof; the capacious yard on the east paved with flat stones. When the cry of fire was raised, Mr. Sheafe turned out a fresh supply of his wine, and with "we will take a parting glass, Mr. Webster," the action was suited to the word; and Mr. W. went home to see his house already on fire. Not much time intervened before Mr. Sheafe found his own house surrounded by burning buildings. The efforts of his company, aided by recruits from the Navy Yard, for some time kept his premises a dark spot amid the flames. The next morning, in writing to a friend in Boston an account of the fire, with characteristic brevity he said, "I have lost about $50,000 and my faithful dog Trim." Notwithstanding his great loss, he headed a subscription for the sufferers by a liberal sum.

It is worthy of note, that no lives were recorded as lost

of more value than Trim's. By a remarkable providence, no person suffered severe personal injury except our late fellow citizen John Smith, who exhibited in his walk ever afterwards the evidence of the breaking of one of his limbs on that occasion.

As in opening the ruins of Herculaneum, not only the remains of edifices but also the little details of the furniture discovered are regarded with interest, so may some of the details of life, which a half a century ago would have passed as scarcely worthy of comment, now be brought out as characteristics or marks of a former age.

We have already spoken of the extent of the ravages of the great fire of 1813, and described some of the buildings destroyed. We will now begin at the river on the north side of State street. Before the Pier wharf was built, more than sixty years ago, the cap-sill of Sherburne's wharf on that site was nearly on a line with the east end of where Mr. Hall Varrel's cooper's shop now stands. Within a few feet of the wharf was a carved statue of a man, with extended arm, and from his forefinger a stream of water was continually issuing. This was a fanciful vent of the Portsmouth Aqueduct, which had recently brought the water from a fountain two and a half miles distant.

On the northwesterly side of the street, there was a two story store extending from the river to a narrow passageway for teams to Langdon's wharf. The easterly end was occupied sixty years ago by Capt. Elisha Lowe as a grocery store, and the westerly end was improved for the storage of heavy imported goods.

Next west of the passageway stood a two story store with the end to the street, which at one time was occupied by Abel Harris, for cleaning flax seed, of which he shipped several cargoes to Europe. It was afterwards occupied as a wholesale crockery ware store by Zebulon Robinson.

West of this store was a small two-story house occupied

as a dwelling by Mr. John D. Seaward. In the westerly end of this house he worked at shoemaking.

The next was a long one-story building which served Mr. Sam'l Sherive for a painter's and glazier's shop and dwelling house for his family, consisting of himself, wife and twenty-two children which she bore him, only a part of whom survived their parents. One of the daughters (Phebe) was married to "Stephen Delande, who makes sugar candy," by which cognomen, being a confectioner, he usually introduced himself and his business to strangers. Mr. Sherive's house was bounded westerly by a narrow passage way, directly opposite Water street, leading to a small dwelling house of Mr. Joseph Stoodley. The intervening lots from the passage way leading to Langdon's wharf were afterwards built upon by Nathaniel W. Fernald, William Varrell and others.

On the lot next to the passageway leading to Mr. Stoodley's house, Mr. George Nutter, house carpenter, erected a two-story double dwelling house, in the northeasterly corner of which he sold groceries, &c.

Next, on the spot where Christian Johnson now resides, was a large double two-story dwelling house, occupied for some years by John Samuel Sherburne, attorney at law, who subsequently held the offices of District Attorney and Judge of the District Court. This house, after Judge Sherburne vacated it for his residence next west of the Court house, was deemed by the superstitious to be haunted by evil spirits and the rendezvous of witches and wizzards who were supposed occasionally to infest the town and dwelling houses which happened to be vacant. The superstitious were therefore very careful about passing such houses by night, especially in dark and stormy weather, when, as many believed in those days, the witches would sally out from the house and if successful in casting a horse's bridle over the head of any person passing by would immediately transform the victim into a horse, and after having him shod with iron shoes, would ride the animal till it became tired, and just before daylight would turn it loose in the street. The persons thus afflicted would the next day find prints of the horse nails on their hands and on their feet, and marks of the bridle bits on the sides of their mouths. Such was the story told and believed by the superstitious, by which relations many children, as well as some of riper years, were greatly frightened. Strange noises in the night time would be heard in this house, and so many voices intermingling on stormy nights as to resemble more the abode of demons than those of human beings. On such occasions, it was said, lights would be seen passing quickly from chamber to chamber, while the witches and evil spirits were carousing below. These scenes generally were represented as taking place in the latter part of the night.

With such superstitious belief, a story obtained credit, of a man who had been absent from his home one night till nearly daylight the next morning, occasioning his family great anxiety and distress. He had been spending the evening with one of his neighbors, and as the family supposed had gone directly home on leaving their house. It was a stormy night. On his return to his home next morning he thus accounted for his absence. He said the moment he had bid his neighbor good night at his door, he saw a woman walking before him with a lighted lantern at her side. He had nearly overtaken her, when she disappeared, but the light still moved on before him and he was powerless to turn from it, and before morning was led by it into an alder swamp near the Pound, worried and greatly fatigued. It at last occurred to him that the woman who had preceded him with the light was a witch, and that if he could turn any one of his garments he had on inside out, he would get rid of her influence. So after great exertion he succeeded in getting his coat off,and, turning the sleeves, put it on again, when the light immediately disappeared and he succeeded in getting out of the swamp into South road, near the place where Dow was executed, and so found his way home.

The impressions which the story made upon the minds of the superstitious were of course confirmatory of their belief in witchcraft. Others, however, who were in the secret that the *bewitched* man had spent most of the night in a gambling establishment, had as strong belief in evil spirits, but in a different mode of manifestation.

The premises of the Judge however, were entirely exempt from the annoyances of those evil spirits when it afterward became occupied by the intrepid Captain Thomas Bell Stevens, if not before that time, as also from the trouble occupants were subjected to by the frequent spirit knocking at the front door by night, which unseen hands occasioned by means of a line attached to the heavy knocker on the door and passing over the house to Daniel street—the weaker portion of the line being attached to the knocker would break upon a sudden jerk, when there was danger of detection, and so elude discovery.

Such freaks of the boys of that day gave a name to "*The Haunted House*," which was retained long after all the natural causes of the light and noises were satisfactorily developed, and until it was swept away in the conflagration.

RAMBLE CXXII.

Central Portsmouth before the Great Fire.—Nicholas Rousselet—The Museum—Sailor Anecdote, &c.

THE last number was a ramble on the north side of State street from the water to where the Sherburne house stood half a century ago.

Next west of the "haunted house" was a tavern and seamen's boarding house, kept by Benjamin Chandler. It was an old affair, of two stories, with an ell fronting on the street, the main body of the house setting some fifteen feet back. A mill stone with a hole in the centre, was used for a door step.

On the southeast corner of Mulberry and State streets was a small two-story building occupied by Joseph Jackson.

Next west, on the opposite corner of Mulberry street, was a large two-story dwelling facing on State street, with a store adjoining extending on Mulberry street. Sixty years ago they were the property of Nicholas Rousselet, who came to this town from Demerara as early as 1787, and married Catharine Elizabeth, daughter of Samuel Moffatt, and sister of the wife of the late Dr. N. A. Haven. Mr. Rousselet was a merchant, and a gentlemen of some taste for the curiosities of nature and art. He changed the name of Mulberry lane, to Demerara street, and over the store he built on that street, he commenced the *Portsmouth Museum*, where he displayed all the curiosities he could gather.

We have seen a schedule of the leading articles, drawn up by him in January, 1800. Among them were two engravings of Winter scenery, two of Parker's dog Bank, two of Lord Howe, two of Cleopatra, two of the King and Queen of France, engravings of an attack by a Shark, group of Dogs, six Landscapes, a full sized Lady, the Graces, the Distress, and painted Flowers. The expense of these imported from London was $200. He also names a pair of Crystal Chandeliers, which cost $60, and a "Mahogany Lady's Cabinet," which cost $160. Whether it had been the property of some West India *mahogany lady*, the schedule says not. This valuable Cabinet, we note in another place, was afterwards transferred to his brother-in-law, Dr. Haven. A picture of Mr. Rousselet, and another representing his being cast away. Six representations of Game. There was a collection of the skins of Snakes and Reptiles, and a variety of animals. A desk with seven drawers contained insects of great variety. A Crucifix of Ambergris. A Sword with agate handle. A trunk of curious female apparel. A Spy-glass, and an Object glass with Pictures. Among the books in the Museum were 52 vols. on Natural History, with illuminated engravings, and about one hundred other volumes.

Nothing was added to the Museum after the proprietor left for Demerara in July, 1800, where he soon after died. He had a daughter, Lucy A. Rousselet, who accompanied him, was married there, but did not survive her father ten years. The property here then came into the possession of Dr. N. A. Haven.

The following document shows that his lady's cabinet was not neglected in preparing a Museum for the public eye:

INVENTORY OF JEWELRY IN HAIR TRUNK, TAKEN APRIL 15, 1799, AFTER THE DECEASE OF MY WIFE, WITH THE ASSISTANCE OF MRS. ODIORNE, OF KITTERY, HER SISTER:

A gold Watch with a gold chain and a gold seal;
A Whistle, small etui, and 5 other small trinkets;
A gold Watch, set in diamonds, on the back a lady holding her head with her left arm;
2 red trinkets, set in gold;
A gold Ring, representing a lady under a tree, with her dog sleeping;
1 with two diamonds and coroline figure;
1 with small diamonds; 1 with corolines;
5 plain gold Rings;
A small Box with my picture and gold chain;
A Snuff-Box with silver plate marked C. E. R., containing a gold necklace and gold locket;
A Snuff-Box as slipper, containing a gold necklace as a chain with gold lock—weight 5 oz.;
A pair gold Bracelets, with ivory representations;
A silver Snuff-Box, marked C. E. R., containing a pair gold bracelets as buckles, with black velvet strings;
A gold Breastpin representing Minerva and ship at sea;
1 ditto representing a woman and her dog;
A Snuff Box of turtle-shell, containing a pair of sleeve buttons and a pair gold earrings;
A Snuff-Box and glass motto, "Look within," containing a gold necklace, with mother-of-pearl circles;
A small Box and motto, containing a gold necklace for a child;
A gold Tumbler in a green case;
A turtle-shell Etui, with silver knife, scissors, penknife, and a silver smelling bottle representing a pear;

John Haven was tenant in this house for several years, up to June, 1800, when he removed to his new house, built by him on Islington street, now occupied by George W. Haven.

The store connected with the house on Mulberry street under the Museum, was at one time occupied as a piece goods store by Mr. Timothy Winn, the third, from Woburn, Mass., who was esteemed a very estimable citizen, but by some persons called "Three-penny Winn," because the inscription on his sign was "TIMOTHY WINN, 3d." He however enjoyed the joke, and would not alter the sign.

The last occupant of this building was another Frenchman named Leonard Serat, a tailor. He used it for a shop and residence. Over his door was an oval sign representing two sailors displaying clothes, with a ship between them. There was a projecting sign with his name and business—on one side "*Taylor*," on the other "*Tailor*." When asked his motive, he replied—"If I have not spelt it right on one side, it certainly will be on the other." He used to say he could spell his name with one letter. He might be seen explaining it, by placing a rat on the sidewalk, and making a C before it. He would say—"Dere is de C and dere is de rat—and if dat don't spell Serat, what does it spell?" Although the fire cleared away the property and his signs, as well as the weather-beaten "Museum" sign, yet the old gentleman still lives in Melrose, Mass., works at his trade, and takes snuff as bountifully as he did fifty years ago.

There is one little story illustrative of sailor character, which occurred in this neighborhood. A sailor once called on a female friend in the tailor's shop of Mr. Nathaniel Fernald on the east, and chanced to break the eye of a needle. He made inquiry where he could have it mended, and was pointed over the way to the blacksmith shop of a wag named George Plaisted, who was asked if he could do the job. Plaisted looked at it, pronounced it rather difficult, but thought it might be done for ten cents. So he sent George Beck to the next shop for a cent's worth of needles, blued the eye of one of them over the fire, rubbed it, and handed it over to the tar. He examined it, said it could not have been done better in England, paid the price and half a pint of rum for his skill, and restored the needle to its owner. The little story has been so often told, we think it has enough of interest now to have a locality.

RAMBLE CXXIII.

Central Portsmouth before the Great Fire—Nicholas Rousselet's Courtship—The eccentric Josiah Shackford—His Unparalleled Feat of crossing the Atlantic alone—The founder of Portsmouth, Ohio.

In the expiring light of the old Museum the reader was left in our last. Let us stir the embers a little to throw some light on a small romantic incident in the life of its old proprietor.

Nicholas Rousselet was a man of good exterior, and when dressed in the official consular costume which he wore on public days, was a man to attract attention. Of his first acquaintance with Miss Moffatt, we have no account, but tradition gives the story, that it was at the Episcopal Church, in service hours, that the most importnnt crisis in their courtship transpired. Sitting with her in her father's pew, Mr. Rousselet handed Miss Catharine the Bible in which he pencilled, in the first verse of the second epistle of John, "*Unto the elect lady*"—and the 5th verse entire—"And now I beseech thee, lady, not as though I wrote a new commandment unto thee, but that which we had from the beginning, that we love one another." Miss Catharine, fully comprehending the appeal, turned down a leaf in the first chapter of Ruth, beginning in verse 16th—"Whither thou goest, I will go; and where thou lodgest I will lodge;

thy people shall be my people, and thy God my God. Where thou diest, will I die, and there will I be buried: the Lord do so to me, and more also, if aught but death part thee and me."

The Bible with folded leaf was returned to him; and after the appeal was thus silently and favorably answered, the happy man doubtless "kissed the book."

After marriage, they became occupants of the Atkinson mansion recently taken down on Court street, the residence where Gov. John Wentworth wedded the widow Lady Frances, in ten days after her husband's death. The strange sounds which, it is said, troubled Mr. R. while residing, there must rather be attributed to the superstition of the times, than to the return of any restless spirit.

While in the vicinity of the old Museum, we will pass to another two-story residence, of some historical interest.

Opposite Mulberry street on the south side of State street, stood the mansion house of Madame Eleanor Shackford, built by her father Nathaniel Mendum, probably as early as 1700. She was twice married, and although she lived to the advanced age of 91 years, she died in the same room in which she was born, and never lived in any other house. By her first husband, named Marshall, she had four daughters—one of them was grandmother to the late Col. John N. Sherburne. Her youngest daughter, Deborah, never left her. They kept negro slaves, as was the custom in those days. The names of the three were Adam, Mercer and Bess. Adam lived to be very old, and one day while left alone he fell in the fire and was burnt to death.

After Mr. Marshall's death, the widow married Josiah Shackford. He had one son then absent at sea, Capt. Josiah Shackford, Jr. When he returned home, he sought the residence of his father. He met Deborah at the door. As soon as he saw her he fell desperately in love, and determined in his mind to make her his wife: but on making a declaration, she refused him, saying she had no heart to bestow, as hers was engaged to another. He however persisted in his suit, declaring she was the one who was raised up before him by an astrologer in Europe, and he should marry her or nobody. She being naturally of an amiable and condescending disposition, like a dutiful child took her parents' advice and married him. After they had been married several years he wanted her to remove with him to New York, as that was the port he always sailed from and returned to, but she refused to leave her aged mother.

Without making known to her his intentions, he left his wife and Portsmouth, and was many years absent, making no communications to his connections here.

In the "Essex Journal and New Hampshire Packet" of May 2, 1787, we find the following announcement, related by a gentleman at New York, "from such authority as puts the truth of it quite out of dispute:"

"A Mr. Shackford, sometime since, from Piscataqua, having the misfortune of discontent with his wife, left that place for Surinam. On his arrival there, he left the vessel he first sailed in, and took the command of one for Europe. He performed his voyage and gave such satisfaction to his owners, that they gave him a cutter-built sloop of about 15 tons. With her he returned to Surinam ALONE, after a passage of 35 days. When he arrived, the novelty of the expedition excited unusual surprise, so far as to induce the government to take notice of the fact. Suspicions prevailed of his having dealt unfairly by the people who were supposed to have come out with him. But he produced his papers and journal, and proved his integrity so far to the satisfaction of his examiners, that they permitted him to take another man on board and proceed to St. Bartholomews, where he arrived in safety, and now follows the coasting business from that Island."

We have understood that the place in Europe which he left was Bordeaux, in France. The vessel appears to have been a personal gift to him. He engaged a man to accom-

man to accompany him, who becoming fearful when he put to sea, jumped on board the pilot's boat, and left Capt. Shackford with no other companion than his dog. He was a man of too stern materials to turn about, so he undertook the voyage of three thousand miles alone. What a resolute spirit! See him on the boisterous mid-ocean alone in his little bark a thousand miles from any land—without a human being to consult when awake, or to aid in keeping watch while he slept; without a hand to aid when the storm beat about him, and his little boat is hid between the mountain swells! With an eye on the compass, a hand on the helm, and a firm trust in Providence, on he goes for five long weeks, witnessing the moon pass into its full, its several quarters, and falling again before he came in sight of the land for which he was steering!

This unparalleled feat he successfully accomplished—the statement of which, however, was not readily believed by the South Americans. To prove his statement, he was required to take his vessel down the harbor of Surinam alone, and bring it in again. This exhibition was so satisfactorily made, that his story received credit, but the government was not fully satisfied until a return was made from Europe confirming his statement.

Some years after, he returned to Portsmouth, put up at a hotel, and in the afternoon called on his wife, took tea with her, in the evening returned to his hotel, and the next morning left again never to return.

He was next heard of in Ohio, where he purchased a large tract of land when that State was almost a wilderness, laid out a township, and in commemoration of the place of his birth called it *Portsmouth.* He erected mills and stores, and built several houses. He lived alone, excepting a boy, and never would suffer a woman to enter his house, having his washing and sewing sent out and brought home by his boy. His wife, after her mother's death, offered to go and live with him. She wrote him several letters, but received no answer. He wrote to his nephews in Portsmouth, and said if one would come out and settle there, he would make him his heir. The late Samuel Shackford, about forty years ago, went and visited his uncle, but returned, not liking well enough to remove there. At his death he left his property to strangers.

He died about forty years since, over 80 years old, living to see his town, so beautifully situated at the junction of the Scioto and Ohio rivers, become a place of note and the chief county town. He was a studious man, intelligent, but of an eccentricity which to some minds bore marks of insanity—but those who recollect him in Ohio will not allow that he was any other than a sane man. He was probably convinced that astrologers' sayings should never have an influence in the selection of a wife; and his wife doubtless was satisfied that the heart which was held by another should not be bartered, even by parental influence.

Mrs. Shackford still lived in the old mansion which her father bequeathed to her and to a grandson, Thomas Jackson, until the fire of 1813, which consumed it, and drove them to another habitation.

Mr. Jackson had been several years an instructor of youth in Portsmouth, and was then teaching at the South School. He conveyed as many things as he could to the school house; they were saved, but the rest were burnt or stolen. The next day he took possession of the old Chauncey house on the South road. No one lived in it but an old man named John Shores, who had been put there to take care of it. He told thrilling tales of the house being haunted, and said there was a closet in the cellar where a minister had laid a spirit twenty years ago, and it had never been opened since. Mr. J. and Capt. John S. Davis had the curiosity to open it. Found two barrels, one containing beef and the other pork, in a good state of preservation. Three or four dead rats were all that indicated any appearance of evil spirits having visited the closet. Mr. Jackson and family lived there unmolested two years, when he built a brick house on his land in State street, and moved back on the old spot again. Mrs. Shackford sold her lot to Capt. Andrew W. Bell, as it joined his property, which is now owned and occupied by Mr. George Henderson. She lived to a good old age, beloved by all who knew her, and would without doubt, like her mother, have breathed her last in the house where she was born, had not the devouring element laid it in ashes.

RAMBLE CXXIV.

Central Portsmouth before the Fire of 1813.—North side of Buck street.

On the north side of State street we have progressed from the river to Mulberry street, and we will continue our route west. Next to Rousselet's premises came the bakehouse of Silas Hunt, at the time of the fire occupied by Robert Yeaton. This location still remains a bakery, owned by George W. Plumer. Next was the dwelling house and grocery of Nathaniel Marshall, owned at the time of the fire by Robert Eaton.

The next was a two-story gambrel-roofed house owned by Major Seth Tripe, the great-grandfather of Mr. Seth W. Tripe of Portsmouth. This house stood on the corner of Chapel and State streets, fronting on the latter, with a shop in the western end. This shop at one time was occupied by the widow Shores, the mother of James F., and at another by George Dame as a music store. On the arrival of Major Tripe's son Samuel with his family from Bristol,

England, he vacated the house and moved into Deer street, where he resided till his death, leaving his house in State street in the occupancy of his son.

On the opposite corner of Chapel street was a two-story gambrel-roofed dwelling house in the form of a T, fronting on State street, the easterly end of which was owned and occupied by Capt. Gregory, the grandfather of Mr. Albert Gregory. The western end was owned by Major William Gardner, and occupied by Mark Chadbourne, hatter, Benjamin Drowne, gold and silver smith, Joseph Clark, gold and silver smith, George Ham, watchmaker, Joseph Akerman, Jr., collector of taxes, and others at different periods.

After the decease of Capt. Gregory, his widow was distinguished as an instructor of small children. With the aid of her two daughters she furnished for several years the shipping of this port with their colors and national flags.

Next was the one-story shop of Mr. John Beck, hatter, whose daughter was the wife of Mr. Mark Chadbourne. He was the father of the late Henry Beck.

Next to the hatter's shop was a large two story gambrel-roofed house owned by Major Gardner, connected with a two story store endwise on the street. This Major Gardner disposed of when he purchased the estate of Ichabod Nichols, Esq., in Gardner street, who removed to Salem, Mass. The house in State street, after Major G. left it, was occupied by Capt. Gilbert Horney, and at the time of the fire by Mr. Phillip W. Currier. The store was occupied by Mr. George Dame, limner, as his studio, from which point of view he painted a very striking likeness, (full stature) of Benjamin Rowe Quint, a tall man who resided in Newington, but who frequently was employed as a stone mason, in building cellars and laying stone side pavements. At that time he was laying stones in front of the dwelling house of Capt. Timothy Mountford, nearly opposite. The position of the painter's subject was that of a stooping posture—his arms towards the ground, his hands clinching and adjusting a flat paving stone, his back towards the painter, his feet wide apart, and his aquiline Roman nose (which was of such extended dimensions that it would have placed him in the highest estimation of Bonaparte,) was visible beneath his body, extending like the point of a plough approaching the ground. The picture when finished, which was previous to the original having finished his labor in the street, was exposed to view in the window of the painter; and so perfect was the likeness that no one familiar with the face of Mr. Quint failed to recognize him as the original of the picture; and being greatly enraged, the subject threatened to demolish the window with his stone hammer if it was not removed forthwith. This was done, but it was afterwards exhibited in a private manner. The ludicrous position and exact likeness of Mr. Q. caused much merriment at his expense.

The store attached to the Horney house in State street, was also occupied as the post office by Mark Simes until 1805, when the post office was removed to the Bass house in Broad street, on the spot where the hay scales now stand.

Next westerly was the two-story dwelling house of Capt. William Edwards, standing end to the street with the front door on the westerly side, approached through a passage-way about eight feet wide. This house was also the residence of Misses Ann and Mary Lanagan, sisters of Mrs. Edwards, and of Mrs. Furniss, mother of William P. Furniss, Esq., now of New York.

Next was a two story-dwelling house standing end to the street, the building of which was commenced by Joshua Pike, "barber and peruke wig maker," but was completed by Mr. John Stavers of mail-stage renown. It was occupied by his son William, and afterwards by his son-in-law Capt. John H. Seawards. It was from this house that the hostler, mentioned in Ramble 101, page 18, stole the bucket of rum, for which he paid the penalty at the town pump.

Next was a long two-story dwelling house fronting the street and elevated six or eight feet above its level. It extended from the yard of Mr. Stavers' house to a narrow passage way at the western end of it, which terminated in a goldsmith's shop, occupied by Capt. Martin Parry, who also occupied the other western part of it as his dwelling house. Capt. Martin Parry died of yellow fever in 1802, which was prevalent in this vicinity at that time and swept off some of our best citizens. He was a merchant of honored standing, and the agent of William Gray, Esq., of Salem, whose ships then were loading at our pier for Calcutta, Russia and other places. Capt. Parry left an only daughter, Ann, who was the first wife of our respected townsman, the late William Jones, Esq., who after the fire built the house now occupied by Rev. James DeNormandie, near the spot. The eastern half of the house was the residence of Madam Bettenham, so favorably known and respected as a lady who never failed to make all happy who had the privilege of her company. Her mother, who was the daughter of George Meserve, ship builder, occupied the same house before her. Capt. James Christie, who married the daughter of Mrs. Bettenham, occupied this house till his death at Philadelphia in 1812. His children John and Mary were born here. The late William Simes, gold and silver smith, was an apprentice of Capt. Parry, and after his master engaged in mercantile pursuits, occupied the shop.

The next building was the long two-story store of Jacob Sheafe, Jr. Esq., standing end to the street and fronting on Washington street. Many amusing reminisences of this of this store might be mentioned. It was once occupied by Mr. William Neil, an emigrant from Ireland, a gentleman beloved and respected by all who knew him. He was the *friend of man* in the full and true sense of the word. He had a very pleasant manner of address, and at times was quite amusing, and made very many sensible remarks to those who traded with him in the store, in which he exposed for sale a great variety of goods. He was distinguished as the seller of Irish linens, of which he was an excellent judge of quality, so that who bought linen of him was sure it was wholly of flax. In teas he was also renowned as a good judge, so much so that the remark was frequently made when tea of the right flavor was served at table, "this is Mr. Neil's tea." Mr. Neil took a hint from this, and had some nice wrapping paper prepared for putting up the tea he sold, and the following neatly printed upon the package :—

"This is very good tea. And where did you buy it? At Mr. William Neil's store, Buck street, Portsmouth. You will call and get some of the same."

William Neil was a native of Belfast in Ireland, and a graduate of Glasgow College. His children were three sons and four daughters. Thomas, Charles and Robert G.; Ann, married George Andrews of Dover; Elizabeth, married Mr. Wheeler of Dover; Sarah, married Daniel Melcher of Boston, and Margaret was the first wife of John Nutter, of Rochester. The children of his son Thomas (who married Sarah, daughter of Capt. Hector McNeil of the Navy,) were William, who died single; Mary A.; Jane, widow of S. H. Sise of New York, and Thomas, now of this city. The latter, of the firm of Neil, Tarlton & Co., is the only descendant which now bears the name of Neil.

The same store was previously occupied for a short period by Pomroy & Maynard, from England, for the sale of hard-ware goods. They soon returned to England.

The venerable William Neil was very sensitive to any remark which unfavorably reflected upon the Irish or his native land, Ireland. So sensitive was he to the publication of any Irish *bull*, that for many years when Mr. Turell had charge of the Oracle, he never admitted any of the amusing anecdotes of this class, assigning as a reason that he would not injure Mr. Neil's feelings. His memory is still pleasant to those who knew him.

Next was the spacious dwelling-house of Jacob Sheafe, between which and the store occupied by Mr. Neil, was a large paved yard, and in the rear of the whole was a fine garden reaching back to the lane. Reminisences of much interest might be related of the occupant of these premises, and of his hospitalities to strangers of distinction who visited the town, and also of his estimable lady, particularly of her kindness and hospitalities to the distressed, sick, poor and needy. Mr. Sheafe, after the fire, occupied his large brick block on the corner of Market and Daniel streets, where he died. Of his large family, Mrs. Charles Cushing, of Little Harbor, only survives. Next on the east corner of Ark Lane, now called Penhallow street, was a square, one-story hipped-roof building, occupied as a retailing piece goods store by William Sheafe, brother to Jacob, and afterwards by Ward Gilman as a brassfoundry.

On the opposite side of Ark Lane, on the corner of State street, stood the Ark Tavern, kept by John Davenport. It was originally a two-story single house, fronting on State street. Mr. Davenport was a silver smith and buckle maker, and had removed to Portsmouth from Boston, where he was born. He had occupied the building on the corner of Fleet and Congress streets, now owned by the Mechanic Association, and had served the town as constable several years. He made several additions to the house in State street, one of which, one-story high, covered a small gore of land on the eastern end, about eight feet in width at the widest end, in which he himself worked at his trade. A connection of Mr. Davenport's wife, (Mr. Welch,) having at Lynn acquired a knowledge of the ladies' cloth slipper manufacture, he with him commenced the making of them in copartnership; at the same time continuing the buckle making business, which soon afterwards became unprofitable by the introduction of shoe strings. Mr. Davenport then opened his premises as a public house, with the sign of Noah's Ark, and denominated his house the "Ark Tavern," exhibiting in front a fanciful sign of the picture of the Ark.

Mr. Davenport's wife died in this house while the Superior Court was sitting in Portsmouth, in the month of February, and as his house was crowded with boarders, which made her burial very inconvenient, she was kept until the court closed its business about three weeks after.

The artist who painted Mr. Davenport's sign, went by the name of James Still. His proper name was James Ford. Under his real name he had been guilty of an offence which cost him a part of his ears. Although he dropped the *Ford* as he did the long hair over his ears, yet as his baptismal name was not changed, it remained, he said, *James still.* Thus in the exercise of his good talent as a delineator and painter he continued till the time of his death under the name of *James Still.*

RAMBLE CXXV.

Central Portsmouth before the Fire of 1813.—James Sheafe's Residence—Abraham Isaac, the Jew—Jonathan M. Sewell, the Poet.

NEXT west of Davenport's hotel on State street, were the premises of Hon. James Sheafe, who occupied the family mansion of his father. The house was large, of two stories and an ell. It somewhat resembled in appearance the Whipple house, the residence of the late Alexander Ladd, Esq. on Market street, and was built at about the same time. The house was on the site of the present residence of J. M. Tredick, Esq. and connected with it was the large garden, now owned by Mr. Tredick. Mr. Sheafe owned the whole of the square south of the Market, excepting the corner lot, on which a building was, after the fire, erected for the N. H. Union Bank, and now occupied by Albert R. Hatch, Esq. and C. N. Shaw & Co. At the time of the fire, on this corner lot was the Adams house, where resided the mother of Nathaniel Adams, the collector of the Annals of Portsmouth. In this house at the time of the fire were shoe shops of Lewis Bruce and Mendum Janvrin. Between this house and James Sheafe's residence, was another double house belonging to him, and occupied in one tenement by Dr. J. H. Pierrepoint, the beloved physician, and in the other by the widow Rachel Isaac, as a variety store and residence.

Abraham Isaac and his wife were natives of Prussia, and Jews of the strictest sect. They were the first descendants of the venerable Jewish patriarch that ever pitched their tent in Portsmouth, and during their lives were the only Jews among us. He was an auctioneer, acquired a good property and built the house opposite the Rockingham House on State street, now owned and occupied by Mrs. M. P. Jones. Their shop was always closed on Saturday, and on almost any other day in pleasant weather, Mrs. Isaac might be seen at the counter or looking over the half door by which the shop was entered. In front of the house, within a foot of it, was a pump. The well is still kept in order for fires, and it may be seen on the outside of the present sidewalk, near the cross pavement which leads to the Episcopal chapel. Mr. Isaac died on the 15th of Feb. 1803, aged 49, and on the stone which marks his grave in the North burying ground, may be seen the following model epitaph, written by our poet, J. M. Sewall:

Entomb'd beneath, where earth-born troubles cease,
A son of faithful Abra'm sleeps in peace.
In life's first bloom he left his native air,
A sojourner, as all his fathers were;
Through various toils his active spirit ran,
A faithful steward and an honest man.
His soul, we trust, now freed from mortal woes,
Finds, in the partriarch's bosom sweet repose.

A better epitaph can rarely be found. Rachael, his widow, for ten years after his death continued her variety store in this house, and after its destruction in 1813, having no children of her own, took up her residence with an adopted son who lived near New Ipswich, in this State. He was the agent of one of the first cotton factories in that vicinity, and at her death, in that place, all her property became his by bequest.

Repassing again the Adams corner, we go up what is now the front of Exchange Buildings, under the shade of large beautifully spread elms, and nearly on the spot where the Rockingham Bank now stands we can see a large white gambrel-roofed house, back to the market, end to the street, approached by a lattice gate. In general appearance, position, and garden on the south, very nearly resembling the mansion of Samuel Lord, Esq., on Middle street.

This house was the property of John Fisher, Esq., who owned the land on which the Market was built. The Fisher family went to England after the Revolution. About seventy years ago this house was occupied by Jonathan Goddard, Esq., the first husband of Mrs. Robert Rice. It was afterwards occupied by Dr. Josiah Dwight until the fire.

The brick market checked the fire in this direction. It was a truly dismal sight the next morning from this standpoint to see a spot cleared which contained one-fourth at least of all the buildings in Portsmouth, and nothing intervening between the market and Portsmouth Pier but naked chimneys and smoking ruins!

We will turn from this scene for a short ramble to Gates street.

Prominent among the poets of the Revolution, whose verses carried spirit into the camp, and stirred up the patriotic fires of those who performed the statesman's duties at home, was that philanthropic man, JONATHAN MITCHELL SEWELL, Esq., whose home was in Portsmouth, and whose last place of abode was the house on Gates street nearly opposite that of Capt. Joseph Grace.

An enquiry has been made who was the author of "The Versification of Washington's Farewell Address, by a gentleman of Portsmouth, N. H., printed in 1798."

This Versification we have before us. It was written by Mr. Sewall and published, with the author's characteristic modesty, without his name. The poem, if such it may be called, occupies forty-four octavo pages, and is almost a literal presentation of the original in rhyme—the author endeavoring to shun any of the tinsel decorations of poetic ornament, "not indulging to his own fancy on such momentous subjects, handled before with such masterly perfection."

Mr. Sewall was born in Salem, Mass., in 1748, and died in Portsmouth in 1808. He studied law with Judge John Pickering of Portsmouth, became a member of our bar, and was of high standing as a lawyer, but no less eminent as a statesman and poet. He was the writer of the stirring song of the Revolution entitled "War and Washington," beginning "Vain Britons, boast no longer," &c., which was sung in every camp throughout the country.

One of our venerable citizens has recently given us a pamphlet containing a Fourth of July Oration delivered at Portsmouth in 1788, "By one the inhabitants." There is no clue in the book to show who that inhabitant was. The title page presents as a motto and apology for withholding his name, the following expressive quotation from Pope:

"Who builds a church to God, and not to fame,
Will never mark the marble with his name."

This was the first 4th of July Oration delivered in Portsmouth after the Declaration of Independence. The modest author was Jonathan M. Sewall. It was a patriotic production of much higher literary merit than many public addresses which have their author's names in conspicuous capitals.

Charity casts a veil over the weaknesses of his latter years, since the record of his whole life showed him an honest man, the advocate not only of the cause of his country, but also of the injured, however humble their situation. His grave stone bears the following epitaph:

In vain shall worth or wisdom plead to save
The dying victim from the destined grave;
Nor charity, our helpless nature's pride,
The friend to him, who knows no friend beside;
Nor genius, science, eloquence have pow'r,
One moment, to protract th' appointed hour!
Could these united his life have repriev'd,
We should not weep, for Sewall still had liv'd.

RAMBLE CXXVI.

Central Portsmouth before the Fire of 1813.—Stories of Escapes, Rescues, &c.

WE close the sketches of the seenes which are forever covered by the ashes of the great fire, with the following sketch, by Mr. John H. Bowles:

The stirring up you have been giving of late in the "*Rambles*," to the ashes of the great fire of 1813, while it has doubtless revived the event in all its freshness to many who were living at the time, has recalled to a still greater number the impressions they received in their youth from others, who were also eye-witnesses of its many thrilling scenes. Names and locations are forgotten, in many instances, but incidents remain ineffacable.

To the children of thirty to thirty-five years ago, it was a theme that was ever new, and never tired. Let us take a backward look to a time, when, to all but the more youthful generation, the great conflagration was an affair of yesterday. It is Christmas eve. A merry group of juveniles, a dozen in number, after an afternoon of unbounded enjoyment in the spacious attic, succeeded by a bountiful repast, are gathered in semi-circular array, around the hearth-stone. An oak-wood fire throws out its genial heat, for the owner of the mansion loves to see the fire-light reflected upon the massive andirons and shining fender, and will admit into the *sanctum sanctorum*, the family sitting-room, no such modern innovation upon old-time comfort as a stove, though it may do very well for the kitchen, whose arctic frigidity nothing else would ever warm. When the entire catalogue of youthful romances, the "Cinderillas," the "Robin Hoods," etc. have become exhausted, the young lady, to honor whose birthday the little party were assembled, suggested to "mother" to "tell them the story about the great fire." "Mother" thinks it is more than a "thrice-told tale;" but it is repeated, and listened to with eager ears by her youthful auditors; and the same story, in substance, has been told again and again, on many others than Christmas eve, and formed the theme of many a winter fireside chat.

"Aunty" has a passage of her own experience to relate, and we will let her tell her own story in her own way. "The china tea-set you saw upon the table, to-night, was among the last articles saved from my father's house, and its rescue nearly cost me my life. It was in a back room closet, whose contents amid the excitement were forgotten, when nearly all else of value had been removed to a place of safety. While I was engaged in removing the china from the shelves, some men were tearing away an out building, into which the closet projected, in the rear of the house, to enable the firemen to obtain water in our own and the adjoining yard; and as I stepped from a chair to place the last remaining article in a basket, the bright blade of an axe came crushing through the back of the closet, in the very position where my head had been but an instant before. My escape seems little short of a miracle as I think of it, to this day. After leaving the house, as we supposed, for the last time, it occurred to my brother that there still remained in the garret a trunk of family relics, including some valuable brocade dresses, once the property of our grandmother, and he expressed a determination to go and rescue it. We tried to dissuade him from the idea, but without success, and I went with him. When we reached the garret, the room was in flames, and the heat was so great that we could scarcely breathe. I was afraid to go further than the door, but my brother went onward, and seizing the trunk by one of its handles, was dragging it to the stairway, when a large portion of the boards of the roof, burnt to a cinder, fell through from the rafters, and covered the floor with blazing coals. It was an awful moment, for through the aperture thus made in the roof, the wind came with the force of a tornado, driving the fire and smoke before it, but my brother kept on with his burden, after an instant's delay, and did not stop until it was safe in the street. Half an hour afterwards, the pleasant home where our childhood had been spent was one bright flame from the foundation to the ridgepole."

"Grandpa," who, in his comfortable chair, has been reading the last "JOURNAL," and a fresh copy only *two days* old, of Major Ben Russell's "Boston Centinel," says, as he picks up the fallen brands and adds a fresh forestick to the fire, that he will tell them a story of a "nice young man," who, he has always thought, did more good than any one else the night of the fire. He was here and there, and everywhere, wherever his aid was most needed for the general or individual good. At one time he could be seen passing water in the ranks; at another helping some poor widow to save from her burning dwelling her little all; here he would relieve an exhausted fireman at the brakes of an engine, and there lend a hand in removing from their homes the sick or disabled; when the strength of others was exhausted, his energies seemed to increase with the amount of labor he performed. About midnight, while resting for a moment, and surveying the fire from the roof of a store, a volume of flame suddenly burst from a barn on the opposite side of the way, and in an instant afterwards a young lady appeared at the second-story window of a dwelling but a few yards distant, which she attempted to raise, but failed in the effort, and fell backwards out of sight. Descending to the ground, he crossed the street, and finding no one below stairs, he ventured to knock at the door of the room where he had seen the young lady, but receiving no answer he lifted the latch and found her lying insensible upon the floor, for she was recovering from sickness, and through weakness and terror, had fainted away. There was no time to lose, for the glass was cracking in the windows from the blaze of the burning barn; and wrapping her in a blanket, which he stripped from the bed, he carried her in his arms to the residence of a relative where he had seen some of the family furniture conveyed an hour before. The next day he was haunted by a vision of a pair of bright eyes, and felt a desire to improve with their owner an acquaintance so oddly begun. A few days before he thought her but a child, as he lifted her across a gutter on a rainy day, and it was benevolence alone that prompted the service he had rendered her the previous night, but as she lay so helpless upon his breast, and one of her soft curls stole out from the folds of the blanket and rested upon his cheek, he fancied that she was changed into something more than a child. There was a very soft spot in his heart for the girls, though he was somewhat bashful in letting them know it, but he mustered courage at last to go to the house where he had left his fair burden, and enquire if she had sustained any injury from her exposure to the keen air of midnight. He soon called again on the same errand, and derived so much gratification from his visits, that he continued to repeat them for four or five years afterwards, when the family mansion had been rebuilt in its old location, and finally carried off the young lady to a snug little home he had built for himself on one of the lots made vacant by the fire. "Grandpa" concludes his story by adding, "The 'nice young man' is living still, and ready as ever to do all sorts of kind acts; and I shall not be surprised if he comes here to-night for this little rogue at my side, who came very honestly by her bright black eyes and her silken curls."

The above are a few of the legends of the great fire, of which enough might be collected to fill a fair sized volume. In the course of a conversation upon the subject recently, with a gentleman who was an eye-witness of the scene from its commencement to its close, he remarked to me that the impression left upon his memory of that terrible night, alike from the awful grandeur of the conflagration, and its many heart-rending scenes of distress, were as vivid as if it had been an event of the previous week's occurrence. In many instances the entire fruits of a life of industry were swept away, leaving the sufferers at mid-winter, without a place of shelter, or a dollar to recommence the world anew. The rapid advance of the fire after it reached the third or fourth building from its starting point, was like the rushing of the flames over a burning prairie. Families, who at first looked calmly on at a distance, never dreaming that danger could reach them, an hour or two afterwards were retreating before the devouring element, leaving half their effects behind to be burned up with their dwellings.

Furniture and other articles of value, that had been taken to places of imagined safety, were afterwards removed to other locations, and finally burnt up in the streets. Such was the consternation when the calamity was as its height and it was feared the whole place would be consumed, that many people seemed utterly bereft of their wits, causing them to commit absurdities which it afforded them much amusement to relate in after years. One good lady, with a houseful of furniture, and the fire but two tenements distant, was running about in a green baize dressing-gown and red woollen cap with an empty bottle in her hand, and another with three bonnets in her hand and none upon her head. A strange sight was revealed the following morning when daylight appeared. The streets and avenues leading in every direction from the location of the fire, were strewed with furniture of every description, from that fashionable article of the time, the sideboard, to the most common utensil in domestic use; family stores, also, added to the variety, even to the pies that had been prepared for Christmas. It was a sad scene, too, and one that many looked upon with breaking hearts, for instead of the comfortable homes of which they were possessed when the sun went down the previous night, they saw only a heap of smoking ruins.

The memorable passage in the history of Portsmouth that forms the subject of this letter, is a most impressive instance of the amount of evil it is possible for a single wickedly disposed individual, by a very slight act, to accomplish. The writer has a recollection of seeing, in his childhood, the author of this great calamity, by which so many were stripped of their entire earthly possessions, and when she deemed the awful secret locked up in her own bosom. A more abject, wo-begone specimen of fallen humanity than she appeared at that time, it would be scarcely possible to imagine. She applied, under an assumed name, (imagining that she would be unrecognized,) to a lady who had been familiar with her face while she was in the employ of Mrs. Woodward, and asked for some out-of-door employment, offering to labor for a pittance that would hardly have saved her from starvation. If those who had been the greatest sufferers from her wickedness had looked upon her then, with a knowledge of the fact, in her utter wretchedness, it would surely have disarmed them of all resentment. Whatever her after life may have been, (of which I have no knowledge,) she was evidently suffering at that period beneath a weight far heavier to bear than poverty, even in its most dire extreme—an evil conscience, and to such a degree, perchance, as sometimes to feel like Cain, that her punishment was greater than she could bear.

RAMBLE CXXVII.

State Street in 1793 – Drown Family – Dr. Lyman Spalding – Capt. Peter Coues – Samuel E. Coues.

In previous Rambles we have given sketches of State street previous to the fire of 1813. Beginning now at Sherburne's wharf, the eastern end of the street on the south side, we will proceed west on that side of the street, and give the residents therein about seventy years ago. First was Capt. Benjamin Sherburne's N. H. Hotel, on the east corner of Water street. On the west corner was a small shoemaker's shop. Next was a long two-story house owned by John H. Seaward, occupied by Griffin's cut nail manufactory, by John Yeaton, tobacconist, and Timothy Winn, 3d. ("Three Penny Winn.") Next comes William Meserve's dwelling house, John Libbey's shoe-shop, then the house of Capt. Josiah Shackford, already referred to in a former ramble, as the adventurer who crossed the Atlantic alone in a boat. This house was directly in front of Rosemary street. Then came the house of Timothy Gerrish, with his silversmith's shop in front. Abner Blaisdell's house was next, and his grocery store was on the east corner of Atkinson street. On the west corner was the dwelling house and grocery and ship chandlery store of Capt. Peter Coues. Next west was the dwelling and silversmith's shop of Samuel Drown. These houses were all two stories, many of them with end to the street, and, as will be seen, affording under the same roof, a residence and place of business. The street was very narrow—from Washington to Atkinson streets, State street (then Buck) averaged only about 22 feet in width.

Mr. Samuel Drown was the third son of Rev. Samuel Drown, the pastor of the Pitt street society. We find among our papers a sketch of the family which is worth preserving. It is said that the first of the name was a child found at sea alone in a boat, too young to give any account of himself, and from his probably intended destiny he received the name of *Drown*. Such is the legend—and as no mention of the name is made in the old English families, it may be correct.

Leonard Drown, born 1646, was a shipwright by occupation. He came from the west of England and married at or near Portsmouth, New Hampshire, Elizabeth Abbott. He lived to the age of eighty-three years, and died in Boston, Massachusetts, October 31st, 1729. He was blind for seven years next preceding his death. His wife died in the year 1704. He married again but had no issue by the second wife. He lived at Sturgeon Creek, about seven miles from Portsmouth, where all his children were born. He carried on ship building there till 1692, when on account of the Indian wars, he was obliged to remove, and went to

Boston with his family, where he followed the same employment.

His children were four sons and two daughters, namely: Solomon, Samuel, Simeon, Shem; Susanna, who married John Johnson of Boston, and Mary, who married Mr. Kettle of Charlestown.

Samuel died near to if not in Portsmouth.

Solomon was born January 23d, 1681, his wife Aug. 18th 1686, and they were married November 8, 1705, in Bristol, R. I. They had eleven children, namely: Solomon, born October 4, 1706; Esther, Oct. 26, 1708; Elizabeth, Sept 8, 1710; Joseph, Feb. 8, 1715; Bathshebah, June 10, 1715; Benjamin, June 9, 1717; Mary, June 7, 1719; Samuel, July 31, 1721; Sarah, July 23, 1723; Jonathan, July 29, 1725; Shem, June 13, 1728; Solomon, the father of these, died in 1730, and his wife in 1744.

Their son Samuel Drown was married to Sarah Reed, in Rehoboth, Mass. He was a Calvin Baptist Minister of the Gospel, but differing from that denomination on account of their practice of close communion, he left it and became an Independent Congregationalist, which sect were sometimes stigmatized by the name of *New Lights*, a name which he and his brethren did not adopt.

About this time, several of the members of the First Congregational Church in Portsmouth, of which Samuel Langdon, D. D., was Pastor, being dissatisfied with the indifference of that Church to spiritual improvement, and the absence of that degree of vitality in a large proportion of the members of the Church, which should, in their judgment, have characterized them as disciples of Christ, together with some differences of opinion in respect to church discipline, induced them to secede from that church; and, being joined by other professing Christians in Portsmouth and from the neighboring towns, founded a new Church, called the "First Independent Congregationalist

Church in Portsmouth, N. H.," and invited Mr. Drown, who had seceded from the Calvin Baptist denomination, to take the pastoral charge of the Church; a place or house of worship being erected in Pitt, (now Court) street, on the site of the Unitarian Chapel, for their accommodation. The invitation was accepted, and he arrived at Portsmouth from Coventry, R. I. with his family, July 7, 1758, and continued the faithful and beloved pastor of this little flock, and by none was he respected and revered more than by the living members and succeeding Pastor of the North Church, from which, mainly, his church were seceders, until his decease, which occurred January 17, 1770, leaving a widow, who died September 12, 1784. They had ten children. The first four were born in Providence, R. I., the next three in Coventry, R. I., and the last three in Portsmouth, in the present Moses house on the east side of Vaughan street, opposite the Toppan mansion.

Mary,	born	August	20, 1744,	died	Angust	31. 1744.
William,	"	September	23, 1745,	"	December	22, 1747.
Sarah,	"	September	3, 1747,	"	May	23, 1820.
Samuel,	"	November	5, 1749,	"	August	7, 1815.
Peter,	"	January	10, 1752,	"	February	4, 1788.
Betsey,	"	November	9, 1755,	"	November	9, 1763.
Thomas,	"	April	27, 1757,	"	September	7, 1846.
Benjamin,	"	July	14, 1759,	"	December,	1793.
Mary,	"	July	19, 1762,	"		1824.
Joseph,	"	Oct.	9, 1769,	"		Nov. 13, 1827.

Peter Drown was killed by Elisha Thomas, for which he was executed at Dover in 1788.

Samuel Drown married Mary Pickering of Portsmouth, sister of Capt. Thomas Pickering, commander of the private armed 20-gun ship Hampden, and fell in battle with an English Letter of Marque, in March, 1779. The children of Samuel were three sons and four daughters. Thomas P., Daniel P., and Samuel. The latter died in 1797, at the age of 18. Lydia married Ebenezer Wyatt; Sarah married Capt. Mark Blunt; Elizabeth married Charles Treadwell. Daniel P., born in 1784, and Sarah, born in 1788.

Sometime in Mr. Drown's ministry here, Robert Sandeman came to Portsmouth and was admitted into Mr. Drown's pulpit. He preached therein several times, but did not fully develop his religious sentiments, (though the doctrines he preached were generally in accordance with those of Mr. Drown and his Church,) until he more fully announced them on the occasion of his preaching from Luke 2d: 28--32.

In opening his discourse, Mr. Sandeman said, some person read this passage in this manner—that he took the child in his *heart*, but my bible says he took him in his *arms*. Mr. Drown from this circumstance, discovered that Mr. Sandeman entertained the doctrine which afterwards distinguished him and his followers as a distinct religious sect. While Mr. Sandeman was making the concluding prayer, Mr. Drown selected from Watts' Hymns 13th, book 1st:

> "If love to God and love to man
> Be absent, all our hopes are vain;
> Nor tongues, nor gifts, nor fiery zeal
> The works of love can e'er fulfil."

When he had concluded his prayer, Mr. Drown rose to read the hymn, and as he was proceeding, Mr. Sandeman took his hat. Mr. Drown observing this, stepped to the pulpit door before Mr. Sandeman reached it, and held it to, so that he could not pass until he had concluded. Mr. Sandeman thus compelled to remain, repeatedly exclaim ed, "I hate the very breath of it." After Mr. Drown had concluded, he opened the pulpit door, saying, "Now, sir, you can go if you please."

The "New Lights" were held in poor repute by Gov. Wentworth, who issued a special notice granting all ministers permission to perform the marriage ceremony "except one Drown."

Since this Ramble was written, two aged members of the Drown family have departed this life, and both were buried on the same day. The young may die, but the old must. To Daniel P. Drown we are indebted for many interesting incidents of old times.

Next east of the Drown residence was that of Capt. Peter Coues; a few rods to the west, just after turning up Washington street, on the east side, was the residence of a son-in-law of Capt. Coues, Dr. Lyman Spalding, one of the most distinguished men of Portsmouth, as a theoretic and practical physician and surgeon, whose services did much in the advancement of medical science.

LYMAN SPALDING, an American physician and surgeon, was born in Cornish, N. H., June 5, 1775, and died in Portsmouth, N. H., October 30, 1821. He graduated at Harvard University, in 1797, and commenced the study of medicine. In 1798, while still a student, he assisted Professor Nathan Smith in establishing the Medical School at Dartmouth College, collected and prepared a chemical apparatus, delivered the first course of lectures at the opening of the institution, and published "A New Nomenclature of Chemistry, proposed by Messrs. DeMovau, Lavoisier, Berthollet and Fourcroy, with Additions and Improvements," (1799.) His medical studies were afterwards continued at the medical schools of Cambridge and Philadelphia, and he entered upon the practice of medicine at Portsmouth, N. H., in 1799. He devoted much attention to the study of the human structure, was a very skillful anatomist, and his admirable preparations, particularly of the lymphatics, are now in the cabinets of our first institutions. In 1812, the college of physicians and surgeons of the western district of the State of New York, at Fairfield, Herkimer County, was incorporated, Dr. Spalding being elected President and Professor of anatomy, and he made annual visits to this school. In 1813 he removed to the city of New York, and, a few years later, resigned his position at the college. With Dr. Spalding originated the plan for the formation of the "Pharmacopœia of the United States," by the authority of all the medical societies and medical schools in the Union. In January, 1817, he submitted the project to the New York county medical society; in February, 1818, it was adopted by the medical society of the State of New York and ordered to be carried into execution by their committee, Dr. Spalding being one of the number. All the medical schools and societies appointed delegates, who at once commenced their labors, and the first edition of the work was published in 1820. To keep pace with the advancement of medical science, a new edition is published every ten years. Dr. Spalding was a contributor to the "New England Journal of Medicine," the "New York Medical Repository," "Lenoureau Journal of Medicine," of Paris, and other medical and philosophical journals; and, beside several lectures and addresses, he published "Reflections on Fever, and particularly on the Inflammatory Character of Fever," (1817;) "Reflections on Yellow Fever Periods," (1819,) and "A History of the Introduction and use of Scutellaria Lateriflora as a Remedy for preventing and curing Hydrophobia," (1819.) Dr. Spalding was active in introducing into the United States the practice of vaccination as a preventive of the small pox. He was a trustee of the only free schools which New York then possessed, and aided in the establishment of the first Sunday schools in that city.

The above honorable mention of one of the citizens of Portsmouth, whose children are now among us, we find in the 14th volume of the New American Cyclopœdia.

Peter Coues, came to Portsmouth from the Island of Jersey in the English Channel, and in this town, Nov. 4th, 1735, married Mary, daughter of Emanuel Long. She was born at Plymouth, Mass., January 19th, 1713. He died at an advanced age about 1783, at the residence of his son Peter, who was born July 30th, 1736, and married Oct. 25th, 1768, Mary, and Oct. 12th, 1779, Elizabeth, daughters of Daniel Jackson; and also married Rebecca, daughter of John Elliott. Of his thirteen children all died in infancy, but Elizabeth, who married Lyman Spalding, M. D., Anne, unmarried, and Samuel Elliott Coues.

Among the venerable citizens of Portsmouth of half a century ago, we well remember Capt. Peter Coues, a gentleman of independent circumstances, who might be seen, with his cane under his arm on State street, or in the vicinity. His residence previous to the fire of 1813, was on the southwest corner of Atkinson and State streets, on the spot where W. J. Laighton's house now stands. In the old dwelling house was a store where for many years he kept ship chandlery, merchandise, groceries, &c. In early life Capt. Peter Coues was pressed into the British service. He was at one time sailing-master of the famous "Royal George," which was afterwards, in 1782, sunk in the British Channel with 800 men on board. He also served in the capacity of midshipman. After several years service in the British Navy he returned to Portsmouth before the American Revolution, where, by that urbanity of mind and simplicity of manners for which seafaring men of liberal views are generally distinguished, he obtained a good standing among his fellow citizens, and died on the 29th of Nov. 1818, at the advanced age of 83 years.

Samuel Elliott Coues, who died July 3, 1867, was the last survivor of the children. In early youth he was a lover of books, and received a good education preparatory to mercantile pursuits—but it was evident that his active mind was better fitted for some profession where his mental powers could be brought into full exercise in the literary world. He early took an active part in promoting those literary clubs and lyceums which have been so beneficial in times past. A ready and fluent debator and good lecturer, he was frequently called before the public, and interested his auditors. Radical in his ideas, he frequently ventured on ground where few were ready to follow him. He even called in question the truth of the Newtonian system of philosophy, and published a volume to prove the truth of his own peculiar theory. He enjoyed the confidence of his fellow citizens, and was for several years a Representative in the Legislature. Humanity was a principle of his nature, and in no better way did he ever display his philanthropy than in his active and successful efforts to establish the Asylum for the Insane in this State. He was a devoted advocate of peace principles, and some of his lectures on this subject were the best productions of his pen. On the death of William Ladd, Mr. Coues was elected President of the American Peace Society, which office he held for several years. As a member of the School committee he took deep interest in our public schools, and labored efficiently several years for their elevation.

In 1853, Mr. Coues received an appointment at Washington, connected with the Patent Office. His health failing, he returned to Portsmouth in 1866, to close his life, surrounded by the scenes of his early days. He might not always have been right in his philosophy—he might not always have been judicious in his business matters—but under the influence of a strong nervous temperament, his active mind had a keen perception of the beauties and mysteries of nature, and the ever pervading feeling of philanthrophy gave a living vivacity to his conversation, in which he ever exhibited a desire to make those around him happy.

RAMBLE CXXVIII.

Seizure of Arms and Powder at Fort William and Mary—The finale of Provincial Government in New-Hampshire.

THE seizure of arms and powder at Fort William and Mary, (now Fort Constitution) in Portsmouth harbor, was the first capture made by the Americans in the war of the Revolution. We give the following extracts of letters of Gov. John Wentworth, communicated to the New England Historical and Genealogical Register of July, 1869, by Hon. John Wentworth of Chicago.

In a letter to the Earl of Dartmouth, dated "Portsmouth, 20th Dec. 1774," Gov. Wentworth says:

"On Tuesday, the 13th instant in the afternoon, one Paul Revere arrived express with letters from some of the leaders in Boston to Mr. Samuel Cutts, merchant of this town. Reports were soon circulated that the Fort at Rhode Island had been dismantled, and the Gunpowder and other military stores removed up to Providence, and an Extract of the circular letter directing the seizure of gunpowder was printed in a Boston Newspaper of the 12th in consequence, as I have been informed, of the said letters having been communicated to the House of Assembly at Rhode Island. And it was also falsely given out that Troops were embarking at Boston to come and take possession of William and Mary Castle in this Harbour. These rumors soon raised an alarm in the town; and, although I did not expect that the people would be so audacious as to make any attack on the castle, yet I sent orders to the captain at the Fort to be upon his guard.

On Wednesday, the 14th, about 12 o'clock, news was brought to me that a Drum was beating about the town to collect the Populace together in order to go and take away the Gunpowder and dismantle the Fort. I immediately sent the Chief Justice of the Province to warn them from engaging in such an attempt. He went to them, where they were collected in the centre of the town, near the town-house, explained to them the nature of the offence they proposed to commit, told them it was not short of Rebellion, and intreated them to desist from it and disperse. But all to no purpose. They went to the Island; and, being joined there by the inhabitants of the towns of Newcastle and Rye, formed in all a body of about four hundred men, and the Castle being in too weak a condition for defence, (as I have in former letters explained to your Lordship,) they forced their entrance, in spite of Captain Cochrane, who defended it as long as he could; but, having only the assistance of five men, their numbers overpowered him. After they entered the Fort, they seized upon the Captain, triumphantly gave three Huzzas, and hauled down the King's colours. They then put the captain and men under confinement, broke open the Gunpowder magazine, and carried off about 100 Barrels of Gunpowder, but discharged the Captain and men from their confinement before their departure.

On Thursday, the 15th, in the morning, a Party of men came from the country accompanied by Mr. [Gen. John] Sullivan, one of the New-Hampshire Delegates to the Congress, to take away the Cannon from the Fort also. Mr. Sullivan declared that he had taken pains to prevail upon them to return home again; and said, as there was no certain intelligence of troops being coming to take possession of the Castle, he would still use his utmost endeavours to disperse them.

While the town was thus full of men, a committee from them came to me to solicit for pardon or a suspension of prosecution against the persons who took away the Gunpowder. I told them I could not promise them any such thing; but, if they dispersed and restored the Gunpowder, which I earnestly exhorted them to do, I said I hoped His Majesty may be thereby induced to consider it an allevi. ation of the offence. They parted from me, in all appearance, perfectly disposed to follow the advice I had given them; and having proceeded directly to the rest of their associates, they all publickly voted, about five o'clock in the afternoon, near the Town House, to return home; which it was thought they would have done, and it also was further expected that the gunpowder would have been restored by the morning.

But the people, instead of dispersing, went to the Castle in the night, headed by Mr. Sullivan, and took away sixteen pieces of cannon, about sixty muskets and other military stores, and brought them to the out Borders of the town.

On Friday morning, the 16th, Mr. Folsom,* the other delegate, came to town that morning, with a great number of armed men, who remained in Town as a guard till the flow of the tide in the evening when the cannon were sent in Gondolas up the River into the country, and they all dispersed without having done any personal injury to any body in the town.

They threatened to return again in order to dismantle the fort entirely, and to carry off or destroy the remaining heavy cannon, (about seventy pieces, and also to seize upon the Province Treasury, all of which there was reasonable ground to fear they would do, after what they had already done; but, on the Gunpowder's being taken away, I wrote to General Gage and Admiral Graves for assistance to restrain the boisterous temper of the people; upon which the Admiral ordered the armed ships Canceaux and Scarborough here, and they arrived (the former the 17th and the latter on the 19th) in time to prevent the further dismantling of the fort."

*Nathaniel.

Further on, Gov. Wentworth says the government has no power to bring the offenders to punishment.

No jail would hold them long and no jury would find them guilty; for, by the false alarm that has been raised throughout the country, it is considered by the weak and ignorant, who have the rule in these times, an act of self-preservation.

Again he says:

I tried to dissuade them by the civil authority, sheriff, magistrate, &c., and did all I could to get the militia raised, but to no purpose.

He had assembled the Council at the beginning of the tumult, but it was of no avail. In his letter to Lord Dartmouth, dated 28th December, 1774, he says:

It is with the greatest concern I perceive the unlimited influence that the popular leaders in Boston obtain in this Province, especially since the outrage of the 14th instant. Insomuch, that I think the people here are disposed to attempt any measure required by those few men; and, in consequence thereof, are arming and exercising men as if for an immediate war.

In a letter to George Irving, Esq, dated Portsmouth, 5 January, 1775, referring to the 14th December, when the Castle was seized, he says:

The powers of magistracy have been faithfully and repeatedly tried. Governor, Council, Chief Justice, Sheriff and Justices of the Peace personally appeared; Proclamation made according to law for all to desist and disperse; the militia ordered out; drums beat, &c.; yet all to no avail. Not one appeared to assist in executing the law. And it was impossible for me, with four councillors, two Justices, one sheriff, Mr. MacDonough and Mr. Benning* Wentworth, to subdue such multitudes, for not one other man would come forth. Not even the Revenue officers. All chose to shrink in safety from the storm and suffered

*This Benning Wentworth was son of Samuel and Elizabeth (Deering) Wentworth, a brother to Gov. John Wentworth's wife. He was born at Boston 16th March, 1757, graduated at Oxford, England, and died at Halifax, 18 Feb. 1808, whilst secretary to Gov. Wentworth. He has no descendants living in the male line.

me to remain exposed to the folly and madness of an enraged multitude, daily and hourly increasing in numbers and delusion.

He says Captain Cochran and his five men defended

A ruinous Castle with the walls in many places down, at length knocked down, their arms broken and taken from them by above one hundred to one, the Captain was confined and at last would not nor did not give up the keys notwithstanding every menace they could invent; finally they broke the doors with axes and crowbars.

In a letter to General Gage, dated "Fort William and Mary, 15 June 1775," he says—

—— The ferment in this province has become very general, and the government hath been very much agitated and disturbed since the affair of the 19th of April last. Two thousand men are already enlisted, two-thirds of whom I am informed are destined to join the insurgents in your province, and the remainder are to be stationed along the coast in different parts between Portsmouth and Newbury.

The spirit of outrage runs so high that on Tuesday last my house was beset by great bodies of armed men who proceeded to such a length of violence as to bring a cannon directly before my house, and point it at my door, threatening fire and destruction unless Mr. Fenton, (a member of the assembly then sitting,) who happened to call upon me, and against whom they had taken up such resentment as occasioned him some days before to retire on board the man-of-war in the Harbour out of their way, should instantly deliver himself up to them, and notwithstanding every effort to procure effectual assistance to disperse the multitude, Mr. Fenton was obliged to surrender himself and they have carried him to Exeter about fifteen miles from Portsmouth where he is, as I am informed, kept in confinement.

Seeing every idea of the respect due to his Majesty's Commission so far lost in the frantic rage and fury of the people as to find them to proceed to such daring violence against the Person of his Representative, I found myself under the necessity of immediately withdrawing to Fort William and Mary, both to prevent as much as may be a

Repetition of the like insults and to provide for my own security.

I think it exceedingly for the king's service to remain as long as possible at the Fort, where I now am with my Family in a small incommodious House without any other prospect of safety, if the prevailing madness of the people should follow me hither, than the hope of retreating on board his Majesty's ship Scarborough, if it should be in my power. This fort, although containing upwards of sixty pieces Cannon, is without men or ammunition.

In a letter to Paul Wentworth,* dated at Fort William and Mary 29 June, 1775, he says:

Admiral Graves has sent a transport under convoy of the Falcon, sloop-of-war, and entirely dismantled this ungarrisoned Castle of all the ordinance, stores, &c.

Besides the inconvenience of being crowded into this miserable house, confined for room and neither wind or water tight, I am inevitably obliged to incur some extra expense for my safety and existence even here. Being of necessity compelled to make some small repairs to render it habitable and to employ six men as watches to prevent my being surprised and made prisoner. These, with my three servants, and Mr. Benning Wentworth, and Captain Cochran are divided into three guards of four hours each; by which means I have some security of getting on board the Scarborough. The six men are at the expence of Twelve dollars per month each, including their dieting, allowance of Rum, &c.; under which expence no trusty man can possibly be had for so unpopular a service in this time of general opposition to Government. The repairs will not exceed fifty guineas.

In a letter to Lord Dartmouth, dated at Fort William and Mary, 17 July, 1775, he says: "From five to eight men have been usually kept in this Fort in time of Peace."

The latest letters dating from Fort William and Mary are those addressed, 17 August, 1775, to Hon. Theo. Atkin-

* This Paul Wentworth was a native of one of the West India Islands; but had passed sometime at Portsmouth, N. H. He was agent for the Province of New Hampshire at London, and had been appointed a councillor whilst at London, but had not returned to be sworn in when the revolution broke out. Dartmouth conferred the degree of L. L. D. upon him in 1789. He died at Surinam in December, 1793.

son, of Portsmouth N. H ; and 18 August, 1775, to the Earl Dartmouth, London.

In Sept. 1775, from the Isle of Shoals, he dates his last official paper in New-Hampshire, proroguing the General Assembly, which was to meet that month, to the next April.

RAMBLE CXXIX.

The Navy Yard.

Our Navy Yard is now so completely a work of art, that it has almost gone out of mind as a work of nature; the days of its youth are forgotten, or remembered only by a few, and those few not sufficiently interested to snatch from oblivion the record of those early days.

The Navy Yard Island, containing about sixty acres, formerly called Fernald's Island, was up to the present century used for farming and drying fish, and had but one house upon it. In 1806 it was purchased by the United States of Capt. William Dennett, for $5,500, for the establishment of a Navy Yard. A lady who has recollections of the island in past years, has kindly aided us in a Ramble, by the following interesting sketch of her recollections.

My recollections of it date from the early years of its establishment as a naval post, when most of it was still in a wild state; and we, children, could gather wild strawberries and black berries, bouquets of violets and white everlasting, and branches of the glossy-leaved, fragrant bayberry, on every hill and in every hollow. But years have brought strange changes! Now it has become almost a regular fortification; not a furlong of its natural shore, or a rod of its original surface, is to be found.

Years ago destiny removed me from the spot—but I still

cling to it. Occasionally, of a summer, I go, for a day, to look with bodily eyes upon that "greenest spot in memory's waste;" but it is like visiting the grave of one long dead, whose quiet resting place it is hard to find. Busy, ambitious life starts out upon me from all the old quiet places where once we could dream for hours undisturbed; the fine brick quarters of the officers stand where once was "our wild strawberry patch;" the "old house" on the hill, as we ascended from where the landing now is, containing two tenements under one roof, (and occupied, as necessity required, by the lieutenant, surgeon, sailing master, or naval storekeeper,) has disappeared, and the hill along with it, from the surface of the earth. It stood about where the steps now descend the declivity in the basin of which is the Dry Dock; and just beyond the house, on the summit of the hill, was a flag-staff within a hexagon or octagon shaped enclosure, built of timber, with embrasures for cannon in time of need, though no cannon were in it then.

Behind the *old* ship house, (which for half a century sheltered the well seasoned Alabama,) just on the water's edge, were two small, white-washed, one-story houses, honored with the name of barracks, and occupied by a sergeant and a small detachment of marines. And between these barracks and the blacksmith's shop was an old yellow, two-storied, frame house, used as the sailor's lodge: the spot now occupied by the *brick* lodge being then a grassy hollow, containing a solitary well, where occasionally the marines came to wash and spread out their linen to dry.

But all this is with the past, and now I look around and feel bewildered by the change that has taken place. The old elm in the enclosure around the Commodore's house is the only object that looks familiar—the only old land mark remaining unchanged—the original proprietor of the soil, whose claims are better *grounded* and of earlier date than

Uncle Sam's. The house itself is an old land mark, but it has been frequently altered and repaired, till it can hardly be called the same. The most striking feature of its *interior* used to be the paper on the walls of the two front rooms. That on the eastern room, represented a mingling of smoke and carnage on a field of battle—soldiers in scarlet and blue uniforms, wounded and dead, prostrate upon the ground or borne upon litters, falling from their horses or trampled under foot by them. These figures were a foot in length, and the horses were the size of cats. I never felt happy in that room—in turning the eyes from one scene of horror they fell upon another; but in the western room it was different. There the walls were covered with a series of sketches from Italian scenery, (with trees the height of the room,) representing ladies, accompanied by gaily dressed cavaliers, stepping from marble palaces into waiting gondolas, or leaning over richly decorated balconies; public marts, where were collected groups in all the gay costumes of the Levant; marble fountains, from which handsome peasant girls were bearing away pitchers and jars of water; and lazy looking men, lounging among grass-grown ruins, playing upon musical instruments; while a group of both sexes were dancing. We never tired of looking at these scenes, and never thought whether there was furniture in the room or not. Such paper must have been designed as a substitute for furniture.

The house now used as a hospital is an old landmark, but is too shabby to be recognized as an acquaintance by those who knew it in better days, with its well kept though not handsome exterior, its highly cultivated garden sloping to the very water's edge, and when comfort and profuse hospitality reigned within. Like many a *human* being, it has fallen, after a long and useful life, into a shabby and neglected old age.

In those days we had no bridges connecting us with

Jenkins' (now Bridge's) Island to the south and the main land to the north, and making the Yard a highway for the multitude. We were a little world to ourselves, and daily sent our greeting to the neighboring town and islands through the mouth of our sun-set gun. This greeting is no longer necessary, because the bridges have made the Navy Yard a sort of continuation of Portsmouth and Kittery, which is doubtless a great advantage to all; but I have less sympathy with its present diffusive and elaborate state, than with its former simplicity and isolation.

The portion of the island now occupied by the marine barrack and parade ground was then a tolerably high hill, rising abruptly from the shore on the south-eastern side, and terminated on the top by the powder house, built of rough stones, white-washed, and with a conical roof. On this hill we played, in sun and rain, summer after summer; on this hill we used to kill quantities of snakes, trying to make it rain (as we had been told we could); to the top of this hill we ran to get a view of the neighboring main land, with its two little straggling villages of Kittery Point and Foreside. But suddenly there came an order from Government to to build a new barrack, and this hill was selected for the site. The powder-house was to be removed, and one half of the elevation to be levelled for a parade ground. I was not sorry to have the powder-house taken away, for it was the cause of some of the most cheerless days of my childhood, those days when early after breakfast came an order from the commandant "to put all fires out," because powder was to be removed, and all the houses which it was to pass must be fireless, lest a chance spark (almost an impossibility) should fall among the kegs or canisters as they were carted by. And there we sat shivering, wrapped in cloaks and shawls, (in mid-winter,) until such time as the transportation was over, and we could renew the fires, doff out-of-door garments, and make an evening of unusual glow and warmth compensate for a day of gloom and chill. I was glad to have the recurrence of these days put an end to, but I was sorry to have the hill, our favorite play-ground, taken from us. And now I watched each day the movements of the prisoner soldiers as they worked at the levelling of the parade ground, with a long iron chain fastened to their waist, to which was attached a heavy iron ball, which they had to lift and carry wherever they went and whichever way they turned. This was the punishment, then, for all attempts at deserting. They seemed cheerful enough, laughing and talking among themselves; but I could not help pitying them, as I watched them through a whole summer, working with shovel, pick axe and wheelbarrow, in the hot sun, with that ball and chain, and I freely forgave them for digging up and wheeling off the soil which had been a little world to us.

RAMBLE CXXX.

Capt. Daniel Fernald — Residence — Ownership of the Navy Yard — War Adventures — Diddling the Spencer 74 — Putting a British Frigate on the rocks.

A FEW rods west of the South Ward Room, on the corner of Manning and Howard streets, stands an old gambrel-roofed house, which numbers almost as many years as the old Church itself which was removed from the spot in 1865. It was in a central part of the town when it was built, and the elevated position it then occupied must have made it a desirable residence. It was built by Capt. Samuel Frost, who died before the recollection of the late occupant, the venerable Capt. DANIEL FERNALD, the oldest person in Portsmouth at the time of his death, which occurred March 7, 1866, at the age of 98 years 3 1-2 months.

About the time of the close of the Revolution the house was owned by Capt. Nichols, a merchant, brother of Nathan Nichols who occupied the Gardner house, and of Ichabod, who at the same time occupied the Buckminister house. Nathan and family occupied the southern half of this house, and his mother and a maiden sister occupied the end on Howard street. Rev. Dr. Nichols of Portland was a son of Nathan.

In 1788, Capt. Daniel Fernald married a daughter of Samuel Nichols, and became an occupant of this house, half of which he purchased, and the other half became his wife's by inheritance.

We called on the old gentleman a few years before his death. He was feeble, and his hearing somewhat impaired, but he was as warm-hearted, and his recollection of early events as good as ever. The events of the day he was also able to keep in mind: for he told us he had attended church a few weeks previous and listened to his good pastor, Dr. Peabody. To the inquiry what did he preach about? he readily responded, "about Mary and Martha, and the one thing needful. I could not hear all he said, but was able to spell out much of it." How few church attendants there are who are able to repeat a text a fortnight after listening to a sermon.

He showed us his old long lost family record, which had recently been found, written on the leaf of an old bible, and wafered to the cover. By it we learn that his father was George Fernald, who was born on the Island now the Navy Yard, in 1724, and was married in 1764 to Anna Leach, born in 1744. He was a regular descendant of Dr. Reginald Fernald, who was one of the first emigrants to New Hampshire.

The island was a family inheritance, and would now be

the property of Capt. Daniel Fernald, had not the right of primogeniture been abolished by the laws of Maine. The old gentleman informed us that at the time the United States purchased the island, in 1806, (when it was purchased of Capt. Wm. Dennett for $5,500,) lawyer Mason searched the records ta Alfred, Maine, for the title. He found by the records that the island was to descend to the oldest male heir from generation to generation, "so long as the grass grows and the waters run." Had not the laws of Maine annulled all entailments, Mr. Mason said he could put Capt. Fernald in possession of the island at the time for not more than ten dollars expense. He looks with some interest yet upon the yard, for one of those great ship houses is erected over the grave of his father and family. Dr. Reginald Fernald, the original proprietor, says he was buried near the Brown place, on the main land near the Navy Yard.

When a young man, Capt. Daniel Fernald participated in the Revolutionary War, and also in the war of 1812. He was ever a kind-hearted, humble man, and was treated with respect by every one. In the war of 1812 he was in command of the schooner Sally, a coaster, and might sometimes take a freight to Boston, and at others down east. It was in the dangerous days of that War, when the British men-of-war were off our coast, and sometimes in sight from the land, that Capt. Fernald took on board at Portland two 24-pound cannons needed at our Navy Yard, and 13,000 lbs. of powder, [130 kegs of 100 lbs.]—100 boarding pikes and cutlasses. The guns were placed in the keelson, and the kegs of powder around them. He then heaped spruce wood around them, and piled some cords on deck over the hatchways. With a speed far inferior to steam he left Portland for our harbor. Off Saco he was becalmed. The British 74 Spencer hove in sight. A tender commanded by a lieutenant was soon sent alongside. After inquiring, "Where from?"—Portland. "Where bound?"—Portsmouth. "What is your cargo?"—Firewood—the Lieutenant not satisfied, ordered his men to remove the wood from the hatch, and see what was in the hold. They worked until tired, and when within one tier of the guns left the job, reporting that there was nothing but wood on deck and in the hold; and as the Captain appeared so inoffensive, the lieutenant, whose name was Robert Lashley, concluded to let the Sally pass.

The sailors were in favor of making her a prize. Why, said the lieutenant it would cost just as much to condemn this poor man's wood craft as it would a large ship, and your prize money would not amount to a penny apiece. So saying they gave him up his papers, told him the way they had piled his wood was too heavy for the bows, and he had better right it, and left the Sally "a bone prize for John Bull," said Capt. Fernald, "if he had but known it."

The interview was seen, and news reached Commodore Hull at the Portsmouth Navy Yard that the vessel was captured by the Spencer, and the guns and powder were of course supposed to have "gone off." But ere long the Sally, slow and sure, appeared below, and the surprised Commodore speedily sent down his boats to tow her up to the Navy Yard, where, after the other wood was removed, the "*big logs*," and "*kindlings*" were rolled out. The Captain tells of this escape with much satisfaction.

On another occasion, when preparations were making for building the Washington 74 at our Navy Yard, Captain Fernald was sent to Portland for a load of timber, &c. He took on board 48 knees and the breast hook of the 74, the knees hanging over the sides of the vessel. He pursued his course as near shore as practicable, being well acquainted with the whole coast. He was discovered, however, by the British frigate Tenados, and seeing his cargo, determined to make the Sally a prize. They were approaching Wood Island, and Captain Fernald took his course so near shore that his men cautioned him that he was among the kelp. No matter, says the Captain, throw over a few of the knees, and we will bring all up right directly. Four of the knees were thrown over, and on the Sally sailed between the rocks, while all of a sudden the frigate was resting upon them, and became a fixture! The exasperated Commodore ordered two 18-pounders to be discharged, to blow the Sally to pieces. The balls however did not hit, but one of them struck upon the rocks on shore, and after he made himself safe, Captain Fernald went on shore and found it. The frigate laid on the rocks until the rising of the tide enabled her to back off, leaving the Sally the victor. When the Sally came in, Commodore Hull inquired whether she had been fired upon. Capt. Fernald replied in the affirmative, presenting the 18-pound ball to the Commodore as a *token*.

Commodore Hull replied, " You are a good fellow, you stand fire well—go up to the Yard and we will unload you." Some years after the peace, Capt. Fernald fell in with a British tar, who was on board the frigate at the time. He said the Tenados was so much injured on our coast that she leaked badly, and was compelled to return immediately to Halifax and re-copper.

Other of the old gentleman's recollections have been given in previous Rambles.

RAMBLE CXXXI.

Shapley's Island — Small Pox Parties — Incidents and Pastimes.

Before the introduction of vaccination for the kine pox, which was not discovered until just before the close of the last century, all who wished to be secure from taking the small pox in the natural way, were vaccinated for it, and withdrew for three or four weeks from intercourse with the world. We have before us a letter in the hand-writing of Doctor Hall Jackson, dated at the Essex Hospital, Dec. 17, 1773, at which time he was a small pox patient. It was on his return that arrangements were made for "a general inocculation in Portsmouth." From that time up to 1797, Shapleigh's Island, in this harbor, was used as the "Pest Island," and every few years parties went there to have the small pox.

These small-pox parties were frequently made social gatherings—there were more who spent a summer month in this way than at the watering places; they had one advantage over the latter amusement, for as they could but once be of such a party, it remained a *novelty* through life.

We have before us a letter from Joseph Barrell, a merchant of Boston, dated July 8, 1776, addressed to Col. Joshua Wentworth, of Portsmouth, in which is this postscript:—

"Mr Storer has invited Mrs. Martin to take the small pox at his house: if Mrs Wentworth desires to get rid of her fears in the same way, we will accommodate her in the best way we can. I've several friends that I've invited, and none of them will be more welcome han Mrs. W."

What a subject for so courteous an invitation! We will adopt for this Ramble the following interesting communication from Mr. Bowles on this subject.

There is a passage in the history of Portsmouth, at the close of the last century, to which I have never seen any allusion in print, that is, I think, worth preservation from being entirely forgotten; at least so far as it may be done in the columns of a newspaper. I refer to the time when in the months of May and June, 1797, the young ladies and young gentlemen went to Shapleigh's Island to receive vaccination for the small-pox. There are but few living, who, from personal recollection can recall the event, but others, of a later generation, still retain much that was related to them in former years, by those who were participants in it.

That little green isle in the Piscataqua, whose still life, at the present day, is disturbed only by its few inhabitants, and the travel to and from Newcastle was for the time a scene of great animation. The flower of the youth and beauty of Portsmouth were congregated there, and as nothing more unpleasant was experienced than the ordinary results from vaccination, a majority of them were perfectly well, and remembered the affair as little else than a holiday festival of the gayest description.

A gentleman of Portsmouth, still in the full vigor of life, with whom I conversed recently upon the subject, recollects the pleasure he enjoyed in watching their sports, by the aid of a spy-glass from the roof of his father's residence in Buck (now State) street. One of the party then in her 17th year, often said to me, in her maturer years, that those were among the very happiest days of her whole life. There was about an equal proportion of both sexes, and as most of them had arrived at an age to understand that order of animal magnetism referred to in Genesis XXIX. : 20, the little knight of the bow and arrows, with the benevolent idea, doubtless, of giving them something to occupy their time during a season of so much leisure, made himself particularly busy among them. A greater amount of that species of amusement known as "love-making," was, probably, never concentrated within a briefer space or more limited period. While some of it lasted out a lifetime, the larger proportion, tradition says, was of the ephemeral kind that some crusty bachelor, who probably never knew anything from experience of "the tender passion," has termed "puppy-love," and did not long survive the change from sea-air to the atmosphere of *the metropolis;* still, it was a very harmless pastime, and furnished a theme for many a pleasant thought and enlivening chat in after years.

The following reminiscences, that have survived through

a period of more than three score years, will give some idea of a season that left so agreeable an impression of itself upon the young of a past generation.

Among the evening enjoyments, candy-parties were highly popular; occurring, by turns, at the different dwellings where the patients were quartered. A ludicrous affair happened at one of these saccharine gatherings, that was long remembered. A fresh supply of molasses had been procured from town, which unfortunately proved of an obstinate quality, still to be found, that cannot be induced to boil into candy. It came off the fire but little thicker than it went on, and was turned into a gallon punch bowl, which it nearly filled, and placed upon a bench in the yard to cool. A brother of the young lady who placed it there, by way of a joke removed it a short distance to a position directly under the eaves of a shed, where it had remained scarcely a minute, being still in a liquid state, when the family cat, returning from an evening walk, leaped head foremost into the bowl, and the next instant came bounding into the house, presenting a spectacle at which even the most tender-hearted, who sympathized with her in the misfortune that had befallen her, could not help laughing. A benevolent young lady (who retained a soft spot in the heart for the unfortunate through a life-time of nearly fifty years,) procured some warm soap-suds and attempted to relieve her from so uncomfortable a predicament; but pussy preferred to be her own laundress, and had ample employment for a week or two thereafter, in efforts to restore her sable garment to its pristine sleek and glossy appearance.

"Dutch-dolls," then much in vogue, formed another of their pastimes. With the exception of its occasional revival among the Christmas festivities, of families who love to keep up the ancient customs, this grotesque invention of a past age is now but seldom seen. It was of

English origin, in the younger days of the Prince of Wales and his friend Beau Brummel, and its name evidently emanated from the ever-existent propensity of the English race to caricature their Teutonic brethren. As it is possible there may be some who were never favored with an introduction to a "Dutch-Doll," a few words of explanation as to their construction may not be amiss. A round splint broom, or something equally convenient for the purpose, was enveloped in a dress, with a mask for the face, a wig, and surmounted by a bonnet or cap. This was elevated in the hands of a person who was partially concealed beneath the skirts of the dress, and wholly so by a sheet or second dress below it. The ordinary height of these gigantic "dolls" was eight to ten feet. Any one who will fancy the surprise it would give them to have their slumbers disturbed at midnight, or in the small hours of the morning, and discover by the moonlight, such an object looking into the window of their second-story sleeping-room, can form an idea of what some of the young ladies experienced during their sojourn on the island. The young gentlemen all acknowledged to have *seen* "Dolly" during her nocturnal ramble, but the particular individual who to "all of which I saw," might have added, "and *part of which I was*," could not be found.

On a beautiful evening in June, as a party of six were enjoying a leisurely stroll along the shore, a small island in the distance had so much the aspect, in the brilliant moonlight, of fairy-land, a wish was expressed to visit it, and the means for its accomplishment soon presented itself, though, as the result will show, it proved a somewhat dangerous one. While pursuing their walk, a few yards farther on, they found a small boat lying high and dry upon the shore, and without taking into consideration the possibility that it might not prove an entirely seaworthy conveyance, they launched it into the water, and, with pieces of board selected from drift-wood on the beach, to serve as paddles started on their voyage. It was soon learned that their bark was by no means water-tight, for a little cascade was visible at every seam, and while two of the young gentlemen were engaged in propelling it, the third found full employment in keeping it free of water. They reached their destination in safety, and, after exploring the little islet without meeting a Selkirk or a Fernandez, but instead thereof plenty of bushes that gave promise of future whortleberries, they gathered a few memorials of their visit from the sand, and started on their return. The precaution had been taken to haul their boat upon a ledge of rocks, fearing it might take in, during their absence, an inconvenient supply of the briny element; and in the process of setting it again afloat, some hard knocks were experienced, which, unlike Mr. Weller's watch, did not have a tendency to improve it, for it leaked worse than ever; how many "strokes an hour," as the logbook is not at hand to determine, cannot be stated with nautical precision, but the young gentleman who took his turn at bailing found it harder work than he had fancied, and soon after leaving the island met with a mishap that placed the adventurous navigators in a situation on the shady side of comfort. The article used for throwing out the water was a broken pitcher, found in the boat, which an unlucky blow against the gunwale shivered to atoms, and left them without anything that would answer as a substitute. The tide was, besides, against them, and their progress necessarily slow; fortunately, however, they reached in safety the starting point, but not until the water was a foot deep in their craft. The adventure being a contraband affair, entirely against the rules and regulations, their mysterious absence, during which search was made for them, remained unexplained until after they had returned to town.

The last of these reminiscences for which space remains,

relates exclusively to the young geutlemen. As the sea air, by which they were surrounded, naturally sharpened their appetites, the hospital diet, prescribed by Doctors Cutter and Jackson, was to them a sore trial. •The supplies of pastry, etc., sent from town, might do very well for the girls, but they wanted something more substantial. The children of Israel in the wilderness did not hunger more for the flesh-pots of Egypt, than they for the roast beef and similar viands of Portsmouth. Pierce's Island could be reached then as now, at low water, by land, and thither by way of variety, they often resorted. One afternoon, when about a dozen had assembled there, a Spring Market fisherman, just returned from a successful trip to the ocean, recognizing among them the sons of some of his customers, came along side of the island to have a chat. The tempting display of the finny tribe that his boat presented, suggested thoughts of *chowder*, and it was proposed, although all amateur cooking was strictly prohibited, to get one up on their own account. As a preliminary step, a fine cod was procured from the fisherman's stock, and hid beneath a pile of rocks in their place of retreat; and before they slept, a pot, and and all the other requisites for chowder making, found their way to the same locality. At a specified hour the next forenoon, they assembled at the rendezvous, and set about putting their project into execution; each one having his allotted task to perform. The result was a complete success; such a chowder, it was the unanimous opinion, had never before been seen on the Piscataqua. Each was provided with one of those mammoth clam shells everywhere found on the Eastern coast, with a smaller one to serve as a substitute for a spoon, and, all unconcious of the surprise that awaited them, they had assembled around the pot to do justice to its contents; when a sound saluted their ears as if some one one was feeling his way with a stick over the rocks, on the other side of the high bank behind which they were sheltered from observation, and a moment later a glimpse was had of a cocked hat, and Dr. Jackson was looking down upon them! The rogues had been betrayed by the smoke seen rising from their place of concealment, which combined with the continued absence of so many of them, led to their detection. How the doctor took the matter, history does not say; but we will imagine that he adopted the most sensible course he could have chosen, and after a gentle reprimand, good naturedly accepted an invitation to partake of a compound, that no one better than himself, doubtless, knew how to appreciate.

The old Shapley mansion, from its capacious dimensions, presented the greatest array of inmates, for whom it ever had the happiest recollections. Its walls re-echoed to many a scene of merriment in after years

> "Recalled 'mid memories of their far-off youth,
> Of sorrows past, and joys of long ago."

The island was re-awakened into life some thirty years subsequently, when the bridges had been built, by the opening for a time of the Shapley homestead as a public house, and the conversion of the large warehouse, still standing at the waterside, into a bowling alley. On the afternoon of a fast-day occurring during that period, a large representation of the youth of Portsmouth, of the male gender, were again assembled there, and the amount of the once popular fast-day beverage, "egg-nogg," consumed on the occasion between intervals of base-ball playing, would have aroused the sympathies of that excellent man and unwavering friend of temperance, the late Father Matthew, of whom some wag has related that he proposed "administering the pledge" to the money market when he heard it was "tight." The ancient edifice has since disappeared, and not a trace now remains upon the spot to show that it once had an existence.

RAMBLE CXXXII.

The Old Spring Market—The Neptune and River Nymphs of the Piscataqua.

IN 1761, the town built a Market house on Spring Hill. The site was that now occupied by Mr. Blaisdell's store, No. 2 in Merchants' Row, next to the south store.

On the south side of the Market was a pump in a well, and a dipper attached. Between thirty and forty years after, when the block of brick stores was erected on the spot, the Market was removed to the wharf east, its present site. In digging for the basement story of the southern store, the well was brought above ground, and a log was then laid to the boat-landing under the market, through which pure water has continued to flow in an uninterrupted stream to the present day.

What a host of recollections cluster around that old site, and how grateful the remembrance of that old awning like shell, which used to be open on three sides,—that map of business life which fifty years ago and up to a later date gave a town attraction to the old Spring Market. About fifty years ago, an attic was built over what had been a simple board awning, and the Market was extended perhaps twenty feet on the east over the water, to give better accommodations for the sale of fish. And twenty years since the progress of the age seemed to require a new market house, so the old one was sold and removed to Noble's Island, where in front of the Noble house it still stands in all its ungraceful proportions. It was a great mistake to change the form of the old free market; where every one who had anything to sell could find a location, and any one who was desirous of purchasing could obtain supplies from *first* hands. The present arrangement of the building for fish dealers has driven the market women from their old favorite location—and the paltry sum received by the city for the rent of stalls, is lost ten times over by the prices which individuals by monopoly have the chance of obtaining.

One day several years ago on a solitary seat in the centre of the Spring Market, with fish rooms on the water side and the butchers' stalls on the other, sat two of the old market women of fifty years ago. Spread around them were their baskets of beans, peas, berries, cucumbers, &c. as of yore—but as their old companions in trade had ceased to appear so had also their old customers—and we stood alone before them, the sole inquirer for a peck of peas. "Well, Mrs. Flanders, you have been a long while here." "Yes, I am now eight-four, and I've traded here since the war times of 1812." "Well, this young lady at your side is Mrs. Furbish, I think."—"Oh, yes, she is only seventy-four. Our old associate Mrs. Carter, now nine-two, is at her home, as sprightly as either of us."

Mrs. Flanders and another female had come down from Eliot that morning in their boat, through the bridge, in the style of former years,—all but the substitution of a modern wherry for the old style canoe. They conducted their craft in seaman-like manner, and landed their cargo in good order. Their boat was then the only one which was plied by females to the old market landing.

Fifty years ago, the canoe was the boat used almost exclusively by our market folks on the river. On a Saturday morning in summer, as well as on other days, might be seen what was called the Kittery fleet, consisting of some twenty canoes, deeply laden with provisions of all kinds, mostly rowed by women, coming down the river, or up, as the tide served. These canoes were handsomely brought in to the stairs near where the spring was pouring out its unceasing libation into the river. As the boat-rings became occupied, the painters of the last canoes which arrived were fastened to the other boats, and over a bridge of canoes, the intrepid boat women bore their baskets and boxes to the landing—and to the seats they were to occupy under the canopy of the old market roof. This movement was not easily done in silence. The upsetting of a basket by the careening of a boat, or a slip on the wet stairs as the heavy loads were borne over them, would call forth many a loud exclamation. In our earliest recollection, there was one master spirit in that company, whose voice was law, and whose decision must be respected, or fearful would be the consequences. HANNAH MARINER was called "the commander of the fleet on the Kittery station." Our good old master Turell came near receiving a flogging from her once for giving her this respectable title. She was the regulator of the position of the market occupants, and from her decision there was no appeal. One day a man at the market did not speak respectfully, as she thought, so seizing a whip from the hands of a truckman, she administered blows with no sparing hand. The man fled, and Hannah, with whip in hand, fire in her eye, cursing on her tongue, pursued up spring hill, lashing him as he went. Hannah was of a noble as well as an independent spirit. She was the saleswoman of the products of the Rev. Mr. Chandler's garden—and of course as she did so much towards the support of the ministry in Eliot, she felt a right to sustain her position elsewhere. There was Mrs. Wherren, who kept her knitting always by her, and Mrs. James, and Mrs. Gould, and Mrs. Tripyear, and Mrs. Remick,—but to give the names of the market women of that day would be a record of the mothers of many of the enterprising men and thrifty housewives of the present day, located on both sides of the river. It was before the times when the girls found employment in factories—and when they aided their mothers not only in the dairy, and the garden plot, but also in rowing the canoes to market, while their fathers devoted their attention to their fields. No slight dexterity was often exhibited when the mother took the paddle for steering, while the daughter plied the oars cross-handed. We should like to pit one of these old canoes under their management, against the shells of Harvard or Yale. Don't think the canoe would run in the shortest time really, but think it might relatively; and taking all disadvantages into account we might hope to see an Eliot boat nymph bearing off the silver cup.

One large sail-boat from Sturgeon creek, with twelve women, could sometimes be seen, with their market cargo, all handsomely arranged. When the wind did not serve for their sail they would be seen standing manfully at their oars.

But the market women were not all that gave life to the old market house. It was a time when sailors were seen at our wharves—and they would make no small excitement among the baskets scattered around the premises. They would buy liberally—not always because they wanted the articles, but because they liked to please the market girls. Old Ben was in the habit of always getting boozy when he came to market, and on him the roguish sailor boys loved to play their pranks. Never shall we forget one of them. The old man was quite happy, and his jug quite empty. Huckleberries were three cents a quart, and pretty ripe and juicy. The tars borrowed the old man's hat, to give him a treat. On returning it filled with about two quarts of berries, one roguish fellow put it on his head, and then placing both hands on top forced it down with all his might! The dark streams came running down on every side, leaving it a matter of no doubt that Ben had become a *black* as well as a *blue* man! His empty jug they then tied to the wheel of a dray going up the hill—and the ridiculous object was seen in pursuit of his dear companion, exclaiming at the top of his voice, "Stop that jug!—stop that jug!" Such was some of the Spring Market life in former times.

There was also a fish department in the old market—and the fishermen, not hucksters, sold in person the avails of their labors.

It has been thought that Neptune had only an existence in heathen mythology—but fifty years ago there was a personage here who so nearly resembled the fabled sea-king, that he bore the name. "Old Neptune" and "Cap Spinney" were the names given to John Spinney, a veteran of the Revolutionary stock, who became of age in the time of the old war.

It is said that Thomas Spinney was the first of the name who came to this country from England, about two hundred years ago. He settled in Eliot, on the spot now occupied by Wentworth Fernald. About thirty years after, Joseph Spinney took up his residence at Spinney's Neck on the river. They were some months residents before one day Joseph in an excursion in the woods called at a house for refreshment. They found in the course of conversation that they were of the same name, and that they were brothers! Thomas had left home when Joseph was an infant, who knew not in what part the country his brother had located. From Thomas Spinney the families of Thomas and Joseph Spinney in this city descended. Our "Neptune" was a descendant of the first Joseph, and lived on the family homestead.

We knew Cap Spinney many years, and time and again witnessed his arrival and departure from the spring market. He was portly in person, upright in posture, of dark skin, long beard, and was invariably clad in petticoat trowsers, and a pea-jacket so covered with patches of every color that it was a matter of doubt what was the original—a blue knit cap was drawn close to his head, and red edging and ear pieces turned up around. His adhesion to this cap gave him the above designating name. He was a man of system and independence, and his routine for business was strictly adhered to. He would leave his home at Eliot at any hour between midnight and day-light, that the tide served, and alone in his canoe proceed to the mouth of the river. When the tide required him to leave before he had done up his sleep, on reaching the fishing ground he would bait his hooks, giving one turn of his line around the thole-pins, and then another turn around his wrist, compose himself to sleep. When the fish bit, the check at the thole-pin would secure it, and the slight pull at his wrist would notify him to take it in. He would then rebait, redrink, and continue his nap,—and in due time he might be seen coming up the river and rowing into the Market landing. To the calls, "Have you any fish," no reply would be made. As soon as his painter was fastened, he would raise his cuddy cover, take out his cocoanut shell, visit a particular shop near the market, get it filled with "O-be-joyful," then return to his boat, take his seat, raise his cocoanut to his mouth and take two or three swigs, resting between each with a smack of his lips—then depositing it safely in the cuddy, he uncovers his fish and gives notice, "Now, gentlemen, I am ready for business." By the time his fish were sold, his shell would need replenishing, and then with another swig he would push off into the stream, and his boat proceed almost intuitively to his home. Thus year after year he went through the same routine, until in 1832, on the 4th day of July—a day which he regarded as worth a particular observance in his way, his boat struck against Portsmouth bridge, and at the age of 73 he closed his life in that river in which he had almost lived for three score and ten years. He left about fifteen hundred dollars as the results of his labors, and the reputation of a friendly disposition to man and beast, as well as to his cocoanut shell. His like we have never since looked upon.

This is the last of the Neptune and the River Nymphs of the noble Piscataqua.

As an additional item to this account of our Piscataqua Neptune, an eye-witness describes the following scene:

It was nearly high water on a very pleasant day in autumn, when to save the tide it was usual for old Neptune to return from his fishing ground to the Spring Market, dispose of his fare, replenish his cocoanut shell, and return to his domicil, that his cap-covered head, and the upper portion of his body were seen from the wharves, about midway between the Navy-Yard and our shore, gradually ascending the river without any exertion or any use of his arms excepting occasionally to lift his nut-shell to his mouth while his head was thrown back sufficiently to receive its contents into his mouth. Every beholder was satisfied that the veritable Neptune of Spinney's Creek, was the object of their vision. But, where was his craft? Had he lost his canoe? And how could he walk in the water? were questions they could not solve. All were astonished till a *wight* at hand, suggested that the object of their wonder and astonishment had by *spiritualization* so diminished his specific gravity, that it had become less than that of ocean water, so that he could not sink if he would! and that although he was not the fabled Neptune, he could occasionally imitate his ocean feats. But when he neared the port of destination it became necessary for him to use his paddle, which he did successfully, and before "breaking bulk" proceeded to his Custom House to enter his craft and return with evidence of his legal entry, by the replenished condition of the far-famed cocoanut.

The mystery was now satisfactorily solved. A gondola laden with wood on the preceding ebb tide had been filled with water, and a large quantity of the wood with which it was laden was spilled and floated down to the mouth of the river. Taking advantage of this mishap, he piled as much of it on board of his canoe as it would hold, which brought it down to the gunwale, so that all was under water, and himself leisurely setting on the after seat as the flood tide gently carried him and craft up the river. It is needless to say the salvage decreed to him by the Court was the whole amount of the property saved.

We append to this Ramble the following sketch by Mr. Bowles:

No feature of the busy life of Portsmouth, thirty to forty years ago, is more agreeably impressed upon the memory of the youth of that period who yet survive, than Spring Market. The native, whether his home be still at his birthplace or far away, remembers with heartfelt pleasure, the time

> "When with pole, and hook and string,
> He fished for pollock at the Spring."

The scene is sadly shorn of its old-time glory since the Kittery fleet, under the command of another "ancient mariner" than Coleridge's, were wont to fill the dock from side to side; and the substantial modern structure that has taken its place, does not compensate for the loss of the

> "Grey, honored, worn Venitian pile,"

(quoting Mrs. Partington again) once serving the purposes of a market-house. Another change, by no means for the better, is the absence of the thriving grocery trade that in former days surrounded the market, and extended along the wharf towards Church Point. The exhaustless crystal fount, from whence so many generations have slaked their thirst, and the lobsters, good and cheap as ever, are about all that remain to remind one of Spring Market in bypast time.

It was a pleasant scene of animation, truly, when those sun-browned specimens of the feminine population of Kittery gathered there in such large numbers. No fruit to the schoolboy of that day will ever taste so good again, or the vegetables that relished the "Cape Ann turkey" on Saturdays ever bear such a flavor, as those that came from their capacious baskets. The whortleberries, too, each as plump and round, and almost as large as buck shot—if memory, which perhaps it may, does not magnify them through its perspective glass—are not forgotten. Bartlett pears were not then known in the world of horticulture, but there were the St. Michael's," and plenty of the more common sorts, all as good as they were cheap. A school-boy could fill the pockets of his round about, or the youngster taking his first lessons in trade, those of his "long-tailed blue," for less than it costs now-a-days, in some seasons, to buy a single specimen of the choicer pear varieties. Those semi-aquatic ladies, who, from all points on the Kittery shore between Boiling Rock and Pepperell's Cove, drove their light barks so skillfully across the Piscataqua, have all passed away. Another branch of the Kittery trade, distinct from that at the market, was in the line of stocking yarn and milk. Queer tricks were sometimes played by young rogues upon the venders of these necessary articles, as they journeyed, through town, stopping from door to door to dispose of their goods. One was to attach a torpedo to the rapper of a door when one of them was seen approaching, and enjoy from a distance, the start of surprise that followed the explosion sure to occur. (Portsmouth boys were always sad rogues.)

Foremost among the fishermen was that venerable individual known as "Cap Spinney." His peculiar taste in dress, including his woolen cap, and a pea-jacket, that like the garment of the "Shepherd of Salisbury Plain," had been patched with so many different colors it was difficult to decide which was the original, rendered him at all times an object of interest. He might readily have been taken, indeed, from his stalwart figure, and rough, weather beaten visage, as he landed from his boat, for old Neptune himself, had he not brandished, instead of a trident, his cocoa-nut shell. It was a fixed principle with him, as you state, unalterable as the laws of the Medes and Persians, never to sell a fish until that vessel had been replenished with "Santa Croix" or "Old Jamaica," and he had fortified himself with a refreshhing draught of its contents. That pleasant exercise performed, he was then ready for business; and as he was generally very successful in his piscatory excursions to the ocean, his pockets were well lined with cash on his return home. An intelligent traveller from the South, who had visited the market with the landlord of the Eastern Stage House, (now the Franklin House,) gave a sketch of him in a letter to a Southern journal, which was copied into Turell's Commercial Advertiser. When it was read to him on the morning it appeared, by a grocer in the neighborhood, he chanced to be in an unusually good humor, having had remarkable luck in his fishing the previous night, and promised to "give the feller a drink from his cocoanut," if he ever came again to Portsmouth.

Another of the fixtures of the fish market was Lewey, an Italian, I think, by birth, a small man, and always, from some infirmity, seen in a stooping posture. One day when the market was rather bare of fish, and Lewey's stock consisted only of a few perch, that inveterate wag, George Schaffer accosted him with the enquiry, "Why do you have so many of these sharp fins in your fish? One might as well undertake to eat a paper of pins." "I no put de fins in de fiss—I no make 'em," was the reply. "If you want 'em, I cut 'em out." And George having had his joke, and willing to pay a trifle for it, acceded to his proposal to the amount of a dozen, which he gave away a few minutes later to a worthy old lady, with a very light purse, who had come to market in pursuit of a dinner.

Among the habitues of the market, was a lady, of elephantine dimensions, bearing the name of Gillett, who was famed as a vender of unusually long sticks of candy, the advantage of which quality, was thought by a portion of her youthful customers to be more than overbalanced by the amount of sediment they contained. Her family mansion was situated not far off, on the rear of a lot on Bow street, where she kept a boarding house of a not very ambitious order. Her name was pronounced *Gil*lett, but in the fancy that some at present have for altering both the spelling and pronunciation of the names of their ancestors, it would now, probably, be styled Gil*lette*.

Besides the activity visible about the market, in strange contrast with its present deserted aspect, the descent of the hill from Bow street was occupied on both sides for business purposes. At the left, near Slade's corner, Eunice Hoyt could be seen with her baskets of fruit and other notions. The very first of the earliest fruits of summer, and the last of the latest to be had in the spring, could be found among her stock. She knew the contents of every fruit garden in Portsmouth and vicinity, and was always on the alert, with the ready cash, to tempt some one of the owners to dispose of a portion of their earliest products. Her store of luxuries had a powerful attraction for the youthful fraternity, who, when finances permitted, often went far out of the way to pay her a visit on their way to school. She did a thriving business, too, in the essence trade, of her own and Barsantee's famous manufacture; also in the line of the two-penny ballads—termed "vairses" by the good people from the rural districts—any one of which she could furnish, from that peculiarly touching ditty, "The Major's Only Son," to "Barbara Allen."

On the other side of the hill was a range of bakers' carts—small vehicles, drawn by hand—bearing the names of Plumer, Clapham, and Barry, kept there with an eye to the country trade. While the general mauufacture of the two former was most in favor, the latter had a monopoly of the bun trade, being the only producer of that article. "Berry's Buns" were in high favor with the boys, and in after years, in connection with the foreign accent of the manufacturer, were inseparably associated in memory with those red-letter days of their youth, the "general musters" at the Plains.

Farther down the declivity, upon a primitive style of table, was a display of New York oysters, which could be had until a late hour of the evening. The proprietor of this establishment, were he still living, could bear testimony, in one instance at least, to the roguish propensities of Portsmouth boys. A party of a half-dozen youngsters were in the habit of meeting together for social chat at a second floor room in Market street, and at one of their gatherings, when they were in a greatly depressed state for want of some species of excitement, a member suggested that one of those mammoth packages, a New Orleans sugar hogshead, which emptied of its contents stood at a grocer's door at the summit of the hill, should be started downward *in the direction* of the oyster stand, which was unanimously agreed to; and, groping their way through the Egyptian darkness of the evening, they proceeded to put the project into execution. Some minutes afterward, the ringleader who *chanced* to go down to the Spring for a drink, found the unfortunate dealer in bivalves in an unwonted state of excitement, and after uniting with him in bestowing sundry anathemas upon the perpetrators of the outrage, volunteered to assist in re-gathering his stock in trade, which lay scattered over a large space upon the ground. One *lad*, numbered among the conspirators, has still, I think, a residence at Portsmouth, who will be reminded of this, among the youthful indiscretions of his early life.

The last of my schoolboy remembrances of the neighborhood, is that of a scene of merriment that occurred there one afternoon at the expense of one of a couple of the hangers-on about the market, who had devised a novel mode of catching fish in a basket, by means of the hoisting apparatus connected with one of the packet landings. On the return of one of them from dinner, he was very sarcastic at the want of success, during his absence, on the part of his partner, in adding to their stock of the finny tribe, recommending that he should devote his talents unless he could do better, to some other pursuit. The other took it very good-naturedly, and suggested that he should try himself, which he proceeded to do, re-adjusting the bait and ballast, and letting down the basket with considerable flourish into the water. On raising it again, to his chagrin and the infinite amusement of a dozen bystanders, all it contained was a mammoth sculpin, with a block of wood attached by a string to his tail, and one of those worthless flounder-shaped fish, with three caudal appendages, known as three-tailed bashaws.

RAMBLE CXXXIII.

A step over the River—The Celebrities of Kittery in former days—The Spinney Family.

David Spinney died in Eliot Nov. 24th, 1862, at the age of 92 years. He was the last of six brothers, who all lived and died old men, after spending years of their lives in canoes, and much of the time three or four miles outside of Fort Constitution, fishing. Mr. David Spinney was probably the last survivor of the workmen on the U. S. Frigate Congress, built here on Badger's Island, 1799. The pay roll for the month of August of that year we have before us. Mr. Spinney's pay was 58⅓ cents. He was then 28 years old. The highest pay on the roll of eighty-nine men is two dollars per day, and but two master-workmen received that sum. The average pay of the whole was about 83 cents.

A remarkable incident marked his old age. Mr. Spinney's hair, after he became advanced in life, for many years had been very white. Within the last few years it all came off, and a new growth of fine silken black hair grew out, covering his head (except a part which had been previously bald) and so continuing until his death. His wife was Mary Mariner, sister of that well-known market woman, Hannah Mariner.

There were six of these brothers, nearly all of whom lived in the same neighborhood in Eliot, a mile or two above Portsmouth Bridge. There was Samuel Spinney, who died about half a century since. His business was to catch lobsters and plaice, and he was ever punctual to his post in the market.

Jeremiah and George were also fishermen. William Spinney, however, was not content to be confined to his canoe, and was a skipper of a Chebacco boat.

Then there was John Spinney, or as more generally known from the perpetual knit covering of his head, Cap Spinney, an account of whom is given in Ramble 132.

The first of the Spinney family who came to America was born in the interior of England, near Manchester. He went to Wapping Stairs, near London, and shipped to go Cod Hauling, (as fishing was then called,) to the Bay of Chaleur, on the northern coast of America. From the fishing ground he was carried to the Piscataway by a Capt. Fernald, and about the year 1630 he settled in Kittery, Me. He was the first schoolmaster of the place, and the ancestor of all the Spinneys on the American continent, so far as known. [The first one of the name came from Normandy to England with William the Conqueror. The name, according to English Heraldry, was three times knighted—first "DeSpiny," second "Spiny" and third "Spinney" as it is now spelt.]

There is a legend in the family that after Thomas, the

first settler, came over, a brother who had not seen him from childhood, emigrated, having no knowledge that his brother was living. The new comer landed at Kittery Point. Taking his gun one day he struck up through the woods on the shore of the river in pursuit of game. He came to a small house and asked for refreshments. They were provided, and it was not until after some general conversation, in which the stranger said he came from the same town in England in which the host was born, that the name was given and they discovered themselves to be brothers.

As Thomas Spinney had a grant of 200 acres of land and lived on Eliot Neck, in 1657, it is probable that he was a son of the first settler; and as the residence of the family is still on the same spot, it has probably never been alienated from the name.

About the year 1690 there appears to have been James, Samuel and John Spinney living in Kittery. They were probably sons of Thomas.

Samuel had eight children, Samuel, James, John, Thomas, Nathan, David, Jeremiah, and Jonathan. His son John married Mary Waterhouse in 1727, and their son John was the father of the family of hardy fishermen, the death of the last of whom is mentioned at the beginning of this Ramble.

Thomas Spinney, who died in 1850, at the age of 83, and Joseph Spinney, who died in 1852, at the age of 83, were the sons of Thomas Spinney, and grandsons of (probably) John Spinney of 1690. We cannot make out the line distinctly from the records.

The location of the small cottages of the Piscataqua tribe of Zebulon was at Eliot Neck, near the site of the old Salt-works. Their cottages which, a few years since made a small village, are now either enlarged and modernized or torn down, so that the appearance of former days, like the inhabitants, has passed away.

RAMBLE CXXXIV.

Our Wharves—Privateering—The Portsmouth Record.

Our wharves afford a depth of water sufficient to float the first class ships at low tide without grounding. Church hill is on a bluff of perhaps forty feet above the water. In former times there were no buildings on the north end of Chapel street—and where Deacon Day's store and house was afterwards built, and west of it, there was an abrupt precipice open by the road side down to the river. It was about the year 1790 that Stephen, the only son of John Greenleaf, the keeper of the Bell Tavern, was riding with full speed in a sleigh from Chapel into Bow street, when the sleigh slid round over the precipice and down went the horse, sleigh and rider! Our informant was present, and saw the horse taken up at the market. Strange to say, nobody was hurt. We shudder as we now look at the place.

At the present day we do not see the busy wharves, the fleets of West Indiamen, the great piles of bags of coffee, and the acres of hogsheads of molasses which we used to see; nor do we see Water street crowded with sailors. and the piles of lumber and cases of fish going on board the West Indiamen for uses in the Tropics.

But if that day is gone by, we have other occupations, and the old town seems as bright and handsome as ever.

The following will recall to our elder men a glimpse of the stiring scenes which some of our people had a part in at no very remote day,—and yet how few can say they "freshly remember" them!

Here we are, in the ever memorable year 1812, standing on the old wharf at Point of Graves, beholding the first privateer fitting out after the declaration of war. That schooner is the Nancy, and that man with two pistols in his belt, and his vest pockets filled with loose gunpowder, is Captain Smart. There is a large company of spectators on the wharf looking at the little craft. But off she goes to the mouth of the St. Lawrence, and like a small spider entrapping a bumble-bee, she soon returns with her prize.

In the last war with England, Privateering was a great pursuit. The Privateer Portsmouth of Portsmouth was a conspicuous cruising vessel. She was commanded by John Sinclair and made a great many valuable prizes. His widow, a very respectable lady, was still living and resided in Brooklyn, New York, in 1856.

The following are among the Privateers belonging to Portsmouth in the war of 1812:

Fox,	Capts. Handy and Brown.
Gov. Plumer,	Capt. Mudge.
Harlequin,	" E. D. Brown.
Ludlow,	
Mars,	
Macedonian,	" R. Townsend.
Portsmouth,	" Sinclair & T. M. Shaw.
Science,	" Fernald.
Squando,	" W. Watson.
Thomas,	" Shaw.
Nancy,	" Smart.
Champlain,	
Liverpool Packet,	" Watson.

The "Harpy" hailed from Baltimore—but sailed one if not two cruises from Portsmouth.

The Harlequin was a promising craft, and among her crew were several who had been ship masters. She was aiming for great returns. They had been out but a short time, when a noble ship hove in sight. The Harlequin bore down upon her, and when at a near approach the port holes of the enemy were thrown open, they played the Harlequin no longer. The *prize*, which *took them*, proved to be the Bulwark of 74 guns!

If any apology is necessary for men fighting against the common enemy "on their own hook," it may be found perhaps in the great disparity of forces of the contending powers. The British fleet comprised 1060 men-of-war, of which 800 were in commission. The American navy had seven effective frigates, and 12 or 15 sloops-of-war!

The disparity is absolutely ludicrous, and yet what glory was acquired by our gallant navy! The fights of the Constitution, the Essex, the Enterprise and their noble compeers, quite eclipsed in history the deeds of daring performed by the Fox, the Portsmouth, the Gen. Armstrong, the Decatur, the young Wasp, the Yankee, the Teazer, the Rolla, the Globe, and a hundred others.

But in the story of man's boldness and bravery, nothing excels the deeds of the *American Privateers*, in the war of 1812. The record, however, so far as we know, is very slight. There was published in New York in 1856, a crude and skeleton sketch of them, entitled "History of the American Privateers and Letters of Marque," &c. by George Coggeshall, captain of a Privateer.

We well recollect, Capt. Tom Shaw as well as Capt. Elihu D. Brown, who led two "private armed" ships against the commerce of Great Britain. No doubt our readers will be interested in the following extracts of the work referred to. The book is a valuable addition to the History of the United States, though compiled by an old sailor of 72 years of age from such materials as he could command. Cooper's Naval History perhaps has something on the subject, but we know of no other History of the American Privateers,—an ample detail of their wonderful and romantic daring, bearding the British Lion in his den, and capturing his ships on every sea, has yet to be written.

The affair of the General Armstrong, Capt. Reid, which was attacked in the harbor of Fayal by two or three British men-of-war, has been before Congress within a few years for indemnity. The enemy lost more men in their attempt to capture her, than in some actions where fleets were engaged. She was scuttled by her own crew.

.These private armed vessels appear to have carried almost invariably a "Long Tom," and besides, from 2 to 18 guns, and from 50 to 150 men. New York had 26 afloat, scouring the seas, Baltimore 18, at one time, in the early part of the war; while Newport, Charleston, Boston, Newburyport, Bristol, New London, Salem, Portsmouth and other ports had their share.

They were commissioned by the United States "to take, burn, sink and destroy the enemy wherever he could be found, either on the high seas or in British Ports."

But the object of this article is merely to give *Portsmouth* as recorded.

1812,—Ship Richmond, 14 guns, 25 men besides officers, 400 tons, deeply laden with W. India produce, worth $200,000, was captured on a voyage from Jamaica to London, snd sent into Portsmouth by the Privateer Thomas.

Ship Falmouth, 14 guns, 30 men, from Jamaica for Bristol, (E.) with a cargo valued at $200,000, was captured by the Thomas of this Port and sent into Portsmouth, Aug. 18, 1812. The privateer sch. Thomas, Capt. Shaw, 11 guns and 100 men, and Privateer sloop Science, Fernald, sailed from this port on a cruise. *Two other Privateers were fitting out at the same time.* Sch. Phœbus and Phebe sent into Portsmouth by the Squando of that Port. The Squando was only a pink stern schooner.

The English brig Resolution arrived at Portland a prize to the privateer Nancy of Portsmouth.

Barque Fisher from Rio with a very valuable cargo and considerable spice was sent into Portland by the Fox of Portsmouth.

1813—Brig Mars, from Jamaica for Halifax, sent into Portsmouth by the Fox. [This was afterwards the privateer Mars.]

Ship Dromo, 12 guns, from Liverpool for Halifax, with a cargo valued at $70,000, was sent into Wiscasset by the Thomas, of Portsmouth.

A Brig sent into Boothbay by the same, with a very valuable cargo. It is said these two vessels produced the captors more than $500,000.

A Brig was sent into Portsmouth by the Gov. Plumer of this port. A Brig was captured and burnt by the Gov. Plumer—she was bound from Hull to Halifax.

Brig Daniel from Waterford to Halifax, laden with provisions, sent into Portsmouth by the Gov. Plumer, privateer. The noted schr. Liverpool Packet of — guns, carried into Portsmouth by the Thomas of that port. Afterwards fitted as a Privateer called the the Liverpool Packet, Capt. Watson.

Brig Nelly, Cork, for Newfoundland, captured by the Fox of Portsmouth, and burnt after disposing of her valuable articles.

Sloop Peggy, Greenwhich, for Limerick, captured by the same and ransomed.

Schr. Brother and Sister, captured by the same and burnt. Brig Louisa, captured by the Fox and ransomed. Sloop Fox, from Liverpool, for Limerick, valuable, captured by the Privateer Fox and sent to Norway. (4 more prizes are recorded in this chapter to the Fox, but there was another of that name from Baltimore, and she may have been the vessel.)

But we grow weary of the task. This was only the first year of the war. The oceans of the world swarmed, literally swarmed, with Privateers, and British ships were captured by hundreds. Our own merchant ships were cooped up at home, not daring to face the gauntlet of the British naval forces. The sailors who should have manned them, gladly turned privateersmen, and thus the war was waged till the Peace of 1815.

We still in imagination see our streets filled with jolly privateersmen in groups, with blue ribbons tied around their hats inscribed in large letters "SUCCESS TO THE FOX," or whatever vessel they were to sail in. And then another scene, of the sailors paid off, with so much money that they knew not what to do with it. It was one of these men who one day near Market Square, put his arm round the neck o a cow, kissed her, and put a five dollar bill in her mouth for a cud. They might be seen, too, sporting their parasols, and in dresses most ludicrously fine.

Some men grew rich by the war—they piled thousands upon thousands—but now, ere half a century has passed away, scarcely any mark of the riches obtained by privateering, is visible in their families. Their mansions have generally passed into other hands, and their descendants are many of them poverty stricken. If Solomon's proverbs on fleeting riches had not been written earlier, they might have been based on the results of our privateering acquisitions.

RAMBLE CXXXV.

Our Wharves -- West-India Trade -- Capt. Gilman—Admiral Nelson—Emperor of Russia, &c.

The Navigation of Portsmouth for twenty years previous to 1812 was much more extensive and employed a larger fleët of vessels, but of smaller tonnage, than are now owned here. It is true the capital now invested is much greater, but our ships now are seldom seen here after they are built. We will for a moment take a retrospective view of the Navigation of Portsmouth some seventy or eighty years ago. The trade was then principally with the West Indias, in schooners, and brigs of from 100 to 200 tons. Some of these vessels were always at our wharves, either loading or discharging. Their outward cargoes were fish, lumber, beef, pork, &c., in the hold and cabin—with a deck load of horses, mules, oxen, sheep, pigs, chickens, geese, turkeys, &c., and would appear at the wharf when loaded, like a farmer's barn-yard, with hay piled up almost to the lower yards. Live stock would always pay largely when it could be got out safe; but of this there was only one chance in ten. Bad weather will soon clear the decks, and the deck load will soon be a-swimming without shore or bounds. The return cargoes were rum, molasses, sugar, coffee, &c., with some specie. This trade was a great advantage to the laboring classes, also to coopers, and fishermen. Our wharves from the North End to the Pier, and even to the Point of Graves, were lined with vessels, and our community busy and happy.

This West India trade was however quite a lottery. Sometimes good voyages would be made, but oftener losing ones; so that few made fortunes by it, and many became bankrupt. One voyage now in mind was considered a good one.

The brig Oliver Peabody, owned in Exeter by Gov. Gilman, Mr. Peabody, Col. Gilman Leavitt, and others in Portsmouth, the master Capt. Stephen Gilman of Exeter, left here in 1803, with a full cargo of lumber, provisions, &c. and a deck load of stock, oxen, sheep, poultry, &c.

Capt. Gilman had been about twenty days from Portsmouth, when, concluding by his observation the day before he must be in the latitude of the Windward Islands, the next morning by day-light found himself surrounded by a large fleet of men-of-war. At that time, as our vessels were daily captured by a French fleet under the command of Victor Hughes, he concluded it was a *gone case.* He soon however was released from his fears, for a cutter immediately boarded him from the Admiral's Flag Ship, with an officer, who stated to him that the fleet in sight was that of Admiral Nelson blockading the French West India Islands, and that he was sent by the Admiral with his compliments, saying that his officers had seen him since daylight, and they had concluded he had a deck load of live stock, of which they were much in want; and also told Capt. G. if he would go on board with him, the Admiral would purchase his deck load at his own price. He accordingly went; the Admiral received him in his cabin and treated him with a glass of wine and great politeness, and after the price of the stock was settled, gave orders to his Purser to pay him the amount, which he did in Spanish dollars. Capt. G. then returned to his brig, and the stock was taken on board the fleet. Capt. Gilman would often after his return home relate his interview with Nelson, with much satisfaction: said he was a man about five feet in height, of a very gentlemanly, and polite appearance, with only one arm, and limping considerably in walking, from a wound received in the knee. He said he thought him a handsome man, and considered him between thirty and forty years old. This was about two years before the battle of Trafalgar—where Nelson lost his life.

Admiral Nelson told Capt. G. he had liberty to go to any Island and dispose of the balance of his cargo. This he soon did, and returned home with full cargo of West India produce, and 10,000 Spanish dollars for his deck load. His outward cargo was invoiced at $5,000.

It was not unusual to see twenty or thirty vessels loading for foreign ports in Portsmouth at one time. We also had a number of vessels engaged in the Russia, South America, and some in the India trade.

In the year 1802 William Gray, Esq., then of Salem, (often called Billy Gray,) loaded a number of ships here for India. They took in spars and naval stores. The specie carried out was brought from Boston in large wagons and put up in small iron-bound kegs. These ships usually returned to Boston.

Portsmouth had merchants in the India trade. Col. James Sheafe and Matthew S. Marsh, Esq., father of George M. Marsh owned two or three ships in this line. They built a ship on Peirce's Island in 1804, and sent her to India. Messrs. N. A. & J. Haven also sent one there called the Hamilton.

Nearly seventy years since, Capt. Charles Coffin, in connection with Thomas Sheafe, was engaged in the Russian trade. In one of his voyages he took a black man as a steward. Soon after the vessel was in port, there was a grand military display of troops to be reviewed by the Emperor. The steward requested permission to go on shore to witness the pageant. He was not aware that a black man had rarely been seen in Russia, and was surprised to find that himself and the Emperor became the observed of all observers. Nor did the Emperor himself overlook him. The next day a messenger was sent to Capt. C. by order of the Emperor, asking if the services of the black man could be obtained for the Royal household. Capt. Coffin offered to dispense with the steward's services if he could better his condition, and the black man in due time became a Royal butler, and being faithful, was distinguished in his position. A few years after, our informant says, he saw him in the streets of Portsmouth, with gold-laced dress, silk stockings, etc., returned to take to Russia his ebony wife and their dark diamonds, to sparkle in the outer court of the Autocrat.

The trade to Russia, Sweden, South America, Liverpool, &c. was then good: iron, hemp, and duck were imported from Russia and Sweden, as none of these goods were then of American production; and hides and tallow from Montevideo and Buenos Ayres. The trade to Liverpool and Bristol was considerable. Messrs. Abel & Robert Harris then owned a ship called the Bristol-Packet, which run regularly to Bristol with cargoes of flax-seed, pot and pearl ashes, and some lumber. These men have now all passed away from us, as well as the trade they prosecuted. Some of them have left large estates, which we daily see in the substantial brick buildings and stores built by them.

RAMBLE CXXXVI.

The Old Welch House on Bridge Street—Johnny Cunningham.

WHO that has been through Bridge street in the past century, has not noticed the long, low black house, with a camel-back ridgepole, end on the street, next South of that on the corner of Hanover street? Passing this spot one day a few years since, we were surprised to find that the house had disappeared, and nothing left but a stout chimney with bricks set in clay.

Of the exact date when this old house was built we have no record. The first occupant we can find was Benjamin Welch. He was born about 1710, and probably he located here as early as 1740. He occupied it in the time of the Revolution. There was no house nearer to it on the south than the Call mansion; and on the North and East were none nearer. Our old folks can yet remember when this house set thus by itself, with several handsome trees on the north side, (where the corner house now stands,) under which the patriarchal proprietor might frequently be seen sitting, enjoying the clear prospect of Christian shore, before any railroad depot or distillery was built, before the first grave was made in the old North Burying Ground, or even a bridge built where the mill now stands. He too could see the full tides by their free ingress, flowing nearly up to his premises.

For many years there was a well curb just inside the door on the street, at which the wayfarers, from a spring in the cellar, quenched their thirst, and the wants of the house were supplied.

This was a cottage of the olden time—and it probably was not wholly without its romance, although its history is not all recorded. Before that broad fire-place happy faces have shone, and as the story of the "Regulars" has been there told, fearful eyes have been looking out to see if they were coming. Here "olive plants" might be seen around the family board. Among the daughters was Betty, whose bright eyes and comely person, as well as her pleasant manners, were the attraction of the foreign gardener of Col. George Boyd. Whether Johnny Cunningham met Betty Welch first at the well, or whether he fell in love with the cottage in the distance as he tilled the great garden of Col. Boyd, (extending from the mill to the depot,) history does not inform us,—but the fact that he here won her heart and hand is better established.

Johnny Cunningham, as he was familiarly called when the writer knew him, was a small man, his head generally turbaned with his handkerchief, sans suspenders, quick in his movements, strong nervous temperament, and very irritable at small matters. He was of Irish descent, but found in England by Col. Boyd, and sent here before the Revolution to be his gardener—for which business he had been educated. As a penman few could surpass him. We recollect an illustrative anecdote of the old man. He had been at work for Maj. Wm. Gardner one day, and presented his bill. Maj. G. was struck with the bold beauty of the writing, and priding himself on his own skill with his pen, inquired of the little rough man, who made out his bill for him! "Myself, sir." The Major expressed doubts, and to test him, asked him to go to his desk and write his name. " Your penknife, if you please," said Johnny. Having adjusted the nib to his liking, the pen was applied to the paper, and Maj. Gardner soon saw in the freedom and ease with which his letters were cut, a penman whom he could not excel. The bill was paid, and a dollar extra added as an acknowledgement of his skill.

After Johnny's marriage, the trees on the north of the house were cut down, and he built the two story house now standing there. How long he occupied it we know not. He for many years rented it, and lived in the old house. They had one son, Andrew, to whom he gave a good education. He died in early manhood. After the death of his wife Betty, he chose to put his effects into the care of the town, and take up his residence at the town farm, where he had opportunity, under the charge of Superintendent Morrison, to follow his favorite pursuit, gardening, when he had the inclination—and if his hoe or a spade was ever out of its place when he wanted it, there would be no peace on the farm until the article was found. That hitching up of his pants, that extension of the arm, that flash of the eye, and that quick expression of irritation when the boys asked of him the hour, none who knew him will ever forget. He died about twenty-five years ago, at the age of 94 years. Thus the old house and its inmates have now all passed away.

RAMBLE CXXXVII.

John Simes and his Descendants.

On the lot of land on Market street now occupied by the stores of C. H. Mendum & Co. and Hill & Carr, in the last century stood an old fashioned gambrel-roofed house, with a shop on the street, and in which was done as much of the dry goods trade as in any other store around it. The house was built by Mr. John Simes, the first of the name among us, who came from England about 1736, and located on this spot. His land extended west to High street. A deed dated in 1760 conveys to two of his grandchildren, Elizabeth Hart (afterwards the wife of Rev. Dr. McClintock,) and Mary Parker, (widow of Capt. William Parker, and mother of Capt. Samuel Parker,) children of Humphrey Fernald, as probably their share of the estate, the house and land on High street, which has long been known as the Parker house, and was recently purchased by C. H. Mendum, of the widow of Capt. Samuel Parker. He held other real estate at the time of his death, which took place before the Revolution. He left but one son, Joseph Simes—and five daughters. One of the daughters married Cyrus Frink of Newington, from whom the extensive family of that name descended; another married Humphrey Peavey of Newington; the third married John Nutter of Newington; the fourth married Moses Noble, from whom the family on Noble's Island have descended; the fifth married Humphrey Fernald of Portsmouth, the grandfather of John W. Fernald, who is now the only male descendant in that line.

Joseph Simes was Chairman of the Selectmen of Portsmouth in 1776, and a highly esteemed citizen. He occupied the homestead on Market street till his death, near the close of the last century, and after his death the widow continued the dry goods business at the same store in the house. They had ten children—six sons and four daughters. The eldest son John was a painter. His shop was in the rear of the house, approached by an avenue, probably the same that is now on the north side of Lafayette Laighton's store. The other sons were Thomas, landholder and livery stable proprietor, the father of Stephen H. Simes; Mark, merchant and postmaster, the father of John D. Simes; William, goldsmith, the father of Bray U. Simes; George, landholder and livery stable proprietor, the father of John P. and William Simes. Mark, William and George owned handsome mansions in the same neighborhood on Court and State streets.

The daughters were Ann, the wife of Capt. Martin Parry, and mother of the first wife of late William Jones; Mary, wife of Capt. Thomas Lunt; Hannah, wife of George Massey; and Elizabeth, who was unmarried.

Our older citizens well remember the mother of the large family when she sold English goods on Market street, not on quite so large a scale as some of her descendants, but large for the times. Mrs. Simes was highly respected for her many virtues. Habits of industry and enterprise had a marked influence on the children and grandchildren of this family, which is not yet eradicated. Of John Simes's six children, and his son's ten children, fifteen were married and settled in Portsmouth and its vicinity. Of their descendants many are now located among us, and are making their mark in the world—but "our fathers, where are they."

RAMBLE CXXXVIII.

Toppin Maxwell—"Commodore" Mifflin.

THE following from the pen of Rev. T. H. Miller, gives a true and graphic sketch to which most of our citizens who are over fifty years of age can attest. The tannery extended from the foot of Deer street, near where the Concord Railroad depot is now located, to Parker street. The site of the windmill is the very spot where is now the engine house of the Concord & Portsmouth Railroad.

Why such a man ever drifted away from sweet Ireland, where he was born, or why he happened to drift into the old harbor of Piscataqua, in which he lived, and on whose shores he died, your deponent knoweth not and therefore sayeth not. But the fact that he did drift away from the one and into the other is about as well established as any similar fact can be; inasmuch as the writer in his boyhood has often paddled in the water (not to mention the mud) which surrounded the Maxwell mansion, rendering the whole domain a landscape very much like a sketch of Noah's view from his window, shortly after the ark rested. That he had drifted up the harbor and was moored to the shore thus, rests on the testimony of an eye witness. That he had drifted away from the green isle was no less manifest to every ear which listened for once to the richest and most unctuous brogue that ever rattled from the tongue of a native.

But—but—the reader may ask, how and why did he live *in* the harbor when land was plentiful all around it, and when a little money would have given him a dry acre? The *why* of this question can only be guessed at; the *how* will soon be plain to the mind of the reader, almost to his eye. Perhaps the reason why he planted himself in a mud-hole on the flats was, that such a lot, being worth little, cost little; or that, being a tanner, he was not afraid of water; or that, being an old bachelor, he thought it was not much matter where he lived. It might be any one of these reasons; or it might possibly be all of them together; for he loved money, he was an excellent tanner, and he never married. Or it might be none of them. For, as "there is no disputing about tastes," he *might* deem his location the most delightful and desirable of all the lovely spots on our shores. If this was so, one happiness he doubtless enjoyed, viz: a home which no one envied him in the possession. And, though probably nobody else thought so, he always acted as if he thought it the best place in the world.

Let no one infer from the hint about Noah, that Maxwell's ark rested on Mount Ararat, or any other mount, whence he came down at certain seasons to enjoy himself in the mud, or disport himself in the water like a dolphin. No sports had he, that his neighborhood knew of, but work, work, work, was his practice, whatever might be his theory. And his ark was at once shop and house, tannery and palace. The harbor of Piscataqua abounds in bays, great and little, in creeks and inlets of all sizes. One of these creeks, formerly deep enough for ship-building on its banks, was turned into a tide-pond a hundred years ago, by the erection of Levis's mills, and on the shore—no, in the shore of this pond, at its south eastern extremity, Toppin Maxwell built his castle exactly at the point which sailors call "between wind and water." Small and frail it was at first, and at every spring-tide, when the winds blew and the floods came, the neighbors' eyes were turned that way to see it go off; but it did not go, and from year to year, as he threw out much tan from his pits, but sold none, his land emerged from the tide, as Venus did from the sea. Now and then a stray log, a waif from the waters came along; it was moored, and very gradually but certainly buried; and by a slow process, as some geologists describe creation, dry land appeared, drier and drier, wider and wider, till a goodly lot, like Boston on a small scale, had emerged from the water, and none but the highest tides dared show their heads above it. As land and money grew in his hands, so did buildings rise. Addition upon addition, patch upon patch, were hitched together, incongruous and inconvenient, but the owner was a conservative, and would throw nothing away. He built stronger and stronger, and always at some cost, till he had a large building. Then all at once a new idea shot across the mind; he would have a wind-mill to grind his bark. This he had done before by a horse, and sometimes hired it done at a water-mill; but now, quoth he, "I'll have a wind-mill, and grind for *meself* and for half the *toon*."

Big with this one idea, he took no counsel of flesh and blood as to the expediency of the proposed measure, but went about the work like a man determined to be "supreme over his accidents. Money would buy lumber, and hire workmen. He bought and hired the best. But money would not buy true ideas, either in castle building or the building of wind-mills. On this latter subject Toppin Maxwell had ideas of his own, which he thought cost nothing, but which in the end proved to be very valuable, if articles are to be prized at their cost. Remonstrances from the workmen or bystanders as to the style of the building, were overruled in a summary manner. He would build the mill to suit himself, and so he did. It was framed strongly enough for a den of lions, and braced so as to resist the most tempestuous wind. Should the top of the mill be rotary, so as to meet all the winds, as wind-mills usually are? "No," was the answer; "make it fast facing the northwest; that's the strongest wind that blows here." And so it was done.

Every thing was finished to his mind; and when the wind blew from the favorite quarter, the wooden sails moved round, and turned the iron mill and ground the bark—but it was not perfect. The machinery was heavy and clumsy; and except in a high wind it would scarcely move. The arms were now made as long as they could be without striking the ground, and the width of the fans was doubled. Now the mill went well with a high nor'-wester; but too furiously with a stiff topsail breeze! What was the remedy? Take in sail, reef the fans, says some *green* reader. Alas, that was impossible! for two reasons—first, you could not throw the mill out of the wind to get hold of the sails; and second if you got hold of them you could not take them in, for instead of cloth they were made of boards, nailed fast to strong timbers. The only way to stop the mill was to choke it with bark, rammed into the hopper by armfuls. Of course it would not always stay choked, but would start off again and run round like a thing of life, compelling Toppin and his workmen, or boys, not exactly to make hay while the sun shone, but to grind bark while the wind blew. After a windy day sometimes would come a windier night, and then they would grind till they were tired, choke the mill as well as they could and go to bed. About the time they got warm and dozy, the breeze would freshen, the mill start, and the music begin — jingle, jingle-rattle, rattle — whiz, whiz, whiz-z-z. "Out of bed, all hands—the mill is agoing, it will soon be on fire." "Will ye—nill ye" up they must get, and grind or choke as best they could, while the breeze lasted.

In the winter, north-west breezes often swell to gales, lasting two or three days. One day and one night the mill had ground and ground and groaned—another day passed and a second night drew on: the pile of bark went down rapidly, but the wind did not go down at all—on the contrary it seemed to rise. Every body was tired and sleepy, and discouraged. Orders were given to stop the mill; but it was easier told than done; however, in a lull of the wind the wheels were brought to a stand—the lights were put out, and all hands went to bed. They might sleep, but not long, for a flaw started the mill, and the mill roused the sleepers. Wide awake, and cross enough, they choked and clogged the machine as best they could, and when at last it stood still, they sought repose once more. But the gale increased; and as the flaws became more violent, away went the mill again. This was too much. Breathing out threatenings, the man of the house not only called the hands, but arose himself, resolved like Don Quixote, to have a tilt with the wind mill; but not like the redoubtable Don, to come off second best and sneak off in his wounds. No, not he! There was the machine with wide-spread wings revolving in hot haste, hotter and hotter, making all *gee* again. No time was to be lost. He seized the first weapon that came to hand—a heavy iron crow bar—and, poising it with his stalwart arm upraised, as lightly as a dandy flourishes his rattan, he stepped upon the platform, and, suiting the action to the word, roared out, "There! (with an oath too big to put in print,) see if I can't stop ye!"

Down went the crowbear among the teeth—round went the mill one whole turn, swallowing the crowbar, and bending the strong iron like a piece of cap wire—but the meat was too hard to digest, and like the Baylonish Dragon after eating the pitch, the mill burst asunder. The shaft broke, one or two fans broke and fell off, and every thing came up with a jerk. One grand crash and all was still—so still that it never moved again. All hands slept soundly that night, and for all the noise made by the mill, they might have slept till this time. This was Toppin's last scheme. He went back to the horse mill; backward in many of his affairs; and without living to be very old or very rich, he some forty years since passed off the stage. Peace to his ashes; he made room for greater men—we were going to say wiser, but let that pass. Corporations which he never heard of, machines and inventions he never dreampt of, occupy his old tanner's paradise. A steam mill made of his house has since ground bark where his wind-mill broke down—a steam tannery now does in a week what he used to do in a year—steam cotton mills are planted on the shores of his pond—the pond itself is cut up with a multitude of railroad tracks—the telegraph near by speaks of new things—and old men and old things are rapidly forgotten.

This biography is written merely for the love of the thing—no chick nor child nor friend of Toppin is there left to reward the writer for giving their relative a good character,—nor foes, that we wot of, to exult over a bad one—but hundreds of men in middle life there are, who can see his round, rosy face, and portly bulk once again, as in a glass—and then, perhaps, think of him no more. But then he had his uses, his aims, his purposes, his thought and life—and who can say that such an one as he had no place in the divine and beneficent plans of the great overruling Providence, or that he did not fill it? If any think or say so let them do it better.

A character, quite as prominent on the shores of the North Mill Pond, has furnished the subject for another sketch from the same writer. We refer to Commodore Mifflin.

The title was honorary or fanciful, but the name was real, and Mr. Mifflin lived and labored in Portsmouth through a long life and died something more than forty years ago.

He lived in Rock Pasture. Well, where's that? No where, now; because the Rocks are gone, and the pasture also, for though the land remains, it is now cut up into streets and squares, occupied with houses, shops, mills and iron works. But Rock Pasture did extend, in Commodore Mifflin's day, from where the west end of the Portsmouth Steam Factory now stands, to the westerly side of Cabot street, and from Islington street to the North Mill Pond.

On the bank of this pond stood the Mifflin mansion, on the spot where is the house and former home of Capt. Robert Shillaber, and close to the Partington estate: for strange as it may seem, be it known to the moderns, that while the middle of the pasture was bare of buildings, the water lots, or rather mud lots, on the shore, were all occupied by houses, from the Partington mansion down to 'Squire Adams's wharf.

On the pond swam and fished Mr. Mifflin's geese, that healthy, vigorous, never-failing flock, whose memory is honored in a poem of Benj. P. Shillaber, the medium through whom the Partington spirit's utterances are given to the sons of earth.

And they fed, as they listed, on the green grass which carpeted the moist even surface of the pasture, during the livelong summer, fearless alike of stone throwing boys and impertinent dogs, both of whom (?) stood in wholesome fear of the old gander's prowess: for verily he had been victorious in many a battle ere these youthful men and dogs had come upon the stage.

When the ground became frozen, or was covered with snow, and commons were short, the geese would march, in the most exact military order, down through the town to the Parade (now vulgarly called Market Square,) where in those days there used to be many teams from the country, and where many grains, and sometimes quarts, of corn, oats, and hayseed were scattered by the oxen and horses.

When the geese had eaten what they could find, and sometimes received a few slashes from the teamsters' whips, they would rise and fly to their home, clearing the tops of trees and houses, and arriving safe.

But leaving the geese, let us go back to the Commodore, inquiring what manner of man he was, and why he was called Commodore.

James H. Mifflin, so he wrote his name in a plain and bold round hand, was a military man, an English soldier, said to be born in London, educated in the blue coat school, and enlisted in the British army, in which he fought at the battle of Bunker's Hill.

The story used to run that he was wounded there, though we never heard *him* say so; but by some mischance he became a prisoner, and preferring to stay in this country he was not exchanged, but came to Portsmouth, married and settled here, where he lived and died, and where some descendants now live.

His occupation here was that of a mason's tender; i. e. he made mortar and carried bricks, and in his day was deemed one of the best in that business.

On training days, when our land forces took the field, Mr. Mifflin, as waiter to the field and staff officers, made a fine appearance. Erect and soldierlike, with hat in hand, head well powdered, his clothes all antique, and his well-preserved blue coat adorned with large brass buttons, he was hardly less conspicuous than Gen. Storer himself.

Our hero lived, as the reader will remember, on the bank of the North Mill Pond. Indeed in that day, the house was nearly at the water's edge, and as he built no wharf, a storm would now and then dig a hole in the bank, and the winds and waves threaten the mansion itself; but to preserve the premises from these perils, the bank was thickly planted with the good old-fashioned Balm of Gilead trees, to break off the winds, and a great pine log, belonging to Robert Ham, was laid alongside at high water mark moored and staked, to break the force of the waves.

In those days, almost every housekeeper carried or sent his own bushel of corn to the mill,—and several of the Rock Pasture people had canoes, floats or skiffs in which they navigated the pond for this and other purposes.

Mr. Mifflin had a canoe, something like the western dug-out of a later day, which he kept tied to the log, and which was shaded by the trees. The boys of the neighborhood were apt to borrow boats without leave, and once in a while would take his. When they did so, his lion-like voice rung out over the pond, and the boys coming as near as they dared, would shove in the boat, and jumping overboard, go ashore elsewhere, glad to escape.

This watchfulness induced other owners to put their boats under his watchful eye; and thus quite a fleet was moored to his log. The joiners' and masons' apprentice boys, among whom he labored for years, dubbed him Commodore, and he answered to the title. In those days laborers drank spirits; and the Commodore labored and drank heartily. His voice, always loud, grew louder as the day declined, and at sundown, when any one, as he passed addressed him as Commodore Mifflin, he responded, Sir!! in one that might ring through a battalion.

Like a true Englishman, he would not speak of his military life, except in answer to questions,—but the military steps, positions and motions, and habits of his youth, were part of his life, and endured as long as he lived.

RAMBLE CXXXIX.

My Brother Bob.

THE genuine truthfulness of the following story, from the genial pen of our old townsman, B. P. Shillaber, Esq., as well as its lively account of no less a character than Commodore Mifflin or Toppin Maxwell, induces us to give it as one of the Rambles. Like the two above named, "My Brother Bob" had his home on the South shore of the North Mill Pond.

It was the remark of a distinguished orator who once discoursed about the Father of his Country, that "G. Washington was not a loud boy." I may, with some propriety, apply the same remark to my brother Bob. He is not a "loud boy," in the sense wherein the term loud might be supposed to apply. He does not stand at the street corners and brawl, to the disturbance of neighborhoods; he has no particular fancy for the boisterous; but he is a quiet man, full of good sense, practical to a fault, honest, plain spoken, industrious, prudent. He possesses very little of the ornate or ornamental, and yet he attracts by qualities the opposite of those which usually control. A hardy, gnarled, rough man, yet he is respected more for his integrity of character, and the qualities enumerated, than hundreds who wear far better clothes and make more pretension to refinement. Bob is not an Adonis, for per sonal grace is not a quality much to be vaunted of in our family, compensation being found in those excellences which the best people discern.

My brother Bob is a character, and from the earliest point to which my memory recurs, he has maintained the same position in the estimation of the people as now. It will not do to call him an old man yet; and though years have severely tussled with him, and taken a little away from his elasticity, it has added to his wisdom, and less impulsiveness characterizes his speech and actions. For instance, he would scarcely now do as he did years ago, when the little boy was drowned in the pond near which he lived :—throw his clothes off piece by piece as he ran to the rescue, and almost naked venture among the crackling and brittle ice, breaking beneath his every movement, in his humane endeavor. That half hour of fruitless effort, in the eyes of the assembled town, covered him with glory—the only covering he had, until his clothes were brought him, and he had made his toilet on the hard-set ice, within a few yards from where the poor boy met his fate. Neither would he do as he did at the time the boys got upset in the boat, when with no other means of rescue than a half-hogshead tub, he gallantly pushed from the shore to aid them. With a bold spirit, actuated by the warmest feelings, Bob had no thought of danger or reward, though he sometimes found compensation in shaking those whom he benefitted for the trouble they had caused him; and there were frequent opportunities.

He was always a favorite of the boys, and his boat on Wednesday and Saturday afternoons was an object of great competetion, for he had a water privilege then on the pond, which a railroad many years since cut off, leaving Bob minus a small income, and a prospective suit against the corporation, in case they refuse to compensate. I can recall many instances of juvenile charter parties for navigation upon the North Mill Pond at such times, and Bob was as well pleased in their sport as though he were not to receive the dime, or less, in payment. Grave and busy men, often, in referring to those times, make mention of that dear delightful sail upon the little pond, then, however, larger considerably than the Atlantic, and speak of Bob in the kindliest spirit of remembrance, recalling him by some amusing anecdote that gave a zest to the good old time. But there were times when he would swear like a tornado, if such expression may be employed, when juvenile depredators attempted to overreach him; and it has been said that in his earlier days there was more profanity in him to the square inch than in any one around. This, however, has changed for the subdued temper that years bring with them, and but moderate scope is allowed for passion.

Speaking of this, I was wont to try him fearfully in the olden time, and well did I rue it in the lofty indignation that fired him; but now, a right philosophy that submits, murmurless, to destiny, governs his conduct to me. This must be the case, else would he denounce me for my failure to answer his letters, and the other indignities of neglect and silence. Even when he called upon me in town in the drive of business, and I begged him, for heaven's sake, to go till I was at leisure—a rudeness which I repented of in dust and ashes—he turned without a complaint, and I did not see him again for six months. In reply to an abject apology I made, he said it was all right; he knew me well enough to believe that I was actuated by right motives, and he had no cause to fret about it. I wish, for myself, that such understanding could more universally prevail; that, when in our honesty we use a friend in this manner, he might not imagine an offence and abuse us for the virtue of candor, which may be the only one we have.

Candor is a virtue which Bob especially possesses. He was entrusted for many years with the care of the Court

House, in the town where he lives, and was intimate with those comprising the Bench and Bar; Pierce, Christie, Hackett, Marston, Hayes, Eastman, Harvey, by all of whom he was held in high regard—one of them, who was after-President, having borrowed money of him, upon which he based a claim for an office under his administration, that he didn't get. He was, as I have intimated, not a very dressy person, therein proving an exception to a rule of our family, and strangers underrated him on account of it. A plain suit of clothes, perhaps a green baize jacket, his collar turned back, cravatless, revealing his stout neck, presented an appearance somewhat different from the beau monde, but it was tolerated by all those who were not more nice than wise. There was but one who ever attempted to meddle with him on this point, and he tried it but once. Bob knew everything that had ever transpired in town. It was said of him by an admirer, somewhat irreverently, that he was next to Omniscience in penetrating human secrets. He had an intuition that was infallible, and could read men like a book. Concerning this one alluded to, Bob had obtained the fact that he was owing a large tailor's bill in town, about which there was some fear. As Bob entered the Court House one morning, there was an extra number of lawyers present, and the individual named among them. "There, gentlemen," said he, pointing to the green jacket and the open shirt collar, "there is a dress in which to associate with gentlemen!" "True," replied Bob very quietly; "I don't dress very well, but if I had gone down to Snip's and run in debt for my clothes, I might have appeared as well as you do." This was a stunner, so to speak, and Bob was declared the winner by a full bench.

He was always ready with replies that had a salutary smart in them. Though an early and ardent Jackson man, in honor of whose inauguration he illumined his house from attic to cellar in 1829, and inheriting the Democratic chart in politics, he turned over to the free soil side of the question, for which he was abused by those with whom he had previously acted. About this time a movement was made against the banks of his State, and Bob, having a few shares of bank stock, took a decided stand in support of the banks, against his old associates. "Well, Bob," said one of these, "I hear you have gone over to the enemy. That's just the way; as soon as a man gets a dollar's worth of bank stock and a house to his back, off he goes among the aristocracy." Bob was all the time pursuing his work of grafting trees—he is a famous grafter, and buds will grow if he but look at them—and only stopped long enongh to to say: "Adze, if you paid less attention to politics and more to your business, you might pay off that mortgage on your house in a little while." Adze made no further remark.

Bob's idea of family discipline would hardly be adopted yet, though we are fast gaining on it. All great ideas have found the course slow before they are established. He has had a fine family of children, though they have become divided—some here and there, and some yonder, beyond the reach of earthly care and sorrow. When they were young, he was asked the question if he ever flogged them. "Flogged them!" said he in a tone half indignant; "no, that would be too cowardly, I am going to wait till they are big enough to strike me back, and then pitch in. It is mighty mean business to strike a child."

He has filled offices of trust and emolument, but has been more distinguished for those he didn't fill. He has been captain of an engine, fence-viewer, constable, and keeper of the court-house, the latter of which offices he now holds in connection with that of messenger to the Fire Department. He was invaluable on election days, before his town was divided into wards; and stationed by the polls, no man passed that he did not know—that fact being regarded as prima facie and sufficient evidence that the unknown one had no right to vote. They might do away with the check list in the town and no inconvenience be experienced. How he does now, I don't know, but have no doubt that at the last election he exercised the same watchfulness over the ballot-box of his ward.

He is well posted in the news of the day, but living so far from Boston, he receives his paper but twice a week. Asking him how he liked this, he replied that he liked it very well, for he had found that news was like beef steak, much better after it had been kept a little while.

This little matter of personal biography may recall the individual to the memory of many. It is the story of a little life, rather than a large one, but it has been usefully and honorably spent. I know no stigma that attaches to his name. Odd, rough, abrupt, he proves in a thousand ways, that sterling stuff rests beneath the at times forbidding exterior of My Brother Bob.

When I published the first paper describing the peculiarities and idiosyncracies of My Brother Bob, there were those who said I had not given the world the best illustrations of his character—each one of them having some pet anecdote of his own that should have stood luminous in the foreground. There are indeed many such that might be told, and to present a few more features of a similar character I have been induced to venture this paper.

I believe I hinted in my previous sketch that Bob was meditating a suit against a railroad for damages in cutting off certain privileges. This he has actually commenced, and a vigorous fight he is making of it, with a certainty of winning if justice is at all regarded. The specifications in his claim are very funny. They are more savory than elegant, and I cannot use them here, but the close is a triumph of magnanimity and a number of other virtues. He says if the directors of the road will only come and endure for eighteen or twenty years what he has done—the villanous smells and noises and sights, the interrupted view by day and the interrupted rest by night—and then refuse to allow him the modest amount he demands, he will pay it to them. This, however, needs the choice strong words of Bob's vocabulary to give it due force. His rhetoric is unapproachable in its distinctness and point. While on the stand as a witness in this case, he was asked if there was not a mutual dislike betwixt him and some other party of the opposition. He said there was not. "Do you deny, sir," said the lawyer for the Road, "that there is a mutual dislike between you?" "I do," said Bob, "most decidedly; he has a dislike for me, but I hate him." I am sorry to record the fact, but the distinction is very nice, and I cannot omit the incident though it tell against him.

One of our most honored and respected naval officers asked me the other day if I was the brother of my Brother Bob, which was at once an introduction to a most delightful acquaintance. Bob had been his right hand man in beautifying and adorning his grounds, and if a plant by any chance didn't grow, it wasn't Bob's fault; Nature had to bear all the responsibility of the failure. But they rarely failed. There was such a thorough understanding betwixt him and them that they seemed to make up their minds to flourish at once after he had looked at them. Like the housewife who was boiling soap and kept it from boiling over by the force of her will, saying it didn't *dare* to, so they didn't dare depart from the directions he gave them. There always seemed a trembling among the more sensitive of the vines when he went through them for fear that they had transgressed in some way. He is wonderful in grafting. Grapes from thorns and figs from thistles are no impossibilities with Bob.

At the commencement of the war when gold took its first start, Bob had some hundred dollars or so in gold pieces that he had put by for a rainy day. No one who knows him will accuse him of extravagant practices, and his economy has enabled him to secure a respectable pile, the gold being simply the dust that rolled off in the piling. He saw the rise one per cent.! two per cent.! three per cent.! "It must be down to-morrow," thought Bob, as he counted over the ingots, like the broker of Bogota. But no; the next day it was four, and Bob grew nervous. Then it was five—six—and, at seven, he could contain himself no longer, but put his yellow boys in the hands of Discount, the broker, who gave him *seven dollars* in greenbacks on the hundred. The next day it leaped to ten and in a very short time it was up to fifty, at which time he told me the story of his want of shrewdness. There was one thing, however, to comfort him. As to every deep there is a lower deep, so if we but think that to every misery or disappointment there is a greater, we gain comfort and thank heaven it is no worse. So reckoned Bob. "Why," said he, with a tone of great satisfaction, "there were some —— fools here that sold at *four*."

The idea of being outwitted pained him most. There is one man in his town whose shrewdness he holds in the highest respect. He marvels at the positive genius he shows in his operations. It is to ordinary shrewdness what the genius of Sherman is to common clodhoppers in the science of war. It was Bob's fortune to sell him some hay by the lot, at the shrewd man's own valuation, who a few days afterwards came to Bob with a long face, telling him that the hay fell short about one hundred pounds, and asked allowance for it. Bob told him he should make none. "Well," said the genius, "I will tell it, all round town, that you cheated me." "Do it," said Bob, "by all means; only let it get about that I was sharp enough to cheat you, and my fortune is made."

There is no man more loyal than my brother Bob. He has a bright eye on the conduct of the war, and criticises everything with the sharpest discrimination. No one is exempt from his strictures, were he a thousand times his friend. At a time of terrible inertness in the army, when active service seemed suspended forever, Bob was terribly exercised about it. He was engaged in his garden, and his spade went into the soil as if he were throwing up entrenchments. "Dead enough," said he, as he worked his spade by some obstacle; "dead enough; why, a defeat would be better than this." There were certain emphatic words interspersed that gave the sentence a gothic massiveness.

My Brother Bob comes to town but seldom, holding the city in but poor esteem. The sun rises here, as he avers, when he stops over long enough to prove it, in the south west and sets he don't know where. He has never seen the great organ yet and says he don't want to, which is an offence not to be forgiven. His early musical education, however, was neglected, which may be submitted in palliation. When asked during a visit which he liked best, Boston or his own town, he replied gravely that he liked the latter best, because he could lie down there in the street and sleep with no danger of getting run over, while here he was in danger all the time with his eyes wide open.

I have written thus far and my pen cleaves to the subject, but I dare risk no more, at present. I received a letter from him yesterday, dated "Poverty Cottage, Highlands, Wibird's Hill"—the location may be remembered by some—where Bob lives enjoying the *otium cum dig.*, cultivating a potato patch and rendering himself useful for a consideration, taking care by a judicious advance in the value of his service to make a depressed currency go as far as ever he did.

RAMBLE CXL.

The Brick School-House in State Street—Teachers former and recent—School Dramatic Exhibitions—Struck by Lightning.

THIS edifice was within the range of the great fire of 1813, and all of it that was combustible was then consumed by the insatiable devourer. It was a building of no little note, for it was at that time not only the place for two schools; one the High School of the day, kept by Master Eleazer Taft, and the other but a slight grade lower, kept by Master Samuel Bowles,—but within the building on the north side, was a room for the Town Records and the Town Clerk's office, and another for the Selectmen. On the north, six feet from it, extending into State street, was a brick watch house of one story. The entrance to the school-house and offices was by a door on the centre of the north side; and where the recitation rooms have since been erected was an avenue to the play ground on the south side of the house. The building was then symmetrical in form, surmounted by a belfry, in which a good bell was hung. We give the particulars, for it is a matter of some interest to hundreds now living, to go back half a century to the scenes where they were "boys together."

This spot has been used for a public school house since 1735, previous to which time the only public school-house was one below the south mill. The house was at first individual property, belonging to the Wenworth family, and by Ebeneazer Wentworth was given to the town in 1735 in exchange for a school lot on Daniel street, given by Mrs. Graffort for school use.

The original house, probably with some additions, remained until about eighty years ago. It was of one low story, built in the style of the old south school-house. We can find no record of the early teachers. Before and after the Revolution, Major Samuel Hale here taught for many years, and gave the right bend to the twigs of those days, as the after life of some of our best citizens, who have continued with us until the last thirty years, show. Another teacher who kept in the old house after Major Hale, was Mr. Morse, of whom we only know that he requested such scholars as Dr. William Cutter and others of his class, to leave the school, as they knew as much as the master.

The last teacher who filled the chair in that old schoolhouse, in about the year 1787, was Salmon Chase, a recent graduate from college. Boys then, as they sometimes have been since, were unruly. Master Chase, who was a portly, athletic man, had occasion one day to chastise young George Turner as he deserved. The boy looking out of the open window and seeing his father, Capt. George Turner, coming up Buck street, sprang out and ran to him, complaining of the whipping. Capt. Turner was rather excitable, and rushing into the school room commenced a torrent of abuse. Master Chase was calmly seated at his desk preparing the boys' writing books. He looked up, told one of the boys to open the door, and pointed the visitor to it. He still continued his abuse. Standing up at his desk, the master raised his round solid ruler in such a manner as to show what he could do, and bade him depart! The old sea captain saw but poor chance in a personal contest, and departed, leaving the master to govern his school in his own way. Mr. Chase was a good teacher, but did not long remain here. He removed to Portland, and we think there studied law. He afterwards settled in an interior town in New Hampshire, and in 1808 was born to him a son named Salmon P. Chase, who has been Governor of Ohio, Secretary of the U. S. Treasury, and is now Chief Justice of the United States.

The next teacher of whom we have account was Deacon

Amos Tappan, probably the first teacher in the new brick edifice. The Deacon was a single man, and the Selectmen of the town thinking it desirable to secure his services permanently, respectfully requested him to get married, and further they recommended him to marry the sister of the Rev. Dr. Buckminister. He doubtless had thoughts of the same proceeding before the suggestion was made. The matter being agreeable all around, the Deacon was married to her. But it appears that the principal marriage the Selectmen sought was not consummated—that of being wedded to the town as a schoolmaster. For in those days corporeal punishment was deemed a duty, and deacon Tappan having done his duty rather severely on one of the boys, his parents prosecuted him. This led the deacon to leave the public school, and open a private school, which he continued as long as he lived, in an old building located on the west side of High street, between the mansion of C. H. Ladd, Esq., and the corner of Congress street. Soon after the fire of 1813 the west side of Mulberry street, near State street, where it now stands. He was a successful teacher, although the boys regarded him a severe disciplinarian.

In 1805 Mr. Tappan was succeeded by Eleazer Taft. Mr. Taft received his classical education in Brown University, and subsequently officiated as a Congregational minister. Changing his religious sentiments, he renounced his ministry, and after serving in the asmy as one of Washington's Life Guards, became an instructer of youth, first in Vermont. In 1805 he came to Portsmouth and succeeded Mr. Tappan in the instruction of the High School, then kept in the chamber story of the school-house, where he remained until the building was burned out in the time of the great fire of 1813.

We here present the names of all the scholars we can gather who attended Master Taft's school between the years 1805 and 1814, when he retired from the school.

Leonard Akerman
Daniel Adwers
Supply J Akorman
Joseph Ayers

John Blunt
Charles E Blunt
Robert Blunt
John Samuel Blunt
Mark Blunt
John Bowles
Charles Bowles
William Briard
George G Brewster
Charles W Brewster
Joseph Brewster
Hosea Ballou
Massena Ballou
George Blunt
Enoch Brown
Archibald Blaisdell
Robert Blaisdell
Thomas Brierly
Wm Bagley
William T Bell
Ira Brown
Nehemiah K Butler
Daniel J Bigelow
Bartholomew Barri

Samuel E Coues
Hugh Clarkson
Benjamin Clarkson
Nathaniel Currier
Charles W Cutter
Charles Conner
J Warner Conner
Daniel Clark
Benjamin Carter
William Coxe
Charles W Coxe
Leonard Cotton
Nathaniel Cotton
Stephen Chase
Ichabod Clark
Charles Cutts jr
John Clark

Theodore S Davis
George Dearborn
Gilman Dearborn
William Dickson
Joseph Dodge
James Dodge
John M Davis
Thomas Deverson
James Drisco
Joshua Drisco
Wm DeRochemont

Mark Ewin
Joseph Ewin
Richard Ela
John Ewen

Theodore Furber
McLaughlin Furber
J Foster Flagg
John Flagg
Supply Foss
Samuel Foss
Augustus Frothingham

Arthur Folsom
Simeon Fernald

Alphonzo Gerrish
William Goddard
Charles Goddard
Oliver Gerrish
Nicholas Grace
William Grace
Joseph Grace
Charles Grace
George Gerrish
George Grouard
Edward Grouard
Phineas P Goodrich
Alden Gove

Tobias Harrold
Benjamin Harrold
George Hill
J Brackett Hutchings
Samuel Hilton
John Hilton
Morris Ham
Oliver Ham
Nathaniel J Ham
William Hardy
George P Ham
Edward Hart
Nicholas C Hart
Daniel J Huntress
Leonard Holmes
Oliver Holmes
Timothy Hall
Thomas Hall
Theodore J Harris
Abel Harris
Herman Harris
Lewis Harris
Joseph Hill
Daniel Haselton
Ira Haselton
Benjamin B Haselton
Charles Harratt
Daniel Haslett
J Byram Hall
Ashton S Hall
Samuel Ham
Robert Ham 3d
Gilbert Horney
Charles Horney
Hanson M Hart 2d
Charles Humphrey
Samuel Hutchings
Edward Hardy
Oliver Hall
Joseph Hall
Renning Hall
E Ricker Hill
J Marshal Hill
William Haven
Henry Haven
Henderson Haven
Howard Henderson
William Henderson
William Ham
Samuel Ham

William Jones
Thomas Jones
Clement Jackson Jr
Edward Jones

James Jones
Arthur Jones
Zaccheus Jones
Samuel Jackson
Samuel Jones

Moses Locke
Jesse Lombard
Oliver Larkin
David Lyell
John I Lane
John Lake
John Laighton
Elias Lowe
John Lowe
Granville Lowe
Sylvester P. Lowe
John Lowe 2d
Jermiah L Lunt
John Collings Long
Samuel P Long
Samuel L Langton
Samuel Lamphire
William Lamphire
Luke M Laighton
George D Libbey
Oliver Livermore
Joseph C Langford
William Libbey

Edward S Manning
George Melcher Jr
Henry McClintock
John McClintock
George Manent
Charles Manent
Benning Morrill
Joshua Morrill
George Morrill
Oliver Merriam
Gershom F Melcher
Daniel Melcher
Nathaniel McIntire
Samuel Marshall
John F Mendum
Thatcher Mather
Nathaniel J March
Samuel Moses
Isaac Mudge
Joseph Mann
Nehemiah P Mann
Thomas Morton
George Morton
William Marden
George Moore
George Moses
Samuel Moore
John Moore
Edward J Marshall
Benjamin Marshall
Andrew Marshall
Samuel Marshall
Joseph Marshall
Woodbury Melcher

William Nowell
William Neil
William G Nowell
Anthony F Nowell

Thomas Odiorne
Benjamin Orne

James Orne
William Orne
Herman Orne
William Overton

Oliver W Penhallow
Samuel Penhallow
Hugh H Pearse
Leonard Peabody
Jeremiah Pike
John M Pillow
Daniel Peters
Edward Parry
Edward Peirce
William Peirce
Nathaniel Peirce

Samuel Rowe
Eben. Rowe
Thomas Roach
Edmund Roach
John E Ross

Samuel Smith
Jacob Sweetser
John N Sherburne
H Hoskins Seaward
Parker Sheldon
Stephen H Simes
John P Simes
George Simes
John H Sheafe
Oliver Sheafe
Samuel Shackford
Henry Shackford
Benjamin Salter
J Billings Shepherd
J Marshall Shepherd
Oliver Simes
George Sherive
Jonathan W Sherburne
William Sherburne
John Sherburne
Henry Schroeder
Samuel Shaw
Joseph Stiles
Samuel Sprague
William Sprague
Thomas Simes
Moses Safford
Charles Stavers
James S Stanwood
John Sparhawk
George K Sparhawk
Washington Sweetser
Henry Salter

Seth Tripe
Hall J Tibbetts
Henry B Tredick
Edward Tredick
Thomas Tredick
Moses Taft
Henry Taft
Alonzo Taft
William B Tappan
William Thompson
Eben Thompson Jr
Hugh Tuttle 2d
John Trundy
William S Tullock
John Turner
Benjamin T Tredick
James Thomas
William Thomas

William Varrell
Samuel Wyatt

Joshua B Whidden
John M Whidden
Samuel W Waldron
Peter Wilson jr
George Wentworth
George Wentworth 2d
George W Walker
William Walker
Edward Watts
Richard Walker
John Wendell
John Winkley
Daniel Wendell

Robert Yeaton
Charles Yeaton
William T Yeaton
Joseph Yeaton
Richard C Yeaton

The tuition of the school consisted of reading, spelling, writing, geography, grammar, natural philosophy, mathematics, and the Latin and Greek languages. He fitted several of his pupils for college, who subsequently graduated at Harvard University.

The reading of the record above given will bring back to many the names of their early associates, many of whom have long since passed away. But in those who remain, there is but one feeling for the old master, whose mildness, dignity and affection for his scholars endeared him in their memory.

After the rebuilding of the school-house in 1814, the teachers were Messrs. E. Hathaway, Ezra A. Stevens, William C. Harris, —— Snell, William H. Y. Hackett, Isaac Adams, Israel W. Bourne, Moses P. Parish, Chandler E. Potter, John T. Tasker, Israel Kimball, A. M. Payson, Lewis E. Smith, and some others, we think, but we have no record for reference.

We have before us the original contract made in 1748 between Samuel Hale and the Selectmen of Portsmouth, in which he obligates himself to keep the grammar school of Portsmouth, and instruct in the languages for five years; and the selectmen bind the town to give him an annual salary of £45 during that time. Salmon Chase received about £80 per year. We find he left the school in 1789.

We have seen Deacon Tappan's receipts in 1791, written in a beautiful hand, showing that his pay as teacher of the high school was £100 per year. He was a keeper of the school about twelve years. Between his time and Mr. Taft's entry in 1805, the school was kept by Mr. Peter Cochrane. His memory is vividly impressed upon the minds of his scholars—whose hands can almost feel the tingle of that awful ferrule, which was in constant use.

In the next generation some of the boys were better prepared for the reckoning—especially when the cowhide was the dispenser of punishment for playing truant. In one of the schools of a second grade in those times, a boy who was certain of receiving punishment for truancy the day before, went like a martyr to his post, and received his punishment without flinching, though put on perhaps rather more severely to overcome his stoicism. He walks to his seat without a tear, and while the boys admired his bravery, they pitied him for his suffering, as was very evident from the *stiffness* of his gait. There was however a good shout at play-time, when he withdrew from under his jacket the remains of an innocent salt-fish his sister had aided him in placing there to receive the punishment.

[illegible] this same school, kept i[illegible] [illegible]oom under Mr. Taft's, in the time of the embargo in 1809, the children were taught the first principles of writing, without the use of pen, ink, pencil or slate. The whole length of the desk, in front, was a level about eight inches wide, and sunk about half an inch below the other part of the desk. This place wa[illegible] covered with yellow sand, smoothed by a guage with projections in it, giving the lines to conform with those in the copy book. In this sand, with sticks formed like lead pencils, the young urchins would make their pot-hooks and trammels—and every form their imagination suggested, on to the mystery of joining-hand. One of our Market-street merchants informs us that in this way he took his first lessons in chirography, without wasting a quill or blotting a book.

Mr. Bowles describes his recollection of the old brick school house, in the following communication:

Among the ancient edifices that have been used for cational purposes, there is none where so many of the past and present generations of Portsmouth have received their earlier instruction, and with which so many memories are associated, as the old Brick School House in State street. Boys have gone forth from its venerable walls not only to fill almost every station in life, from the most humble but useful calling to the highest positions in the state and national councils of the Republic, and, better far, to become faithful watchmen on the walls of Zion, and to elevate the American name in other lands beside our own. Neither have the girls, when weighed in the balance, been found wanting. In every place where woman's duty and destiny call her, they have acted well a woman's part—crickets of the hearthstone, bringing joy and gladness to their husbands' firesides—and better mothers never fulfilled

"Life's highest, holiest task."

The scholars of some forty years ago, when a bell upon the roof rang out its stirring notes to call them to their tasks, had a more extended play ground than those of the present day enjoy; for School House Hill was then an open thoroughfare between Pitt and State streets. Although the school building had risen Phœnix-like from its ashes, other memorials of the great conflagration of 1813 were visible around, in the form of old cellars and bricks, innumerable, the latter affording an inexhaustible fund of amusement in recess time. Upon the summit of the hill, on the State street side was an old well, with the stump of a half-burnt pump in the centre. It was a hid eous trap, into which it is a miracle that more than one unfortunate wight did not fall, during the years its open mouth stood ready to receive them. One day it occurred to Master Stevens, in connection with the above, that he would bring the boys' play to some practical account. Having interested them just before recess hour with the incident in ancient history where a river is recorded to have been filled up, by each soldier of one of the conquerors of old throwing a stone into it, he then suggested that they should thus fill up the old well with a portion of the bricks that lay so profusely scattered around. It would be such rare fun, they were not slow to act upon the hint thus given them, and before the bell rang for their return, (delayed a little probably in honor of the occasion,) the dangerous aperture had been filled to the surface of the ground; the last course of brick laid with the smoothness and precision of a Russ-pavement.

Let us cast a backward look to the days when school dramatic exhibitions were in vogue, and see what it pre sented to our view. It is a winter evening. The first floor of the school-house is converted for the time being into a theatre, with a crowded audience. A partition ex tends across the lower end of the room, one-half the enclosed space answering the purpose of that mystery of mysteries in a theatre, the green room, and the remainder as a stage, with its green curtain. There is no gas to cast its brilliancy upon bright eyes and fair faces, where bright eyes and fair faces still are seen, (for no visionary had ever dreamed of such a corporation as the Portsmouth Gas Company,) but Tetherly's "dips" in tin candlesticks suspended from the walls supplied the deficiency, and a range of oil lamps furnished the "foot lights" for the stage. The orchestra, located in the green room, consists of Esido-Victor, from Water street, professor of the tamborine, and another colored gentleman, professor of the violin. The bell rings, and the curtain rises to scenes from Shakespeare's "Midsummer Night's Dream." As Peter Quince calls over the names of his actors who are to play before the duke, and "Nick Bottom, the weaver" "Francis Flute, the bellows-mender," "Robin Starveling, the tailor," and "Tim Snout the tinker," severally answer, "Here!" the oddity of their names, combined with the ridiculous dresses they have assumed, call forth shouts of laughter from the juveniles, and the humor of the scene is well enjoyed by the audience generally. Nick Bottom is an especial favorite, and creates much mirth by promising, that if permitted to play the lion, he will so roar that the duke shall say, "Let him roar again!" nor less so, when, on being told that he might frighten the ladies, he replies that he can, at will, "roar as gentle as any sucking dove." The entrance of Snug, on all-fours, (enveloped in a buffalo skin) as the lion, is the signal for a fresh outbreak of merriment.

Peter Quince, bidding adieu to Athens, retires to the gentlemen's dressing-room in the entry, (*under the stairs,*) transforms himself, by the aid of a Gilman Blues' uniform into a fine looking soldier, and reappearing, recites with much spirit Campbell's stirring poem of "Hohenlinden." A blooming young lady then favors the audience with a popular song of the time, "Wreaths for the Chieftain," and is succeeded by a young gentleman, who in the costume of an American sailor, sings one of the war songs of 1812. A *very* young gentleman, in a broad frilled ruffle, (his "first appearance on any stage,") then recites, with the most most approved accent, the somewhat familiar lines, commencing—

"You'd *scarce* expect one *of* my age,
To *speak* in *public* *on* the stage."

School dialogues, of a varied character, intervene, but enveloped as they are in the shadows of the past, they present a confused and misty appearance. Among other passengers of less note, Queen Zenobia, with a train of attendants, appears in one of them. The performance concludes with an entire two-act play, entitled the "Military School" very well done, but the special life of the piece is "Old Pipes," a decayed soldier with a crutch and a wooden leg, who, perpetually smoking, perfumes the room—not with tobacco smoke, but the more agreeable odor of pennyroyal. *Exeunt omnes*—the curtain falls.

The scene changes now to a day in summer. The rain that commenced early in the morning has increased in violence, until school-house hill is a fair sized cataract, and the street at its base a running river. Mingled with the deluge of the watery element, are thunder and lightning so terrific and oft-repeated, that the more youthful pupils hide in terror beneath their desks. At last there comes a shock more terrible than all that preceded it—like a broadside from Nelson's fleet at Trafalgar, or the Allies' fire at Sebastopol. The room is filled with sparks, and without the whole atmosphere seems a blaze of fire. When it has passed, revealing faces livid with affright, the stillness of death succeeds, for simultaneous with the last great shock, the rain has almost instantly ceased, and teacher and pupils rushing out of doors, discover that the belfry has been shattered to fragments, one of the chimneys rent asunder, and the bricks scattered upon the roof and the ground below. Looking in the direction of the residence of William Jones, Esq. they see that one of the chimneys has entirely disappeared, and the windows of the first floor are in a sadly damaged condition. A man in the door of Wiggin & Story's grocery, at the corner of State and Penhallow streets, is telling some people that while standing in that position a few minutes before he saw in the air a large ball of fire, which separated, one portion taking the direction of the school-house, the other that of Mr. Jones's residence, and while nearly blinded and stunned by the blaze and explosion that followed he was suddenly brought to consciousness by a heavy blow upon his knee from a brick still lying upon the door step. There is no more school for the day, for the lightning has struck in a dozen places, and the boys are given a holiday to enable them to take lessons in electricity. Among other locations they visit the old South Church, and climb the fence on the opposite side of the way, to get a peep at two promising spring pigs, which had been brought to an untimely end by the electric fluid. They think the catastrophe rather of a comical character, yet it brings to mind a fact the master endeavored to impress upon them before they were dismissed for the day, that had the classes recited that morning in their usual position beneath the belfry, a miracle alone could have saved some of them from being instantly killed.

RAMBLE CXLI.

School House Hill — School Books — Amusements — Slides—Mrs. Maloon's Shop—The Catastrophe—Parson Walton's Meeting-House—Services—The Beloved Disciple.

If the Brick School House has its agreeable associations to the school-boys of past and present generations, School House Hill, the scene of their pastimes in recess hours, is not forgotten. Pleasant memories of the old play-ground have been borne away to every spot on the globe where thehomes ofcivilization are seen, or commerce has extended its enterprise. We have recently seen a venerable copy of the "American Preceptor," one of the reading books used in conjunction with "Æsop's Fables," by a school-boy of the time of President Madison. It is printed with the long ſ, that must have caused much perplexity to young beginners in distinguishing it from an f, I can fancy one of them just fledged from "b-a ba, k-e-r ker, baker," puzzling over the following extract from Dr. Franklin's story of "The Whistle," half oblivious whether the boy *found* the whistle, or if it was the *sound* that attracted him. "I went directly to a ſhop where they ſold toys for children; and being charmed with the ſound of a whiſtle, which I met by the way, in the hands of another boy, I voluntarily offered, and gave all my money for it."

A later day than this, however, is embraced in the writer's memories of the old locality, but within the period that the avenue remained unclosed, between Pitt and State streets. While groups of boys could then be seen engaged in various sports on the southern side of the hill, others never tired of playing among the ruins on State street; standing the bricks on end in rows or circles, to see them fall again in quick succession, or forming them into forts, and storming out imaginary foes with missiles of the same hard material—illustrating one of Mr. Punch's "Facts in Natural History," that "among *bats*, the brickbat flies with the greatest force, if not with the greatest velocity."

An exciting scene was visible on a winter's day, when scores of boys could be seen enjoying the fine slides the hill afforded. Although the boys who lived in the neighborhood, as they worked out the slide after each fresh fall of snow, regarded it as their especial domain, they never quarelled with any others who came to share it with them. It was the resort of youngsters from all quarters; a neutral ground, from its central location, where the hatchet was buried by "Northenders" and "Southenders," who seemed to forget the feuds existing between them, which ran so high in hoop-time, as they went down the declivity upon their sleds, side by side, together.

At the foot of the hill, in the old building demolished ten or a dozen years since, a widow lady kept one of those little shops so numerous at Portsmouth in former years. On the outer shelves was an array of crockery and earthern ware, the latter with an especial eye to country trade, embracing, (from Dodge's pottery,) capacious milk-pans, pots for beans or brown bread, jugs and pitchers for the haying-field, and white mugs that would hold a full quart of cider. Among the older stock, were relics of a former day, mugs and pitchers adorned with Porter, Perry, Bainbridge, Hull and other heroes of the war of 1812, and that now almost forgotten personage "Toby Philpot." Behind the counter were barrels and boxes of groceries, and upon the shelves above, pins, needles, thread, and other notions, with slate pencils, nuts and apples for the school-boys. A cheese, whose excellence could always be relied on, occupied a particular spot on the counter, and near by, arranged upon a line, were skeins of yarn, stockings, gloves, and mittens, taken in trade from country customers. There was one peculiarity about the *mittens*, that, among the reminisences of their boyhood, is not forgotten by some of the wearers to this day. No matter how high upon the wrist they came when first put on, after an afternoon's service in snow-balling, they could rarely be induced again to reach above the thumb.

The sun was not more regular in its course than the proprietor of this establishment. If a neighbor's time-piece stopped, it could be set from her movements, about as correctly as by the Old North clock. Adjoining the shop was a cosy little sitting-room, with its antique furniture—the walls adorned with engravings of so old a date they would be a rare prize, now-a-days, to collectors of such curiosities—and there she could be found, when not called to wait upon a customer, sitting upon the same spot, year in and year out, engaged in knitting; her favorite cat "Tibby" lying upon the rug at her side. It was a cheerful scene of domestic comfort when a bright wood fire was burning upon the hearth, for she eschewed stoves, and would admit no such modern innovations upon her premises. She had long occupied her mansion, and could remember a time when a ten-foot building stood upon the site of Mrs. Abbott's dwelling, and a blacksmith's shop was on the garden in the rear. One evening, while engaged in her occupation of knitting, thinking of the days that were gone, and of her youth that would return no more, her meditations were suddenly disturbed by the bursting in of the door of her shop with a crash that shook the house to its foundation. On opening the door to learn the cause, she discovered to her astonishment, as much of a horse-sled projecting inside the shop as its huge dimensions would allow to enter, a boy of some six years old clinging to it through the aid of a hole in the centre, and no one else to be seen, far or near, in the bright moonlight. The tale he had to tell, related with much fear and trembling, while assisting to remove the unwieldy obstruction, bore sufficient evidence of its truthfulness, as it was very clear that he, unaided, could never have used so ponderous a conveyance. While some of the smaller boys of the neighborhood were engaged in sliding, two of the largest and roughest specimens of "Southenders" made their appearance among them, and after amusing themselves for a while with borrowed sleds, started off in pursuit of something more exciting. A few rods distant on the northern side of Pitt street, was a depot of old gigs, carts and other vehicles that would have done honor to Shepherd Ham's collection of sadlery articles mentioned in Rambles 41. Selecting from among them a dilapidated horse-sled, they dragged it to the summit of the hill, and getting on themselves, and inducing the smaller youngsters to follow their example, they started for a slide. When once underway, it went with locomotive speed, and as there was no such thing possible as guiding so clumsy an affair, it finally brought up at the point mentioned above—all the others making their escape, with the exception of one small specimen of young Portsmouth, before the final catastrophe occurred.

I cannot close these sketches without at least a passing notice of the venerable church, known as " Parson Walton's Meeting House," that in former years adjoined the widow's residence; the same structure that, afterwards remodelled, was finally torn down to give place to the new chapel of the Unitarian Society. It was one of the most antique of the old New England churches, now fast passing away, and of which not a vestige will remain, ere many years have elapsed, in the most sequestered country village. It stands before me now, both in its interior and exterior aspect, just as it looked when untouched by the hand of modern improvement. The plain and unpainted, but not ungraceful pulpit, and its faded velvet cushion whose tassels swayed to and fro in the summer breeze; the solemn-looking sounding-board, exciting childish wonder how it was ever raised to its seemingly lofty height, or what sustained it there; the square pews, nearly large enough for a small family to live in, city tenement-house fashion; the long galleries, that creaked at every footstep! the gayly colored chandelier, suspended by a painted rope from the ceiling; the queer looking poles, well filled with hooks and nails, rising above the pews, designed for coats and hats, but looking, in more modern times, like some arrangement for the suspension of a clothes-line; the long pews, one on each side the centre aisle, where a choir had once been located, (the ladies occupying one, the gentlemen the other,) with seats that turned upward on a pivot while the occupants were standing, and elevated forms in the centre for singing-books; all are daguerreotyped in unfading hues upon my memory, mingled with remembrances of early childhood, when my home was almost within the shadow of the ancient bell-tower. Nor is the exterior—weather-beaten, black with age, and moss-covered—less familiar, or the belfry, with its spire and vane, that vibrated at every revolution of the ancient bell. On every Sabbath day, and on afternoons when "conference meetings" were held, hitched to the church-railing, might be seen a horse, of *very* "certain age," attached to an antique pattern of a gig or sleigh, the conveyance of a worthy pair from Long Lane. When absent in the winter-time, it was an unerring indication that the snow had fallen very deep in the country, and that the roads must be badly blocked up. Accompanying them was a long hound-shaped dog, of iron-gray color, who was left in charge of the vehicle during church-hours. If a mischievous boy attempted to invade his castle, he was too well principled to bark, especially if it were Sunday, but he displayed a double row of ivory that never failed to send the offender away in terror, glad to escape at so cheap a rate. Others too, who came from far distances, seldom failed to be seen in their accustomed places.

How many prayers ascended to the throne of grace from that sacred edifice, and how often its walls echoed to the good old tunes of 'Lisbon,' 'Corinth,' 'St. Martin's,' 'Mear,' 'Coronation,' that most sublime of sacred lyrics 'Old Hundred,' and many others not less remembered, or less loved. But the old church is no more; those who offered up the prayers have had their "faith changed to sight," and the singers are numbered with the choir who sing the song of "Moses and the Lamb."

There probably never existed, since the apostolic age, a more devoted body of Christians than those who constituted the church of Rev. Joseph Walton; a people, truly, who were "good for goodness' sake," and whose daily life illustrated the truth and beauty of the faith they professed. Many of them long survived the good man who for so many years was their teacher in things spiritual, but all have passed away to those mansions where they have laid up much treasure for eternity. Some of their descendants yet have homes at Portsmouth—others are scattered far and wide abroad. Wherever they may be, it is to be hoped the good seed has not become extinct within them, but that it has yet a living principle, springing up and germinating, and bringing forth much good fruit.*

RAMBLE CXLII.

The Old South Church.

THE departure of time-honored edifices creates a feeling of regret, however dilapidated they may have become, or by however superior buildings they are to be supplanted,—for there are associations connected with the old which the new will be long in giving.

It was about twelve years since that the steeple of the Old South Church, that prominent point in our city landscape, was cast upon the ground, after having occupied its position 132 years. The oak posts around the belfry which supported the steeple, were as sound as when first put there. The house was vacated by the society in 1826, when the Stone Church was prepared for occupancy. For a short

---

* One of the most distinguished divines of the American pulpit, Rev. Dr. Stow of Boston, in a brief eulogy at the time of the death of one of these good people, said, "His faith in God I never saw equalled, and I doubt if it has been surpassed in many instances, since the days of Abrabam. *He lived for God.*" Among the sacred spots in the North Burying-ground, where the ashes of the righteous dead await the resurrection morning, there is none more so than that where rests the dust of this holy man. "That disciple whom Jesus loved" is inscribed upon the stone that marks his grave with a truthfulness equalled only by the pure taste that indited it.

time the old meeting house was occupied by a portion of the Society who did not wish to leave the place in which their fathers worshipped. It subsequently became the property of a member of the Free-Will Baptist Church; and was occupied at several different periods as a place of worship by that denomination, which afterwards erected the church on Pearl street. In the intervals of this occupancy, it had been for a considerable portion of the time, kept open for religious worship, sometimes by series of Sunday afternoon or evening services, arranged by the clergymen of the city; sometimes by regular services conducted by the city missionary. Several years before its destruction a floor was laid between the two tiers of windows. The second story was converted into an audience-room, with a pulpit, while the lower story was divided into a ward-room and two school-rooms.

The first pastor settled after the house was erected was Rev. William Shurtleff, in 1733, who died in 1747. His remains, the record says, were "deposited in a grave *under* the communion table." It appeared on the removal of the upper flooring, that a hole the size of the coffin was cut in the under boards about *ten feet west* of the communion table, and that here his remains, with those of his successor, Rev. Job Strong, had lain for more than a century. It was not a matter of great importance, but the discrepancy of the record and the fact we will explain.

On going from the house about the time it was taken down, we met standing on the hill, the venerable Captain Daniel Fernald, who seemed to look with much interest upon the departure of the place of worship of his early days. Among his interesting recollections of the house, he said, that originally the house was some twenty feet shorter than it now is. Nearly a century ago it was cut in two, the eastern half moved about twenty feet, and a new piece put into the centre of the house. This was at once an explanation of the position of the pastors' graves, which were actually beneath the communion table when buried, but by the enlargement of the house, the pulpit, to be in the centre, was removed several feet towards the eastern end.

On the 22d June, 1767, the following vote passed in a parish meeting, of which Daniel Jackson was moderator:

"Whereas a number of subscribers being desirous for their own convenience, and of being accommodated with pews, to have the meeting house cut and made twenty-four feet longer, and the broad alley, pulpit and fore door to be in the middle of the house as near as possible, and the addition proposed to be made to be all in readiness as soon as the house is cut and moved to the distance proposed, to be joined together immediately thro' frame and interlays to prevent the house being damaged or overset by any sudden gust of wind. * * * To be completed entirely at their own cost and charge, and they to have the benefit of the disposition of the pews to themselves. * * * n Voted, that Mr. John Griffes, Mr. Thomas Hart, Deaco- Mark Langdon, Capt. Titus Salter, and Capt. Samuel Lang don, be a committee for the proprietors of this Parish to receive the bond (£2,000) from the subscribers."

Turning over the parish records, we find the following interesting entry made at the time of the death of Rev. Mr. Strong, which we copy verbatim. It presents in itself a picture of the past.

October 1. 1751.

At a meeting of the parishoners of the South Parish, in Portsmo. assembled on the occasion of the decease of our Rev. Pasture, Mr. Job Strong, and to know the minds of the parishoners with respect to ye decent interm't of our deceased pasture, they proceeded unanimously and made choice of Mathew Livemore, Esq. mod'r, and it was put to vote whether they would do any thing at all or not relating to the funeral, and it passed in the affirmative.

Voted, Neminie contra dicente, That there be a grave and decent coffin.

Voted, That the bearers have rings.

Voted, That the following persons have gloves, viz:

1st The Paul Holders and their wives.

2dly, The Under Bearers.

3dly, The Doc'r and his lady.
4thly, The Rev. Mr. Brown and his lady.
5thly, The Watchers.
6thly, That the Govern'r and his lady have gloves.
7thly, The Saxten of this Parish.
8thly, The other two Saxtens, if they or either of ym toll ye bell, shall be pd for ye service.
9thly, The Ministers that attend the funeral.
10thly, That Sam'l Hart Esq'r & his wife for the paul.
11thly, Coll. Gilman and lady and three sisters of Mr. Strong.
12thly, The Tenders.

Voted, That the widow of our deceased pasture have a suit of mourning.

Voted, That their be seventy pounds, old ten'r, given to Mad'm Strong to put herself in mourning.

Voted, That the grave be dug for the iterm't of the remains of the Rev. Mr. Strong, be as near to Mr. Shurtleff's coffin as may be.

Voted, That Mad'm Shurtleff have a pair of gloves.

Voted, That the church wardens be, and hereby are, empowered and authorized to put the above votes in execution, and raise money on the parishoners for effecting the same, together with ten or twelve pounds old ten'r, for unforseen contingences, if there be occasion for it.

Voted, That Mad'm Fitch have a pair of gloves.

Voted, That the Rev. Mr. Langdon of Portsmo., Mr. Addams of Newington, Mr. Wise of Berwick, Mr. Rogers of Kittery, be four of the paul holders.

Voted, That the other two paul holders be left to the appointment of the friends of the deceased, and in want thereof, to the church wardens.

Voted, That the church wardens be hereby desired to make provision to have a sermon preached the same day before the interm't of our deceased pasture. MATHEW LIVEMORE, Mod'r.

Capt. Fernald says that when he first attended the meeting there was but one house on the square south of the church,—a one story house occupied by a Mrs. Wyatt, nearly opposite the present residence of Ichabod Rollins, Esq. The house of Mr. Thatcher Emery, near the bridge was also then standing. The square on the North of the church was owned by Capt. Nathaniel Pierce at that time, and upon it was only the Pierce house on the northwest corner, and a barn on the southwest corner. Capt. Pierce, after the Revolution, sold to Capt. Drisco the whole square, excepting the small lot reserved for his own residence, for $300.

It is said that when this church was built, some of the

timber used was cut on the ground. The lot was presented to the parish by Capt. John Pickering, who was a liberal supporter of the ministry, as well as an active citizen in temporal matters.

On the 13th Sept. 1863, wewere present at the exhuming of the remains of Rev. William Shurtleff, who was pastor from 1733 to 1747: he died May 9th of that year, and was buried under the communion table;—as were also the remains of his successor, Rev. Job Strong, who died Sept. 28, 1751, and was buried by the side of Mr. Shurtleff.

In the boards of the under floor, as we have stated, a place of the size of a coffin was found cut, which indicated the position of the graves. Directly under the opening the remains of one of them was found, and by his side, the coffins probably touching, was found the other. There was a difference of opinion as to the identity, but to us it was clear that the remains of Mr. Shurtleff were removed to the side, to admit those of Mr. Strong to be lowered directly into the grave. On first opening the grave, which was between three and four feet deep, it was doubted whether any remains were to be found, after having been buried in the earth 112 and 116 years. This doubt was soon removed by the disclosure of the skull, hair, and principal bones of the one whom we regard as Mr. Strong. Some of the bones were undecayed—the teeth in the section of the lower jaw white and apparently as sound as when he died, at the age of 27. The bones of Mr. Shurtleff, who was about 40 years older when he died, were more nearly approaching decomposition—of the skull only a piece of the size of a dollar was left. There was but one rib left in a good preservation, and that belonged to Mr. Shurtleff. No remains were left of either coffin except two little strips of 3 and 6 inches long, which appeared to have been the bands of the coffin lids in which was a row of brass nails, about an inch apart. There were two pine knots found, so well preserved by the pitch they contained, they were as white and sound inside as new wood. An iron hinge in one of the graves showed that the coffin lid was made to turn down.

The remains of each, under the direction of the Wardens of the Stone Church, were put in appropriate boxes, and placed in the Auburn Cemetery where a suitable monument is now erected.

The coffins in the Rindge tomb, under the centre of the house on the south side, have all been removed to the cemetery. This tomb must have been built more than a century ago, for when the house was enlarged and the porch erected in 1767, the entrance to the tomb was covered by the porch. The idea that the entrance to the church was made over the tomb was so abhorrent to the feelings of the family, that they changed their place of worship in consequence, to the Episcopal church.

In casting our eyes over the records of the South Church, we find a few matters worth giving. The subscription paper, on which the names are given of those who contributed to the support of Rev. Mr. Emerson, for the years 1714, 1715 and 1716 is summed up by the committee with the following entry:

"All that we can find that Mr. Emerson has had that we can make out at present is £175 2s 2d."

Mr. Emerson gives his receipt as follows:

"I allow of ye one hundred seventy-five pounds two shillings, as so much paid for my salary ye first three years after I came to town." J. EMERSON."

1753. *Voted*, That the scriptures of the Old and New Testament be publicly read every Lord's day as a part of the public worship in God's house.

1756. *Voted*, That ten pounds old tenor, of the Charity Money in the hands of the Deacons, be laid out in practical books for the use of the poor of the Parish.

Voted, That the hundred pounds, old tenor, given by Capt. Geo. Walker to the church, and now in the hands of the Deacons Langdon and Jackson, should be laid out to the best advantage in silver and gold coin, that the church may sustain no further loss by its lying in a depreciating medium.

1757. *Voted,* That the remainder of the proportion of the charity money appropriated to purchase practical and instructive books, for the use of the poor in this parish, be given into the hands of the Pastor to be laid out in books for said use.

Voted, That the £32 in stock of the church's money, now in the hands of Deacon Jackson, be by him converted into silver or gold coin.

Sept. 27, 1760. Received of the hands of Deacon Jackson one silver tankard, being the gift of Mrs. Mary Shurtleff to the South Church in Portsmouth, for the use of the Minister for the time being.

1760. A list of books belonging to the South Parish in Portsmouth, for the use of the Minister for the time being, and to be lent out among the people under his direction:—Pool's Synopsis, vol 5, Dr. Watts' Sermons; Dr. Doddridge's Rise and Progress, 3 vols.; Shaw's Welcome to the Plague, &c. 4 vols.; Christian Piety; Dickinson's Letter.

1762. The church likewise voted that the Deacons Langdon and Jackson be and hereby are desired to purchase with the silver money in their hands (being the gift of Capt. Walker) a decent christening basin, as soon as a sufficient sum shall be raised to pay for the forming of said basin, by subscription, the whole of the silver now in their hands to be applied in the weight of the basin.

The church likewise having further considered the proposal made for the introducing the use of Dr. Watts' version of the Psalms instead of the New England version, into their public worship, desired the Pastor to menti on said proposal to the congregation.

At a meeting of the church, Sept. 9, 1763, at the meeting house, the church voted the use of Dr. Watts' version of the Psalms, instead of the New England. Voted, likewise, that the congregation should be desired to make a stop after public worship, and that the vote of the church be proposed to them for their concurrence. The congregation voted their concurrence, and likewise that said Psalms should be sung without being read line by line.

RAMBLE CXLIII.

The Old Bell Tavern.

THE old landmarks of a city, if not of great beauty, have an interest which time gives to many things of antiquity. Four or five successive generations have been wont to look upon this old tavern, as one of the matters which formed the hub of the busy wheel of Portsmouth. In the recollections of our older inhabitants, the Court House, the old North Church and the Bell Tavern have an association, together with the Parade and the old oak still standing, which has fixed a lasting picture on the mind.

They have revolutionary associations. When the patriot Manning on the west Court House steps threw up his hat, declaring that *King* street should no longer bear that name, but in *Congress* street should in future the Bell Tavern be found—from that day the name of the street was changed.

In 1727, the Gains house was built on the west side of the Bell Tavern lot, having a front yard 40 or 50 feet deep. In 1738, a building occupied by Robert Macklin, the baker, who lived to the age of 115 years, was burnt on the present site of Congress Block. Soon after, a portion of the first meeting house was removed to the spot, from the south mill dam, and made a dwelling house for John Newmarch, a merchant. Five years after, in 1743, Paul March, who married a daughter of John Newmarch, built the Bell Tavern. The building was framed by Hopestill Caswell of New Market, a mulatto, half brother of Paul March. That it was strongly made, the test of a century and a quarter has shown. On the completion of the work there was, according to the custom of the day, a merry gathering to commemorate it. Though Hopestill had performed an important part of the work, he did not venture to approaca the board, until it was decided by the company that he should be permitted to come in and partake with them on the joyful occasion.

How long March occupied it, and whether it was at first a public house we know not. An old lady, who saw the house erected, once told us that several years after its erection she had seen the yard filled with hogsheads of molasses, rum, and such goods as showed that March was extensively engaged in mercantile pursuits. Previous to the revolution the house was occupied by Mr. John Greenleaf, and the sign of the Bell (painted blue) was hanging from the post. Whether or not it was intended to represent the "Blue Bells of Scotland," it is not in our power to decide. At that time there was another public house kept by Mr. Foss in the neighborhood, on the spot where the stable of the Franklin House now stands.

To the old Bell Tavern the patriots of the revolution used to resort, while the tories made their headquarters at the Earl of Halifax. The venerable Theodore Moses of Exeter, has told us that this was the place for resort of such patriots as Thomas Pickering, who commanded the Hampden, and his fellows, and we may well imagine the nature and spirit of the meetings at the bar room and parlors in those days, when punch-bowls were in fashion. Horses were kept at the stable in the rear in those days as now. Mr. Greenleaf's son, on a winter day, was using one of his father's horses and a sleigh for a ride round town. After passing in front of St. John's church, in turning into Bow street, the sleigh went over the bank, where the Day building now stands, and passed down some fifty feet into river. Not much damage was done, excepting a wetting of the horse and driver. It was a perilous adventure.

The keeper after Greenleaf was Fursell, whose widow afterwards kept a boarding house in the present residence of Samuel Lord, on Middle street, where John Paul Jones boarded. It was also kept by Col. William Brewster, previous to his occupancy of the house on the site of Richard Jenness' mansion. It was also kept by Mr. Jacob Tilton, the father of the well known idiot Johnny Tilton, who for many years was an inmate of our almshouse. Johnny was not a very bright child, but was not born an idiot. When a boy he was in his father's stable in the rear of the Bell Tavern, and seeing the hens fly out of the loft window, supposed he might do so to. He stood upon the window frame, and flourishing his arms in imitation of the hens' wings commenced his flight—but he reached the ground rather sooner than he expected, injuring himself so as to affect his mental faculties during his after life. He is well recollected as seen carrying corn to the mill for the almshouse, usually decorated with feathers in his hat, as if in remembrance of the hen adventure. He died about forty years ago. It was he who said, when asked at the mill what he knew, " Some things I know, and some things I don't know—I know the miller's hogs grow fat, but I don't know whose corn they fat on."

It was afterwards kept by Ebenezer Chadwick, who left it to take charge of the Jail, about 1790. It was afterwards kept for a time by Col. Seth Walker, the Register of Deeds.

Early in the present century, Nathaniel Brown, from the Governor's farm in Wolfborough, took charge of the Bell Tavern, and remained there until 1821.

In a letter from a friend who had spent many years under its roof, during Esquire Brown's administration and afterwarbs, he says:

"It was not a beautiful structure—an architect would not hold it up as a model. I don't think its proportions are exactly laid down in the books. It had no stately columns, pillars, dome or tower. But it had a history, and hallowed memories which are more significant and enduring.

On those walls, in invisible letters perhaps, are written many a legend which if compiled would swell to a volume as large as "Greeley's Conflict," and some of them perhaps quite as thrilling. We had come to think it fire proof. Four times it was enveloped in the flames of its more stately neighbors, and like Moses' bush it consumed not. It had seemed to mourn since the demise of its old companions, the North Church and Court House. It was the retreat of a little band of Patriots who used to gather around the midnight lamp, in that quiet ante-room, for the double mission of social improvement and political reform: which latter, was at that time much needed. Sometimes those sessions were continued into the small hours ; not from want of harmony, but solely from press of business. Imbued with the *spirit* of the times, self-denying and earnest, they were bold to do and dare. On its roll were New Hampshire's most honored sons. Sad to say, most of them have passed away. How much of this recent glorious triumph had its germ in that little gathering I will not say. I suppose there may be some mischief-loving persons who as they pass will laugh at its destruction. Well! let them laugh—so did *Nero* on another occasion. For one, I shall mourn its loss, and with Mrs. Partington take our cup of tea and recite its story in our own humble way."

To those anniversaries of the "Gilman Blues," where, after the evil spirits the bottles contained had disappeared, the bottles were arranged in a pyramid on the table to be made a target for those who were able to aim a blow at them—and the appearance of the sedate landlord to know what the "pesky fellows" were doing with his glass ware,—it would be well to pass over in silence—and with many other like scenes bury with the ruins of the old tavern.

It will be recollected that here were held the corporation meetings—here in that front parlor, the probate courts were held for many years. And who will forget that projecting cellar-case door, on the east corner, in front of Pritchard's barber's shop, to which the old truckman Daniel Lowd was daily carried to receive the alms of the public, and the terror he inspired in the school boys at his shrill call for his dog Lion, when they annoyed him as they stopped to gaze.

It has since been kept by Samuel Robinson and Oliver Potter; by Samuel Rea, who changed the structure from a gambrel roof to a three story building. A second Mr. Tilton, Hiram Locke, Jackson & Rowe, and we know not but some others, were the landlords after Mr. Rea.

In 1852, the building was sold to J. P. Morse, Aaron Akerman and Henry M. Clark. The old sign post of the blue Bell was soon cut down, and three stores made in front. Thus it remained, until the fire in March, 1867, swept it away. Nobody is sorry for its departure—as its place is supplied by the handsome three-story block, an ornament to the city, built by Messrs. Henry M. Clark, Aaron Akerman and Samuel S. Frye.

RAMBLE CXLIV.

Witchcraft in Portsmouth and Newcastle—Death of Molly Bridget—Stone Throwing Devils of Newcastle.

For a large portion of the century which terminated some thirty years since, witchcraft was regarded as a relic of ancient superstition; but now, in the modern developments of mesmerism, spiritualism, etc. we have again brought up under the auspices of a new science, developments everybody in olden time called witchcraft and charged to Satanic influence. It is science now—it was witchcraft then.

Although belief in witchcraft in late years has not been general, yet at no time has it been without some who have had a belief in it. There are many stories given in proof of the agency of evil spirits in conferring superhuman powers upon those over whom they had an influence.

In the time of the Revolution when our almshouse was kept by Mr. Clement March, there was among the inmates a woman who bore the name of Molly Bridget. She had been notorious as a fortune teller. She was regarded as a witch in those times, and to her was attributed many of the domestic evils of that day. Her fame as a witch was wide spread. Finding her way to Boston, the police gave her warning to leave the city forthwith. "Why?" she asked. "Is not your name Molly Bridget?" "No, sir," she replied—"do you think I am such a despicable creature as Molly?" Although she denied the identity, she took pains to return by the first opportunity. It was in the year 1782, when she was at our almshouse, that there was trouble in the pig stye. The pigs were pronounced bewitched, and the remedy resorted to was to cut off the tips of their tails and ears. The evil spirits however were not cast out. It was then said that those tips must be burned. But nothing could be found of them. Mr. March directed that all the loose chips and leaves in the yard should be scraped up and burned in the several fireplaces in the house. After the fires were kindled, Molly hastened from room to room in a frenzied manner. She soon went to her own room, and as the flames began to subside her sands of life began to run out, and before the ashes were cold, she was actually a corpse. At the hour fixed for her funeral, arose one of those dreadful storms which are said to occur when witches are buried. These are facts—how far the results were induced by the superstitious feelings of that day, the reader is left to judge. The poor creature might have believed herself a witch, and the expectation expressed that the burning of the pigs' tails would kill the witch, might have so wrought upon her mind as to produce the result.

The principal object of this ramble is to bring up some of the strange developments which were made in early times in what was once a part of Portsmouth, but afterwards became the town of Newcastle. Cotton Mather, who lived in that age, refers to the Stone-Throwing Devil of Newcastle, and thus notices it:

"On June 11, 1682, showers of stones were thrown by an invisible hand upon the house of George Walton at Portsmouth, [Newcastle.]—Whereupon the people going out found the gate wrung off the hinges, and stones flying and falling thick about them, and striking of them seemingly with *a great force*, but really affecting 'em no more than if a *soft touch* were given them. The glass windows were broken by stones that came not without, but from within; and other instruments were in like manner hurled about. Nine of the stones they took up, whereof some were as hot as if they came out of the fire; and marking them they laid them on the table; but in a little while they found some of them again flying about. The spit was carry'd up the chimney, and coming down with the point forward, stuck in the back log, from whence one of the company removing it, it was by an invisible hand thrown out at the window. This disturbance continued from day to day; and sometimes a dismal hollow *whistling* would be heard, and sometimes the *trotting* and *snorting* of a horse, but nothing to be seen. The man went up the Great Bay in a boat onto a farm which he had there; but there the stones found him out, and carrying from the house to the boat a *stirrup iron* the *iron* came jingling after him through the woods as far as his house; and at last went away and was heard of no more. The *anchor* leaped overboard several times and stopt the boat. A cheese was taken out of the press, and crumbled all over the floor; a piece of iron stuck into the wall, and a kettle hung thereon. Several cocks of hay, mow'd near the house, were taken up and hung upon the trees, and others made into small whisps, and scattered about the house. A man was much hurt by some of the stones. He was a Quaker, and suspected that a woman, who charged him with injustice in detaining some land from her did, by *witchcraft*, occasion these preternatural occurrences. However, at last they came to an end."

Thus wrote the reliable Cotton Mather, one hundred and sixty-eight years ago. Although he says these things had an end, yet there have been some reliable witnesses to events of a similar nature on the Pest Island, in the vicinity of Newcastle, nearly a century after. When there were but two men on this island, things were mysteriously moved about the pest house, and unaccountable noises heard. Later days have shown as strange things produced by mesmeric powers, since table-moving has become an every day occurrence.

A pamphlet published in London in 1698, gives in quaint style, a detailed account of the strange proceedings by an eye witness. As the whole account would occupy too much space, we make only extracts from the work, which bears every mark of authenticity.

"I have a wonder to relate; for such (I take it) is so to be termed whatsoever is Præternatural, and not assignable to, or the effect of Natural Causes. It is a Lithobolia, or stone throwing, which happened by Witchcraft, (as was supposed,) and maliciously perpetrated by an elderly woman, a neighbor suspected, and (I think) formerly detected for such kind of diabolical tricks and practices; and the wicked instigation did arise upon the account of some small quantity of land in her field, which she pretended was unjustly taken into the land of the person where the scene of this matter lay, and was her right; she having been often very clamorous about that affair, and heard to say with much bitterness, that her neighbor (*innuendo* the forementioned person, his name George Walton) should never quietly enjoy that piece of ground. Which, as it has confirm'd myself and others in the opinion that there are such things as Witches, and the effects of Witchcraft, or at least of the mischievous actions of evil spirits.

"Sometime ago being in America, (in His then Majesty's service,) I was log'd in the said George Walton's house, a Planter there, and on a Sunday night, about ten o'clock, many stones were heard by myself and the rest of the family, to be thrown and (with noise) hit against the top and all sides of the house, after he the said Walton had been at his fence-gate, which was between him and his neighbor one John Amazeen an Italian, to view it; for it was again (as formerly) wrung off the hinges, and cast upon the ground; and in his being there, and return home with several persons of (and frequenting) his family and house, about a slight shot distance from the gate, they were all assaulted with a peal of stones, (taken we conceive, from the rocks hard by the House,) and this by unseen hands or agents. For by this time I was come down to them, having risen out of my bed at this strange alarm of all that were in the house, and do know that they all looked out as narrowly as I did, or any person could, (it being a bright moon-light night) but could make no discovery. Thereupon, and because there came many stones, and those pretty great ones, some as big as my fist, into the entry or porch of the House, we withdrew into the next room to the Porch, no person having received any hurt, (Praised be Almighty Providence, for certainly the infernal agent, constant enemy to mankind, had he not been over-ruled, intended no less than death or maim) save only that two youths were hit, one on the leg the other on the thigh, notwithstanding the stones came so thick and so forcibly against the sides of so narrow a room. Whilst we stood amazed at this accident, one of the maidens imagined she saw them come from the Hall next to that we were in, where searching, (and in the cellar down out of the Hall,) and finding nobody, another and myself observed two little stones in a short space successively to fall on the floor, coming as from the Ceiling close by us, and we concluded it must necessarily be done by means extraordinary and præternatural. Coming again into the room where we first were, (next the Porch) we had many of these lapidiary salutations, but unfriendly ones; for shutting the door, it was no small surprise to me to have a good big stone come with force and noise (just by my head) against the door on the inside; and then shutting the other door, next the Hall, to have the like accident; so going out again, to have another very near my body, clattering against the board-wall of the House; but it was a much greater, to be so near the danger of having my head broke with a Mall, or great Hammer brushing along the top or roof of the room from the other end, as I was walking in it, and lighting down by me; but it fell so, that my Landlord had the greatest damage, his windows (especially those of the first mention'd room) being with many stones miserably and strangely batter'd, most of the stones giving the blow on the inside, and forcing the bars, lead and hasps of the casements outward, and yet falling back (sometimes a yard or two) into the room; only one little stone we took out of the glass of the window, where it lodg'd itself in the breaking it, in a hole exactly fit for the stone. The pewter and brass were frequently pelted, and sometimes thrown down upon the ground; for the evil spirit seemed then to effect variety of mischief, and diverted himself at this end after he had done so much execution at the other. So were two candlesticks, after many hittings, at last struck off the table where they stood, and likewise a large pewter pot, with the force of these stones. Some of them were taken up hot, (and it seems) coming out of the fire; and some (which is not unremarkable) having been laid by me upon the table along by couples, and numbered, were found missing; that is, two of them, as we return'd immediately to the table, having turn'd our backs only to visit and view some new stone-charge or window-breach, and this experiment was four or five times repeated, and I still found one or two missing of the number, which we all mark'd, when I did but just remove the light from off the table, and step to the door and back again.

"After this had continued in all parts and sides of the first room (and down the chimney) for above four hours, I, weary of the noise, and sleepy, went to bed.

"In the morning (Monday morning) I was inform'd by several of the domesticks of more of the same kind of trouble; among which the most signal was, the vanishing of the spit which stood in the chimney corner, and the sudden coming of it again down the chimney, sticking it in a log that lay in the fire place or hearth; and then, being by one of the family set by on the other side of the chimney, presently cast out of the window into the back-side. Also a pressing iron lying on the ledge of the chimney back, was convey'd invisibly into the yard. I should think it (too) not unworthy the relation, that, discoursing then with some of the family, and others, about what had past, I said, I thought it necessary to take and keep the great stone, as a proof and evidence, for they had taken it down from my chambers; so I carried it up and laid it on my table in my chamber, and lock'd my door, and going out upon occasions, and soon returning, I was told by my landlady that it was, a little while after my going forth, removed again, with a noise which they all below heard, and was thrown into the ante-chamber, and there I found it lying in the middle of it; thereupon I the second time carried it up, and laid it on the table, and had it in my custody for a long time to show, for the satisfaction of the curious.

"August 1. On Wednesday the window in my ante-chamber was broken again, and many stones were plaid about, abroad and in the house, in the daytime, and at night. The same day in the morning they tried this experiment; they did set on the fire a pot with animal fluid, and crooked pins in it, with design to have it boil, and by that means to give punishment to the witch or wizard, (that might be the wicked procurer or contriver of this stone affliction) and take off their own; as they had been advised. This was the effect of it: As the liquor began to grow hot, a stone came and broke the top or mouth of it, and threw it down, and spilt what was in it; which being made good again, another stone, as the pot grew hot again, broke the handle off; and being recruited and filled a third time, was then with a third stone quite broke to pieces and split, and so the operation became frustrate and fruitless.

"Friday after, I was present, being newly come in with Mr. Walton from his middle field, (as he called it) where his servants had been mowing, and had six or seven of his old troublesome companions, and I had one fall'n down by me there, and another thin flat stone hit me on the thigh with the flat side of it, so as to make me just feel, and smart a little. In the same day's evening, as I was walking out in the lane by the field aforementioned, a great stone made a rustling noise in the stone fence between the field and the lane, which seem'd to me (as it caus'd me to cast my eye that way by the noise) to come out of the fence, as it were pull'd out from among the stones loose, but orderly laid close together, as the manner of such fences in that country is, and so fell down upon the ground.

"Some persons of note being then in the field (whose names are here under written) to visit Mr. Walton there, are substantial witnesses of the same stonery, both in the field, and afterwards in the house that night, viz: one Mr. Huzzy, son of a Counsellor there. He took up one that having first alighted on the ground, with rebound from thence hit him upon the heel; and he keeps it to show. And Captain Barefoot, mentioned above, has that which (among other stones) flew into the Hall a little before supper; which myself also saw as it first came in at the upper part of the door into the middle of the room; and then (tho' a good flat stone, yet,) was seen to rowl over and over, as if trundled, under a bed in the same room. In short these persons being wondrously affected with the strangeness of these passages, offer'd themselves (desiring me to take them) as testimonies; I did so, and made a memorandum by way of record thereof, to this effect, viz:

"'These persons underwritten do hereby attest the truth of their being eye witnesses of at least half a score stones that evening thrown invisibly into the field, and into the entry of the house, hall, and one of the chambers of George Walton's, viz:

Samuel Jennings, Esq. Governor of West Jarsey.
Walter Clark, Esq Deputy Governor of Road Island.
Mr. Arthur Cook
Mr. Matt. Borden of Road Island.
Mr. Oliver Hooton of Barbados, Merchant,
Mr. T. Maul of Salem in New England, Merchant.
Capt. Walter Barefoot.
Mr. John Huzzey.
And the wife of the said Mr. Huzzy.'"

In reply to some inquiries made by us of Rev. Mr. Alden of Newcastle, we have received the following letter, giving some interesting historical memoranda.

NEWCASTLE, N. H., Jan. 1, 1862.

C. W. Brewster, Esq.

DEAR SIR:—Agreeably to your suggestion, I would communicate the following in regard to an article in the Historical Magazine for November last, purporting to be the reprint of a tract, entitled "Lithobolia," by R. C. Esq., and published in London in the year 1698. The writer states that he had been in America, at Great Island (now Newcastle, N. H.) was employed in His Majesty's service and lodged in the house of Mr. George Walton.

It is an inquiry of some interest to the antiquary whether this curious and unique treatise will be found to be *genuine* and *authentic*, on an application of the proper tests in similar cases used. In the instance before us, we are furnished with a specification of the names of persons and of places. An examination shows the authenticity of the writer in these respects.

Prominent among the names is that of *George Walton*. Adams, in his Annals, states that in the year 1661, George Walton claimed the land at Fort Point, on Great Island, and commenced building on it. He subsequently says that one of that name here was a long time President of the Provincial Council.

"*John Amazeen, an Italian.*" He is well known to have been an emigrant from Europe, to have settled here at an early period. His posterity is numerous in Newcastle.

"*Mr. Randolph,*" in 1680, was appointed by the King, Collector of Customs for New England, and in 1683, he was Attorney General for the Province of New Hampshire.

"*Captain Walter Barefoot,*" was Deputy Collector under Randolph, and subsequently Captain of the fort, a judge, and President of the Council.

"*Mr. Jeffereys, a merchant.*"— George Jaffrey was a prominent citizen in this place in 1684. His ancient mansion built nearly 200 years ago is still standing, and this review is being written in one of its chambers.

"*One Mrs. Clark.*"—None of this name now reside here, but tradition says that there was once a family of that name, the proprietors of Clark's Island, now so called, and that they resided at a little distance from the Walton estate.

The localities specified. — The traditions of many aged persons concurrently testify that the estate of the Walton family was situated about one-quarter of a mile from Newcastle Bridge, on the north side of the road leading to Fort Constitution and now owned by the Locke family. Some of the inhabitants of advanced age recollect the mansion house, which was spacious—of two stories and with a gambrel roof; the exact spot is known from the remains of the cellar.

"*The fence gate between him and his neighbor John Amazeen.*"—The Walton estate adjoins that of Amazeen; the latter having been entailed, remains esentially as it was at that period, and is now owned by Capt. John Amazeen of the sixth generation from John the Italian.

"*A Cove by his house.*"—There is now a small and beautiful cove a few rods south of the ancient cellar of the Walton mansion.

"*Great Bay*" is a well known sheet of water, and a very prominent locality in Rockingham county.

"*The Stone Fence between the Field and the Lane.*" — No road passed through the Walton estate till the Newcastle Bridge was built, about the year 1821. Previously the only passage way to Amazeen's and Walton's was a lane, as is well remembered by the present inhabitants.

As regards *authenticity* of the narration, it may be readily allowed, in so far as relates to the unquestionable fact of a popular delusion concerning Witchcraft, which at that period extensively prevailed. All who are familiar with the history of New England in the 17th century, need not be informed of this fact. The occurrences detailed in this treatise, as absurd and ridiculous as they are, and, if allowed to be real, must be classed with the miraculous, yet are not more marvelous than those relating to the same subject as recorded in Bancroft's History of the United States, Felt's History of Salem, Barber's Historical Notes on Andover, Mass., and Adams' Annals of this Settlement, under date 1656. It is well known that Rev. Joshua Moody, minister here at that period, stood almost alone in opposing this pernicious delusion, and was the means of saving the lives of some persons of eminence, accused of Witchcraft. And there are now among the older citizens here traditions of this "Lithobolia, or Stone-Throwing Demon." And it is said, that at a later period, gravel on the beach has been thrown at some persons, as was supposed, by invisible hands.

As regards the *definite object* of the writer and publisher of this Treatise, it may be no easy matter to decide. On supposition that the production is spurious, and got up by some wag as a hoax for the antiquary, it may be said of the author, he has outdone his own hero, "Lithobolia," the Stone-Throwing Demon himself.

Most respectfully, LUCIUS ALDEN.

RAMBLE CXLV.

The Former Men of Portsmouth—Ancient Furniture.

IN 1862, John G. Brewster, then in his 83d year, furnished the following record of the deaths of old people in Portsmouth. He himself passed away October 10, 1867, at the age of 89 years 9 months.

"When the mind is active, and we look back to former years, even to our childhood and youth, and remember well the looks and appearance of many of the aged men of those days, we can say in the language of the prophet of old—"Our fathers, where are they? And the prophets, do live forever?" The Scriptural answer is—"Few and evil are the days of the years of thy servants here on earth."

Died.	*Name.*	*Age.*	*Profession.*
1787—	Clement March	78	Keeper Alms-
	Daniel Fowle	72	Printer[house
	Noah Parker	64	Rev. Univ.
	Edmund Roberts	46	Sea Captain
1788—	Clement Jackson	83	Doctor
1791—	Jacob Sheafe	76	Merchant
	Daniel Hart	50	Joiner
1792—	John Langdon	41	Tanner
	John Fernald	50	Founder
1795—	Joseph Alcock	77	Trader
	George Hart, jr.	40	Laborer
	Michael Wentworth	76	Gentleman
1797—	John Sherburne	77	Merchant
	Hall Jackson	58	Doctor
	Stephen Hardy	68	Tailor
1798—	Eleazer Russell	76	Naval Officer
	Elisha Hill	55	Blacksmith
1800—	Jeremiah Hill	48	Joiner
1801—	John Noble	66	Keeper Alms
1802—	Joshua Brackett	69	Doctor [house
	George Jaffrey	86	Merchant
1803—	Samuel Rice	59	Sea Captain
	John Fernald	58	Captain
1805—	Woodbury Langdon	66	Merchant
	John Pickering	68	Judge
	Thomas Martin	73	Merchant
	Stephen Chase	61	Merchant
1806—	John Mendum	68	Sea Captain
	Samuel Haven	79	Rev. Dr.
	Eliphalet Ladd	63	Merchant
1807—	Samuel Hale	89	School teach'r
	George Hart	77	Blacksmith
1808—	Richard Billings	75	Captain
	Jonathan M Sewall	60	Lawyer
	Walter Akerman	71	Tanner
1809—	George Gains	73	Town Agent
	Theodore Furber	58	Captain
1810—	Nathaniel Jackson	69	Farmer
1811—	Supply Clapp	69	Merchant
1812—	Richard Salter	68	Captain
1812—	Samuel Hill	67	Merchant
	Neil McIntire	68	Tobacconist
	Jos Buckminster	61	Rev. Dr.
1813—	Timothy Gerrish	60	Goldsmith
	John March	55	Sadler
1814—	John Peirce	68	Bank Officer
	James Hill	58	Blacksmith
1815—	Benjamin Slade	80	Trader
	Rich'd Champney	71	Merchant
1816—	Joseph Whipple	78	Naval Officer
1817—	William Cutter	48	Doctor
1818—	David Brewster	79	Joiner
	Wm. Brewster	77	Taverner
1819—	John Langdon	79	Governor
1820—	Wm Langdon	82	Tanner
	Ammi Cutter	86	Doctor
	Micha'l Whidden	87	Joiner
	Richard Hart	87	Merchant
1821—	George Massey	70	Gentleman
	Timothy Ham	79	Joiner
1822—	R. C. Shannon	77	Lawyer
	Joseph Walton	80	Reverend
1823—	Robert Ham	85	Farmer
	John Flagg	59	Captain
	Nath'l Kennard	68	Captain
1824—	Jere'h Libbey	76	Gentleman
	Nath'l Jackson	60	Tanner
1825—	Samuel Ham	83	Farmer
1827—	John Bowles	72	Captain
1829—	John Goddard	73	Merchant
	Gideon Walker	63	Miller
	Jacob Sheafe	84	Merchant
1830—	Thomas Sheafe	80	Merchant
	Clement Storer	70	Merchant
	Samuel Fernald	74	Town Clerk
1832—	Joseph Akerman	92	Cordwainer
1838—	William Ham	84	Merchant
1844—	Kendal Fernald	92	White smith
1849—	Thomas Spinney	83	Laborer
1851—	Mark Green	89	Boat builder

"'Tis but a few whose days can count
To three score years and ten
And all beyond that short amount
Is sorrow, toil and pain."

A venerable bureau was recently exhibited at a town fair in Connecticut, which was brought to this country at its early settlement, and is still preserved in the same family. A chair that has been in one family 150 years, and another some 200 years old, were also exhibited.

We have in daily use, and as good as new, four chairs made by our great grandfather, John Gains, in 1728. He built the house in the rear of the Mechanics Reading Room in that year, and these chairs he made for his parlor. The Marseilles counterpane which was in use in the family before our grandmother's birth, in 1739, we also have in as good condition as it was a hundred and twenty years ago. A looking-glass which formed a part of the furniture when "that old house was new," bears more the marks of age, and has for several years reflected the countenances of the inmates of the Journal office. When our venerated ancestor used to look in this glass, there were but four newspapers published in the United States.

[NOTE.—The old mirror hung unharmed in the Journal office until the Friday evening previous to the death of the writer of these Rambles. Then by a singular coincidence, just as the last number of the last paper previous to his decease was worked off, the glass was broken by an accidental blow.—*Ed.*]

RAMBLE CXLVI.

The Episcopal Church Yard.

IN the last Ramble is given the names of some of the Portsmouth citizens who took an active part in public affairs between the time of the war of the Revolution and that of 1812. The list might be considerably extended,—but we will not not now attempt it. While thus marshaling this company of the past, it is not out of place to enter one of the sacred enclosures where some of them are resting from their labors.

Among the early cemeteries of Portsmouth was that of the St. John's Churchyard. This was used as a cemetery some twenty years before the first interment was made in the old North Burying Ground. Within the walls of this Churchyard rest the remains of the principal and highest in rank, in their time, of the inhabitants of Portsmouth previous to the Revolution. Here are the remains of the

Governors, Counsellors, and Secretaries of the Province of New Hampshire, in the colonial days—for it was then in the Church of England that all felt obligated to worship who held an office under the Crown. So the Ground around the church was the place where they also, with the humblest citizens, mingled in one common dust, at death.

The Church that stood on the spot where St. John's Church now stands was built in 1732 and was called "Queen's Chapel." About ten years since, on rebuilding the wall around the Burying Ground, the tombs became for a short time exposed. They were large, and quite full, some containing the remains of upwards of one hundred persons. One was, however, opened with the remains of but one person, in the centre of the tomb, who no doubt was the proprietor. It belonged, according to the records of the Church, to Mr. Christopher Rymes, and no doubt had not been opened for one hundred and twenty years.

There is also a tomb in the middle of the yard called the Governors' tomb. In this tomb were placed the remains of the several Governors Wentworth (except the last), with their families. Some sixty years ago this tomb was opened, disclosing the coffins of occupants, their standing designated by the escutcheons, coats of arms, lion, unicorn, etc. that were on their lids. The rusty remains of a highly polished sword, laid on one, reminded, with these coffin ornaments, of the words of the poet:—

> "Shall we build Ambition! Ah, no;
> Affrighted it shrinketh away,
> And nothing is left but the dust below,
> And the tinsel that shines on the dark coffin lid."

The whole enclosure on the north of the church is sufficiently elevated to permit entrance to the tombs from the street. Here are the tombs of the Atkinsons, the Sherburnes, the Jaffreys, the Peirces, the Sheafes, the Marshes, the Mannings, the Halls, the Gardners; and the remains of many others of latter days here repose,—among them honored names, whose fame needs no tomb-stone to perpetuate them.

By the liberalty of one of the descendants of the Sheafe family, (J. Fisher Sheafe, Esq. of New York,) a handsome and substantial iron fence was erected on the walls of this ancient churchyard a few years since; thus not only making more secure the sacred depository of the dead and conferring an acceptable present to the Church, but also making the enclosure a city ornament.

Could we in imagination go back through a century, we might here see many splendid arrays of carriages with footmen, servants, and military display paraded around these tombs, to pay the last respect to the illustrious dead, and hear the beautiful service of the church, consigning them to their last resting place, read by the venerable Arthur Brown, as in later days it has been read by the talented and sympathizing Burroughs:

"I am the resurrection and the life, saith the Lord: he that believeth in me, though he were dead yet shall he live; and whosoever liveth and believeth in me shall never die."

RAMBLE CXLVII.

The Oldest House in Our State.

THE oldest house now standing, built in Portsmouth, is the quaint brick house on the Week's farm in Greenland. This is no blunder, although it may seem like one—for at the time that house was built, Greenland was a part of Portsmouth. We can find no written record of the year of its being built, but a family tradition dates its erection in 1638, by the father of Leonard Weeks. Leonard was born not far from that time, and had four sons, John born 1668, Samuel born 1670, Joseph born 1671, John born 1674, Mary and Margaret. From Samuel the present ownor ol the farm descended. The house was built on the main road—but the straightening of the road half a century ago, throws it on a circular lane several rods on the side. The speckled appearance of the house is made by having black headers scattered among the bricks all over the front. The bricks were burnt in front of the house. The walls of the house are eighteen inches thick. It is of two stories: the lower story is 8 1-2 feet, the second 8 feet. The windows were originally of small diamond glass set in lead. Some of them have been in the house within the last fifty years. The timbers used throughout the house and for the roof are all of hard wood. The beams in the cellar are squared 12 by 14 inches. The sleepers are of red oak, about 10 inches in diameter, with the bark on. There are planks on the inside of the walls, and the plastering is on reft wood nailed to the plank. There are marks of the house being injured by an earthquake, probably in 1755. If tradition is correct, this is the oldest house in New England, being 228 years old.

In the old records we find that "On the 8th of Oct. 1663, at a meeting of the Selectmen (of Portsmouth,) at Greenland to lay out the hiwayes a hiwaye laid out from Winecote river falls east or thare aboutes to Samuel Haines is house and from thence the hieway is to rune to Hamton hiwaye where it now lies by Ffrances Drake feild which is now inclosed, these hiwaye is to be tow rod in bredth.

"There is also a hiwaye lade out over against Leonard Weikes house and is to goe through his land soue and by west or thare abouts until it comes to the common land."

The same year a contract was made for making a foot and horse path through Great Swamp.

It is probable that the early connection with Strawberry

Bank was by the river. The house was evidently built as a sort of garrison, with a view of safety from being burnt by the Indians.

Feb. 4, 1660, we find "Leonard Weikes'" account for town services allowed. In 1662, he was a Selectman of Portsmouth.

RAMBLE CXLVIII.

The Dead Elm on South Road.

GREEN and fresh as early childhood is the general aspect of Auburn-Street Cemetery. No wilted shrubbery, no decaying tree, is to be met with in its extensive avenues. It seems more like a place of life than a residence for the dead. But such is not the aspect of the whole vicinity outside of its walls. Opposite its north-west corner on the north side of the road, stands as a "*Memento Mori,*" a huge skeleton, sixty to seventy feet in height, with sinuous feet stretching far beneath the soil, and from a body of masterdom size, extend five long weather beaten arms far into the air, seeming to say to all visitors to the spot,

> "I am Old Mortality—
> As I now am, so you must be:
> Once a fresh and vigorous tree
> Was this sear Mortality."

That old elm, on which the lightnings have so often played, that it has been without a leaf for many years, should not pass away, as it now appears to be gradually, without a slight sketch of its early history. As trees do not travel, they have not much to tell—but are content with casting a cooling shade upon those who may come under their branches. Do you see the peculiar form of that old trunk? It has the size of twenty feet in circumference up to twice your height from the ground, and then divides off into five branches of nearly equal size—each branch six feet in diameter, as large as almost any of our forest trees. Now when that tree sprang up, about 135 years ago, it was as regular in form as the beautiful elms generally are. So it grew for a few years. We will look at it in 1732, perhaps on the very day on which Washington was born, but for this we cannot vouch.

This was then the main road to the Plains and Rye, and was the principal thoroughfare. Here comes along a man on horseback with his bag of meal from Pickering's mills. The horse is soon to go up a little elevation in the road, and needs something to quicken his pace. So the rider approaches this young elm and breaks off, for a switch, the top of the thrifty tree. It is done with a twist, leaving the broken end fibrous. Thus the main body of the tree was stopped in its progress, and the five branches, which otherwise would not have appeared, shot forth at this place.

This old elm has never parted with its five venerable children, but continues still to bear them up, although they are all alike dead, well representing a decayed family standing solely upon its high pedigree. One main branch has become disintegrated from the main body—but seems not ready to depart, for above it interlocks its arms with its old associates—and thus is left, perhaps for years, to be in a state of suspense ; if not fearful to itself, it is to the passer by. But the branches are not held up in vain, every one of them points towards the cemetery—some inclining earthward and others towards the sky. This Old Mortality thus appears in its huge vegetable skeleton to preach its sermon on the transitory nature of earth, exhibiting in its own image the changes which may be made through life, in animal and moral as well as vegetable formation, by influences in youth which are hardly thought of by those who are the agents that use them. Was there ever a more impressive illustration of the adage—"Just as the twig is bent, the tree is inclined."

Within sight of this tree have some of the most exciting local scenes transpired. Here was the training field before the Plains were laid out for the purpose. A few rods west of this old tree was buried in the road the body of Eliphaz Dow, who in 1755 was hung on a gallows in that neighborhood for the murder of Peter Clough. And thirteen years after, a few rods from it was hung Ruth Blay, also for murder. By the side of this tree Gov. Burnet passed in 1729, and Gov. Belcher many times in years after, when "Boston was so distant from Portsmouth, and the roads so bad, that he could only make one annual visit." This tree Gov. Wentworth made his turning point when he came from his Little Harbor seat into town, and when its shade was larger, John Hancock, George Washington and a host of eminent men passed near if not beneath its shadow. And in later years, as the cemetery gates are opened to receive some new comer, the huge skeleton stands out to the mournful procession in its full proportions, like the apocalyptic angel, who proclaims that time shall be no longer.

[NOTE.—Shortly after this Ramble was written, in 1862, by the hand that, after the labors of a busy lifetime, is now at rest in the cemetery just across the way, the old elm was felled by the woodman's ax. But the Ramble remains, and we give it an appropriate place at the close of this book.—*Ed.*]

RAMBLE CXLIX.

Fifty Years in a Printing Office — Our Own and the World's Progress.

THIS day* closes a half-century since the senior proprietor entered this office as an apprentice to the art and mystery of Printing. That memorable day was the 16th Feb. 1818. The paper was then called the "PORTSMOUTH ORACLE" and was published by Charles Turell. In 1821, it was purchased by Nathaniel A. Haven, jr. who changed the name to "THE PORTSMOUTH JOURNAL OF LITERATURE AND POLITICS." The plain style of heading adopted by him has never been changed. The paper then had four columns to the page, and contained about half as much reading as now. After Mr. H. had conducted the paper four years in a manner which gave it a high standing in the community, in July, 1825, the Journal establishment was purchased by the present senior proprietor in connection with T. H. Miller. It was then removed into the room now occupied as the office, and for four years Col. C. W. Cutter was assistant editor. In 1833, the present senior proprietor purchased the establishment and took the sole management of the paper. There has been no change since, except the admission of his son to joint-partnership in 1853.

The Oracle was published in a chamber in Market street on the site of C. H. Mendum & Co.'s store. As it was removed to Ladd street in 1825, the senior, who removed with it, has really been in the same office fifty years—never having worked a week in any other office.

---

* NOTE.—In his publication of the number of the Portsmouth Journal dated Feb. 15, 1868, the Rambler gives this record of a busy lifetime. It is copied just as written, and, while more particularly prepared for his newspaper, is such a chronicle of individual and general changes and characteristics, that it forms one of the most interesting features of this book.—ED.

His relaxations from business in that long term have been few and short—never having been absent at the publication of two successive papers in the whole time, excepting five weeks in 1830, from sickness. Only on *one day* besides, does he recollect being absent from his office from indisposition, in the whole fifty years. Twice to Bangor, thrice to the White Mountains, twice to New York, once to Philadelphia, and once to Canada, comprise the whole circuit of his distant excursions. He has attended four sessions of the State Legislature and the State Constitutional Convention—but not to the neglect of the paper, spending some time in the office each week.

When he entered the office in 1818, he well recollects the load of wood it was his lot to carry over two flights of stairs, and how grateful was the privilege of then resting at an old pied brevier case, on which he took his first lesson in type-setting. It was some relief, after setting a column of pi, to have a regular paragraph to put in type. The first line for which he explored the case was this: "*The passions, after having been tyrants, become slaves in their turn.*"

Another early paragraph has never been forgotten: "*The follies of youth are drafts on old age, payable forty years after date with interest.*" It is as fresh to him now as though put in type yesterday, and certainly has never produced any injury in leading to a total abstinence from alcohol and tobacco.

The first manuscript he put in type was an article from the pen of Rev. Dr. Burroughs, then a young man of thirty. His chirography has not changed in the half-century. It was on the Lancasterian system of education, just being introduced. The Dr. finished the corrections of his proof at midnight on Friday, and then the printing of the paper for the morning issue was begun. This late hour was the custom of the office in those days. The whole of

Friday night was usually spent in the office, as our fellow apprentices, John T. Gibbs, John R. Reding and George Wadleigh, will recollect.

As he has resided in the same locality the whole fifty years, (only removing " over the way" when he commenced housekeeping forty years ago)—the distance from his residence to the office, 2300 feet, has been walked at least four times every day on an average. Thus has he passed over 27,150 miles in one beaten track, compassing more than a circuit round the world,—and that too without the notoriety a short and hurried walk to Chicago* might give.

Has not this sameness been tiresome? may be asked. O no, it has had its variety in scenery—it has its variety also, in the change of fellow travellers.

The changes of the seasons present in the hundred and twenty trees daily passed, the bud, the blossom, the full foliage, the autumnal tinges, and the strong and muscular bare limbs of the winter months. They are all company to him in their associations. He has seen, in fifty years, other trees in the same spots where the largest and loftiest elms, of eight or ten feet in circumference, now stand. That at the opening of Pearl street, he saw Ricker Hill put down when a twig. The spot where stands the 10-ft. elm in front of Geo. W. Haven's, was occupied less than fifty years ago by a large horsechestnut, which had taken the place of a lofty Lombardy poplar. And that 8-ft. elm in front of the Academy has its historical remembrance. The Commissioner of the Sandwich Islands now at Washington will recollect the day when his father applied to him the ferrule for aspiring so high as to break off the tree twelve feet from the ground, where the large branches now spread from the main trunk. T. Starr King was witness on the occasion. There have been trees on the way set out by lady hands, which are held sacred by their departure. One might have

---

* Reference is here made to Weston's walk in 1868.

been seen a few years since, which had no claim to beauty or vigor, but was for years in a dying state, and like a tombstone told only of affection for the departed.

Even from the pavements over which he walks, some associations arise. Passing fifty years ago over a long gravelly walk lined by a row of posts on one side, and the red fence of the Adams garden on the other, he did not reach any pavements until arriving at Mrs. Buckminister's premises. Thence the flat stones were laid to Market street. Now the brick walk extends the whole distance, and far west. As we pass the old granite at the street crossings, the mysterious seams in the rocks bring up thoughts of primeval times—the square and the octagon stone passes bring up the mechanical contest of years gone by—and when these stones on a frosty morning display the rich traces of the frost, who cannot find 'sermons in stones?'

Of the male heads of families resident on Islington and Congress streets fifty years ago, there now survive only John P. Lord, Samuel Lord, James F. Shores and Henry Goddard.

All the old occupants of the houses on these streets fifty years ago have passed away, and their places have been supplied by another generation, just then entering upon manhood. He can now look upon these as men of three score and ten,—but somehow they do not look as old men did to him fifty years ago. Among the old residents he might name Messrs. Akermans, Ham, Jackson, Fitzgerald, Halliburton, Barnes, Story, Fernald, H. S. Langdon, Hill, Folsom, Haven, Storer, Abbott, Sheafe, Parrott, J. Melcher, Treadwell, Dean, Cutter, Rogers, Bell, Dearborn, Lakeman, Brewster, Gerrish, Goddard, Rice, Webster, Clark, John Langdon 2d, N. Melcher, Sowersby, Call, Robinson, Bishop, Bartlett, McIntosh, Isaac Waldron, Wildes and others. Only step for an hour into the shop of John Gaines, the watchmaker, where politics were always on the tapis, and you would meet the leading politicians of the day discussing the affairs of the nation. They are now all gone. In the shop next east of John Gains's might be seen John Somerby, apparently not five years older now than then, industriously engaged in upholstery. Next comes the old Bell Tavern, where 'Squire Brown and Samuel Rea reappear, with Jacob Pritchard the barber. whose shop was in that tavern. Daniel Lowd is sitting on the cellar casement in front, leaning on his staff—and Supply Ham in the little shop behind his window of watches, as regular as a chronometer, and as reliable. Then George Ham might be seen in the old Billings house, with a magnifier held by his eyelids, and his sons Nathaniel and Daniel aiding him in regulating time. Then the old Walker house, where Robert Metlin the baker lived, who probably knew nothing of saleratus, for he died in 1787 at the age of 115 years. Then came the mansion where "Sally Allen" kept her millinery store—and next the "fortunate" lottery office of G. W. Tuckerman, which afterwards became Peduzzi's confectionery. There, too, is the ancient Court House on Market-Square, and the venerable North Church behind it.

There are now in Portsmouth eight handsome Churches, and four Chapels, none of which, (except the Episcopal and Universalist Churches) were built in 1818. The two latter were built in 1808. One other large brick church on Pleasant street was built about forty years ago, and has been made into a dwelling house. Fifty years ago the Unitarian Society occupied the Old South Church—the Congregational Society the Old North, in neither of which the parishioners had confidence that the cold blasts of winter could be overcome by the heat of stoves—and so only those who could endure with philosophic firmness the cold house for three hours on the Sabbath, were punctual in their attendance. The ladies were generally provided with foot-stoves and moccasins—gentlemen wore galoches—India rubber shoes had not then been discovered. The Methodist Society then occupied the building in the avenue on Vaughan street, now used as a stable. The Free-will Baptists occupied what is now called the Temple. The germs of what after became the Middle-street Baptist Church, were gathered in the church of the Independents on Court street, on the site of the present Unitarian Chapel. The Sandemanian Society worshipped in the chamber of the brick school house on State street. The Society is now extinct. These were all the religious societies in Portsmouth fifty years ago. *The* Brick School house readily designated a locality, for all the other school houses were old wooden buildings, better fit for pigs than for children. Now we have seven brick school houses—one of which cost more than all the school houses in Portsmouth fifty years ago. Not one of the public school houses of 1818, except that on State street, now remain.

The only organ then, was that in St. John's Church. There were no Sunday Schools, no Temperance meetings, no Lyceum lectures. There was no Hearse in Portsmouth. The bier might be seen in the entries of the churches, and the friends or neighbors of the deceased bore them to their graves. There were no carriages used for funerals then—nor was there an Auburn street or Harmony-Grove Cemetery.

Fifty years ago the present lower room of the Atheneum was an insurance office, and the chamber over it was St. John's Masonic Hall. The Atheneum was just incorporated, and its five hundred volumes were on shelves in the room over John H. Bailey's store on Congress street. There were then no bridges to connect Portsmouth with Maine, or with Newcastle, or with Rye over Sagamore creek. Lafayette road was not then opened, and Rye Beach was less thought of as a place of resort than Newington—Piscataqua Bridge being then the great place of attraction to parties of pleasure. The Assembly House at what is now Raitt's Court, was then the only place in town for public exhibitions and balls.

Fifty years ago, an old dilapidated building on the present site of the Court House, was the "Work House," as it was called. In it was "Union Hall," where the Selectmen held their meetings, and enjoyed an annual supper. That noble brick edifice which now stands on the City Farm well supplies its place. The Stone Jail has been built in that time, and within fifty years the iron staples have been taken from the top of the corner of the fence in front of the jail, to which we have seen the hands of many a culprit fastened, while his bare back received the cat-o-nine-tails, every blow leaving a ridge, while the cries for mercy rent the air. It is but a few years more than half a century that these scenes were witnessed at the close of almost every term of the County Courts. And we have seen also the branding process, when the horse thief was pinioned down on the broad stone at the west door of the jail, and with a cork filled with needles, India ink was pricked in over his forehead and down his nose, to form the letter T. The erection of our State Prison happily terminated these legal barbarities.

There was no imposing factory building in Portsmouth fifty years ago. The spinning wheel was then as much more common than the piano, as the piano now exceeds in number the spinning wheels. Mrs. Tucker's loom in Tanner street used to do the weaving for many families. There was a windmill for grinding bark on the spot where the car house of the Concord railroad stands—and on the spot where the Concord station house now is, stood that long black building, the Old Distillery. On the highest point between Russell and Green streets stood Bowles's windmill for grinding grain.

But enough of local for our present purpose. To look

at Portsmouth now and compare it with what it was fifty years ago, no one will deny that it has made steady progress in many important particulars—such as we may well be proud of.

The changes in the outer world have been as great as in any half-century since the flood. The printer's eye is naturally cast first on the progress of that art which is the preservation of all arts. In 1818, he put in type a paragraph which announced a new discovery in paper making. In March of that year, Messrs. Gilpin, on the Brandywine, gave notice of a discovery whereby paper can be made by machinery, in a continuous sheet of any length. Until then every sheet of paper was made singly by hand, and when used for paper hangings, sheets were pasted together to make the roll. This discovery saved more than half the expense of labor in paper manufacture.

Fifty years ago the most rapid Printing Presses in this country could not print more than 300 impressions per hour. The London Literary Gazette, in March 1818, announced that a wonderful invention had just been made in England, whereby one thousand sheets of that paper could be printed in an hour. It says that it is an improvement on the steam press of the London Times, which had been in operation about three years. Now, 30,000 impressions are made per hour by the Hoe presses, and only last month it was announced that a new press in Paris is sending out 600 impressions per minute! Although this statement needs confirmation, yet the known facts show that the progress of Printing in the last fifty years has been greater than from the time of its discovery in 1429 to 1818.

Fifty years ago he thinks there was not a City in any New England state, excepting Connecticut. The town of Boston contained about fifty thousand inhabitants. The cities of Lowell, Lawrence, Nashua and Manchester had not even received a name,—and the flowing waters of the Cocheco and Salmonfalls were only used for grist and saw mills. Boston then had but one daily paper, the *Boston Daily Advertiser*, three or four years old. It was about half the present size of the Journal. The Boston *Chronicle & Patriot* was published on Mondays and Thursdays, the *New England Palladium* on Tuesdays and Fridays, and the *Columbian Centinel* on Wednesdays and Saturdays. These were all the regular commercial newspapers of Boston fifty years ago. The Daily Advertiser, now the first newspaper in New England, is the only survivor.

There are but few papers on our exchange list which have remained for fifty years. The Boston Daily Advertiser, the Salem Gazette, the Salem Register, the Newburyport Herald, the Keene Sentinel, the Concord Patriot, and the Amherst Cabinet, were in 1818 and are now on our exchange list.

Fifty years ago the art of Lithography was undiscovered. He well recollects the admiration excited by the first specimens of the new discovery. Daguerre had not then dreamed of enlisting the services of the sun to produce truer pictures than the fifty preceding centuries had ever known.

In 1818, the application of steam to propelling river boats was but just commenced. Fulton made his first expedition in 1807, and died in 1815. In 1818 there were on the Mississippi but 23 steamboats, where there now are over 1600. In 1818 the first outside boat commenced running between New York and New Orleans. In 1819 a company in Georgia built a steamer, called the Savannah, and sent her to Europe. This was the first time the ocean had been crossed by steam power. But nearly twenty years elapsed before any regular line of steamers was established. In that time the foreign news was received with no regularity. Thirty and forty days from Europe was not unusual, and sometimes we were favored with the latest dates by arrivals at Portsmouth.. But the regular ten-days trips of the steamers are now put in the distance by another discovery of the day, the Telegraph, which will make a circuit round the world in less than the "forty minutes" of Shakspeare's fanciful imagination.

Fifty years ago our golden fields in California, then belonging to Mexico, were unexplored—and the present fuel of our whole country laid in its undisturbed beds in Pennsylvania—the "great unknown,"—as was the author of Waverly, then at work on that array of novels which long after were acknowledged the productions of Sir Walter Scott.

In 1818, Napoleon Bonaparte who had been a terror in Europe, and was still the lion of the day, was yet alive, held in St. Helena. His brother Joseph was in Philadelphia, Louis in Rome, and Jerome in Austria; their mother was also alive in Italy. Lafayette and his son were also then in France, and six years after came to America. All have since departed and passed into history.

Turnpikes were the only internal improvements made previous to 1818. There had been but two inconsiderable canals constructed in the whole country previous to that time—the Middlesex canal, connecting the Merrimac river with Boston, 27 miles; and the Santee and Charleston canal of 22 miles. The Champlain canal was constructed in 1824, the great Erie canal of 365 miles in 1826, the Ohio canal of 300 miles in 1832, and twelve other large canals were constructed in the country up to 1832—when Railroad facilities took the place of many of them, and stopped this mode of internavigation. The project of connecting lake Winnipisseogee with the tide water of the Piscataqua was also abandoned when the steam horse promised to do the labor better and more speedily. These improvements have all been brought forth in the country while the writer has been quietly noting their progress from his "loop hole of retreat."

When he entered this office, but one President of the United States had deceased. The progress of the Republic was then looked upon and still aided by the counsels of John Adams, Thomas Jefferson, and James Madison. Monroe was then the favorite President, whom no party opposed. In various positions were then scattered through the land the "coming men." John Quincy Adams, Andrew Jackson, Martin Van Buren, William H. Harrison, John Tyler, James K. Polk, Zachary Taylor, Millard Fillmore, Franklin Pierce, James Buchanan, Abraham Lincoln and Andrew Johnson have all since that day been elevated to the Presidency, and twelve of the sixteen have also departed this life in the period he has been chronicler of public events.

In the fifty years, the population of our country has extended from 9 to 36 millions. The 1,500,000 slaves of 1818 had increased to 4,000,000 and then, a joyful event not anticipated in our day, were all made freemen.

In 1818, there were only twenty States in the Union. Since then Illinois, Alabama, Maine, Missouri, Arkansas, Michigan, Florida, Iowa, Texas, Wisconsin, California, Kansas, Minnesota, Nevada, Nebraska, Oregon, and West Virginia, have been admitted; and the territories of Arizona, Dakota, Idaho, Montana, New Mexico, Utah, Washington and Wyoming will soon be presenting their claims to become States. But not again will the claim be made as heretofore, that no free State shall be admitted without a slave State being received as an offset. He well recollects that Maine could not be received to the sisterhood, without Missouri as an offset. And so the admission battle has raged for half a century.

He might go into the public history of times past, and bring up matters relating to the twelve Presidential elections which have been the subject of newspaper record,—speak of the party spirit which in 1824 brought forward four candidates for the Presidency, Adams, Jackson, Crawford and Clay, which resulted in Adams's election--of the contest in 1828, between Adams and Jackson, in which the latter was elected. But these contests are a matter of national history, and need no repetition here. He has only to say, that through the whole series of Presidential elections, the Journal has sustained such candidates as were esteemed patriots of the soundest political principles on the side of a righteous government. Such a man was Adams in 1824 and '28, and Clay in 1832. In 1836, the anti-masonic elements entered into the election. Van Buren was the Democratic candidate, and Webster, White and Harrison from other parties. New Hampshire was so decidedly democratic at that time that no opposing candidate was sustained in our State. In 1840, Harrison was elected by a large majority over Van Buren. The effort in New Hampshire that year gave Harrison about 6000 votes more than Van Buren received in 1836, but the latter received the vote of the State by a small majority. In 1844, Clay was again our candidate. In 1848, Gen. Taylor was elected. In 1852, Gen Scott was our candidate. In 1856, Fremont was nominated. In 1860 and '64, the lamented Lincoln was elected—and in 1868, Gen. Grant will find his election secure. None of these men whom the Journal has sustained is it now ashamed to bring up in a review of the past.

The misfortune of the country has been in electing Vice Presidents who were not sound in principle. Beware in the future.

While it has ever been the aim in the management of the paper to make it interesting to readers, care has been taken to exclude such matters as might not be fit for reading in any family circle. To preserve this negative quality has kept out many sensational articles, which would perhaps, have been more popular than beneficial. Though at times pressed hard with work, it never has been performed in the office on Sunday for the half-century, except on one occasion, about 1820, when the paper, being kept open for the President's Message, was issued on Sunday morning. The strong inducement to employ the leisure of Sunday in writing articles for the paper, led to an early resolution to write nothing on that day. This resolution has been so strictly observed that he has not written a dozen lines for the paper on that day for forty years. This is not stated in any pharisaical spirit, for he is conscious of failing in far more important matters, but long experience has shown that cessation from the usual labors of the week on Sunday gives vigor for the better performance of duties through the week.

When he entered the office, the yearly Vol. at the head of the paper was XXIX. After two or three years he made up the paper regularly, and has each year changed with his own fingers these characters until they now stand LXXIX.

And yet with all the responsibilities, constant care, requisite close application and unceasing labor, the toil has been pleasant to him, nor has he ever had a wish to change it for any other business. What another decade may bring forth is only known to Him who has strewed the writer's path with matters pleasant to the recollection, and not the least among them is the good feeling of a large class of the community, many of whom have travelled in his company the long term which he this day notes.

To show time's mutations, we present at the close an impression of a fancy rule, as the only thing in our office which was in it fifty years ago.